the
goodness
of
GOD

THEOLOGY,
CHURCH, AND THE
SOCIAL ORDER

the
goodness
of
GOD

D. STEPHEN
LONG

Brazos Press
A Division of Baker Book House Co
Grand Rapids, Michigan 49516

Published by Brazos Press
a division of Baker Book House Company
P.O. Box 6287, Grand Rapids, MI 49516-6287

Printed in the United States of America

Library of Congress Cataloging-in-Publication data is on file at the Library of Congress, Washington, D.C.

For current information about all releases from Brazos Press, visit our web site:
http://www.brazospress.com

For my mother, Beverly Sue Long, who labored to give me birth and taught me to tell the truth; and my father, Ralph Wayne Long, who taught me the art of shooting free throws and tending to family. Both set me out on a journey toward the good, which found its deepest yearnings and rest in Christ.

Contents

7

8. **Polis**

Preface

This work can be read by either beginning at the beginning or in the middle. It is intentionally structured in two parts. The first part tends to be more "theoretical" and engages the philosophical and theological tradition of "the good." The second part tends to be more "practical" and develops both traditional Christian responses to questions of social order and some concrete cases that help us think theologically about family, race, economics, crime, and the like. Readers could begin in either place, but both parts are necessary to make sense of the argument in this book. The "form" of the first part informs the "matter" in the second part, and the "matter" in the second part does not matter without the "form" of the first part. If both parts could be read simultaneously, the purpose of the work might be more easily accomplished, but that would require a divine activity of which few are capable. I am not suggesting that divine inspiration is needed to read this book, though I would submit that divine inspiration might be necessary to read any book, for such inspiration allows us to see the depth behind sensual, everyday material existence that can too easily be missed. This tempts us to think that we can begin with concrete, material cases and develop accounts of the good without the necessity of speaking of God. By writing this book in terms of its two parts, I am trying to avoid that temptation. God matters for the good, and what matters only makes sense when it can be seen in God's splendor of luminosity that gives it existence. My hope for any reader of these reflections is that she or he will neither forget material questions of the good when thinking or speaking about God nor forget God when thinking through material questions of the good.

This work owes a tremendous debt to a number of people. Dan Bell gave it life after an earlier draft languished on a shelf for several years. I knew it was not yet ready for publication. I still wonder if this work or any work is ever ready. Like marrying, giving birth, rearing children and, I assume, dying, published works just seem to happen whether we are ready or not. Dan read it and offered excellent criticisms that helped "fix" it. He thought it might be worth fixing. Though that does not make him responsible for this final draft, it does make him a good friend whose encouragement allowed this work to see publication. Stanley Hauerwas, John Howard Yoder, David McCarthy, Martin Tripole, Robert Brimlow, Tobias Winright, Ed Philips, and K. K. Yeo read versions of this work and offered helpful criticisms. This is the second work Michael Budde has read of mine with a thoroughness that made it much better than it would otherwise be. That a political philosopher of Budde's high caliber continues to take theology seriously gives me reason to hope that a book such as this might gain an audience for theology beyond the walls of seminary life. His friendship and excellent leadership of the Ekklesia Project give me hope. I owe a particular debt to Rodney Clapp, whose keen vision for theology led him to establish Brazos Press so that those of us who do unapologetic theology, seek to keep the tradition alive, and engage in theologically-based cultural criticism have a place to publish. This work is dedicated to my parents, whose gifts I have received and benefited from throughout my life.

I would like to thank the following publishers for allowing me to reprint these essays:

Part of chapter 7 appeared earlier as "A Global Market—A Catholic Church: The New Political (Ir)realism," *Theology Today* 52 (1995): 356–66.

"A Dilemma for Faith Communities," *The Journal for Peace and Justice Studies* 7.2 (1996): 81–89.

Part of chapter 8 appeared earlier as "Humility As a Violent Vice," *Studies in Christian Ethics* 12, Number 2 (1999): 31–47.

"Making Theology Moral," *Scottish Journal of Theology* 52.3 (1999): 306–28.

Chapter 2 appeared in earlier versions as "A Dilemma for Faith Communities" and as "Making Theology Moral."

"The Economics of Dying," in *Growing Old in Christ*, Carolyn Stoneking, ed. (Grand Rapids: Eerdmans, 2001).

"Those who have abandoned God cling more firmly to faith in morality."

NIETZSCHE, *THE WILL TO POWER*

"We destroy arguments and every proud obstacle to the knowledge of God, and take every thought captive to obey Christ."

2 CORINTHIANS 10:5

Introduction

I recently attended a conference where a trained theologian responded to a question on a moral issue by saying, "All moral norms are social constructions and subject to revision." I do not know precisely what she intended by this statement, but she did not put it forward as a mere descriptive statement explaining the problematic nature of moral claims. Her statement was not bemoaning the "crisis of humanism" that has befallen the modern era, the crisis Gianni Vattimo explains as the reduction of being to values.[1] This statement was not uttered with any sense of loss or despair; in fact, it was put forward as a beneficial form of knowledge. After all, if all moral norms are social constructions subject to revision, we must realize the limitations of our own moral convictions and never impose them on other persons. Her proposal functions to create a more tolerant society where no single community or individual's account of the good takes priority over that of any other's.

I have little doubt that this theologian's statement expresses what many people in North American culture *think* about the nature of the moral life. Having taught ethics to undergraduate and graduate students for a number of years, I am no longer stunned when persons put forward the claim that all moral norms are social constructions and thus relative and limited. It is standard fare, even if (as I shall argue) it is nonsensical standard fare.

MORAL NORMS AS SOCIAL CONSTRUCTIONS

For example, the majority of my students, when I taught at a Catholic university for several years, were not from secular backgrounds but had gone through the Catholic educational system and had received instruction in morality and religion. One might have expected them to have a different account of morality than that put forward by the liberal Protestant theologian cited above. Yet my students often suggested something quite similar about the moral life. I regularly began an introductory class on social ethics with a test case from a novel, Walter Miller's *A Canticle for Leibowitz*.

Toward the end of this novel, rival powers engage in a nuclear exchange, the fallout from which creates great suffering. To respond to this suffering the government establishes the "Green Star" relief agency. People who are beyond help can go to a Green Star clinic to have their pain "relieved" through physician-administered death. Doctor Cors oversees the clinics and asks a priest, Abbot Zerchi, to use his monastery for the "relief" efforts. Zerchi agrees as long as no euthanasia is practiced on church property. But Dr. Cors is a man of deep principle who lives by one moral norm: "pain is the only evil I know." Everything that can be done to relieve pain, including physician-assisted suicide, should be done. Father Zerchi is also a man of deep principle who believes in the church's teaching that directly intending to kill ourselves or another is intrinsically evil.

For both Zerchi and Cors, these principles are part of the fabric intrinsic to their existence. But these two principles come into conflict over the fate of a single woman and her child, who are irremediably suffering the effects of the fallout. While at the monastery, Cors counsels her to receive the treatment the Green Star offers for both herself and her baby in order to avoid the further suffering they will inevitably face. Whereas Zerchi believes he must do what he can to prevent them from receiving the "remedy," Cors believes he owes it to the woman and child to save them the inevitable suffering the superstitious priest seeks to impose on them.

When confronting students with this conflict, I was initially surprised how often they refused to make a judgment on the position of either Cors or Zerchi. Many students refused to recognize the differences in the two positions and sought to allow space for both. Many would explain, "I personally believe that euthanasia is wrong, but I would never impose my values on another person. Each person must decide for herself what her values are and then live consistently with that decision." Students would then suggest that their moral commitments were primarily "values" that they held, personal preferences that should not be "imposed" on others. Moral values were nothing but social constructions. This position made them appear to be tolerant and allowed them to "agree to disagree" with others holding different values because of alternative social constructions. However, in trying to be tolerant of both positions, students failed to recognize that they had already sided with Dr. Cors, not on the content of the particular issue, but with how moral language functions. Unlike Zerchi, Cors thought that morality was fundamentally a question of individual preference. If, because of her religious convictions, the woman had agreed with Zerchi that euthanasia is wrong, Cors would not have imposed the remedy of the Green Star. But she was ambivalent, uncertain that she agreed with Zerchi. Therefore, Cors was obligated to assist her in her own decision.

The intriguing part of Miller's novel is that Cors and Zerchi represent not merely two contrasting moral positions but different sociopolitical accounts of the moral life. Of course, they do represent the basic textbook distinction between consequential (Cors) and deontological (Zerchi) moral theories. But what Miller recognizes is that these "ethical theories" come with social formations behind them. Cors represents the power of the modern nation-state. He is a functionary of the state, just as Zerchi is a functionary of the church.

Thus, the conflict between Cors and Zerchi is not merely a struggle between ethical theories but a conflict concerning which social formations make sense of our "ethics." For instance, to ensure that each individual is allowed to pursue his or her own values, Cors draws upon the power of the state to create a "neutral" playing field where the woman is allowed to make the decision for herself. Zerchi, laboring under his own conscience, seizes the woman and child and places them in his car to take them to safety in the sanctuary of the monastery. He seeks to incorporate her into the space of the church. In response, Cors calls the police, who pull Zerchi over and physically prevent him from enforcing his views on the woman.[2]

This brief incident portrays the stark contrast between the two men's "ethics." It is not merely a difference in decision-making theories, or the difference between a priest committed to a tradition and social formation (church) and a physician who wants people to think for themselves. The decisive difference between them concerns *which* social formation helps make sense of their particular reading of what goodness is. For Cors, the nation-state secures the social conditions in which each person is given the freedom to decide what the good is. Cors's good happens to be that pain is the only evil he knows, but he recognizes that this is not the only account of goodness. Still, this account of the good needs the power of the state to secure the individual against encroachments from other accounts of the good. It is as committed to a "tradition" and social formation as is Zerchi. Zerchi lives in a different world, which is just as real as Cors's. For Zerchi the good is part of God's good order and is even present in God himself. This goodness produces a world in which certain things are intrinsically good and certain things intrinsically evil. Because the purpose of life is not merely to avoid pain but to live unto God, his world conflicts with that of Cors. An essential difference between them is the social formation that makes sense of their ethics: the life of the church and its traditional teachings or the power to be an individual secured by the modern nation-state.

Thus, when a contemporary theologian states that "all moral norms are social constructions," she speaks a profound truth. All moral norms do assume an underlying social formation. The exchange between Cors and Zerchi discloses that truth well. No account of goodness can be present in our everyday lives without some social formation being the condition that allows us to make sense of it. Ethics does not happen in a vacuum; it always takes place within social and political formations.

At one level my argument throughout this work agrees with this contemporary theologian: the good is a *social* construction. We can see it only as we participate in and actualize particular orderings of social formations. I hope to convince the reader that the goodness of God requires our participation in a hierarchical order of social formations that privileges the church above all others. Such an order is necessary for us to participate in God's goodness. This does not move the church beyond critique, but it assumes that moral critique always comes from some location, from within some particular social formation and not from the perspective of a neutral observer.

When, however, this theologian argues that all moral norms, as social constructions, should be subject to revision and critique, she assumes the location of some neutral and universal space where such critique and revision can take place. But such a location is difficult to establish. It is a position located only by the constantly present but ever-disappearing norm of critique and revision. Like my students who sided with Dr. Cors's moral reasoning, this theologian has simply accepted a dominant form of moral language in the modern era, one that is inextricably connected to the nation-state and the free market. With the second part of her moral aphorism, she has subordinated the centrality of the church for an account of goodness to that of the state and/or the market. She has exchanged goods, and this occurs such that "goods" are more determined by their "value" in exchange than by their being goods. The result will be a thoroughgoing loss of the ability to speak or think truthfully about the goodness of God.

To say that all moral norms are social constructions and thereby imply that they are limited, relativistic, and always (a priori) subject to critique not only subordinates the social formation we call *church* to that of the state and/or market; it is also inherently contradictory. Anyone who utters such a statement, if he or she truly means it, is either arational or irrational, for the statement contradicts itself. To make this statement is to put forward a *moral* claim about moral norms. If the statement is true, then it must also be subject to revision and therefore potentially false. That is, we must subject to revision the moral utterance that "all moral norms are social constructions and subject to revision." If the statement is meant as a *truth* statement, then it must also call itself into question as nothing but a social construction that is subject to revision. That is, proponents of this view must say more fully, "All moral norms are social constructions and subject to revision, and this moral norm falls into this category as well. Therefore, we must also be open to the possibility that all moral norms are not social constructions and therefore not subject to revision." While that *can* be said, it makes no sense. It is a statement that lacks meaning. It is "language on a holiday."

Further, the statement is ridiculous not only because it contradicts itself and therefore cannot be true but also because no one actually lives this way, at least no one who still thinks being good matters. The statement lacks the obvious *practicality* of everyday goodness. If anyone lived as though "*all* moral norms are social constructions and subject to revision," then everyday life would be worse than it is, if not impossible. What if my neighbor decided to revise the moral prohibition against murdering one's neighbor? my children, the prohibition against patricide? my nation, any prohibition against genocide? Of course, we do live in a world where all these things are possible, but to affirm this possibility as a positive affirmation about the character of morality is beyond absurd. The claim that "all moral norms are social constructions and subject to revision" contains sufficient truth to provoke fear, but it can never be intended as a positive example for "moral" practice by any serious-minded, moral person, let alone for a serious *theologian* who believes that we live in a world created and redeemed by God.

God and the Good, and Goodness As a Transcendental Predicate of Being

If God creates and redeems the world, should we act as if all moral norms are social constructions always subject to revision? Is not such a statement a species of atheism? Does not this view reject God's creating and redeeming activity as the basis for the possibility of living a good life? Perhaps not. Of course, to avoid this atheism, we will need to retrace our steps to see where modern ethics has gone wrong. This does not mean that we adopt a romantic nostalgia for the past, simply that we discern why this journey ended as it did and contrast it with other paths that might move us forward. There is no reason to continue to bump into a wall at the end of a journey when one can easily turn around and find some other path.

The quest for the good that Immanuel Kant set us out on has ended in such a dead end. By retracing some of his steps back into the Middle Ages, we can find other possible paths. In fact, this work will draw on Thomas Aquinas to identify some of those paths. Aquinas can help us conceive of *social construction* so as not to assume atheism. We can affirm God's creating and redeeming activity as the basis for any knowledge and existence of the good, which is not subject to revision. At the same time, we can affirm that both the knowledge and the reality of this goodness are mediated to us through a sensible, *social* formation. In other words, we can both affirm an absolute ground for our ethical thinking and living (God, who is good) and recognize the contingent nature of that thinking and living (it takes place in a particular, historical social formation, namely, the church).

This work draws on Thomas Aquinas not because it falsely assumes we could, or would desire to, repristinate the thirteenth century. Thinking with Aquinas—even if we cannot, nor seek to, think as he thought—offers an alternative path out of the dead end in which we find ourselves at the end of modernity. Those of us who are Protestant theologians must recognize our own tradition's complicity in bringing us to the end of modernity. This does not mean the protest is now finished, but by looking to Thomas we might find a way to end the protest rather than merely repeating protest as an end. Aquinas's quest for the good took place alongside a quest for truth and beauty, which understood them all as related to each other and as secure in God, even though they were not so secure with us. This quest for the good sought after it as a "transcendental predicate of being."

In the medieval world, truth, goodness, and beauty were understood as "transcendental predicates" of *being*. "Being" here means that which truly *is*—whose essence is the foundation upon which all things are and in which all things participate. The *existence* of things was not a mere existence; things could exist only because being itself is true, good, and beautiful. The transcendental predicates of being are being in another form in the form of truth, goodness, and beauty. What *is* is not defined simply by its mere empirical givenness or its mere existence as a discrete entity. Instead, to say that something "is" is at the same time to say that it participates in what is true, good, and beautiful. Its truth, goodness, and beauty will be correlative to its achieving its "isness." Thus reality is not merely a mirror of some pure transcendental forms, but what "is" participates in the transcendental predicates of being through becoming what the "is" should be. Anything that "is" can only be understood in its existence against the transcendent depth that the transcendental predicates provide. That depth prevents the thing itself from becoming a mere thing disconnected from other things. It relates each thing to the beauty, truth, and goodness that God is.

Being was understood to be the first transcendental because "it is the primary act of all things." Truth, goodness, and beauty relate being to ensouled bodies, such as we are. Truth relates being to a mind. While it is "convertible" to being, it also adds something to it. It adds "conformity to intellect."[3] As Thomas Aquinas suggested, truth is "correspondence" or "adequation" of the thing to a mind, but this adequation cannot take place without goodness and beauty,[4] for the truthfulness of things participates in an aesthetic judgment where a thing's "fittingness" or *convenentia* to its true end, which is the good, is determined by a subject's judgment as to the harmony or *proportio* of this thing to its truth and goodness. In other words, to recognize that a tree *is* does something more than state a proposition that a tree exists. It expresses a judgment that the thing before us attains the purposes that "tree" designates. Such a judgment is "beauty," and Thomas Aquinas claims that "beauty and goodness in a thing are identical fundamentally; for they are based upon the same thing, namely, the form; and consequently goodness is praised as beauty."[5]

They differ logically. Goodness relates to a thing's "end," while beauty is related to cognition based on the senses' delight in things. Thomas states that "even sense is a sort of reason."[6] Thus the truthfulness of things is not simply the mind's mirroring of reality to itself in detached speculation. Truth's relation to goodness and beauty means all the transcendentals are inseparable from the senses and desires that constitute created being.

Goodness is the relation of being to the appetitive part of the human soul. As Francesca Murphy notes, "The good is being as desirable."[7] In both the true and the good, the central relationship between them and being is their *"convenientia"* or *"fittingness."*[8] We don't desire for its own sake; desire assumes an end. The end of our desire is the good. Likewise, we don't *think* simply because of some bare power to do so; we think for some purpose. Such purposes assume truth. The "fittingness" of being with our appetite depends upon and affirms the good. The "fittingness" of being with our intellect depends upon and affirms the true. But goodness and truth are not simply cognitive faculties in the subject; they are also in the things themselves. Otherwise there could be no harmony, no *proportio.* Yet the aesthetic judgment also assists in a thing's attaining its end. It is made true by our delight in its fulfillment of its end. Thus truth, goodness, and beauty are neither merely objective nor subjective, they are both simultaneously.

Even God's relationship to the world is not one of an abstract essence that the creation merely imitates. Instead, the "archetypal idea" through which the Divine mind creates is the second person of the Trinity—the Word made flesh whose temporal existence was radically contingent, even dependent upon Mary's "yes" and the ongoing re-presentation of his body in and through the church. Through him creation is made, and in him creation returns to God. We do not "make" Jesus possible, but we are called to make him present through our participation in this movement. We do this through our own "yes," our own acts of obedience. History matters, and our "makings" are received by God as gifts that will then always contain more than they could have by themselves because they are always graced makings. They cannot be explained solely in terms of our own activity; God is present in them—before we ever offer them back to God—such that we participate in God's redeeming work. Like Mary's "yes," our acts of obedience become sites of divine activity whereby God's goodness is fulfilled and completed in time. But this adds nothing to God's goodness, which is always already complete and lacking nothing. Because God's goodness is present in God "in a most excellent way," his goodness is always the source and measure of ours and never vise versa. As Aquinas put it,

> God is the supreme good simply, and not only as existing in any genus or order of things. For good is attributed to God . . . inasmuch as all desired perfections flow from Him as from the first cause. They do not, however, flow from Him as from a univocal agent . . . , but as from an agent which does not agree with its effects either in species or genus. Now the likeness of an effect in the univo-

cal cause is found uniformly; but in the equivocal cause it is found more excellently, as, heat is in the sun more excellently than it is in fire. Therefore as good is in God as in the first, but not the univocal cause of all things, it must be in Him in a most excellent way; and therefore He is called the supreme good.[9]

In other words, the goodness that is God can only be related analogically to the goodness that we know. Thus God's goodness cannot be equated with our goodness, for that would make it univocal and make "goodness" a genus under which both God and creation can be subordinated. But nor can our "goodness" be so thoroughly equivocal that no relation exists between it and God. That would deny our participation in God's goodness through creation. God's goodness, then, is the measure of our goodness, but it is a measure that is never securely present to us. It is discovered through what is added to us by God's gift, which is grace.

The transcendentals are not then free-standing forms separate from theological content. Knowledge of them is discovered through the existence of the Word made flesh. In fact, they do not exist outside of God's eternal processions. They only make sense within a theological framework where the processions that are the Triune God—the Son from the Father and the Spirit from the Father and the Son—generate the superfluity that makes creation possible without the creation being divine or limiting God. Creation does not occur because of some primal eternal matter that "is." Creation arises "out of nothing." That is a Jewish and Christian confession that proclaims that apart from God there is nothing, and this nothing is not an "is," an eternal potentiality that awaits actualization. *Creatio ex nihilo* preserves the idea that what "is" comes only from God's abundance and not from God's containment or fashioning of some preexisting matter outside of God. Creation out of God's abundance adds nothing to, nor subtracts anything from, God. That means that the "good" is not an independent criterion by which we can assess God and creation. God and creation cannot be brought under a larger category called "good" any more than they can be brought under a larger category called "being."

The transcendentals do not mediate God's presence to the world such that the goodness found in the world is God. If that were the case, there would be no reason for the redemption found in the incarnation, life, death, and resurrection of Jesus. Rather, the goodness we find in the world points to and participates in, but is not identical with, the goodness that is God. For this reason, the specificity of the form through which this goodness is revealed to us is indispensable. That form is Jesus of Nazareth. He is our way to the goodness that is God. Only in him do we have the infinite in the finite in such a way that the latter is not destroyed by the former, but restored, preserved, and maintained. In pagan Greek incarnations, the presence of divinity in finitude destroys the finite by unleashing a catastrophe upon it because the boundary between them has been transgressed. But in the Christian incarnation, our finite participation in the infinite makes possible participation in a goodness beyond us, a goodness that is transcendent, an infinite goodness. For Christian theology, to desire Jesus is to desire the good. Jesus is the bodily presence of the infinite who ruptures the immanence of being, but without destroying being through catastrophe. Instead, being is restored to its proper goodness. Jesus is the full and perfect manifestation of God's goodness, which needs no progressive unveiling. He is this as an infinite goodness fully given in history but never fully exhausted. This makes the church indispensable for both our knowledge of and participation in the goodness of God, for the church represents Jesus to the world as an object of desire. This also makes it possible for us to confess that moral norms are, in fact, "social constructions." But we cannot give the blueprints for such construction. Only when we recognize that God's goodness is the measure that we must perform in time and space is it safe for us to confess that moral norms are social constructions and not by that confession deny God's existence.

THE GOOD AND THE HOLY SPIRIT

Although Jesus is the form of goodness present in human existence, medieval theologians often attributed the transcendental predicate of goodness to the particular work of the Holy Spirit. This makes good theological sense, for as Yves Congar has noted in his magisterial work on the Holy Spirit, "The Spirit is regarded as responsible for our sanctification, inhabitation and intimacy and he 'inhabits our hearts'."[10] The role of the Holy Spirit in the Christian moral life gives its account of morality a peculiar and almost amoral character, for such a pneumatological rendering of the moral life means that it cannot be viewed primarily as an achievement. The Holy Spirit is central to the Christian moral life because he "gifts" believers for works they cannot achieve in their own autonomous power.

The Spirit gifts us in (at least) three distinct ways. First, the Spirit makes possible the mission of Jesus and his church. At Jesus' baptism, the Spirit identifies Jesus as the one who fulfills this mission. As the Spirit formed Jesus in Mary's womb, so the Spirit shapes Jesus' mission in his baptism, his crucifixion, and his resurrection. And just as the pouring out of the Spirit enabled Jesus' mission, so Jesus pours the Spirit out on his church to continue that same mission (Acts 1:8). In other words, the economy of salvation mirrors the theological relations present in the Triune God; this economy takes place "in the Spirit."

This leads to the second distinct work of the Spirit that makes the good possible. The Spirit represents the ongoing presence of Jesus in the church that gives it the necessary charisms for its institution in time. As Congar put it, "The Spirit does not invent or introduce a new and different economy. He gives life to the flesh and words of Jesus."[11] The church is not the routine institutionalization of an original charism that has now been domesticated. This distinction between an original charism and its institutionalization, a distinction created by the sociologist Max Weber, cannot do justice to the pneumatological constitution of the church. Because of the Spirit's work, the charism does not get "routinized" in an institution, but the ongoing presence of the charisms makes the institution possible. Both the offices within the church (symbolized by the laying on of hands) and its sacramental and prophetic roles can only occur because of the ongoing presence of the charisms in and through the Holy Spirit. But the purpose of these offices and roles is not merely to maintain an institution; their purpose is to produce in us holiness.

The third distinct work of the Spirit is as the agent of sanctification, applying the benefits of Christ's sacrifice to the believers in their common life. The Spirit produces those gifts, fruits, and infused virtues without which the Christian moral life cannot make sense. Thus the medieval correlation between the Holy Spirit and goodness as a transcendental predicate of being makes perfect theological sense. This correlation of course never excludes the other two persons of the Trinity from their role in the moral life as well; but the Spirit's unique role is to actualize that which is potential in the mission of Christ and his church, bringing it to its perfect fulfillment. To participate in this mission is to be ordered toward that good that characterizes God's own life.

Goodness as a transcendental predicate of being prevents us from saying that moral norms are only social constructions, while at the same time it allows us to recognize that the social formation we call "church" is indispensable for goodness. The church is necessary for the possibility of a historical performance of God's goodness, while, at the same time, this goodness stands over and against the church. But goodness transcends the church only through the categorical shape given to it through the church's mediation. Just as Mary's "yes" makes God present in the world such that Christian orthodoxy confesses that she gave birth to God, so in the proclamation of the Word and the celebration of the Eucharist, the church *makes* God present in the world. This making is never a mere social construction crafted by an immanent human power. It is always only present through God's original gift, a gift mediated in and through specific social formations. This means that the good is not a self-evident category by which we can assess God and creatures. It is a gift discovered in and through our location in social formations. The good here is inextricably related to God. God is the ground for the ethical life. Thus, God is the ground of the ethical life, but its actualization only occurs through contingent social formations.

Needless to say, the first part of the equation (God as the ground of the ethical life) is not widely accepted either in the world or in the academy. Such is the influence of Immanuel Kant, who argued that the good itself is independent of God and our knowledge of God. Although Kant also asserted that God is at least a necessary postulate for the *possibility* of the good (his moral argument for God's existence), the damage had been done. God's necessity became only hypothetical, subordinated to the priority of universal reason and will, and ethics cast off the shackles of any theological grounding.

Kant's legacy has deeply marked our moral thought and practice, both by those who preserve and those who oppose his ethical thought. Nietzsche and much of postmodern philosophy deny both the existence of God and the good. In this view, any appeal to the good is most likely a disguised power move by which some persons maintain control of others. Although we may *think* that the good and the true exist somewhere as stable beings capable of measuring and ordering our lives, no such entities exist. Therefore, they need to be deconstructed. God is dead, and *good* and *evil* have ceased to exist. Others accept the existence of the good but deny any intrinsic connection between it and God. Iris Murdoch, for example, argued for the "sovereignty of the good" over other concepts, including "theological fictions."[12] This allows the good both to transcend mere social construction and to remain independent of theological claims or considerations. Against all these views, I will argue in this book that the only feasible basis for *truly* human existence must be grounded in God who is good.

One would think that the second part of the equation, that our ethical thinking and living take place in a particular, historical social formation is broadly accepted, but looks can be deceiving. In the first place, Kant's elevation of the individual will to a transcendental status means that individual freedom and the all-powerful nation-states that guarantee this freedom inevitably seek to destroy the particularity of all other social formations. Likewise, the putatively free exercise of the individual will in our postmodern world feeds into an all-consuming global market, which likewise engulfs any social institutions, including the state, that stand in its way. Thus, although most moderns claim to recognize the social and contingent nature of ethical thought and behavior, the reality of our current situation belies this claim.

It is within this context that I will argue for a Christian approach to "ethics" that is grounded in the God who is good and socially located in a particular institution, the church. To do so, I will focus attention not only on the goodness of God but also on Jesus Christ as the complete incarnation and revelation of God and God's goodness. Only in the Second Person of the Trinity are we able to discover the unity between the transcendental and the temporal, the absolute and the contingent. Only in the incarnation can our finite participation in the infinite make possible participation in a goodness beyond us, a goodness that is transcendent, an infinite goodness. Consequently, only in the body of Christ known as the church are we able to develop the good through the performance of the sacraments (baptism and Eucharist) and the ongoing activity of the Holy Spirit, who both gifts and enables us to carry on the mission of Christ in our everyday lives.

It should be obvious such an "ethic" will be decisively theological. In fact, I hope to persuade the reader of a theological rendering of the good in which the question regarding the relationship between God and the good can barely arise. Indeed, even to pose the question assumes that we can have one without the other, which renders morality independent both of theology and of the church. But if all morality assumes social formations, then what social formation allows for this question itself to arise? It could be, as Emmanuel Katongole has argued, that such a question only arises when "the state replaces the Church as the social mediation of common 'salvation'."[13] In the argument that follows, I hope to present a compelling account of the good in which theology is not reduced to ethics nor ethics understood independently of theology, but in which ethics is rendered intelligible by theology.

The Christian social ethic developed in this work will be dismissed by many in the guild of Christian ethics out of a charitable concern. In our pluralistic society we cannot expect all persons to be participants in the life of the church, but we can expect all persons to be moral and to satisfy the basic requirements of the natural law. Therefore, some will argue, my argument introduces an unnecessary element of divisiveness in an already overly fragmented society. I hope to show that this legitimate concern has led us to an illegitimate concentration on a common, universal morality at the expense of a catholic, theological particularity.

Beginning with the flesh of Jesus and its presence in the church, theology alone can give due order to other social formations—family, market, and state. The goodness of God is discovered not in abstract speculation but in a life oriented toward God that creates particular practices that require the privileging of certain social institutions over others. The goodness of God can be discovered only when the church is the social institution rendering intelligible our lives. This, of course, leads inevitably to a reordering of other institutions, such as the family, market, and state. For this reason, our analysis of the goodness of God necessitates a discussion of church, family, market, and state.

THE QUEST FOR GOODNESS

The following work is divided into two parts. The first part subordinates ethics to theology and discloses the dire consequences of the alternative subordination of theology to ethics. In chapter 1, "Beyond Evil and (Toward an Enchanted) Good," I argue that, despite our debased use of moral language and Nietzsche's predictions, we seem unable to do without the good in everyday practice. Why is this so? Ethics without theology cannot explain this, because the surprising hold the good has over us remains a mystery. Theology is necessary to make sense of the moral life precisely because it allows for a mysterious and enchanting good that calls us to itself rather than to some good that we achieve, define, create, or explain through our volitional activities alone. Christian theology calls this good, God. Thus, philosophy should be in service to theology if it is to make sense of everyday moral experience. The moral life cannot do without God. But God, then, will give shape to the moral life.

However, contemporary moral philosophy is perhaps irremediably separate from theology.[14] Thus, in the second chapter, "Kant's Ethical Revolution against Religion: Questing for Freedom," I argue that the reason for this unfortunate circumstance is that moral philosophy took a wrong turn and went on an inappropriate quest, the quest for freedom at the expense of the quest for the good. Immanuel Kant's self-designated "Copernican revolution" is largely responsible for this other quest. Modern people seek to be free, but we no longer seek God. Surprisingly, it is not Kant's critiques of God's existence that harmed the quest for God but his defense of God's necessity for morality that renders God useless for moral practice. The moral life cannot do without God, but Kant's moral proof for God's existence does more harm to theology than those philosophers who have developed ethics without God. Kant asked a profound question: How can we think of God intelligibly, given our inseparability from sensibility? Kant's question was profound, but his answers were misleading. Those answers meant the loss of theology in the moral quest. We cannot act as if Kant's Copernican revolution did not happen, but we need not merely repeat his answers. Unfortunately, many Christian ethicists repeat Kant's answers and avoid addressing his question. By answering his question in terms of a practical reason that is *theologically* practical we can set out on a different quest.

Once we set out on a new quest, a quest for the good rather than a quest for a freedom that lacks substantive goodness, then we might find ourselves discovered by God. In chapter 3, I shall argue that the revelation of God in Jesus reveals to us what it means to be human and thus what it means to be good. Because evil is the privation of good and not merely some function of the human condition, we must first know the good before we can recognize evil. Good is more fundamental to our being than is its lack, which we call evil.

Then, in the final chapter of part 1, "Christian Ethics As Repentance," the social practice of the church's sacramental life will provide the basis for an account of goodness that recognizes both that the good is a social construction and that such construction does not take place through the immanent powers possessed by a self-enclosed humanity. It is in the discrepancy between what we are given in our baptism and what we should be in our eucharistic celebrations that ethics becomes both necessary and possible. This is a historical and a theological claim. It is indebted to Troeltsch's historical arguments. He has shown us that Christian ethics arises with the sacrament of penance. But unlike Troeltsch, I do not see in the practice of penance a *spiritual domination* that denies individual freedom. Instead, I see in this practice the possibility of a true freedom where our lives are directed and redirected toward that which is good. Christian social ethics makes no sense apart from the virtue and sacrament of penance. But that requires the importance of the virtues to which the sacrament points and the laws that guide us toward those virtues.

Part 2 seeks to show how these theological musings lead to the proper ordering of social formations. I set the groundwork for this ordering in chapter 5,

"Ecclesia: Ordering Desires," demonstrating how such a proper order follows the order of the law given to Moses by which all persons should live. For this reason the church (and synagogue) is given a primary place in a virtuous economy. The church makes possible the right ordering of desires that are also produced by such social formations as the family (chapter 6), the market (chapter 7), and the state (chapter 8). The reversal of this proper order has led to disastrous consequences in the modern world. For example, why is it that democratic nation-states have been some of the more violent and warlike political institutions yet created? Why does the "enlightenment" that produced these modern states end with the "enlightenment" of uncontrolled atomic destruction waged directly upon the innocent at Hiroshima and Nagasaki and then ritualized politically in the Cold War? I shall argue throughout that one reason for this disordered state of affairs is that modern states are based upon the will to power alone. They know nothing other than the will that makes them possible. Without the church, the family, and the necessary exchanges that the market requires, the modern state would have destroyed us all long ago. Any quest for the good must so order our desires after the example of Christ that we render to Caesar that which is Caesar's but to God that which is God's. Some roads, airports, and communication systems may be due to Caesar, but God is the condition for the possibility of all things.

As dangerous as an unlimited desire for state power is, the rise of the global market and its dominance over all aspects of human existence also poses a serious threat to the proper order of human desiring. The global market may be the last catholic social institution, albeit a heretical one, that tries to redeem us. The chapter "Agora" argues that Christians have a stake in resisting the much-celebrated rise of the global market and its technological fascinations precisely because it is a theological text that seeks to offer a heretical salvation. Thus throughout the second part of this work, the role of the church as a social institution will be juxtaposed to other social institutions, such as the state, the military, the family, and the market. The heart of the matter is that these institutions are divinely ordained, but what that means is that they are unintelligible in and of themselves. Any intelligibility they possess can only be rightly determined when the centrality of the church is recognized. The church bears the divine law. Only it can direct our desires and everyday activities toward their proper end, which is God. To be "divinely ordained" is to have a society where each social institution is ordered toward its appropriate good. In this sense, the good is a *social* construction. We discover it by our participation in a proper social ordering that makes up ordinary, everyday life. For a Christian account of this good, the church is the social formation that orders all others. If the church is not the church, the state, the family, and the market will not know their own true nature. Only when the church is the church can these other social institutions know their proper place. The church is, rather than has, a social ethic.

the

Subordination

of

ETHICS

to

THEOLOGY

ONE

Beyond EVIL and (Toward an Enchanted) GOOD

"Good" still seems to enchant us. This catches us by surprise, for our everyday use of language often debases it to such an extent that we might have expected "good" to be rendered meaningless generations ago. In everyday conversation, the word *good* signifies nothing more than "pleasant," "fine," or "well." "How are things going today?" someone asks. Another responds, "Things are going good." How could such a trivial use of the term enchant us? How could it maintain any power over us? Yet this debased use of *good* does not exhaust its meaning for us. *Good* still signifies something more, something almost inexplicable, something enchanting.

If someone utters something deeply offensive, such as, "Slavery was good for the African people," he means something more than that it was pleasant. What he might mean cannot be discerned from this statement alone, but this single statement arouses passions that seemingly come from outside of us, prompting us to decisive action. We feel the need to respond, "Oh, I can't let you get away with saying that" or "How can you say that?" Our passions compel us to speak against this perverse use of "good."

From whence come these passions? Why is the statement "Slavery was good for the African people" so different from "Slavery began in the seventeenth century"? That statement does not have the same effect on us. We might disagree with such a person—"No, it really began in the sixteenth century" or "it existed from time immemorial"—but we would not think such a person evil for this judgment, merely wrong. But the person who says "Slavery was good" is evil, and that seems to matter to us.

To say this person is evil is to do something more than merely give an opinion. If someone replies, "I think that is only your opinion," then she reacts against the judgment by seeking to limit its scope. She suggests, "Such a person may be evil to you, but he is not evil per se; it is *only* your opinion." But even in her effort to diminish the scope of the judgment of evil, she bears witness to the power that the term *good* still holds, for she seeks to undo the damage *evil* invokes by reducing it to mere opinion. In so doing, she acknowledges evil as a power. This betrays the fact that the power evil wields depends upon something other than evil itself. To limit evil, to seek to contain it and diminish its power, tacitly bears witness to something that is not evil, something against which this evil makes sense. If all we knew were "evil," then evil would have no power. We would all be its victims, and no one would be surprised by it.

If evil depends on something other than itself for its intelligibility, something that is not-evil, then it would seem appropriate to think of that not-evil as good. As long as the term *evil* has some power over us, it must be because the term bears witness in some fashion to good. Perhaps the relationship between good and evil is that of a tragic dialectic. That is to say, good requires evil for its intelligibility and evil requires good. Perhaps this tragic dialectic is grounded in the nature of things such that we cannot escape it. If so, then evil would be (as Kant suggested) "radical," going to the very root of our reality. But if this is the case, then we should not be surprised by evil. Evil is as much a phenomenon of everyday life as is good. Yet it could also be that evil depends upon good in a way that good does not depend upon evil. Here evil would be understood as privation, much as it was in Plato and in a great deal of the work of Christian theologians. We cannot know evil in and of itself because such an "in and of itself" does not exist; evil has no "substance." This makes evil nearly inexplicable, but it also avoids making human existence depend upon a necessary victimization in which evil and good necessarily depend upon each other.

Whether good and evil are related in a necessary, tragic dialectic or evil is narrated as the privation of a more substantive good, in both cases *good* still seems to matter. This seems to reflect ordinary life for most of us. Despite the debased treatment that *good* receives at our hands, our language and actions still betray that it has a power over us that other words, such as *yellow, tall, short,* or *plump,* do not have. We have not yet moved beyond good and evil.

Over one hundred years ago, the philosopher Friedrich Nietzsche prophesied that modern life would require a new system of ethics that would take us beyond these terms altogether, "beyond good and evil."[1] For Nietzsche, *good* and *evil* designated little more than the relationship between master and slave. *Good* originally named the nobility of the master. Because the good signified strength, nobility, vitality, and power, the strong were the "creators of values." Goodness was a social construction whereby the noble gave value to what they honored.

However, under the influence of Christianity a revolution occurred, exchanging strength and nobility for weakness. Like Judaism, Christianity disguised the fact that goodness was strength. Christianity reacted against imperial strength and "transvalued values" by making weakness appear to be strength and vitality. The deleterious influence of Christianity led to the development of moral philosophies that conceal the true basis for morality. No longer were we capable of recognizing morality as simply the value we place on vital and noble sources of strength. Instead moral philosophy sought to "rationalize" morality by subjecting it to objective and impersonal criteria. In so doing, it took the passion out of the moral life. Thus Nietzsche described morality as a "soporific appliance." By that he meant something more profound than that moral philosophy is boring; he meant that it is anaesthesia, an aesthetic that numbs us. Moral philosophy conceals the true nature of good and evil. It works like novocaine, separating us from our passions so that we no longer feel and know that "good" is nothing but that upon which we "confer honor." We are desensitized from the reality that "the good" is grounded only in our will to power, that morality is nothing but "self-glorification."[2]

If Nietzsche were correct, perhaps we should have expected the terms *good* and *evil* to fall into disuse once he awoke us from our dogmatic slumber. Yet even though Nietzsche's work has now become standard fare in "Western civilization" courses in university curricula, and even though Nietzsche's will to power has become the ordinary understanding of the moral life for many people, wittingly and unwittingly, the terms *good* and *evil* still seem to enchant us. If a gunman opens fire on a subway train, we do not think of this person merely as some vital force let loose to inflict damage like a tornado. We regard his actions as evil, particularly if his victim is someone we know or love. Anger, hatred, even the desire for revenge all stem from the assumption that this person did something evil, something that did not have to be done, something that should not have been done. Our passions betray us; they do not take us beyond good and evil. They constantly remind us that good and evil still have a hold on us. Whether we need them or not, we still *want* them.

This might not mean that Nietzsche was, in fact, wrong. These terms could enchant us even though we find ourselves in agreement with him. The question is, Why do the terms *good* and *evil* have this hold on us? Is this enchantment a mystery for which we cannot finally give a definitive account, or is it merely a lack of maturity, a residual superstition that haunts us like a ghost in the night?

GOOD AND EVIL IN LIGHT OF "THE SOPORIFIC APPLIANCES"

To answer this question, we usually turn to the philosophical discipline called "ethics," and we assume that it represents something more than a sleep-inducing aid. Ethics should help us understand why the terms *good* and *evil* possess power over us, for ethics supposedly helps us make sense of why and how we use moral language.

According to William K. Frankena's standard definition, ethicists both ask and answer questions concerning "what is right, good, or obligatory" (normative ethics) or the prior metaphysical question, "What do we mean when we speak of the right, good, or the obligatory?" (metaethics).[3] Ethics should explain to us what is good and what we mean by it. Yet does *ethics* accomplish this? Is the scientific understanding of ethics sufficient to explain why good and evil matter? Or does it merely assume that ethics matters and thus ignore Nietzsche's critique? A brief review of recent approaches to ethics reveals that the latter is the case.

For example, the philosophical discipline of ethics has developed impressive taxonomies of moral systems. Usually these systems are divided between two main types: teleological and deontological. Teleological theories (e.g., utilitarian and consequentialist theories) focus on the *telos* or end of actions, while deontological theories (monistic, pluralistic, and contractarian theories) focus on being bound or tied to do the right thing despite consequences.[4] A third type, H. Richard Niebuhr's "responsible self" approach, refrains from both the *ought* of deontology and the *goal* of teleology in favor of "response." This approach asks the question, "What is going on?" and seeks to find the fitting response.[5] For Niebuhr, we are not solely the creators of our own action; rather, we are respondents to something that is going on outside of us that is not always easily named. Theology helps us name what is going on.

Even though Niebuhr helps move us beyond *philosophical* ethics and thus points in a direction that proves fruitful in explaining why good and evil still matter, the moral taxonomists incorporate Niebuhr's third type within the standard taxonomy by referring to it as a "mixed" type. In the end, nearly every form of ethical theory is located somewhere in the taxonomy. Once we have this taxonomical system, ethics as a discipline appears "scientific," and the task of "ethics" becomes to introduce students to the various types of ethical decision-making models. Teachers of ethics seldom "impose" one model on their students; instead, they let students decide which model fits them best. But of course this approach to ethics is just one more particular model, one that fits well within the dominance of the market over human action. The result of this taxonomical approach to ethics is that students are treated as consumers who choose one decision-making model over another. Ethics is understood primarily as value-preference.

As a result, no substantive account of the good can appear. The question ethics answers is not why good and evil hold power over us but where we place this action and its justification or meaning within the classificatory schema.

The only purpose of such an approach to ethics can be to help the student "know thyself," but now in a reductive fashion. It helps the student know himself as that which gives things their "value." Perhaps such a periodic chart of elemental action serves some purpose, but it certainly does not help us understand from whence come good and evil.

We find a similar explanatory vacuum with casuistry, a different form of ethical "theory" that, at least in one version, seeks to eschew theory altogether. Casuistry was once understood as the deductive application of general principles to particular cases, but recent advocates, such as the theologian Paul Ramsey and philosophers Albert Jonsen and Stephen Toulmin, present casuistry in a different light. Ramsey, a student of H. Richard Niebuhr, argued that casuistry allowed for the application of exceptionless principles but not by way of a deduction from general rules to concrete particular cases. Instead, casuistry is the effort to "surround the particular" by traditional, exceptional principles so that we might understand what is going on. We do not know what the particular is unless it is so surrounded by a tradition-rich moral language. Whether a human act is murder or a justified act of self-defense cannot be known either from first principles alone or from some self-evident nature of a concrete case. It is in the interplay between principles and the concrete cases that both are clarified.[6]

Jonsen and Toulmin take a completely different approach in their important work, *The Abuse of Casuistry*. They see casuistry as a form of practical reasoning free from theoretical argument, in particular, from universal major premises. Casuistry begins with the "present fact situation," the "particulars of the case," and then moves to a "general warrant based on similar precedents," arriving at a "provisional conclusion."[7] Whereas Ramsey views casuistry as a tradition-rich practice, Toulmin and Jonsen see it as a way to build consensus among persons from differing traditions and moral perspectives. Because we have no singular account of the good in our pluralistic society, casuistry gives us a method to move forward ethically without getting bogged down in questions such as the one I have asked, namely, What is the good and from where does it come?

These three approaches—teleology, deontology, and casuistry—are the three most widely used and discussed methods in the discipline of ethics. They have value in helping us explain why and how people use moral language, but can these ethical theories help us explain why good and evil still seem to matter? Can they help us explain why many persons are still enchanted by these terms? Here their usefulness vanishes, for these theories seek to explain actions that are already assumed to embody something called morality. They assume their object (morality) as given fact and then proceed to dissect it into its parts. They seek to explain why and how we use moral language, but seldom do they seek to demystify the object they presuppose. The taxonomy of ethical positions assumes its objects just as Mendeleev's chart of the elements assumes its objects. It avoids the obvious fact that in producing such a chart we do not discover an object but merely invent a way of speaking about it.

ON GETTING CAUGHT UP

Ethics as a philosophical discipline always comes after the fact. Just as no one first learns her native language by learning its formal grammatical rules, people do not learn morality by first learning its formal logic. Few people, if any, were taught morality by first learning the language of deontology, teleology, or casuistry. Instead, most of us learned certain ways of life through our participation in regular activities with specific boundaries. We learned not to cheat on examinations, not because we sought to be deontologists, but due to pressures, both noble and less noble, brought on by our families or other social communities.

Most of us did not first learn to describe such ways of life as moral, immoral, ethical, or unethical, let alone as deontological, teleological, or casuistical. We were already involved in those activities, and if we ever learned the language of ethics, it functioned retrospectively to describe, justify, or find fault with activities within which we were already caught.

Graham Greene's novel *The Power and the Glory* illustrates this well. After a revolution has occurred in which the new regime persecutes priests, a scandalous priest finds himself remaining under the new regime when others more faithful than he have fled. This priest has fathered a child, allowed others to die in his place, and has been more concerned with acquiring his next drink than performing his priestly duties. Nevertheless, he remains behind as the last priest available to assist the people in the church's service.

The priest tries to escape, but finally fails to do so because his role as priest keeps detaining him within communities that need his services. A noble revolutionary lieutenant captures him, and they evidence the kind of mutual respect combatants often develop for one another. The lieutenant explains to the priest why he must kill him despite the fact that he holds nothing against him personally. The whisky priest responds that the lieutenant is not fighting against him, for he is not worthy of the lieutenant's animosity. Instead, suggests the priest, the lieutenant fights against God. The lieutenant disagrees. He is fighting against the whisky priest's "ideas." He says,

> You are so cunning, you people. But tell me this—what have you ever done in Mexico for us? Have you ever told a landlord he shouldn't beat his peon—oh yes, I know, in the confessional perhaps, and it's your duty, isn't it, to forget it at once. You come out and have dinner with him and it's your duty not to know that he has murdered a peasant. That's all finished. He's left it behind in your box.

The priest concedes that the lieutenant is a genuinely good man who seeks the betterment of the people, but that does not change his opinion. The lieutenant's war is with God, not some inconsequential priest like himself, and certainly not with something as ephemeral as "ideas." In fact, precisely *because* he finds the lieutenant noble, he recognizes that the lieutenant is fighting against something more than the priest's irrelevant "ideas." He must be fighting against God.

The conversation then shifts, and the lieutenant begins to query the priest as to why he stayed in Mexico when other priests left. At one point the lieutenant blurts out, "Well, you're going to be a martyr—you've got that satisfaction." The priest quickly demurs; he is not worthy of martyrdom. Of course, the priest is correct; he is not worthy. Nevertheless, the lieutenant also speaks the truth—the whisky priest is being prepared for martyrdom. How can this scurrilous figure be called to martyrdom? How can he possibly become a saint? The lieutenant asks the same question, "That's another thing I don't understand, why you—of all people—should have stayed when the others ran." The priest responds, "Once I asked myself that. The fact is, a man isn't presented suddenly with two courses to follow: one good and one bad. He gets caught up."[8]

The words Graham Greene places in the whisky priest's mouth can help us understand our enchantment with the moral life. Most of us would recognize that our morality has been more formed by "getting caught up" in certain adventures rather than by adopting some moral theory through an objective and impersonal observation of types of behavior. But if morality is nothing more than "getting caught up," how can we be certain that it is not a mere social construction? Perhaps the best answer is that we can never be certain, and thus there will always be philosophers, theologians, politicians, clergy, and teachers who think it revelatory and liberating to teach that morality is nothing but a social construction.

But what if we refuse to narrate this "getting caught up" simply in terms of an immanent human power at social construction? What if we listen to the whisky priest, who views his surprising situation as guided by something more than the sum of his own actions and the actions of his social situation? In his own strength he would be incapable of martyrdom, but now he discovers a capacity for something more. Only in light of this "something more" can he begin to see that the lieutenant is fighting against God. The lieutenant is as caught up in this something that is beyond him as is the priest. The moral life is not an achievement of our actions alone. The moral life is our actions and something else, something that beckons us that we do not quite understand but that we cannot quite do without. It is something that catches us. In "catching us," it does not destroy and subvert our sense of things; it makes them more fitting. In its catching of us, we come into our own.

But if this is how the moral life is identified, then how can we know that the priest's reading of these events is any more true than that of the lieutenant's? If morality is getting caught up in something greater than ourselves, then Nietzsche could be correct: morality is not an antithesis between good and evil in which we choose one or the other; it is more a contingent historical reality that we avoid by mystifying it with moral language. Good and evil are seldom obvious choices we make in the midst of an unusual situation. Instead, we merely "get caught up" in a way of life, and then, fortuitously or tragically, we find ourselves in need of justification for our way of life. Perhaps ethical language serves a useful purpose in assisting our reflection upon those ways of life; perhaps it merely serves to justify our actions with a technical language alien to our actual practice.

The philosopher's ethical taxonomy is not helpful in explaining why the terms *good* and *evil* have a hold upon us because this taxonomy is merely epiphenomenal; that is to say, its theoretical descriptions are only indirectly related to the actual practice of morality. Surely Graham Greene's novel offers a more compelling explanation of good and evil than does the taxonomy. But if we are merely "caught up" in certain ways of living, then the terms *good* and *evil* may be similar to terms such as *deontology, teleology,* and *casuistry;* they are merely used retrospectively to justify or mystify what we did when we "just got caught up."

Perhaps the use of terms like *good* and *evil* is a sickness, a residual element of immaturity. Perhaps a future generation will look upon the phrase "good and evil" as a sign of a not-yet developed civilization still bound by superstitious myths. Much like we are condescending toward those who thought the earth was flat, those who come after us will find our judgments of persons and actions as good or evil quaint and naive. "Notice how ethical judgments permeated their culture," they might say of us with a detached fascination. Perhaps, but who wants to live in such a disenchanted world? Who wants to observe genocide, murder, rape, and other hideous "evils" and regard them as only so many contingent vital forces of nature? We seem to need to bear witness to the good even when we cannot explain it.

When we begin to analyze why good and evil have such a hold on us, we lack the ability to give an adequate explanation. This is the reason I have used "enchantment" to explain *good* and *evil;* they are words we cannot (yet) do without, yet we lack adequate explanations as to why we seem to need them. They are there like magical incantations, and in a scientific and rational age, little room remains to take seriously what appears in such a mysterious guise. Perhaps, some would say, we would be better off facing the reality of our situation. G*ood* and *evil* have had their day; let us be done with them.

GETTING CAUGHT UP IN THE TRAGIC

This option is returning as a viable "ethic" in our postmodern culture. It is the return of a Greek paganism. Through the influence of Nietzsche, some moralists and philosophers now revel in the tragic, moving beyond good and evil toward play and beauty alone. They claim that good and evil are only names we give to forces that press down upon us as so much quanta of uncontrolled energy. *Good* and *evil* merely name those fates that inflict us independent of our actions or discoveries. Thus John Caputo informs us,

> You and I, all things, this very moment, this innocent child here who suffers needlessly, these prosperous white upper classes who flourish at the expense of others—that is all so much will to power, so many quanta of force charging and discharging their energy, a veritable monster of energy, decreasing here, increasing there, blessing itself in its sheer innocence. . . . You and I stand on the surface of the little star and shout, "racism is unjust." The cosmos yawns and takes another spin. There is no cosmic record of our complaint.[9]

Has Caputo seen something that many of us have not yet seen, or is this just a tired imitation of Nietzsche? Is this now our reality? No, it is merely the logical conclusion of a quest to achieve good and avoid evil that has ended in failure. If Caputo is correct, terms such as *good, evil, justice,* and *injustice* cannot matter; they are tragic illusions.

Caputo's argument makes little sense. To say that racism is unjust *and* that human actions are only the discharge of energy seems illogical. Either the statement "racism is unjust" signifies something substantive, or it is only the assertion of Caputo's will, a meaningless discharge of energy. But then "racism is unjust" has no significance. Perhaps that is Caputo's point. If it is, why would he seem to be bothered by the fact that the cosmos yawns? Why do these moral terms still enchant him? Is he a superhuman moralist who has risen above the language of good and evil and now seeks to tell the rest of us herdlike masses what he has seen? Or is ethics still for Caputo (as Nietzsche suggested) nothing but philosophical autobiography?

When philosophers do not know what makes the conditions for their own existence possible, they dismiss the moral life altogether. Or they claim to have seen it—to have looked behind the veil of the real—and find it tragic, the unleashed forces of fate. But having viewed "reality," our philosophers do not have the strength of an Oedipus; they refuse to pluck out their own eyes rather than see such a hideous reality.

Nietzsche first appealed to the tragic literature of fifth-century B.C. Athens as a corrective to Western obsessions with the unity of life that the notion of the good makes possible. In this literature, even if one knows the distinction between good and evil, such knowledge is irrelevant; one's fate cannot be avoided. The best that can be hoped for is to embrace the tragic character of one's life and to turn it into something beautiful. Perhaps this is best demonstrated in Sophocles' play, *Oedipus the King*.[10]

In the play, an oracle comes to King Laius that his newborn son Oedipus will kill him and sleep with the baby's mother, Laius's wife, Jocasta. Upon hearing this, Jocasta takes her son and gives him to a henchman to cast into the desert to die. But the henchman gives him away to be raised by a family in a different city, where he grows up thinking that his adopted father, Polybus, is his natural father. In this other city, Oedipus hears from the fates that it was foretold that he would kill his father and sleep with his mother. Because he is a good and honorable person and seeks to avoid this fate, he leaves the home of Polybus and exiles himself. As he travels one day, a driver and passenger in a wagon attack Oedipus. Oedipus swiftly and decisively defends himself, not realizing that the aggressor he kills in self-defense is his true father, King Laius. The dreaded prophecy is realized. Later Oedipus answers the riddle put forward by the Sphinx to save the people of Thebes and is honored by being made king. He marries Laius's wife Jocasta, his own mother, and together they bear children. In his ignorance, Oedipus is blind to the conditions of his own possibility.

Oedipus's obsession to discover who murdered the former king brings him self-knowledge, and with this knowledge he discovers the "truth." The blind prophet Tiresius reveals to him "the corruption of his life." When Oedipus sees the truth, the vision is ghastly: "I see myself stained with such corruption, stained to the heart." Oedipus's knowledge is not redemptive; the "truth" does not set him free. He had no tragic flaw, nothing that deserved such a hideous turn of events in his own life. Yet despite his admirable character, he kills his father and sleeps with his mother; his own children are his brothers and sisters—all events that we might think even a person of less than ordinary moral character should be able to avoid. If Oedipus could not avoid them, what are we to say about the structure of reality? What are we to say about truth and goodness? Are they not rendered to be mere illusions for weak-minded persons who cannot see what Oedipus has seen?

It would be more than inadequate to tell Oedipus, "So what! You slept with your mother and killed your father, but you didn't mean to do it. It is not your fault. Cease your self-flagellation. You are not culpable. Leave your eyes alone. Affirm your being." But this seems to be the kind of advice modern moralists are reduced to when our moral culpability is based primarily on the choosing will. Any moral philosophy that makes the choosing will the center of the moral life cannot adequately explain tragedy. If we assumed Oedipus could dismiss his circumstances simply because he was not culpable for his actions, then we would fail to recognize the depth of his suffering. For the tragedians, evil is not a choice, but a fate; it is something that we "get caught up in" despite our best intentions.

Perhaps the only redemptive element in Sophocles' play is that we as an audience get to look upon the tragedy, see life as it is, and embrace it nonetheless. We are not the authors of good and evil; we are its captives. But we need not let it victimize us. We can take the horrible "truthfulness" of our lives and turn it into something beautiful. This seems to be the path Nietzsche thought we should take once we have moved beyond good and evil.

The tragic vision does not require a complete dismissal of the terms *good* and *evil*, but it does require a dismissal of an end, a *telos* termed *good* toward which we are moving. Everything does not come out good in the end; no redemption is found there. As Lou Ruprecht suggests, "The Greek theater was far from thinking teleologically, tragedy has no interest in the end."[11] For Ruprecht, tragedy functions as an undeniable, universal, common human experience. Tragedy is an anthropological given. Thus any account of good and evil needs to be situated within the terms of the tragic structure of our lives. Even the Gospels should be read as tragedies.

Ruprecht finds the Gospel of Mark tragic because of its lack of an ending. Ancient copies of this text end the Gospel at 16:8, where the angel tells the women who have come to tend to Jesus' dead body that he is not there. If the Gospel ends here, Jesus makes no physical appearance. The end is not in sight. The ending is left open. Although the church's tradition thought this inadequate and thus supplied the rest of the story, Ruprecht finds the Gospel more compelling without the physical appearance of Jesus. The conflict of wills evident in the garden, the agony, and its lack of resolution point out the fundamentally tragic nature of our lives. This lack of resolution tells us that

> salvation is through suffering, not from it. Suffering is not necessarily tragedy's last word, but it is decidedly the first; if it is not "the end," it is definitely "the beginning" of a tragedy. And here is precisely where tragedies and gospels are speaking the same language: in the performance of human suffering, in the refusal to accept it blindly, in the will to understand something through it, and in the understanding, to see it transformed.[12]

Yet Ruprecht cannot tell us what that "something" is that we understand by opening our eyes to suffering. Jesus does not appear. All that appears is our will to understand the tragic and see it transformed. He gives us no compelling alternative to Caputo's yawning abyss, only a tragic view of evil as our ultimate reality.

To say that Graham Greene helps us understand our enchantment with the terms *good* and *evil* by recognizing that the moral life is best understood as "being caught up," I do not mean something as hideous as a tragic fate where good and evil are locked in an inevitable conflict. We do, of course, get caught up in such a pagan understanding of the moral life. But getting caught up itself is not laudable. The question is, Toward what are we caught? What do we want? Toward what do our desires compel us? Is it possible to get caught up in a good that is not in primordial conflict with evil? And how would we envision our lives in such a world—a world that bears witness through our actions to God's goodness?

BEYOND EVIL

Ruprecht's effort to renarrate Christianity as tragedy is not surprising. Evil and suffering have dominated theological imagination for some time. A preoccupation with the rise of evil and an effort to explain it has resulted in evil constituting too central a place in Christian theology. Evil is no longer viewed as merely a lack, as a privation from good, as it was with the church fathers. Our modern preoccupation with evil makes it a thing, a substance that is, and thus is explainable in terms of the "human condition." Evil and its subset, "sin," are the last Christian doctrines capable of universalization with a good conscience in the modern era. If they describe the human condition, then anyone can understand sin even if he or she has no relationship to Judaism or Christianity. When all of theology must be done in such a way that the maxim of its action is a universal law, radical evil as an anthropological given dominates our theological imagination.

Curiously, many Christian theologians have been quite comfortable with universalizing the doctrine of sin and turning it into a general anthropological condition while being increasingly hesitant to universalize Christian redemption or the *logos* of the incarnation as the basis for all creation. This is an odd circumstance in modern theology. Any argument that would see in the particular contours of Jesus' life the good end, which all creation should serve, often appears to us too parochial in a world defined by so many different cultures and religions. But for some reason, the same suspicion has not circulated among theologians against explaining that "the human condition" is caught in a tragic web of sinfulness. Yet the idea of a generalized human condition bound by sinfulness is as particular a Christian reading of a shared Jewish text (Genesis 3) as is the argument that Jesus is the Messiah. Why is it acceptable then to continue to speak of this universal human condition, yet unacceptable to speak of the universality of Christian redemption through the particularity of Jesus? Explaining the "human condition" in terms of the antinomy between good and evil is still the dominant strategy for making theological reflection relevant to contemporary human experience.

Robert Williams takes this approach in his essay "Sin and Evil" in the popular introductory theological textbook *Christian Theology: An Introduction To Its Traditions and Tasks*. In this essay, Williams objects to doctrines of sin as found in Karl Barth and Karl Rahner because they tie sin too thoroughly to a particularly Christian narrative of redemption. Williams finds this to be fideistic. He writes, "Fideism is present in the attempt to derive the meaning of sin entirely from soteriology and Christology, for if the meaning of sin is entirely generated out of the symbols and concepts of soteriology, no real insight is obtained into sin and evil as aspects of human experience."[13] That no real insight into human experience is obtained from soteriology and Christology is an odd assertion for a Christian theologian to make. It seems to assume that any adequate account of human experience will present itself solely from human experience itself. But why should christological and soteriological claims not be recognized as decisive for "real insight into human experience"? After all, Christians profess that Jesus Christ is true divinity and true *humanity*. Should we not expect Christology to give us "real insight into human experience"? Yet Williams denies that evil should be construed as the lack of a good that is defined in christological terms. Evidently, something universal will be lost if evil and sin are bound by soteriological themes rather than by an articulation of the human condition. Williams assumes that a particular reading of sin and evil in terms of Christian soteriological symbols will lose the general anthropological insight as to the nature of sin. Instead, human experience alone can give us "real insight into sin and evil."

When Williams explains these general, universal insights into sin and evil, he emphasizes the "tragic depth of evil."[14] He notes the problems involved in locating evil anthropologically. It creates an irresolvable antinomy. Human freedom produces anxiety that leads to sin and at the same time is the result of sin. Once this generalized anthropology becomes the reason for sin, it cannot at the same time be its result. "It cannot be the case, therefore, that autonomy and anxiety are the results of the fall since they are ontological and constitutive of freedom."[15] This argument points in a direction beyond anthropology as a way to explain evil, but Williams does not then move away from explaining evil in generic, anthropological terms. Instead, he resolves the antinomy by finding a "tragic flaw in human existence, coextensive with its essential goodness." This makes evil and good necessary antinomies. Evil is necessary for good just as good requires evil.

This tragic view of life conflicts with traditional Christian theology as found in Augustine and Thomas Aquinas. They both argued that good was possible without evil, but evil was not possible without good. Thus, they sought to move us beyond evil to that which truly is, which is always good. The grammar of the faith as developed by Williams cannot do this. Divine goodness has a necessary shadow side. Yet Williams cannot escape the church fathers completely, thus he argues, "Although divine goodness appears to have a tragic aspect, God is not a 'tragic God.'"[16] But the second part of that sentence conflicts with the first. If divine goodness is tragic, then we do have a tragic God. Otherwise we must separate God's attributes from God's essence. Only then can we say something as illogical as "Although divine goodness appears to have a tragic aspect, God is not a 'tragic God.'" If Williams viewed the good as a transcendent predicate of being, he would not be able to separate God's goodness from God himself. Then he might be able to question whether an apparent tragic notion of the good available to us should be univocally attributed to God himself.

Williams's Christian piety prevents him from following through on the logic of his position. He acknowledges a "tragic depth and flaw of human freedom," and he concludes that sin arises from the ontological constitution of human freedom. Yet because, as Christian tradition insists, the origin of evil and the origin of being must be kept separate, he asserts that this tragic depth and flaw of human freedom is not a necessary ingredient of this ontological constitution. His argument contradicts itself.

Perhaps the problem is precisely that Williams still takes evil too seriously as an anthropological condition. He sees good and evil as a necessary antinomy for being human even when he must deny the implications of that position. This position could be traced back at least to the nineteenth-century theologian Friederich Schleiermacher. He made sin an anthropological condition by the way he explained the Christian doctrine of the fall. Sin became a permanent feature of the human condition; it became ontological.[17]

Schleiermacher followed the Reformed theologian John Calvin in asserting that human creatures were "totally depraved." Original sin created a "complete incapacity for good which can be removed only by the influence of Redemption."[18] However, for Schleiermacher, this original sin was not prompted by some historical fall where cosmic principalities and powers rebelled against God. It was explained in terms of the human condition *qua* human. Although Schleiermacher constantly referred to christological themes to explain the relationship between sin and grace, he emphasized that "sin is anterior to grace."[19] Thus sin is explained prior to grace, and here the damage is done. Generations of Protestant theologians can now speak of sin and evil without first speaking of God.

TOWARD AN ENCHANTING GOOD:
BEING CAUGHT UP IN A QUEST FOR GOD

Schleiermacher's theology made possible a discussion of sin and evil as a condition of being human that can be known without first acknowledging goodness. This possibility, however, arises in opposition to a different insight he had, namely that evil is a lack of God-consciousness, for Schleiermacher also acknowledged that only when we are conscious of God can we resist God.[20] Sin is a derivative concept, secondary to our knowledge of God.

This latter insight of Schleiermacher's was developed by Karl Barth, but it was developed in such a way that sin was not made an anthropological condition. Instead, knowledge of sin was dependent upon Christology. Barth wrote, "In the knowledge of sin we have to do basically and in general with a specific variation of the knowledge of God, of God as He has mediated Himself to man, and therefore of the knowledge of revelation and faith."[21] According to Barth, we cannot speak of sin without first speaking of God, and knowledge of God depends upon knowledge of Christ. So Barth critiqued Reformation theology for its failure to radically reconsider "the meaning, importance and function of Christology in relation to all Christian knowledge." In particular, it failed to do this with the doctrine of sin. Thus Reformation theology was incapable of developing an adequate standard to discern good from evil. Barth wrote, "There is no doubt that in the measure that we think we know what the Law and sin are 'by nature,' and therefore because the Law of God is written on the heart of ourselves, to that extent our knowledge will not in fact be the knowledge of faith."[22]

Barth thought our knowledge of sin became separated from knowledge of faith when the "*lex naturae* is read as the inner *lex aeternae.*" He suggested that this was the mistake Scholastic theology made because of the influence of Thomas Aquinas. But here Barth was mistaken. Although the manualist tradition of the High Middle Ages can fairly be accused of reading the law of nature as the inner core of the eternal law, for Aquinas, the relationship between the *lex naturae* and the *lex aeternae* is not so construed.[23] The law of nature is a participation in the eternal law. The eternal law, the divine plan upon which all creation and nature are founded, is the Second Person of the Trinity. He is true God and true humanity. Separate from him, we cannot know what it means to be human. Aquinas can only speak of grace in terms of law because Christ himself is the New Law. We cannot know ultimate goodness or its defect, sin, without some knowledge of this New Law. This New Law is not merely added on to a nature already complete in itself; this New Law renders intelligible nature *qua* nature.

Therein resides the problem for modern theology. To claim that we must know the Second Person of the Trinity before we can understand evil seems too extreme and parochial. We want a "nature" that we can know without correlating it to any particular theological language. If Barth were correct, then the question of good and evil would be related to a quest for the Triune God. If we make the life of a Jewish Nazarene the basis upon which knowledge of God, knowledge of humanity, and the derivative concepts of sin and evil depend, what will this mean for other religions, cultures, and peoples who do not share our faith? Surely this question drives arguments like Williams's that seek to develop a different side of Schleiermacher and speak of nature and sin prior to, and now separate from, the concrete example of grace found in the flesh of Jesus. But then good and evil are turned into an antinomy universally present in human nature. The question of their resolution is no longer a quest for a community of Jewish or Christian faith. It is now a metaphysical quest, and evil has become a necessary antinomy to good for being human. It is some-*thing*. If we want freedom, we must have evil. Therefore we can excuse Ruprecht for confusing the gospel with Greek tragedy. Protestant theologians made such an error possible.[24] But such an error will have disastrous results for our understanding of the church and the possibility of redemption, for it will inevitably subordinate the church and theology to the state and political philosophy. The latter mediate salvation in a world defined by a tragic dialectic, where to have freedom we must also have an evil that must be contained through a human will to power. When the good is predicated upon a reaction against a prior evil, we cannot help but privilege the modern state, with its philosophical basis in the restraint of violence, as a social institution more universal than the church. Any redemption we can hope for will not be a redemption from sin and evil, but a redemption that at best can contain the always threatening violence of sin and evil through a counteracting assertion of power. Our language about the good will be trapped by the language of that putatively more universal institution, the *polis*. We will become preoccupied with language like "rights" and "justice" and terms such as "the church and society."[25] Such language inevitably results in the subordination of theology to ethics.

To say that Graham Greene helps us understand our enchantment with the terms "good" and "evil" by recognizing that the moral life is best understood as "being caught up," I do not mean something as hideous as a tragic fate where good and evil are locked in an inevitable conflict. Christian theologians once thought such a "being caught up" was a more compelling description of our life than the tragic alternative. We are directed toward a God who is found in the sensible elements of everyday life, a God incarnate in Jesus. The moral task is not to achieve that which can't be an achievement; rather the moral task is simply not to turn away from God, from our movement toward that which is good. (Contra Barth, this movement assumes no final distinction between the *lex naturae* and *lex eternae*.) The moral task is to allow one's self to be caught up in the general movement of all creation toward God. This is no tragic world, but a world filled with goodness, truth, and beauty. Tragedy is not a necessary feature of creaturely existence, but one that we "achieve" by striving for knowledge of good and evil without knowledge of God. Nor is this a world that denies human freedom, but God's good creation cannot be defined by an a priori ontological constitution defined in terms of a necessary conflict between good and evil. Human freedom is not about a capacity to choose between good or evil. Human freedom occurs when our desires are so turned toward God and the good that no choice is necessary. Few of us may participate fully in such a goodness in this lifetime, but Jesus shows us that such a life is possible *in our humanity*—not against it.

Although faced with signs that we are progressively moving toward the tragic as that which gives our lives intelligibility, we are even now not yet fully living in that place. A few overenlightened persons are "against ethics," but most of us remain enchanted by good and evil. An enchanted world does not necessarily need Jesus as the object turning our desires toward God's goodness. There are other possibilities to explain how we get caught up in a journey toward good that seeks to avoid evil.

COMPETING VISIONS/ALTERNATIVE QUESTS

Plato's philosophy can give us one answer. It is often interpreted as a deliverance from the tragic temptation.[26] The tragic view of the world prevents the rule of reason, for if good and evil hold us captive, how can we exercise right reason that will control and sublimate unruly passions?

For Plato, "the good" was a transcendent idea, not an idea in the subjective sense of a thought located in one's head, but more in the sense of an archetype or first thing. The good is a first thing that exists. It is universal and transcendent but not self-evident. It is even "beyond being." Many interpreters of Plato understand him to have posited the good as achieved only through a laborious process of education and contemplation in which we eschew our sensibility to discover a secure ontological presence of the good. Plato's story of the cave provides the basis for such an interpretation.

Imagine a cave, Plato has Socrates state to his interlocutors in *The Republic*, where people are bound since childhood in leg and neck irons so that they can only see the back of the cave facing away from the opening. Behind them is a fire, and between them and the fire is a wall upon which puppeteers carry objects and make noises. The people in leg irons see only the shadows on the wall and associate those shadows with the noises they hear. These people assume, albeit falsely, that the representations they see and hear are in fact a truthful depiction of reality. Such persons "would hold that the truth is nothing other than the shadow of artificial things."[27] This is the condition of human beings. We live in the land of the shadows, unable clearly to perceive reality as it is. Because we live in the shadows of the appearances, we cannot immediately grasp reality as it is. To do so would be akin to immediately bringing people out of the cave to the light of day and asking them to stare into the sun. They would be blinded. Only through a gradual process would people who have lived their lives in the shadows of the cave be able to see in the presence of the sun. So it is with human knowledge. Only through a laborious and difficult process can we actually know and see that which truly is, especially the good that is even beyond being. As Socrates suggests, "the last thing to be seen, and that with considerable effort is the idea of the good; but once seen, it must be concluded that this is in fact the cause of all that is right and fair in everything—in the visible it gave birth to light and its sovereign; in the intelligible, itself sovereign, it provided truth and intelligence."[28] It is the source of being.

What is "the idea of the good"? It cannot be explained without the soul's laborious effort to "journey up to the intelligible place." Only through heroic intellectual efforts to free oneself from the chains that bind to mere appearances can one even begin that journey. But Plato finds an end to that journey. The Good is (but, as Iris Murdoch reminds us, it is by no means God).

This journey is a powerful alternative to the Christian and Jewish journey toward God. Plato's philosophic quest to achieve this good is still embodied in our culture. The image of the hero who overcomes the chains of custom and tradition to climb out of the cave through a laborious process is replicated countless times in literature, film, and everyday life. Likewise, the understanding of reason as representation holds us in its grasp. The world of appearances in which we live cannot be trusted, so we must look beyond it or above it to something pure and not bound by appearances. Through our intellect, we re-present ideas and free them from their sensible connections to their social and historical boundedness. Once these ideas are represented, then because our will can act freely, we can choose to act in the world as enlightened people rather than as people of the shadows.

Or so goes one interpretation of Plato's work, one commonly presented to undergraduate students in first-year philosophy courses. However, the traditional reading of Plato is clearly not the only way to understand him. Catherine Pickstock reads Plato doxologically. She reminds us of those opening sections in many of the dialogues where praise and prayer are invoked for the presence of the *logos*, the very sections we often overlook in Western civilization courses. Such a doxological reading of Plato rejects the assumption that Plato grounds truth in a secure *eidos* (form) achievable through our laborious efforts to discover our being independent of sensible appearances. It finds in Plato an example of a transcendence that is not secured by some interior subjective space but is enacted through praise and glory. The good, then, is a gift discovered through doxology. It is not a heroic achievement secured through a stable philosophic reason alone.

Although Pickstock offers a refreshing and persuasive interpretation of Plato, the Plato of a philosophical heroism who secures the good without doxology remains the Plato with whom many persons are all too acquainted. This is troubling because, as James C. Edwards notes, this other Plato asks us to be something other than liturgical participants questing for God; it asks us to be god. Edwards finds the philosophical quest for the good to ask a question that only gods could ask, for only gods could answer it.

> One way or another, Western philosophy has continually reenacted the heroic ascent out of the Cave; rationality as representation, especially its apotheosis in metaphysics, is itself a heroic conception.[29]

Edwards finds this other Platonic quest disturbing. It seeks to turn us into something other than human beings, for only heroes or gods can climb out of the cave and see what Socrates wants us to see. Plato's quest denies the significance of the everyday.

Edwards's critique of Plato's "metaphysical Good" is similar to Aristotle's critique. For Aristotle, the good is "that at which all things aim."[30] Aristotle stated, "The good cannot be something universal, common to all cases and single; for if it were it would not be applicable in all categories but only in one."[31] For Aristotle, the good is not a first thing separate from its particular instantiations. Divinity, intelligence, virtues, and the like are all good; *the good* cannot be something transcendent, singular, and universal and thus separate from the specific things we call good.

For Aristotle, things can be good in two ways; they are either intrinsically good or good "as being conducive to the intrinsically good." In this latter sense, Aristotle discusses different goods for different practices. The good of medicine is health, the good of military strategy is victory, and the good of the practice of house-building is a completed house. Yet, asks Aristotle, is there one good for the sake of which all else is done? His answer is yes insofar as this, the highest good, is final and self-sufficient and not something conducive to the good of something else. Honor, pleasure, intelligence, and virtue are candidates for the highest good, but they all fall short. While they are "chosen partly for themselves," they also point to something else, the highest good, which is happiness. Happiness results from a person's exercise of his or her *ergon* or proper function. The "good of man," Aristotle writes, "is an activity of the soul in conformity with excellence or virtue, and if there are several virtues, in conformity with the best and most complete . . . in a complete life."[32] When a person's proper function is exercised, such a one cannot help being happy. But happiness is likewise dependent upon humanity having a proper function that can be exercised in everyday living. This entails that we have an end, a *telos*. Any quest for the good requires that we aim for this *telos*.

Aristotle's description of the good explains how, by participating in everyday activities such as rearing a family, preparing a meal, and driving to work, we get caught up in things that are good in themselves and at the same time point to something more. Aristotle was incapable of articulating that something more. For him the ultimate good was finally an achievement that only a noble person could achieve. Thus, his lack of a well-defined transcendent final good lessened the significance of the everyday and failed to see the good not as an achievement but as a gift; no doxology was necessary for his good. However, Aristotle's insight would be developed and completed by Thomas Aquinas with his theological virtues. These virtues—faith, hope, and charity—complete what is lacking in Aristotle's quest for the good. Although we prepare for them, participate in their reception, and cooperate in their exercise, these virtues come to us as a gift made possible through the historical reality of Jesus, who gives us a new law, the law of the gospel. They are not secure metaphysical possessions but gifts received through liturgical enactment.

If the good is a gift, then perhaps Plato's philosophical quest for the good has some strong similarities with Aquinas's quest for God. Perhaps Edwards is wrong; Plato's quest does not ask us to be god but to participate in God. And such a participation is possible not because of something secure in the human person but because God seeks to give himself to us. This interpretation of Plato would find common ground with that of Raimond Gaita, who finds Plato's Good something other than philosophical heroism. The good "is not an object of pursuit, but that in light of which we and our pursuits are judged." The good is not achieved but discovered; it comes as gift. Thus the appropriate response to it is not to seek nobility and virtue but to love the good as a mysterious gift.[33] What unites us with the good is not striving or overcoming, but loving.

Although Edwards and Gaita differ on their exegesis of Plato, this is secondary to their agreement that a philosophic quest for the good understood as a heroic human achievement has not and cannot be successful. The good is not a heroic achievement. For Edwards, the philosophic quest for the good teaches us to be suspicious of the everyday. For Gaita, the philosophic quest for the good cannot account for mystery, and the good is fundamentally a mysterious category. Pickstock gives us the best account of this when she recognizes that the good must ultimately have a sacramental character. If the good is merely an achievement we seek through overcoming our limitations, then the good will be predicated upon a violent striving against our own finitude and historical limitations. Our histories, traditions, and even our own bodies will need to be overcome for the sake of the good. But Pickstock finds an alternative to this pagan and all-too-modern account of the moral life in the church's eucharistic celebration. A "realistic construal" of the Eucharist, she suggests, is the basis for an understanding of all human meaning, including goodness, that does not "evacuate the body" and embrace death as our final "good."[34] In the Eucharist, like the incarnation, we creatures receive God as gift. This occurs not by abstracting from or overcoming the concrete, sensual matter of everyday life. It comes to us only in and through such matter.

Philosophers themselves acknowledge that the philosophic quest for the good ends in failure. Yet this quest is institutionalized in the modern academy, where we bring students away from the communities in which they were reared to an environment where ideas can be re-presented free from the constraints of family, custom, and tradition. Here we often see a poor reenactment of the story of the cave. Yet while this quest may resemble the philosophic quest for the good, the modern academy is not a place where we expect to find the good. Why is this the case?

Iris Murdoch, among others, has pointed out that the problem is that our quest has drastically shifted. Modern people are no longer on a quest for the good but on a quest for freedom. Thus the questions we ask do not assume we are journeying toward something other than that which we make ourselves, and for such a journey all we need is an "immanent" freedom. That is to say, we need a freedom from anything that would challenge our inherent right to build and live in families and cities of our own making. Murdoch sought to reinstate the good as a nonrepresentable and indefinable sovereign over all other concepts.[35] By her own admission, she did not succeed. The reason is that the overpowering quest for this immanent freedom works against the quest for good. She finds the culprit who misled us to be none other than Kant. Thus she writes,

> The idea of life as self-enclosed and purposeless is of course not simply a product of the despair of our own age. It is the natural product of the advance of science and has developed over a long period of time. It has already in fact occa-

sioned a whole era in the history of philosophy, beginning with Kant. . . . Kant abolished God and made man God in His stead. We are still living in the age of the Kantian man, or Kantian man-god. Kant's conclusive exposure of the so-called proofs of the existence of God, his analysis of the limitations of speculative reason, together with his eloquent portrayal of the dignity of rational man, has had results which might possibly dismay him. . . . This man is with us still. He is the ideal citizen of the liberal state, a warning held up to tyrants. He has the virtue which the age requires and admires, courage. It is not such a very long step from Kant to Nietzsche. . . . In fact Kant's man had already received a glorious incarnation nearly a century earlier in the work of Milton: his proper name is Lucifer.[36]

Murdoch notes that Kant himself would be surprised at the consequences of the Kantian "man-god." Kant thought he was defending the philosophic quest for the good and for God, not rejecting it, and he thought that quest required God as a necessary postulate of practical reason. If Kant is not far from Nietzsche, then we must ask ourselves, What went wrong with his defense of the quest for God and the good?

If philosophy has failed by turning the quest for the good into a quest for freedom that ends in nihilism, then perhaps philosophy can recover a search for the good only when it renders itself once again in service to theology. This will require rejecting not only Kant's critique of God's existence but, even more important, his moral proof for the existence of God. Kant's critique of God's existence recapitulated a philosophical error that was introduced into theology in the late Middle Ages. Like Duns Scotus, Kant assumed that *existence* was not a real predicate of anything. It was only an assertive modality of judgment. Thus his critique of the *ontological* proof for the existence of God only works when ontology is defined in Scotist terms: *existence* is a mode of being and not a real predicate of it. After the criticisms of this ontology Etienne Gilson brought to bear on that philosophical tradition, any decent philosopher can point out the problems with Kant's critique of the ontological proof.[37] The problem Kant poses for Christian theology is not primarily found in his first critique, which addresses the so-called ontological proof for the existence of God. The problem Kant poses for Christian theology is found in his second critique, where he makes a space for God in rational discourse solely on the basis of the freedom of the individual will as the basis for the moral life. It is Kant's defense of good and God that renders theology irrational, severing any connection between theology and philosophy. We need a moral quest other than the one Kant has bequeathed us. To set out on that other journey, we must first recognize how the quest for freedom sets unreasonable limits to theological arguments.

The next chapter explains Kant's moral quest. It is a quest for freedom that Kant himself recognized as revolutionary. This quest too often establishes the context within which moral action is understood. To start out on an alternative quest, we must first recognize how Kant's quest has enticed our moral imagination. Only when we find ourselves freed from that quest by acknowledging its failure can we undertake a theological quest that seeks God and therefore goodness. Kant did raise for us a profound question: How does God matter in everyday life? But Kant's answer reduces theology to ethics and makes God, at best, an understudy in the moral drama, always there in the shadowy wings merely to prop up our courage if we doubt the authenticity of our freedom to do our duty. God mattered for Kant in such a way that God's necessity for morality's possibility rendered God useless for actual moral practice. Ethics made theology useless.

TWO

Kant's Ethical REVOLUTION against RELIGION: Questing for FREEDOM

The relationship between theology and ethics has been largely determined in the modern era by the questions Immanuel Kant posed and the answers he gave. This contains a certain irony, because in 1786 Kant's philosophy was banned at Marburg on the assumption that it threatened faith and morals. His demolition of the Scholastic arguments for the existence of God were thought to be a threat to Christian faith. Many neo-Kantians relished this challenge to theology and moved Kantianism in the very direction the orthodox authorities feared.[1] By 1835 Heinrich Heine had written an essay for French publication entitled, "On the History of Religion in Germany." He argued that Robespierre himself was unworthy of comparison with the revolutionary Kant. Robespierre may have lopped off a few royal heads, but "Kant has stormed heaven, he has put the whole crew to the sword, the Supreme Lord of the world swims unproven in his own blood."[2] Perhaps Kant's ethics did not go as far as Heine asserted, but it did result in the marginalization of theology from ethics. Ethics was grounded in freedom alone. Theology could be consistent with ethics but not determinative for it.

Yet God's absence in Kantian ethics is surprising because Kant himself worried that the dethronement of reason, which he assisted, would lead to atheism, and atheism to "libertinism" in moral matters.[3] In fact, Kant sought to defend the notion of a "living" God against what he perceived to be the lifeless God of Spinoza.[4] And Kant understood that many of the proofs for God—ontological, cosmological, and physico-theological—were incapable of rendering intelligible this living God.

Nevertheless, I shall argue that both Kant's orthodox critics and his antitheological defenders misidentified Kant's threat to and/or revolution against theology. Despite the fear of his orthodox critics and the delight of his antitheological defenders, Kant's critique of God's *existence* poses little threat to Christian theology. Kant merely highlighted problems in late-medieval philosophical arguments in which ontology had already been developed with the assumption that *existence* was nothing more than a formal or modal assertion.

Long before Kant, *existence* had become philosophically suspect in metaphysics. The ontology found in such a metaphysics could never prove God's existence, and with a more reasonable ontology, as found in Thomas Aquinas, such an ontology was never intended as a *proof.*[5] Thus Heine was wrong to assert that Kant had obliterated the Trinity. In fact, Kant posed a useful theological question that could have moved philosophy beyond a late-medieval metaphysics: What sensuous, real-life practice renders theology intelligible? Unfortunately, Kant's answer to that question proved disastrous because it made theology dependent on and subservient to ethics. It was not Kant's calling into question our knowledge of God's existence that marginalized theology from ethics; rather, his ethical defense for the *necessity* of God as a postulate of practical reason marginalized theology from the moral life. Kant's "moral proof" for God's existence produced his ethical revolution against religion, a revolution that has exhausted itself even though many "theological" ethicists do not yet want to recognize that exhaustion. Thus, I shall argue that the orthodox authorities were nonetheless correct in their suspicions against Kant's ethics, but for the wrong reasons.

Karl Barth points the way beyond Kant with his revolutionary suggestion that Christian dogmatics is ethics. As Barth put it, "We can speak about man only by speaking about God."[6] Thus any discussion of human action entailed understanding who God is and what God has done. Barth cannot be fairly accused of failing to recognize that speaking about God also requires speaking about human creatures. As John Webster so ably demonstrates, Barth's theology is a moral theology preoccupied with human action precisely because dogmatics is ethics.[7] The common criticism raised by Hans Urs von Balthasar and others that Barth was unable to give full development to the significance of human action by his dialectical method and his philosophical actualism certainly has some merit, but this is not the heart of the difference between Barth and von Balthasar. Even though von Balthasar's work would not be possible without Barth's brilliant theological insight that dogmatics is ethics, they differ on which dogmas one employs. This is the heart of the matter that divides them. The debate between them, as well as among Barthianians and Balthasarians, as to Barth's use of analogy and dialectic is secondary to the more primary debate about which dogmas constitute ethics.[8] For Barth, the dogma of election was the heart of the Christian moral life. This contributed to his consistent concern to avoid any "'false absolutism' of finite things" so that only God's command, and nothing a priori, would constitute ethics. This prevented him from drawing upon certain dogmas von Balthasar envisioned as central to moral theology.[9] In particular, the dogma of infallibility, the role of Mary, eucharistic transubstantiation, and the authority of the early ecumenical councils are the decisive dogmas that separate Barth from von Balthasar.[10] Related to this is Barth's reluctance to incorporate the language of virtue or character in the Christian life. Barth is so concerned to ensure that ethics does not become a philosophical framework within which to read dogma that, according to von Balthasar, he truncates dogma. Dogmas that develop the church's giftedness as a true and "absolute" social formation in time, participating and re-presenting Christ's ministry and mission to the world, do not function adequately for Barth's analysis of human action.[11]

If Barth does not adequately develop the significance of human action, it is not because his theology is "abstract" or uninterested in human action. In one sense, nothing else interests Barth. The charge that Barth has not adequately developed the theological significance of human action only makes sense because of the different dogmas Barth and von Balthasar draw upon for their accounts of human action. The same reason Barth cannot draw on these dogmas is the reason he also does not embrace the theology of Thomas Aquinas.[12] He finds Aquinas to be symptomatic of Catholicism's absolutization of temporal, finite things in its temptation "to lay hands on God."

Oddly enough, Barth himself influenced a rereading of the work of Aquinas through the theologian Hans Urs von Balthasar. Theologians like von Balthasar, who rehabilitated Thomas Aquinas, can help us knit together theology and ethics so seamlessly that the question of what the relationship is between theology and ethics need not even arise. This theological reality of Aquinas's fulfills Barth's revolutionary idea that dogmatics is ethics, perhaps even better than Barth himself. It allows us to construct an "exclusively theological concept of nature" such that no division such as "theology *and* nature" or "theology *and* ethics" arises.[13] Speaking about God entails at the same time speaking about ethics, politics, nature, and vice versa.

In this sense, Kant can be helpful, for he recognized what John Milbank has explicitly stated, "Theology has no 'proper' subject matter, since God is not an object of our knowledge and is not immediately accessible." Because God is not a proper "object," Milbank argues that "theology must always speak 'also' about the creation and therefore always 'also' in the tones of human discourse about being, nature, society, language and so forth."[14] In speaking the "also" we are not merely using a symbolic language with which we can dispense; we are speaking about God, but we are speaking analogically. Nevertheless, we are speaking about God such that we need not speak a language other than that which humans can speak. We do not abstract from everyday language to speak of God; we speak of God in and through it. It is, after all, the only language we speak.

If we can speak *about* God, then Kant's rigid separation between knowledge of God and human sensible knowledge is irrational, for this distinction assumes that we cannot reasonably speak about God. Kant's distinction between these two realms of knowledge implies that we can know without a doubt what we cannot know, for he claims to know what can be known and unknown about the relationship between God and the world with a "metaphysical dogmatism" that Aquinas could never have countenanced.[15] Kant's *Critique of Pure Reason* establishes a limit between "reasonable" human knowledge, which cannot speak meaningfully of God, and transcendental "illusion," which can speak of God but does so unreasonably. This division assumes Kant's limit between things as they are for us (phenomenal) and things as they are in themselves (noumenal). This limit functions as a police barricade that keeps everyone to one side. But such a barricade only works if we also claim implicitly to know what is on the other side. In other words, only if we claim to know with certainty what cannot be known with certainty would we know where to place the barricade in the first place. But this is an unreasonable position. Because Aquinas is *more* agnostic than Kant concerning the limits of our knowledge of the relationship between God and creation, John Milbank finds him more reasonable than Kant.

Milbank's appeal to the necessity of "also" speaking about being, nature, society, etc. should make Barthians uneasy. After all, Barth thought that the vast majority of analogical language about being was nothing less than an anti-Christian speech that sought to master the relationship between God and creation by subordinating it to a larger philosophical system. When Barth read the Catholic theologian Eric Pryzwara's *Analogia Entis,* he thought it embodied everything he detested about liberal Protestantism and Roman Catholicism. Both sought to position theology within an overarching philosophical framework that resulted in the domestication of theology. Theology was domesticated by being subordinated not only to philosophy but more importantly to ethics. For this reason Barth asserted that Christian dogmatics is ethics.[16]

Barth thought that also speaking about being (or speaking about theology "and" society) left theology prey to an accommodation to the modern spirit. For this reason, Milbank's willingness to speak "also" about being, nature, society, etc. should cause Barthians to wonder if Barth's theological revolution has been once again domesticated to the liberal, modern spirit by subordinating it to philosophy.

Yet Barth, like Milbank, finds Kant insufficiently agnostic. Kant still had a metaphysical preconception of who God is and what God could do. He thought he knew the limits of the possibility of our knowledge of God. Barth argued it was impermissible ". . . to exalt [such knowledge] to the level of empirical knowledge on account of its incomprehensibility . . . since in order to do this we should already have to have some prior knowledge of what revelation is, and of what God is."[17] Barth suggests that this residual element of some natural knowledge of God, even when it is a knowledge about what cannot be known, inevitably "leads to Rome."[18] This was not a journey Barth thought we should take, for he assumed such a journey required subordinating knowledge of God mediated through Jesus to a putatively greater form of knowledge, such as being, nature, culture, or society. Such natural knowledge leaves open the possibility for the very kind of analogical thought about creation, being, nature, language, and society that Milbank still finds to be necessary for theology.

Barth's critique of Kant's inadequate agnosticism is consistent with his ongoing critique of the *analogia entis*. Although he later thought it might not be central to all Catholic thought, he still found the *analogia entis* to be the position of the Roman Catholic magisterium, and Barth hunted down every possible vestige of the *analogia entis* in both Roman Catholic and Neo-Protestant theology and tried to kill it. Barth was not so foolish as to deny that language about God is all too human and analogical, but he sought to ensure that the *analogia fidei* and not the *analogia entis* would discipline the language. Language that used the "copulative and," such as church *and* society, grace *and* nature, Barth thought, would inevitably sacrifice the *analogia fidei* to the *analogia entis*, which means that rather than Jesus Christ being the mediator between God and creation, other "natural" forms of mediation would be possible. Knowledge of God would not be christologically determined. Philosophy, particularly ethics, would lay hands on God.

BOTH/AND THEOLOGY

Any Protestant who has worked in Catholic institutions knows there is still good reason to be worried about the "copulative and" within Catholicism. Protestant criticisms of any aspect of modern culture can be easily thwarted by modern Catholic theologians who dismiss such criticisms with the facile argument that they represent the Protestant "either/or" while Catholics are more "culture affirming," and thus are "both/and." Such a facile argument neglects the substance of a specific argument and always moves to an empty formalism. The Catholic political philospher Michael Budde has recently subjected this kind of criticism to a searing critique by showing how such thinking was ineffectual in preventing the killing of Christians by Christians in Rwanda, "the most Catholic country in Africa." Budde argues that the "mainstream of intellectual tradition within Catholicism throbs with both/and affirmations." But, he argues,

The problem with such easy compatibility is that in many cases it is wrong. It often has as much to do with the life and message of Jesus as a GM Pontiac has with real Native Americans—nothing except a claimed, most imaginary, continuity of name. This sort of theology displaces the priorities, loyalties, and allegiances of Jesus—which the state and economic elites of his time correctly recognized as subversive, and for which they murdered him—with safer, more comfortable ones. Being a disciple of Jesus, to which all of us are called, was and is meant to be a primary, ultimate, pivotal vocation. By its very nature it cannot share allegiances with lesser goods and commitments.[19]

The problem with the Catholic both/and is not only its formal vacuousness; it also tempts us to tolerate competing allegiances without recognizing we are doing so. Jesus never says to us, "Let the dead bury their dead," because we can always affirm *both* Jesus' difficult command *and* our cultural and societal customs. Contradictions are easily mollified through an overarching philosophical synthesis. Barth recognized the problems to which such an analogy of being could lead when it spoke the language of "both/and" or "also." He also recognized that the "copulative and" was first used naively by conservative Reformed churches to protect religion and society from each other. Each could have its own domain. The result was that politics and economics gained an illegitimate independence from theology. For this reason, he worried about the "and"; it still allowed for a distinction between things that should not be so easily distinguished.[20]

Milbank is not afraid of the "copulative and" when he states that "theology must always speak 'also' about the creation and therefore always 'also' in the tones of human discourse about being, nature, society, language and so forth." Such language must put any good Barthian on the defensive. But the problem with the language is not that Barth was incapable of calling into question the "supposed objects of other sciences" as Milbank has argued.[21] Barth worried that the "and" separated "theology" *and* "society" or "theology" *and* "politics" too thoroughly, so that the latter was given too much space free from theology. Milbank's work is less a critique than a restatement of Barth's position that dogmatics is ethics (and politics, economics, etc.). Nevertheless, the "copulative and" does not function in Milbank's work as Barth thought it would inevitably function. It does not assert that the God-creation relationship can be discerned outside of the Second Person of the Trinity. Even though Milbank asserts, drawing and extending on the work of Henri de Lubac, "there is no gratuity in addition to the gratuity of creation,"[22] this is not a creation that is known via nature alone. It is a creation always already gifted through the same event by which God redeems the world. The eternal generation and gift of the Son is not a foundation for redemption that is not already present in creation; no "pure nature" exists. Thus while Milbank seeks to maintain Budde's appropriate concern that "being a disciple of Jesus was and is meant to be a primary, ultimate, pivotal vocation," he also provides a way for us to speak about our inevitable "allegiances with lesser goods and commitments" without losing that prior pivotal vocation that must render intelligible all other lesser goods and commitments. As Christians, we still take time to raise families, engage in exchanges, write books, watch television, seek education, and—despite a command from Jesus—we take time to bury our parents. Can we make sense of this without falling into a both/and that implicitly bifurcates grace and nature? faith and reason? theology and ethics (including politics and economics)? The Catholic "both/and" too often assumes that these two things are so distinct that they can be discussed and developed separately from each other. It does not resist an inappropriate Protestant "either/or." Barth's radical move to make dogmatics ethics avoids thinking in terms of either a both/and or an either/or.[23]

Yet Barth approximates something akin to Kant's method of denying a priori sensible knowledge of God by using such a denial to safeguard God's own communicative act. Much as Kant's relegation of God to a noumenal realm resulted in God's historical absence from concrete ethical practice, Barth does have difficulty explaining how God's communicative act becomes embodied in everyday human existence. At his best, Barth explains the embodiment of this act through the human capacity to hear. This does not make the human subject merely passive; in fact Barth consistently critiqued liberal Protestantism for making the human subject too passive with its defense of Christianity as a "feeling of absolute dependence." Barth rejected the notion that the God discovered in the biblical witness merely wanted us to be passively dependent. So Barth insisted that hearing is self-determination. But at his worst, Barth simply refuses to explain how the act of God's grace is embodied and appeals to "miracle."

Von Balthasar defended Catholicism against Barth's charge that it always subordinates the Word of Christ to some overarching systematic principle; this was a misreading of Pryzwara's *analogia entis*. Von Balthasar thought this misrepresented Catholicism, but he also thought that Barth's concern prevented him from finding in creation anything other than a contradiction to God's goodness. He thought that Barth himself had subordinated the God-creation relationship to an overarching philosophical system ruled by dialecticism and actualism.[24] He describes Barth's (early) position as, "the searing fire of God's 'aseity,'" which "does not grab hold of a 'neutral' creature but one who is actively opposed to God's holiness." This dialectical method cannot make intelligible that creation is "first of all a legitimate, good and divinely willed counterpart to God." The theological consequences of this method are found in Barth's ethics, where his first attempts "show that he had not yet reached the Christological foundation that takes seriously the two natures of Christ, thereby giving history and temporal being their due."[25] Thus Barth's early account of the relationship between theology and ethics embodied a basic Kantian problem. Having made room for faith through the critique of reason, this faith was too far removed from any historical practice of reason. The moral agent was bifurcated between a free, supersensible, noumenal realm and a contradictory, historical, phenomenal necessity. Kant's barricade remained too thoroughly in place.

Von Balthasar argued that even though Barth's early dialectical theology was later supplemented with "an exclusively theological concept of nature," it was still unable to give history and temporal being their due. This was because the one theological source that could have helped Barth in his theological revolution against Neo-Protestantism and Catholicism's *"analogia entis"* was the theology of Thomas Aquinas. But Barth remained suspicious of Thomism for good reasons. A poor understanding of Thomism led to the development of "natural theology" based on *natura pura*. This allowed for a politics and ethics based on nature without any theology of grace, which meant that politics and ethics had a certain independence and even autonomy from christological considerations.[26] Such an understanding of nature coupled with the Catholic "both/and" remained as dialectical as Barth's own theology. Ethics and politics were not yet dogmatics; they were still pure philosophy. Barth remained suspicious that Aquinas's theology allowed for a natural knowledge of God separate from grace.[27] But, argued von Balthasar, Henri de Lubac's reading of Aquinas recovered the centrality of grace even for nature, for Aquinas's "transitional place in history finds its clearest expression in the fact that he attributes only *one* end, a *supernatural* end, to the created spirit."

This supernatural end allows Aquinas's theology to accomplish two things not available to theology done within a Kantian problematic. First, the reasonableness of the Kantian distinction between the phenomenal and noumenal is called into question. The barricade is torn down. The sensible is not marked off from the supersensible by a divide only mediated through an abstract freedom because Aquinas's supernatural end is not merely beyond nature, it is an "object" eliciting desire within nature. "Nature" is no more set in opposition to "supernature" than Mary would be in opposition to the Son to whom she gives birth. We cannot be so metaphysically dogmatic in our knowledge of God as to assert that God is unknown through sensibility. Second, ethics becomes inseparable from theology. For Kant, ethics is grounded in a freedom known through practical reason alone. Theology can help explain this freedom, but it cannot have any necessary connection to it. Thus Kant requires the separation of ethics from theology; goodness can be discussed under the categories of freedom and law. Aquinas's supernatural end as an object naturally desired requires situating ethics thoroughly within theology; the journey toward the good entails discussions of God. This is why Aquinas's theology assists us in our quest for goodness beyond the modern subordination of the quest for the good to a quest for freedom.

While von Balthasar drew on Aquinas to reform theology in its relationship to ethics, Barth's suspicions against Rome lead him to be suspicious of Thomism, particularly its language of *habitus* and virtue. He recognized the problem modern Protestantism and liberal Catholicism posed to the relationship between theology and ethics. Ethics stood alone without need of sacred doctrine. Dogmatics was not yet ethics. But without an account of the supernatural embodiment of grace in our temporal existence, can dogmatics be ethics? Barth did not finally give us a sufficient answer to this problem. An adequate alternative is needed precisely because the danger Kant poses to theology is found in his ethical defense of religion, a defense grounded in freedom from the historical that Barth himself can be (mis?)read as perpetuating. To understand the problems with this method and its deleterious implications for the relationship between theology and ethics, we must examine more closely both Kant's useful theological question and his problematic answer.

KANT'S QUESTION: CAN THE SENSIBLE BE THEOLOGICAL?

In his criticism of theology, Kant renders theology beyond any historical practice of reason. To make room for faith, theology is severed from reason. But such a reading of Kant is only true of the answer he provided as to what constitutes the relationship between God and creation, not the question he asked. Notice that he began his critique of the ontological proof by stating,

> In all ages men have spoken of an absolutely necessary being, and in so doing have endeavored, not so much to understand whether and how a thing of this kind allow even of being thought, but rather to prove its existence. There is, of course, no difficulty in giving a verbal definition of the concept [of an absolutely necessary being], namely, that it is something the non-existence of which is impossible. But this yields no insight into the conditions which make it necessary to regard the non-existence of a thing as absolutely unthinkable. It is precisely these conditions that we desire to know, in order that we may determine whether or not in resorting to this concept, we are thinking anything at all.[28]

Kant's critique of the theologians here is misleading. How can he argue that they merely tried to prove God's existence and gave no thought to the question "whether and how" such a "thing" can be thought? Neither Anselm's *Proslogion* nor Aquinas's first thirteen questions in the *prima pars* of his *Summa Theologica* fit the distinctions Kant seeks to impose. Neither were so foolish as to think they were simply proving God's existence through the coherence of logical concepts. Both recognized that they were discussing the conditions by which knowledge of God might and might not be possible. But unlike Kant, they did not think those conditions were policed a priori by a human subjectivity that synthesized intuitions into concepts on the basis of a priori categories.

In one sense, Kant's question is neither new nor unique. Kant asks us not to prove God's existence by way of mere concepts that logically cohere but to ask what sensible conditions might allow us to think God intelligibly. His question is similar to that of Anselm's and Aquinas's. That is certainly why Anselm can put forth his "proof" only in the form of a prayer. For Anselm, such knowledge only makes sense doxologically, though it does make sense. But in another sense, Kant's question is new, for it assumes the answer. Unlike Anselm or Aquinas, Kant assumed that no such sensible conditions exist precisely because he was so certain as to what constituted the conditions for all human knowledge. It is Kant's philosophical dogmatism with its concomitant authoritarianism that calls theology into question. But this prejudiced answer should not deter us from recognizing the profundity of the question itself. If we ask Kant's question without assuming his answer a priori, then his critique of the ontological proof for the existence of God points in the same direction as that of theologians such as Anselm, Aquinas, von Balthasar, and Milbank. The priority of God's speech need not be set against the "always also" of human speech about "being, nature, society, language and so forth."

In fact, Kant's philosophy poses little challenge to Christian theology, for he asked this question and demolished the "ontological proofs" for God's existence based on an ontology that assumes that being is concerned primarily with concepts. God cannot be thought of simply as an essence whose concept leads necessarily to his existence. Aquinas argued this and suggested that God's essence *is* God's existence. *God* is not an essence to which existence is added as an accident or merely as a mode of assertive judgment made by human subjectivity. God's existence is God's essence, and this distinguishes God from creation. Although both must be spoken of as *existing,* both cannot be subsumed under a single, univocal category called "being." "God" does not designate an existence *within* an essence, such as I would be an existence *within* the essence of humanity. My existence does not exhaust the essence of humanity, but God's existence exhausts the essence of divinity. Therefore, when we say that God *is,* we cannot mean by "being" something univocal to the statement that I *am.* Nor can we begin by seeking to prove God simply by identifying the *concept* that expresses God's essence. We begin with God's existence, and that is a beginning that comes only as gift.

Of necessity, God's existence can never be proved through reason alone. Aquinas himself suggested as much when he argued that God "is above the necessary and the contingent."[29] Kant's philosophy only becomes problematic for theology when what he found to be impossible in the speculative employment of reason in his first critique ("insight into the conditions which make it necessary to regard the existence of [God] as absolutely thinkable") becomes *necessary* in reason's practical employment in his second critique. Kant moves beyond an analogical language that assumes a distinction between God's being and ours to assert a necessary relationship between God and creation based on the certainty of "practical reason" because of the "fact" of our freedom. In so doing, he subordinates God's being and creaturely being to a larger category of metaphysical freedom. Because this freedom makes ethics possible, ethics subordinates theology to its putatively more universal basis in freedom. In Kant's world, ethics makes the idea of God possible; the idea of God does not make ethics possible. What is worthy of worship is freedom.

Kant already pointed in the direction of God's necessity through the employment of practical reason in his first critique, when he suggested, "Now since there are practical laws which are absolutely necessary, that is, the moral laws, it must follow that if these necessarily presuppose the existence of any being as the condition of the possibility of their obligatory power, this existence must be postulated."[30] Not Anselm but Kant makes the thought of God necessary on the basis of being *qua* being. Kant's adverse influence on theology arises from the *necessity* this answer entails. His ethical revolution against religion arises precisely in his defense of it, and such a defense has misled countless theologians who seek to make theology relevant through its ethical import via Kant's answer and yet neglect his question.

KANT'S ANSWER AND THE ETHICAL REVOLUTION AGAINST RELIGION: ONLY THROUGH FREEDOM CAN GOD BE THOUGHT

Kant's own answer to the question posed in his first critique—What are the sensible conditions that allow us to think God intelligibly?—is incomplete and mischaracterizes theology. His answer to the same question in his second critique is that God must be thought on the basis of practical reason. This answer is truly dangerous to theology. Even Kant's sympathetic interpreters have treated his answer with contempt. Lewis White Beck ends his translator's introduction to the *Critique of Practical Reason* with the following story:

> There is a tale invented by Heinrich Heine, that Kant demolished religious belief, but when he saw how unhappy this made his servant Lampe, the great philosopher showed that he was also a kindly man by writing the *Critique of Practical Reason* to give old Lampe his faith again. This is, of course, a caricature of the doctrine of the primacy of practical reason and its postulates. But if readers will keep this story in mind as they read the Dialectic, so that at the end they can decide whether there is a kernel of truth inside the husk of error in this anecdote, they can rightly feel that they have at least the beginning of real insight into what is perhaps the most important and profound philosophy of morals produced in modern times.

Kant answered his question by examining reason in its "practical faculty."[31] This turn to practical reason misled Kant's interpreters, such as Heine, for it seemed to give back what was taken away in the first critique, God as a necessary intelligible thought.

For Kant, God is necessary for the possibility of the moral life because God makes possible the highest good and the state of blessedness. Without the highest good, freedom and nature remain too thoroughly separated. Human agents would have the freedom to act in accord with the moral law, but without the highest good, the moral law has no object found in nature. God is necessary for the possibility of morality, for God secures the highest good and gives Kant's ethical system completeness.[32] The state of blessedness ensures that well-being and well-doing can be united.[33] This point is made explicitly in his *Lectures on Philosophical Theology*.

> An indeterminate concept of God does not help me at all. Yet on the other hand, the concept of God is a moral concept, and practically necessary. For morality contains the conditions as regards the conduct of rational beings under which alone they can be worthy of happiness. These conditions, these duties are apodictically certain. For they are grounded necessarily in the nature of a rational and free being. Only under these conditions can such a being become worthy of happiness. But if in the case of a creature who has conducted himself according to these eternal and immediate laws of nature, and who has thus become worthy of happiness, no state can be hoped for where he participates in this happiness; if no state of well-being follows his well-doing; then there would be a contradiction between morality and the course of nature.[34]

God prevents morality from *reductio ad absurdum practicum* by ensuring the state of blessedness. If we are free to will a maxim consistent with the categorical imperative, we must know that the categorical imperative exists for some purpose that would be the highest good and that this highest good will bring a state of blessedness. Otherwise, our freedom would be illusory; it would be vacuous, having no actual object.

This poses an irremediable contradiction in Kant's ethical system. The validity of the moral law requires some highest good, which requires something like God. But the moral law is known from, and achieved through, freedom alone separate from any actual object of the good. Our freedom to follow the moral law must be prior to knowledge of an actual object of the good, yet the highest good prevents this freedom from being illusory. God cannot function in Kant's system as an *object* of desire who compels us through love toward himself. Instead, God must be absent—a shadowy abyss who must be present to ensure that our free moral actions are not mere illusions. God is a necessary postulate for the possibility of exercising our freedom for moral practice, but God cannot be a *factor* in that actual practice. Ethics makes theology possible, but theology itself has no necessary relationship to ethics.

Kant's practical reason functioned in an abstract, formal mode. Morality makes God possible, but actual moral practice cannot invoke specific theological language because freedom alone makes possible the human agent's moral actions. Morality requires autonomy. For Kant, then, God only matters in a purely formal mode through things that can be universalized; God cannot matter in the particular. Thus he stated, "Universal nature and not particular circumstances ought to evoke our thankfulness."[35] The reason for this is that God is to be loved solely because of God's beneficent rule in providing the occasion for us to exercise our freedom for moral purposes. The freedom that grounds moral practice leaves us with the only remaining proof for God, the moral proof, but the freedom that grounds moral practice requires God to be irrelevant for actual moral practice. If we want to find a proof for God in the modern era that does not contradict Kant's epistemology, then only this moral proof works (and the neo-Kantians even called it into question). But herein resides the problem. Why is Kant still looking for "proof"? And why has he misread the Scholastic theologians as putting forth such arguments? Is not Kant desperately trying to find a place for God in a world so thoroughly defined by human freedom that, as Nietzsche recognized, this freedom rendered God dead?

For Kant, freedom is a "fact" known by "revelation."[36] Because freedom can be known, God and the highest good are possible. Why is freedom a fact, and why, unlike God, can it be known with such certainty? Because of the practice of moral responsibility. Suppose someone has done a horrendous act, such as murdered a child. Why are we horrified at such an action? Why do we hold the person responsible? If our actions are necessitated by the immanent causal nexus in which we live, then such an action merely represents an uncontrollable vital force of nature. Holding someone morally accountable for such an act would be akin to holding a hurricane personally responsible for its destructive force. Yet we do not understand a murderous act like an act of nature. Practically, whether it can be proved speculatively or not, we assume some form of individual responsibility and freedom for moral and immoral actions. We hold people accountable for such effects and thus assume as a fact an element of freedom in their actions. Insofar as we do this, which Kant believes to be a universal and necessary implication of action, the transcendental idea of freedom is given a "practical" determination. The immanent world in which Kant's epistemology trapped us appears to be punctured.

We know freedom as a logical and necessary postulate for the practice of the moral life. After we know freedom, then God, the highest good, and the immortality of the soul are credible. Only through freedom do the "ideas of God and immortality gain objective reality and legitimacy."[37] Freedom is more basic than God; freedom is a "matter of fact": "Freedom is the only one of all the ideas of pure reason whose object is a matter of fact and must be included among the *scibilia*."[38] While freedom is listed among the *scibilia*, God, the *summum bonum*, and the immortality of the soul are listed among the "mere credible"; they are "mere matters of faith." "Because," as Kant stated, "they being the sole condition under which, arising to the frame of our human reason, we are able to conceive the possibility of that effect of the use of our freedom according to law."[39] Because of freedom, knowledge of God is possible. Within the limits of sensibility, neither God, freedom, nor immortality can imply anything meaningful. These "transcendental ideas" can be neither proved nor disproved. Therefore, nothing can be based upon them. But "beyond the limits of sensibility" practical reason secures the objective possibility of the transcendental ideas. However, and this is the crucial point, the only way "beyond the limits of sensibility" to the transcendental ideas is through freedom, a freedom that bears no trace of the sensible.

The relationship between God and moral practice in Kant reduces to this vicious circle. Freedom to will action consistent with the moral law is known prior to the highest good, but the highest good is necessary a priori if the moral law is not merely illusory and thus our freedom in vain. Therefore, the *summum bonum* does not function adequately for moral practice. It cannot tread on our freedom. It cannot be specified. It cannot be God as the initiator of our actions nor as the *object* eliciting our desires. Kant rejects all these positions not because he seeks to deny God but because of his apologetic for God. If the only way to God is beyond sensibility by way of the fact of freedom, then God will always be secondary to freedom. The relationship between God and creation is secured through human freedom and autonomy. The immanent world Kant constructed in the first critique only appears to be punctured. Its self-enclosed domain remains intact, and people can still believe that a God exists outside this domain only insofar as it actually makes no difference within the domain itself.

It comes as no surprise that many of Kant's interpreters dismissed his thought of God. But can Kant's question be asked without assuming his answer? I think so. We can answer Kant's question by recovering a practical, moral rationality inextricably wedded to theological particularity. Thomas Aquinas assists us in thinking and speaking of God without assuming the implicit answer present in Kant's question. The Neo-Scholastics are wrong to assume that the threat posed to morality in modernity is "speculative atheism." The threat to God in modernity is not that God can no longer be thought but that God can be thought in such a way that it no longer matters. The problem with Kant's proof for God was that it made God useless; it fostered a *practical* atheism while securing a logical interpretation for God's existence. God may be dead, but we would not know it.

OVERCOMING THE KANTIAN DEBT

Unfortunately, much of Christian ethics has been indebted to Kant's answers mediated via Weber, Troeltsch, and the Niebuhrs. The gospel is essentialized into disinterested love that maintains universal beneficence against all particularity. Anything that threatens to disturb this universality is denigrated as sectarian or utopian. Ecclesiology is essentialized into a principle of cosmopolitanism and universal rights grounded in a constant criticism. The purpose of the church is not to be the church but to point beyond any historical presentation of God in this world through constant negation of all historical pre-sentations. Such negation points "beyond" to a "radical monotheism." The historical existence of the church is lost to a "permanent revolution." The relationship of the church to the state is mediated via a so-called public use of reason, giving us a new orthodoxy, "public theology." All of this occurs without challenging the barricade Kant erected between us and God or puncturing the immanent domain of human freedom and autonomy. We remain autonomous and God remains free in the supersensible realm, so free that the threat to God's supersensible freedom is understood to be any material or historical re-presentation of the Christ event such as is found in the Catholic Mass. Even Karl Barth suggested that this re-presentation remains the central problem in the work of de Lubac and von Balthasar; their "christological renaissance" could not be successful because "the doctrine of the sacrifice of the Mass, the archetype of the whole idea of representation, is still unshaken."[40]

Barth was correct in one sense: this christological renaissance within Catholic theology—and its resonance among some Protestant theologians—has led a number of theologians to emphasize the importance of the Eucharist as precisely that point where temporal materiality and the divine converge into a single history. In its historical performance the Eucharist tears down Kant's barricade; God matters. Catherine Pickstock has even suggested that "the event of transubstantiation in the Eucharist is the condition of possibility for all human meaning."[41] This remarkable conclusion cannot be appropriately understood without her argument that the sensible reality of the Eucharist overcomes the mind-body dualism that always ends in an assertion of mind against body (and essence against existence) and thus in necrophilia. A "realist construal" of the Eucharist, she suggests, becomes an "example of the coincidence of sign and body, death and life." It points us beyond the Western dialectic of presence and absence. A better answer to Kant's question is found, not in human freedom, but in the ongoing practice of the Eucharist. How is this possible in the modern world? Why does the Eucharist still compel people to taste and see that God is good?

A similar argument to Pickstock's, though not quite as encompassing, can be found in the work of the theologian Mariá Clara Bingemer. She argues that "women find themselves and identify themselves with the sacrament of the eucharist" because "feeding others with one's own body is the supreme way God chose to be definitively and sensibly present in the midst of the people." God, whose essence defies definition and sensibility, becomes definite and sensible. God is known through touch. Bingemer also seems to resonate with Pickstock's "liturgical consummation" of being when she suggests that the incarnation "invents an 'other time,' a liturgical time." Finally, like Pickstock, she recognizes that postmodernity means "the need to become conscious that a time for silence and discretion about one's conviction and adhesion to the Christian faith, characterized by modernity and secularization has passed and is over."[42] We need no longer police our theological convictions by containing them within some private realm and assuming some neutral posture in the so-called "public square."

Modern and secularized time bore a tradition of "ethics" that took Kant's answers as given but failed to take seriously his question: Can we intelligibly think God such that God matters, that God is sensibly present? By assuming the answer was no unless God is indirectly present through our freedom, that modern time marginalized theological space—the fruitfulness of the womb could not bear God. Theology was forced beyond the sensible, barricaded into private arational spaces present only through "miracle."

THE REPETITION OF KANT'S ANSWERS: PUBLIC THEOLOGIANS

The "public theologians" who currently dominate the church's ethical discussions too often merely rehearse Kant's answers without taking seriously his questions. In so doing, they continue the Kantian legacy of subordinating theology to ethics. This can be seen in Max Stackhouse's emphasis on a nonconfessional, cosmopolitan Christian ethic based on universal rights and in Ronald Thiemann's criterion of publicity for theological arguments to have a role in the public square. Contextualized ethics that emphasize ethnic identity promise some alternative space to such arguments in that they speak from the perspective of the marginalized and oppressed. Yet even these theological ethicists cannot finally escape the hold of Kant's answers as the means for adjudicating conflict within the "public" sphere, as is seen in Ismael Garcia's development of an ethics through Hispanic eyes.

Max Stackhouse's Universal Moral Order

Of theologians working in the field of ethics today, none is more committed to carrying on the legacy of the Kantian answers than Max Stackhouse. He finds the essence of Christian morality to be a doctrine of universal human rights. He suggests that his position "represents a modest revolution against much of the treasured wisdom of modernity."[43] That universal human rights are in any sense a rebellion against modernity is surprising, for, as Joan Lockwood O'Donovan noted, "The entrenchment of the concept of human rights in contemporary political and legal discourse and practise as beyond dispute is obvious to anyone who notices current political issues and events."[44] Yet Stackhouse disputes this entrenchment and views his argument for universal human rights as revolutionary. He does so because he sees a growing cultural reality that alarms him: the celebration of the particular. Feminist, liberation, postliberal or narrative, and fundamentalist theology are, for him, expressions of a similar problem—a fideism that refuses to acknowledge "that there is a universal moral order under which all peoples and societies live."[45] Stackhouse fears the threat of relativism, which holds forth the dangerous idea that our culture's morality is merely our culture's morality and thus does not stand under any moral order that might interrogate and question it. No external criterion exists to question a morality embedded in cultures. This is a valid and important concern, for if Stackhouse is correct we must recognize that morality has become a legitimating discourse for a mere assertion of power. Morality is reduced to nothing but social constructions, nothing other than an assertion of power. Each culture's ethics would be impervious to correction, and the determinative argument in every moral contest would be, "But that is just my culture."

My own appeal to the good as a transcendental predicate of being could actually be seen by some as consistent with Stackhouse's concern to maintain a universal moral order against all particularity. Like Stackhouse, I agree that much moral argumentation today has a silly relativism to it that does not realize that it is nothing other than a political assertion of power where the good is finally abandoned.[46] But I am not convinced that he has narrated our situation accurately. He does not seem to recognize how his own Kantian solution to the problem created the problem in the first place. That lack of awareness results in an abandonment of the very theological themes that can call into question the barricade Kant erected. One of the reasons I am unconvinced by Stackhouse's appeal to a universal moral order is precisely because of what he asks us to abandon. For the sake of his cosmopolitan social ethic with its universal human rights, we must abandon or at least subordinate Christian confessional theology to a putatively more universal moral order. Following in the footsteps of Kant, Stackhouse continues to subordinate theology to ethics.

In *Creeds, Society and Human Rights,* Stackhouse defends a "Judeo-Christian anthropology" that he finds fundamental for the preservation of a universal moral order. This defense includes a discussion of creeds in which their essential component is not their content but their form. Stackhouse does not defend Athanasius against the Arians or Cyril of Alexandria against the Monophysites. He does not explain why the hypostatic union is necessary for a right understanding of politics and morality. Instead, he argues that the crucial element to creeds is that they provide a "space for bonding." This social space creates the possibility of voluntary associations where particularities such as family, tribe, nation, and race are superseded. He suggests, "The social space defended by the church over the centuries has now been broadened to allow a wider range of voluntary associations, interest groups, dissent committees."[47] What the church gives to the world is not so much the sacrifice made by the Second Person of the Trinity but this social space for voluntary associations, which eventually becomes universal and makes possible the doctrine of human rights. It gives us a freedom to construct associations that are not defined by more particular considerations, such as family, tribe, or confessional communities.

This has led Stackhouse to affirm the global market and its social institutionalization in the modern corporation as the embodiment of this universal social space. The corporation is

> the social form distinctive of every cooperative human activity outside the family, the government and personal friendships. It is historically based on the patterns of association worked out by the church beyond tribe, patriarchy and nation. The modern business corporation could become a worldly ecclesia no less than hospitals, unions, parties, schools, voluntary organizations and cultural institutions, virtually all of which are incorporated.[48]

What Stackhouse finds laudable in the corporation is precisely that it is a putatively nonparticular social space. It is global, universal, catholic.

This emphasis on the social institution of the global corporation as a "worldly ecclesia" fits well Stackhouse's "cosmopolitan social ethics," the ethics Christians need to be relevant to contemporary reality. It is an ethics that reaches beyond "confessional particularities, exclusive histories and privileged realms of discourse."[49] These confessional particularities divide us and prevent the universal cosmopolitan community that social bonding around a creed began. Stackhouse seems to suggest that ethics grounded in our particularities prevents us from being truly human.

Stackhouse's cosmopolitan ethic poses a challenge and a threat to Christian ethics. The challenge is that any ethic that revels in the particular disunites the human family and leads to conflict, strife, and possibly even violence. If we revel in the particular, we will neglect the universal moral order that should bind humanity together. We will miss the universal quest for the good. But how serious is this challenge? This is not a new idea. Stackhouse's ethic merely repeats Kant's cosmopolitan ethic. That ethic has been with us for well over a century. Has it made us more human? Has it made the world less filled with conflict? Have we moved one step closer toward perpetual peace? No. The idea that we will be citizens of a universal cosmopolis assumes that we can develop an Olympian identity. The idea that this cosmopolitan structure is found in the global market and in the corporations that traverse that market is only one more particular, one more privileged realm of discourse. Stackhouse's cosmopolitan ethic is one more heroic ascent out of the cave, away from the everyday and toward the universal.

The central insight of Christianity is not that a universal community is being formed separate from our particular identities. The central insight of Christianity is that God, who is the only resident of any possible cosmopolis, assumed human flesh and was found in the particular. To cling to this exclusive history does not entail strife and conflict. That this exclusive history has lent itself toward such inhumanity is a well-attested fact, but that such inhumane behavior perverts the content of that history is also true. This should cause us to be vigilant against such misinterpretations of Christianity's content, but it should not tempt us to forego the particularity of being the church for some false cosmopolis, for the twentieth century taught us that the quest for the cosmopolis ended in an uncontrolled violence not even the crusaders could have imagined. Did the modern quest for the cosmopolis end at Hiroshima?

The Kantian legacy is obvious in Stackhouse. He assumes that universal human rights will ensure a more humane world, and thus particularity is a threat to the moral life. This is Kant's answer to the condition for the possibility of exercising the freedom necessary for the moral life. Progress toward the cosmopolis is moral advance. Such progress, even if the goal is unattainable, requires the overcoming of particularities into larger social organizations asymptotically approaching cosmopolis. God is a logical concept in such an ethic, but this is the God who merely ensures universal beneficence. It is a God stripped of all concrete particularity. It is a God who is pure essence, not a God who can be found in flesh.

Ronald Thiemann's Dogmatic Political Liberalism

Like Max Stackhouse, Ronald Thiemann is a "public theologian" who points out the dangers of a public life that eschews religion. Unlike Stackhouse, however, Thiemann appears to advocate the importance of the particularities of religious communities, but this is, in the end, only an appearance.

Thiemann advocates religion in the public realm. Without such a role, he writes, "we will be unable to make significant progress toward addressing the moral divisions that plague our society."[50] Because religion is necessary for the moral character of society, democracy in the United States confronts a dilemma. Since the establishment of the Bill of Rights, the role of religion in public life has been mired in confusion. Specifically, the nonestablishment clause forbids the state from assisting religion, while the free-exercise clause "mandates governmental accommodation." Thiemann seeks to clarify religion's role by providing a public expression of religion that will be inoffensive in a pluralistic society.

For Thiemann, unlike Stackhouse, the dilemma is exacerbated because "religious belief and practice are notoriously particular."[51] Thiemann does not advocate translating this *notorious* particularity into something more universal, as do most liberal political theorists. He rejects, in theory, that vague religiosity tolerated under the guise of civic piety. Instead, he argues for the politics of particularity, claiming that it is not a "threat to the historic sense of a national identity." In fact, Thiemann suggests, the "genius" of modern nation-states like the United States is that they do "not require persons to abandon their ethnic identity as the price of citizenship."[52] Therefore, the fact that religious faith and practice are particular should not exclude them from the public realm any more than ethnic identity does.

Thiemann is committed both to the particularity of faith and the liberal political project. This appears to be an alternative to Stackhouse's cosmopolitan ethic, but it is misleading. Thiemann is as indebted to the Kantian legacy as is Stackhouse. The very characterization of work such as Thiemann's as "public" theology assumes the normative role of Kant's bifurcation between *private* religious and theological arguments and a *public* and political use of reason.[53] For Kant, "the many" are the problem, and making them into a cosmopolitan *unum* is the answer. One's confessional particularity is acceptable as a private endeavor, but political arguments should be *public*. Thus any theological claims that will be political must pass Kant's criterion of publicity. For this reason, liberal political theory is usually set against the politics of particularity. Thiemann appears to offer an alternative to Kant, but in the end he merely repeats the answers found in liberal political theory.

Despite Thiemann's considerable efforts, the politics of the particular suffers at the hands of the *unum*. Despite his best intentions, liberal political philosophy still arbitrates, via "public reason," which faith is socially acceptable. The legacy of Kant's public use of reason remains the central criterion to which the political must pay obeisance. Thus, the practice of faith communities remains the problem, and the practice of constitutional democracy remains the norm against which those communities are assessed. They render the church intelligible. The result is that Thiemann's public theology does not deliver what he promises but merely trades on vague principles such as "fairness and concern for the vulnerable" to show how religious convictions can matter in the so-called public realm.

Moreover, if the politics of particularity is no threat to national identity, then why does Thiemann so emphasize the need to recover a "national identity"? He asks whether we "can reknit the fabric of commonalty within our own boundaries, whether we can discover an *unum* within our *plures*."[54] Despite his insistence on particularity, Thiemann still treats "moral heterogeneity" as a national problem. He writes, "Some principles must be discerned that can guide our public life when we are faced with moral heterogeneity."[55] This requires that "diverse interests and commitments" need to be "forged" into "some sense of common aims and purposes."[56] The politics of particularity appears to be more of a threat to national identity than Thiemann first admitted. His central image is still *e pluribus unum*, by which he does not mean that people will come out of every nation to form a catholic church but that our national life will forge a commonalty from our particularities.

What is surprising is that heterogeneity and diverse commitments remain problematic despite Thiemann's continual insistence that "genuine freedom implies pluralism."[57] If constitutional democracy instantiates pluralism, why are religious communities a problem for such a democracy in the first place? What is meant by pluralism here?

From Thiemann's critique of "sectarianism" we know that pluralism does not mean the fostering of "smaller associations and intact communities" that "recover their own traditions."[58] Such communities, he argues, abandon "civil society" and fail to confront the "challenge of pluralism." I can only surmise from his critique of the "sectarians" that pluralism signifies the contribution of any person, group, or organization to civil society whose contribution passes the conditions of publicity. This criterion of publicity is indistinguishable from Kant's "public reason." For Kant, theology based on confessional particularity was permissible as a private pursuit within a community but not as a reasonable public argument. In the public realm, everyone must be freed to speak from his or her own individuality and not merely as a representative of something like a faith community. Thus our public speech had to be consistent with the principle of universalizability. This did not render theology irrelevant to public reason. But the theology that can be relevant must first be acceptable on the basis of the criterion of publicity.

Kant's project appears to foster a civil public argument on the basis of free speech within a pluralistic society so that no single community's good dominates others. But one must never forget the concluding remarks to his famous essay "What Is Enlightenment?" in which he developed his public use of reason: "But only a ruler who is himself enlightened and has no dread of shadows, yet who likewise has a well-disciplined, numerous army to guarantee public peace can say what no republic may dare, namely: 'Argue as much as you want and about what you want, but obey!'"[59] This is important to remember because the celebration of pluralism, diversity, and free speech often forgets the conditions that make these practices possible—a ruler with a well-disciplined, numerous army who fears no threat to his power. Perhaps only when speech is rendered innocuous can it be "free." It is rendered innocuous when it cannot threaten anyone in power. Then speech can easily be tolerated because speech no longer matters. Pluralism results not from a true diversity but from a forged unity that superimposes a new identity on top of all others and then teaches us to forget that forged identity.

What passes for "public" in Thiemann is self-referential; those who constitute the public define the conditions for acceptable arguments. All other arguments are then excluded from political significance by being labeled sectarian, private, or utopian. For example, Thiemann attempts to defend liberal philosophy and maintain a politics of particularity by labeling three of liberalism's critics—Michael Sandel, Alasdair MacIntyre, and Stanley Hauerwas—"sectarian communitarians." This is most unfortunate, because Hauerwas and MacIntyre have explicitly distanced themselves from the communitarian position. Whether they have done this successfully could certainly be argued, but Thiemann does not even suggest the distortion his category brings the self-description of their work. Why has he so badly misinterpreted them? Thiemann's dismissal of their work results from his uncritical acceptance of the Kantian legacy that divides any political use of reason into two categories: public or private. Anyone who bases moral rationality on the grounds of a particular tradition is a priori rendered private and thus, at best, a "sectarian communitarian."

Thiemann further distorts the issue by suggesting that the Methodist-pacifist Hauerwas, Thomist-Catholic MacIntyre, and republican Sandel advocate, via their particularistic claims, a warrior state. Like Stackhouse, Thiemann finds the critiques of liberal society to be dangerous because the only alternative to liberalism is strife, conflict, and violence. However, Thiemann's claim that liberal political society "always prefers non-coercive, non-violent means of conflict resolution"[60] rings hollow. One wonders, When did our pluralistic society disarm? Does liberalism not assume that society will require arming itself against both external and internal aggressors? Does it not ask its citizens to pledge allegiance to this practice? Does it not require all citizens implicitly or explicitly to pledge allegiance to this defense?

If Thiemann's work sought to reconstruct liberal society on nonviolent terms, then it would have been a great advance over the harsh realities of the practices of that society. Yet this is not what Thiemann seeks to do. He assumes that liberal democratic regimes foster nonviolence and then, using them as the benchmark, promises an explanation of how religious arguments can work in the public realm and not be a threat to it once they are made to abide by the "criterion of publicity."

Thiemann wants both church and state to recognize that religious arguments can meet "primary public standards of accessibility." This is the Kantian standard for a political and public use of reason. But is it a priori true that religious arguments can meet this public criterion? Will it not depend on the moral character of both the religion and the state? Moreover, are there not occasions when religious arguments may very well need to remain as clandestine as possible so that we can fulfill our religious duties and at the same time not provoke the state or be a cause of scandal to others? For instance, is this not the case with the sanctuary movement, where "illegal" aliens are given Christian hospitality?

Conversely, some religious arguments do not deserve a hearing although they actually meet public standards of accessibility (i.e., pro-slavery arguments). Thiemann recognizes this and states that all religious arguments should not be welcome in the public sphere, but when he explains this he involves himself in massive contradictions. He says, "The important issue is not whether an argument appeals to a religious warrant; the issue is whether the warrant, religious or not, is compatible with the basic values of our constitutional democracy." Here his argument seems to contradict itself. To explain the apparent contradiction he states that some religious arguments should be *unwelcome* in the public sphere but that all religious arguments should be *heard*. In explaining this distinction, his argument makes four points. First, he suggests without qualification that religious beliefs are "capable of meeting primary public standards of accessibility." Second, he then denies what he has just asserted by stipulating that certain religious beliefs, such as those that "appeal to racist ideologies," are not capable of meeting the criterion of publicity. This could be viewed as merely a qualification to his first point, except that he then makes a third point in a futile attempt to reconcile the apparent contradiction between the first two: even racist ideologies cannot be precluded from the public sphere because democracies must maintain free speech. He concludes with a fourth point, "we cannot by philosophical or political fiat decide in advance which arguments we will accept in the public sphere."[61]

If he holds to his fourth point, then he must disregard his second point. He must acknowledge that we have a moral obligation to be open to the possibility of the truth of racist religious ideologies if they are advanced nonviolently in terms of the criterion of publicity; otherwise, we will have decided in advance and violate the criterion of publicity. But if his argument suggests a moral obligation to be open to the truth of racist ideologies, surely it has more than failed us.

Thiemann's argument fails, but he consistently shows what a dogmatic commitment to political liberalism requires. His conclusion is that faith communities must abandon the "myth of absoluteness." When he explains what truth claims are acceptable to faith communities, he only leads us into further contradictions. On the one hand, if we are to overcome the divisive role of religion in the public realm, then faith communities must forego the assumption that "claims to truth are inevitably absolute." On the other hand, "Communities of faith must come to recognize the compatibility between deep and abiding commitment to the truth claims of one's tradition and an openness and respect for the claims of another tradition."[62] He seems to be telling us that absolute truth claims are divisive for the *unum* while deep and abiding ones are acceptable. What does this mean? Are Christians supposed to have a deep and abiding commitment to the claim that Jesus is the Messiah but not hold it absolutely? For the sake of civil society, must we be open to the possibility that Jesus was not the Messiah? Or does this mean that on certain policy issues, such as slavery, abortion, or capital punishment, people of faith can state that such activities are wrong but they are not absolutely wrong?

Thiemann encourages faith communities to forego the myth of absoluteness while accepting constitutional democracy as a benchmark of political truth. He seems more frightened that faith communities will unite a tyrannical power with absolute truth than that democratic nations will unite tyrannical power with relativistic truth claims. But when it comes to the uncontrolled violence of this century, Thiemann has not helped us develop a social ethic that speaks to the reality of our situation.

Ismael Garcia's Dignidad: Ethics through Hispanic Eyes

Stackhouse's and Thiemann's ethics tempt us to subordinate the practical wisdom of the church to the abstract rationality of the modern nation-state and/or corporation. Can ethicists avoid this temptation? Following Immanuel Kant, the father of modern ethical thought, ethicists too often work with the implicit or explicit conviction that the heart of Christianity has little or nothing to do with dogma, but the heart of Christianity is ethics. Once this assumption becomes operative, ethics replaces dogma. Ethicists are not sure it matters politically and socially that Christ is truly God and truly human, but they are convinced that all people should be moral. So the discipline of Christian ethics becomes one more immanent anthropological discourse that incessantly addresses questions of justice, rights, care, autonomy, and the need for religion to have a role in the public square. But seldom does Christian ethics actually engage with the theology of the moral life, that is, with what difference it might actually make for understanding the moral life if the God whom Christian tradition confesses as Father, Son, and Holy Spirit were true. Christian ethics are short on emphasis when it comes to discussing how God matters, and that seems to be a necessary consequence of relating theology to ethics in its modern modality. In fact, the discipline of ethics not only avoids theology but also often avoids the political and social formations that render accounts of ethics intelligible.

If this characterizes the dominant tradition of Christian ethics, then perhaps ethics intentionally developed from the perspective of those who have been disenfranchised from the public square might create an alternative, might free ethics from its captivity to the modern nation-state and corporation. A *first* glance at a popular development of such a position proves less than promising. Ismael Garcia's *Dignidad: Ethics through Hispanic Eyes* does not appear to offer much of an alternative to the dominant Kantian themes already found in Stackhouse and Thiemann, for *dignity* is the heart of Kantian ethics. Each person is an autonomous individual whose dignity must be preserved so that he or she can freely act based on a universal law. But this account of dignity only further distances the individual from his or her traditional communities by securing the individual's dignity through the coercive power of the modern nation-state against any communal goods that might interfere with individual dignity. The state grants, protects, and preserves the rights of autonomous individuals by first creating *rights* and then defending those rights through coercive systems (judiciary, police, military) against any encroachments by communities such as church and family. But rights are never either universal or individual because they are always *social* entitlements. No other kind of rights exists. Rights always require social and political formations for their possibility. The moment ethics is done in terms of *dignity* and *rights,* we will not be able to escape the all-encroaching power of the modern nation-state.

That Ismael Garcia uses the term *dignidad* to define Hispanic ethics opens his work up to the suspicion that it is one more defense of this kind of ethics, though now put forward with a twist from the perspective of the Hispanic American community. But such a *contextualized* version of the dominant Kantian tradition merely makes it more difficult to expose an ethics of dignity and rights

as that which creates the homogenized power of the nation-state over any competing account of the moral life, especially one located in the church. Do *contextualized* ethics set forth the kind of false difference one finds at the food court
at any mall, where every culture is represented and difference is putatively
affirmed, but the difference is always already contained by the overarching edifice called the "mall"? Rather than being emancipatory, *difference* becomes one
more way we are grafted into a single homogenous social and political reality.

Oddly enough, Garcia's Hispanic ethics, written from the perspective of the
oppressed, uses the dominant traditional ethical language: deontology, conse-
quentialism, ethics of principle, ethics of care, divine command theory, autonomy, rights, and so forth.[63] This kind of ethics puts Anglo critics at a disadvan-
tage, for to suggest that the Hispanic eyes through which this ethics is developed
still seem Prussian is to risk being perceived as one more gringo who does not
appreciate the unique gifts Hispanic American Christians bring to the tradition.

Fortunately, there is a promising turn in Garcia's ethics of *dignidad* that renders it somewhat different from the dominant tradition. A turn occurs in Garcia's ethics that reminds readers that *dignidad* cannot be translated into the
Prussian Kant's *dignity* without remainder. Garcia's refusal to translate the title
of his book makes possible something other than a repetition of the dominant
tradition of ethics, for after giving us one more standard treatment of the language of the ethics of principle with its notions of autonomy and rights, Garcia makes a move that catches us by surprise. He interrupts the all too familiar excursus on ethics that characterized the introduction to his work and
suggests that this language is inadequate. *Dignidad* requires something other
than the modern nation-state to be able to make sense of it. He writes,

> However, the strong commitment Hispanics have to family life and their sense
> of loyalty to their ethnic community necessitates a moral language broader and
> more comprehensive than that provided by the ethics of principle in both its
> consequentialist and duty-based modes. The principle of autonomy and the lan-
> guage of rights, though valuable, remain too cold and impersonal to the His-
> panic way of being. It is a language proper for people who are essentially unre-
> lated to one another and meet in the public square as strangers who are equal
> and free in socially significant ways, to negotiate, assert and affirm their inter-
> ests and rights.[64]

There are, of course, echoes of Marx in this welcome shift in Garcia's argument.[65]
One need not see the world through Hispanic eyes to see that the language of
individual rights, autonomy, and an ethics of principle assumes a political and
social order of strangers whose relationships with one another are primarily
determined by the contractual obligations of the marketplace. But it is surely
significant that ethics intentionally written from the perspective of a marginalized community recognizes the inadequacy of the language of autonomy, rights,

principle, and the like. Garcia struggles to find a different language to express the Christian moral life. What is significant in this effort is not just his recognition that the Kantian tradition of ethics makes us strangers but the way *dignidad* functions as an alternative space to this politics of alienation.

Dignidad cannot be easily translated into the politics of strangers that the language of rights and the criterion of publicity assume. In fact, *dignidad* functions in at least four ways for Garcia. First, it functions something like the premodern notion of the moral life one finds in Aristotle and Aquinas. Here *dignidad* seems similar to their notion of character, *hexis* in Greek or *habitus* in Latin. This account of the moral life assumes that our ability to be moral agents is not discovered in some inner realm of metaphysical freedom where we "do it our way." Instead, our ability to be moral agents is discovered in the moral formation that comes from our communities and marks us; that is, it gives us a "sign" (character) that causes us to live in the world one way rather than another. Here the ethical life is not about decision-making processes but about who we are and how we preserve our identity even when it is threatened.

But *dignidad* does not function only as a character; it also functions as a *telos,* as the goal a community seeks. Thus *dignidad* appears to be not simply something that someone has (which can be protected and defended by coercive power) but something that one brings into being through the way one lives in the world. *Dignidad,* suggests Garcia, is the goal of communal life, to constantly "create and sustain communities of love and care."[66] In this, *dignidad* is a reflection of the Trinity. God is, in God's own self, precisely this kind of community, so the fact that we are created in God's image makes this kind of life possible. *Dignidad* is a reflection of the *imago Dei* and perhaps not unrelated to the role that charity and the beatific vision had in more traditional accounts of Christian moral theology. When Garcia discusses the "theological dimensions" to *dignidad,* he explicitly mentions the "Vision of God" and places *dignidad* squarely within that context.

In addition to being both character and *telos, dignidad* also seems to function as tradition. That is to say, *dignidad* is the character out of which someone can live and act in the world, but this is not merely an autonomous individuated center of choice. Instead, *dignidad* comes as gift, formed in us from our community's effort to sustain and preserve a form of life through time. As Garcia explains, "Dignity is related to the struggle to preserve and perpetuate our unique identity."[67] This is tradition—the passing on of a way to live and be in the world that allows us to participate in that *telos* for which we are given the great privilege of being part of God's good creation.

Dignidad seems to function in at least these three ways for Garcia: as character, *telos,* and tradition. In that sense, it is everything the modern notion of ethics, in its Kantian mode, rejected. But there is a fourth way *dignidad* is used that seeks alliance with that politics of strangers upon which ethics is often predicated. *Dignidad* also expresses something quite similar to Kant's autonomous individual. Garcia writes,

> Dignity is grounded in our capacity to make moral choices in the sense that we are a center of decision making. This is a democratic interpretation of human dignity. It assumes that all adult sane persons have within themselves the capacity, the potential to make moral decisions. Dignity is related to our being moral agents, and as such, beings who have to be respected and given the space and opportunity to live their lives in light of their moral visions. This view of human dignity is foundational for the ethics of principle, the notion of universal human rights, equal citizenship and nondiscrimination.[68]

Despite the three interpretations of *dignidad* that resist the modern politics of strangers, this one seems to bring us right back into that same politics. This fourth interpretation of *dignity* is all too easy to translate into Kantian terms. But is it possible to have all four interpretations with consistency?

Garcia can put forth this fourth interpretation of dignity because he has faith that liberal democratic societies create a "complex" space where Hispanic identity can be nurtured and preserved. He writes, "One of the virtues of our liberal democratic society is that it allows for the establishment of independent institutions and voluntary associations that provide alternative social spaces where we can live in light of the values we hold dear, and which are relatively free from government control and the coercive presence of the state."[69] But is this true? Do liberal societies establish these kinds of complex spaces where "alternative voluntary societies" can flourish? Or do liberal societies create "simple spaces" where all alternative communities are flattened out because every person is first constructed as a rights-bearing individual, where this monolithic identity renders innocuous any true alternative political community?

William Cavanaugh offers an alternative reading of the modern state's ability to make possible the complex space Garcia claims. In an astute theological analysis of the torture present in Chile under the Pinochet regime, Cavanaugh argues that the language of universal human rights was not only ineffective but actually participated in the construction of the hegemonic power of the state. Such language destroys the diffusion of power present in social formations that might be an alternative to the power of the state through its construction of individual bodies. Cavanaugh writes,

> Beyond the question of whether or not universal human rights exist as such, I argue that what accounts for the failure of human rights language to stop acts of torture is a misunderstanding of the nature of torture as primarily an attack on individual bodies. While certainly individual bodies suffer grievously, the state's primary targets in using torture are social bodies. Torture is not merely an attack on, but the creation of, individuals. In this aspect, torture is homologous with the modern state's project of usurping powers and responsibilities

which formerly resided in the diffuse local bodies of medieval society and establishing a direct relationship between the state and the individual.[70]

This makes Cavanaugh much less sanguine than Garcia toward the possibilities the state holds forth for sustaining something like *dignidad*. The construction of the political body as a conglomeration of rights-bearing individuals will not allow for the sustenance of those forms of communal life that can be a substantive alternative to this kind of politics. Only those communal forms of life that are willing to be subordinate to this politics of strangers can successfully develop an ethics based on autonomy and rights.[71] Cavanaugh suggests that only a disciplined form of communal life that does not emulate the power relationship between the individual and the state can stand as a possible alternative to the simple space the latter creates. He writes, "The only hope we have for a discipline that is not demonic is in the Eucharist." When it is appropriately enacted, the Eucharist embodies a form of power where the one presiding is not there to "accumulate power" but to lay down his or her life for the sheep.[72]

Torture is certainly not new in the modern world, but neither is it absent, and to assume that it is absent is to have a romantic and utopian posture toward liberal democracies as they have existed. To suggest that they are better than some monarchical or fascist alternative may be correct, but it still does not say much. To privilege them as the context within which our quest for the good must be made intelligible is problematic, for they are not social formations on a quest for the good. They are social formations that embody the Kantian prioritizing of freedom over the good, and they cannot be otherwise. This makes them prone to the kind of "demonic discipline" Cavanaugh rightly teaches us to fear.

THE CHURCH AS PUBLIC

The social institution of the church is not a private religious institution. It should be for Christians the social institution that renders intelligible both our politics and our morality. It is already the most "public" of all institutions, so to assume that it should be ordered to something more public will lead to a false and idolatrous catholicity. To argue that the church is a social ethic does not imply that the church cannot learn from other social formations, nor does it imply that the church lacks a critical role to play in relationship to other social institutions. In fact, it demands just the opposite. Only when the church engages with these other social institutions can it properly be the church. But the way it engages with these other social formations and institutions is by being the church and reminding them of their limits. It need not rule like a state.

The church exists within a complex social order in which it is central. It cannot afford the "pathos of false humility" that characterizes much of modern theology.[73] If the church is not the church, then the claims other social institutions make upon the faithful will lead us to live disordered lives. Because the church is the central institution necessary for the "order of charity," it should never be referred to as the "public church." This phrase contains an unnecessary redundancy. The church, by virtue of its own life, is public. The phrase "public church" seems to imply that there is one church that is not public, and thus must be private, and another church that engages the task of social justice and is the public wing of the otherwise private church. If this phrase is so interpreted, then it merely replicates Kant's distinction between a public use of reasoning that is nonconfessional and accessible to all people and a private use of reasoning that can be confessional and communal. To avoid such misunderstanding, theologians should refrain from the troubling expression "public church." The church is more than *public;* it is *catholic,* and that is its politics.

The relationship between the church and the modern state as formed by Stackhouse, Thiemann, and Garcia remains within the Kantian scheme. Theology is not itself a public or political enterprise; it is made so when it is mediated via other terms dictated to it by a putatively larger public space. That space seems to be the nation-state, which is assumed to be *public* in a way that the church must be made to participate in this greater "publicity." Thus the form these theologians give to the relation between the church and the modern nation-state remains within the tradition of moral inquiry put forward by Ernst Troeltsch in *The Social Teachings of the Christian Churches.* Drawing upon the methodology of Max Weber, Troeltsch constructed a typological answer to the form of the relationship between the church and other social formations by examining historical movements, abstracting from them, and setting forth those abstractions as ideal types. Three ideal types constructed his answer to the question of the relationship between the church and other social formations: the church type, the sect type, and the mystical type. Briefly put, the church type accommodated other social formations by adopting a social ethic from the culture at large, such as medieval Christianity's adoption of the Stoic natural law. The sect type refused accommodation with the larger culture and maintained its religious purity. In so doing, it became politically irrelevant. The mystical type emphasized a noninstitutional form of Christianity that privileged individual freedom. Troeltsch clearly thought that this third type embodied the direction modern Protestantism would and should pursue.[74]

Troeltsch's typology influenced Christian social ethics in North America through H. Richard Niebuhr's work. His *Christ and Culture* crafted the language many moral theologians use to explain the relationship between the church and other social formations. Niebuhr claimed that an "enduring problem" presented itself for theological reflection: the relationship between Christ and culture or between Christianity and civilization. By *Christ* Niebuhr primarily meant the mediator between God the Father and human creatures, between eternity and time.[75] In his definition of culture, Niebuhr relied upon Troeltsch's work, where culture is understood as the free creativity of human creatures in art, literature, technology, and science.[76] Niebuhr defined culture as "that total process of human activity and that total result of such activity to which now the name *culture*, now the name *civilization*, is applied in common speech."[77] Because Christ had to be made relevant to culture understood as all human activity, Christ was not assumed present within human activity. Niebuhr's description of the "enduring problem" prevents theologians from thinking rightly about traditional Christian themes such as the incarnation and the significance of Mary as *theotokos*. This has important social and political consequences.

Once Christ is defined primarily as mediatorial between eternity and time, and culture is defined as everything people create, the stage is set for the resolution to the question of the relationship between Christ and culture to be *transformation*. The Mediator transforms the world (a timeful nature) through the exercise of his moral influence on peoples' cultural production. But the Christ-mediator remains himself always separate from culture. Expanding Troeltsch's threefold typology to five, Niebuhr's resolution to the question of the relation between Christ and culture became his fifth type: Christ the transformer of culture. It is the norm by which the categories *Christ* and *culture* are related and his other four types assessed. The other four types—Christ against culture, Christ of culture, Christ above culture, and Christ and culture in paradox—are measured against the standard laid out in Christ the transformer of culture.

Even the relevance Niebuhr finds for Christ within his own question is too limiting. His theological types are too generic, the categories too vague, to provide a rich theological analysis. As John Howard Yoder noted, by *culture* Niebuhr seems to have meant "everything people do, every realm of human creative behavior." If so, then relating Christ to culture through five different types will be radically reductivistic. Culture functions as a *monolithic* entity toward which only five postures are posited. As Yoder recognized, "You must either withdraw from it all, transform it all, or keep it all in paradox. Niebuhr cannot conceive of, much less respect, a position which would not make a virtue of such consistency."[78] Thus Niebuhr finds many early theologians, such as Tertullian, to be inconsistent because their work does not fit within the typology Niebuhr sets out.[79]

Niebuhr does not see the church itself as a culture, as a human making that participates in the divine making. Thus the question Niebuhr posed—What is the relationship between Christ and culture?—already assumed a distinction between the two that denied the significance of human making in the divine drama. Niebuhr does not take into consideration the role of Mary in making God present in the world. Neither Mary as *theotokos* nor Christ's hypostatic union challenges the divisions he works with in his fivefold typology. If they were evident, they would qualify the entire project, for then one could not so thoroughly separate Christ and culture to begin with and ask what the relationship between them is. The typology would not work because it could not assume a rigid distinction between *Christ* and *culture*. Niebuhr's theology of culture assumes a Nestorian Christology. It neglects the dogmatic reality that

God himself is "cultured" in the womb of the Virgin who says yes to God. Christianity is essentially a human making, one that is ceaselessly reproduced through the faithful gathered to perform the church's liturgy. This human making is not simply a sociocultural phenomenon to which we must apply theological terms; it is always also a theological phenomenon as well. The church "makes" Jesus possible, but God speaks the church into existence.

H. Richard Niebuhr once suggested to his brother Reinhold that the latter's Christ remained too much on the edge of history, never fully participating in it. Perhaps the same can be said of H. Richard's Christology. *Christ* functions too much as a *symbol* for the transformation of the finite by the infinite through negating every finite presentation of the infinite. Concrete, temporal existence is set against a divine, eternal essence. Niebuhr's Christology remained indebted to the dogmas developed within the tradition of Protestant liberalism. That tradition was unable to think the incarnation adequately. Niebuhr continued that tradition and was perhaps its logical culmination through his insistence on "radical monotheism." For Niebuhr, God was so radically other that God remained in a noumenal realm that could never be represented in historical phenomena. Thus Niebuhr admonished theologians and believers alike not "to substitute the Lordship of Christ for the Lordship of God."[80] What Jesus points to is not his own flesh.

For Niebuhr, like the liberal Protestant tradition before him, Jesus does not point to himself or to something historical that he founds. Instead, Jesus points away from himself toward God. Jesus gives us a *radical monotheism* that relativizes and critiques all historical institutions and their dogmas. Jesus' radical monotheism produces a "permanent revolution" that "opens out infinitely into ever new possibilities."[81] Although this radical monotheism putatively functioned as a critique of all historical presentations of the infinite, it resulted in valorizing democratic institutions above the church itself.

Radical monotheism has its social correlate in democracy, but not in just any democracy. Niebuhr recognized that his radically monotheistic theology produces a "theology of protest against the assumption of any sovereignty by any finite power or against the presumption of any human voice to speak the ultimate word." The "negative side" of this radical monotheism was "pluralism and fragmentation." But this is merely the negative of a positive affirmation in a transcendent "universal Sovereignty" already present, who is good. Responding to that "Transcendent Universal" in loyalty and confidence even when demonstrated through "secular activities" constitutes true faith. The social formation such a transcendent universal makes possible is not a "pluralistic democracy" where each person is sovereign or where a majority is sovereign. Instead, it makes possible a democracy where "loyalty to the universal Commonwealth and its Constitution is maintained through no single human power or institution."[82] But this is not a Christian depiction of social formations. It is Kant's cosmopolis that assumes a permanently revolving democracy where every attempt to actualize the transcendent universal in history is subjected to endless critique and protest.

The social formation Niebuhr's radical monotheism privileges is the constant criticism and ever-present production of the "new" in democratic forms of government. But this conflicts with the biblical narrative because Niebuhr fails to account for the historical presentation of God in Jesus' flesh. Jesus does not simply point away from himself to the One beyond the many. In pointing away from himself by pointing to the bread, Jesus also points precisely to himself and says, "This is my body." Because Niebuhr directs our gaze away from this and away from the theological and political significance of the lordship of Christ *as* the lordship of God, he misconstrues the relationship between the church and other social formations. Because his work has been at the center of Christian social ethics, this misconstrual of the relationship between God, flesh, and church has had devastating consequences for the church's social life. It leads to a subordination of the church to modern political formations.

SUBORDINATING ETHICS TO THEOLOGY:
THOMAS AQUINAS AS THEOLOGIAN

Can ethics be something other than the means by which theologians subordinate theology and the church to the discourses and the practices that sustain the modern nation-state and the global market? Insofar as ethics repeats Kant's answers, it will not be able to resist this subordination. This is not surprising. As is well known, Kant thought that as true religion increased, its relationship to the church would decrease until finally "the humiliating distinction between laity and clergy disappears, and equality arises from true freedom, yet without anarchy, because, though each obeys the (non-statutory) law which he prescribes to himself, he must at the same time regard this law as the will of a World-Ruler revealed to him through reason, a will which by invisible means unites all under one common government into one state—a state previously and inadequately represented and prepared by the visible church."[83] That is the simple space the modern era constructs. Individuals who truly *obey* their own maxim also at the same time obey the universal state. Alternative political spaces, like that of the church, are either collapsed or subordinated into this simple space. Kant's ethics anticipated the dissolution of the church into the state. When ethics is viewed as truly universal and public, and theology is private and confessional, then the state or the market will be the institution that provides the intelligibility for our actions. Likewise, a quest both for the good and for God will be conditioned and constrained by the freedom offered by the state and the market.

Any adequate theological response to Kant will not merely make theology moral but, more important, will make *ethics* theological. Theology will no longer be relegated beyond the sensible to some private, ineffable realm, placed safely behind an arbitrarily erected barrier as to what counts as a reasonable interpretation of the relationship between God and the world. For when theology is first placed behind this barrier, then it will have to be applied to the *public* realm by using the language of ethics. Christian theology must refuse this forced spatialization and confess that the relationship between God and the world is discovered in the ordinary, material reality of everyday life. Such a material theology will lead us rightly to order our desires and the various social formations that produce and satisfy those desires. Such social formations arise from an understanding of Christ's two natures that gives the historical and temporal their appropriate due. This leads us back to Aquinas.

A recovery of Aquinas's "New Law of the Gospel" will offer an alternative to the dominance of Kantian ethics as the basis for Christian ethics. I say *recovery* following Servais Pinckaers's suggestion that, beginning with the seventeenth century, the central place of the law of the gospel was replaced in the Roman Catholic manualist tradition with moral theology as the science of human actions, where "each action was considered as an isolated entity, an independent case of conscience."[84] This resulted in an obsession by moral theologians during "high scholasticism" with legal obligations rather than the life of virtue. Pinckaers views this as the "modernization" of Aquinas's moral theology. The result, he argues, is that "Scholastic moral theory was greatly impoverished by its loss of contact with human and spiritual experience." In opposition to this, he recovers Aquinas's moral theory,

> governed by practical reason, which is in its turn perfected by the infused and acquired virtues. The reference to reason constitutes the principal criterion for forming a moral judgment. Yet this reason is rooted in faith and receives from faith, as well as from the gifts of wisdom and counsel, a higher light. It is also closely linked with the concrete experience produced by the will and sensibility, and their inclinations and desires, rectified and strengthened by the moral virtues and their corresponding gifts.[85]

Pinckaers shows how the theological sources of Christian ethics can answer Kant's question without reproducing Kant's answers.

To understand the significance of the Thomistic alternative, we must realize the marked distinction between Aquinas and Kant on the relationship between the will, the intellect, the good, and objects in the world.[86] Unlike Kant, Aquinas does not posit a will that must be either good or evil before it chooses particular objects. For Aquinas, the will is rational desire, which is constituted through the objects it pursues and that pursue it. The will must be moved by desire because the will is desire. Desire is not an internal, isolated thing; it requires ex-perience; that is, objects outside some safe, secure internal space of a subject first prompt desire. Such objects are pursued not through autonomous, volitional choice but through the intellect ordering the will to a good, either apparent or true, through sense-experience.

At the beginning of the *prima secundae* Aquinas stated that our ultimate end consists in beatitude. That we have an ultimate end is not a normative moral claim per se in Aquinas but a description of human action. Without an end, human action would not exist, because human action proceeds from a deliberate will. If the will does not merely move randomly or formlessly, then it requires an object. "And an object of the will is an end and the good."[87]

In this first article, Aquinas makes an important distinction about the voluntary character of human action; it can be an act of commanding (*actus imperatus*), as when we speak or walk, or it can be an elicited act (*actus elicitus*). Here Aquinas gives us one of the few images in his work. Willing is compared to seeing. He notes that in vision what is first seen is not seeing itself but the object that is seen. Likewise, what is first desired is not the will itself but the object of the will, which is the end. The act of the will is not itself an end, but the object that elicits the will's movement is the end. Desire, then, always has an object, and our desire for an object is what makes possible our actions.[88]

If there is no *reasonable* object of desire, there is no *free* will. If there is no will, there is no movement toward reasonable objects of desire. In fact, even though Aquinas rejects pleasure alone as our ultimate good (contra Mill), he does recognize that "strong desires of sensible pleasures are the beginnings of our knowledge."[89] Such desires are necessary for the beginnings of knowledge, even though the desire for possessed goods cannot be our ultimate good. Ultimate happiness, or beatitude, is a power of the soul, but, even more important, it is found in an object extrinsic to the soul. Thus Aquinas stated that our good is "not only a power or habit or act but also an object which is extrinsic."[90] But this poses a problem for the moral life, for not only does an object extrinsic to us become our end, but that *object* is God, who can never be a possession. The *object* that is to satisfy us remains always beyond us.

Henri de Lubac explained the significance of this supernatural end. It means that human nature is such that it can only be fulfilled in itself beyond itself. By interpreting Aquinas this way, de Lubac safeguarded Christ's mystery against its naturalization through an a priori *analogia entis*. That is to say, de Lubac avoided describing the relationship between God and the world by means of a natural analogy of being that could be known through philosophy alone. He stated, "It is not the supernatural which is explained by nature, at least as something postulated by it." Thus he answered Barth's objection against Catholic theology and rejected Kant's conception of God as a necessary postulate of practical reason. But he also made possible a theologized nature in history, something Barth never successfully accomplished,[91] for de Lubac went on to suggest, "It is, on the contrary, nature which is explained in the eyes of faith by the supernatural, as required for it."[92] We do not know God through knowing our own nature, but we know our nature in knowing God; yet it is *our nature* that we come to know. Thus, this end that is always beyond us—an object extrinsic to us—can at the same time be in us. And it is in us through *desire;* knowledge of God comes through and in desire and not beyond the senses precisely because human desire is not clearly marked off into some sensible realm over and against the supersensible. The supernatural end that elicits our actions does so through our sensible nature.

This recovery of the central role of desire in Aquinas leads to a theological aesthetics that recognizes the bodiliness of our nature in its relationship to God. Not only hearing elicits our desire for God but also seeing, touching, tasting, and smelling. Through the enfleshment of God in the incarnation, on the cross, in the resurrection, in the Eucharist, and in its historical re-presentations through liturgical enactment, our desires become directed to that supernatural object sensibly given to us. And these theological practices become inextricably connected to a Christian understanding of the moral life. Through our doxological participation in the liturgical enactment of Christ's offering to God, we participate in God, who completes our nature even though our nature can never possess this God through some secure metaphysics of presence. Such liturgical enactments are where we discover the good. Aquinas himself argues that the incarnation was necessary for "our furtherance in good."[93]

For Aquinas, Jesus is the concrete sublime. This is not an a priori anthropological statement about human possibilities, as was the Kantian sublime, which stated that the sublime was to think the infinite without contradiction. The Kantian sublime was a statement about us, a self-possession. As Kant put it, "The bare capability of thinking the infinite without contradiction requires in the human mind a faculty itself supersensible."[94] This is an intriguing suggestion that Kant's work never fully accounted for; it requires something more than freedom and law as the basis for the moral life because it requires an *object* given to thought that thought itself could not account for. The apriority of the categories would not be able to explain it. In Aquinas's work Jesus as the concrete sublime is not first and foremost a statement about us, a self-possession, but a gift given that can be received in sensible form yet never possessed. This leads Aquinas to think of Jesus as the "New Law of the Gospel."

While the ultimate end that brings beatitude must exist outside the will, such an end must also be something capable of being created and existing within the person; otherwise, it would not be capable of satisfying and eliciting human desire, and the universal good would not be capable of being enjoyed as our ultimate end. This leads Aquinas to make a distinction between the cause or object of beatitude, which is uncreated (God), and its essence, which is something created.[95] Blessedness is never a self-possession, as were ancient virtues, where someone could be happy through strength of character alone. Blessedness requires participation in the Triune life, because "God is happiness by his Essence for He is happy not by acquisition or participation of something else, but by His Essence. On the other hand, human creatures are happy by participation."[96] The significance of this account of happiness for the moral life is precisely what led Aquinas to do to Aristotle what Aristotle himself never could have done: move beyond the acquired virtues to emphasize the moral life as requiring theological virtues, gifts, fruits of the Holy Spirit, and beatitudes, all of which arise from the sensible presence of the new law.

Using an expression from Paul, Aquinas speaks of the gospel "*per legem fidei.*" The gospel is a new law that affects and effects human reality. It was not given at the beginning of time but came when the hour had come. But having come, human life changed. This new law is both inward and written; it not only shows what a person is to do (*quid sit faciendum*) but also helps one accomplish that which is to be done (*sed etiam adjuvans ad implementum*).[97]

The new law both illumines that which was already present in the gratuity in creation and constitutes that reality anew. So Aquinas stated, "It is fitting that the grace which overflows from the incarnate Word should be carried to us by external perceptible realities; and also that certain external perceptible works should be brought forth from this interior grace by which flesh is made subject to spirit."[98] This new law effects an "external perceptible reality." Aquinas speaks of its impact on us as "a disposition and a use." It produces a disposition both in our *intellectum* and in our *affectum*. Through its operation on our *intellectum* we understand the most important things, such as that Christ was both human and divine. Through its operation on our *affectum* we learn contempt for the world (not to be confused with contempt for creation), which makes us further open to the Holy Spirit. As *usus*, the new law provides a power that produces all the works of virtue. This is not to say that the new law keeps us from sin, since such a state belongs only to the state of glory.[99] However, the new law is not some hidden work of God that cannot be specified (and therefore neither known as true nor false) but a sufficient help given to us such that we need not sin.

The new law of the gospel affects external perceptible reality, or it is false. It accomplishes this because Jesus himself becomes the source of a reasonable object of desire constituting our appetites. Our desire for God issues forth in a movement toward God. This movement is never self-initiated, for the life, death, and resurrection of Jesus always give the definitive form to the object of our desire. This movement comes to us as gift, but we can also cooperate with this gift precisely because it is sensibly present within us through our desires. It is a gift we possess but that is never our possession. Theology and the moral life are united in that we understand God more as we are more thoroughly turned toward that end. This means, as Pinckaers reminds us, "Theology must always remain unfinished in this world, outstripped by the mystery of the God it seeks to grasp."[100] Theology need not be tentative, but it can never be exhaustive. It remains unfinished in this world, yet it also must matter in this world. Ethics is not an appendix to systematic theology based on the various applications of theology to human action. Dogmatics is ethics.

FORGETTING KANT'S ANSWERS, REMEMBERING KANT'S QUESTION

The deep difficulty in Christian ethics, as evidenced in the work of "public" theologians such as Thiemann, Stackhouse, and, to a lesser extent, Garcia, is that Kant's answers are assumed but his profound question ignored. They do not seek to refute Kant. They do not seek to point to concrete, sensuous forms of life to show that Christian faith is reasonable. Instead, they speak in general terms. They speak of cosmopolitan social ethics, a criterion of publicity, and universal human rights. Their work contributes to the production of a generic theology that makes no particular claims on people of faith or people outside faith. The result is a refusal to challenge Kant's designation of freedom as more basic than the goodness of God. This Christian social ethic only continues the Kantian quest. We can use the language of faith and continue to speak of God and a Judeo-Christian anthropology, but the concrete material reality of Christianity (Jesus' flesh) is rendered superfluous to the moral life. This Christian social ethic constantly offers an apologetic for Christianity as inoffensive to the development of modern nation-states. It does not need to suggest that the life, teachings, death, resurrection, and ongoing presence of Jesus is the heart of any Christian social ethic. But any social ethic that seeks to be Christian must surely take Jesus as its center, for Jesus teaches us not only who God is but also what it means to be human. A Christian social ethic need not be embarrassed to argue that what is good is discovered in the concrete life of Jesus and made flesh in the sacraments.

John Howard Yoder, Stanley Hauerwas, and Oliver O'Donovan overcome the Kantian legacy by developing theological ethics with explicit attention to *theology*, particularly through Christology and ecclesiology. Their theological politics refuses the subordination of theology to ethics and the church to some putatively more universal space. Their work holds forth the new law of the gospel as the true end of politics, but they each do this with substantive differences between them. This is reflected in the titles of the works they have produced on this question: Yoder's *For the Nations*, O'Donovan's *Desire of the Nations*, and Hauerwas's *Against the Nations*.

Jesus for the Nations

Yoder finds the church to be "for the nations." He uses this language because he thinks both friends and foes have unfairly characterized his work as "sectarian," failing to recognize that his work is more "ecumenical" and "catholic" than the more mainline establishment churches that are marked by national and regional boundaries.[101] Those who unfairly characterize Yoder's work as sectarian miss the positive role the church plays in God's economy. This role has a place for the modern nation-state. "The reign of Christ means for the state the obligation to serve God by encouraging the good and restraining evil, i.e. to serve peace, to preserve the social cohesion in which the leaven of the gospel can build the church, and also render the old aeon more tolerable."[102] But the church never gains its role in God's economy by being subordinated to the state. The church's identity is not formed by reaction against the state nor by its contribution to the state. The church remains a universal community, always embodied in a specific locality, that is never subordinated to some grand imperial scheme. Thus Yoder's work is truly catholic. However, his catholic church does not mirror the state by taking on the trappings of empire. The church is lived through the local gathered assembly. This makes his ecclesiology radically reformed. This radical catholicity is both for and against the nations precisely because they are no longer the most significant social and political actors within God's economy. This can easily mislead Yoder's interpreters, for his indifference toward all things modern led him to use the language of modernity (rights and democracy) to speak of the "social cohesion" that permits building the church and making the old aeon more tolerable.

Yoder's work could suggest a privileging of modern democracies, but Yoder never assumed that the church was in a position to make democratic regimes or ensure their rule. Instead, he warns us that asking how the church contributes to the nation-state may itself tempt us to faithlessness. Whether it be Christendom's theological apologia for the divine right of kings or Protestant liberalism's apologia for democracy, Yoder sought to redirect our attention from the question, How shall we as Christians rule? He did this precisely because Jesus himself redirects us away from this question. The appropriate question is how the church endures the powers.[103]

That Yoder sought to redirect our question does not mean that he had nothing to say about the form of government under which Christians live in their "normal diaspora situation." Christians in every situation can adopt the language of the rulers and use it prudently. This is the task of Christians living within modern democratic nation-states:

> When I have the good fortune to find myself in a situation where part of the ruler's language of justification is the claim to have the consent of the governed, then I can use the machinery of democracy and am glad to do so. But I do not therefore believe that I am governing myself or that "we" as "the people" are governing ourselves. We are still governed by an elite, most of whose decisions are not submitted to the people for approval. Of all the forms of oligarchy, democracy is the least oppressive, since it provides the strongest language of justification and therefore of critique which the subjects may use to mitigate its oppressiveness.[104]

This is no ringing endorsement of modern democracies. Still, Yoder conveys the impression that the consent of the governed is a preferred form of *social cohesion* for making the old aeon most tolerable. It appears more consistent with the biblical command not to lord it over others. It fits best the kind of discernment under the Holy Spirit that the Christian community should embody.[105] And it provides the clearest "language of justification" that makes possible critique against an idolatrous human sovereignty.

But Yoder's use of the term *democracy* must be invoked with care. He never assumed that a secular account of democracy can be the norm that measures the church. For Yoder, true democracy is present in the gathered community of faith; it is the norm by which other kinds of *democracy* are to be assessed. In this he follows Karl Barth's understanding of *politics,* where the church's "governmental language within the people of God is the norm."[106] He used the term *democracy* in terms of the *politics* of the nations only because his more theological use of the term *politics* was "misunderstood in ecumenical and apologetic contexts." Thus Yoder refused to "impose it in a conversation with the children of Troeltsch and Niebuhr, for whom the pagan definitions are semantically prior."[107] As an act of charity Yoder sought to use the language of the dominant culture to address it (even though he did not hesitate to call it pagan). Any confusion over what Yoder meant by *democracy* may result from his willingness to use the "ruler's language of justification."

But Yoder's positive use of *democracy* is not simply a misunderstanding arising from his generosity. He also argued that the language of justification present in the "consent of the governed" was preferable to the lack of critique toward political institutions that was present in the divine right of kings. Is this true? Does Yoder read the political theology of the Middle Ages too monolithically, as if the king were conceded sole sovereignty without any possibility of critique?[108] Are modern democracies the least oppressive forms of oligarchy? Do they provide more possibility of a critical theological stance on the sovereignty exercised by rulers?

In *The King's Two Bodies: A Study in Medieval Political Theology,* Ernst Kantorowicz raises the possibility that a theological critique of political society was more present in medieval political theology than in the modern nation-state: "After all, the idea of a state existing only for its own sake was foreign to that age. The very belief in a divine Law of Nature as opposed to Positive Law, a belief then shared by every thinker, almost necessitated the ruler's position both above and below the Law."[109] That the king is both above and below the law reflects the christological rendering present in medieval political theology—the king has "two bodies." The one is human and historical and is bound to the positive law of the realm, as is every other historical human being. The other is divine and above the positive law because the realm does not exist only for its own sake but also functions within God's economy. Thus the positive law alone can never rule. A higher law is also present, embodied in the king, to which the positive law is accountable. Political society is not contained by the consent of the people alone—that would be an enactment of positive law that avoids subjecting the positivity of law to anything outside itself, including the judgment of the divine law. When Martin Luther King Jr. sat in a Birmingham jail for disobeying Alabama's positive laws on segregation, he appealed to this medieval political theology and wrote, "An unjust law is no law at all." Without an understanding of a law not subject to the "consent of the governed," is such a witness possible? Does Yoder assume that the language of justification present in liberal democracies bears more possibility of critiquing human sovereignty than the language of Christendom? Or does he simply assume that the faithful must use the language of liberal democracies because they, rather than Christendom, are our reality? Why should we assume that the strength of a government is its ability for self-critique in the first place?

The answer to the last question seems obvious: any government incapable of self-critique will be more prone toward totalitarian excess. But is this answer so obvious? Could a government that tolerates and fosters self-critique also produce a form of hegemony whereby the very ability to critique the government freely becomes the source of its unquestioned power over us? In other words, can the kind of permanent revolution H. Richard Niebuhr advocated become a hegemonic power that we cannot critique precisely because its power functions through a self-imposed critical posture? And is this, rather than Christendom, the true mark of the political reality under which Christians must today learn faithfulness? Yoder's assumption that good government primarily embodies a posture of critique toward any human appropriation of sovereignty may reveal the lingering influence of Niebuhrian realism.

The lingering Niebuhrian realism in Yoder's work influences not only his relative appreciation for democracy but also his ecclesiology. Like H. Richard Niebuhr, Reinhold Niebuhr's lack of any orthodox doctrine of the incarnation led him to reject any strong ecclesiological claim that posits the church as the body of Christ. He wrote,

> The Catholic doctrine of the Church is, in fact, a constant temptation to demonic pretensions, since it claims for an institution, established in time and history, universal and absolute validity. Except for the fact that its institution is actually more universal than a single state, this Catholic claim leads to reactionary political consequences, similar to those of Hegelianism, in which the Absolute is thought to be incarnate in a single state. . . . Protestant theory does not give the historic and concrete institution the same aura of the Absolute. . . . The real Church is always in the sphere of transcendence.[110]

By definition, the church cannot be a social ethic for Niebuhr because it exists only as a metaphysical ideal whose purpose is to critique all historical presentations of the Absolute (presumably God.) Thus Niebuhr's Neo-Protestant theology has one dogma: never dogmatize the historical. The fact that the historical promulgation of this dogma contradicts itself never slows Neo-Protestants from proclaiming it.

Yoder does not share Niebuhr's inability to think the incarnation, but his ecclesiology can lend support to Niebuhr's ecclesiology. Yoder finds any defense of the church's indefectibility to be a form of Constantinianism.[111] Unlike Niebuhr, Yoder claims that God speaks in the community of faith and that we have "marks of validity" helping us recognize that speech. "God speaks where his people gather and are free to be led. The marks of the validity of the conclusions they reach are to be sought not alone in the principles applied but in the procedure of the meeting. Were all free to speak? Was every speech heard and weighted?"[112] The "marks of validity" are found at the local level when the practices of the Holy Spirit are embodied in the community of faith; they are not ensured by an overarching magisterium.

Although these marks of validity could lead readers of Yoder to find resemblances between his "hermeneutics of peoplehood" and the proceduralism of liberalism, such a resemblance must be qualified. It is the charisma of the Spirit that makes Yoder's ecclesiology possible and not an individual right to free speech itself. Thus Yoder's critique of the indefectibility of the church is not that the church is incapable of re-presenting God's speech in history, but that it does so only when the church adheres to the priesthood of all believers. Nevertheless, Yoder's ecclesiology resembles Niebuhr's in that Yoder defines "the criterion of Protestant identity" as its "process of critiquing the developed tradition from the perspective of its own roots."[113] In so doing, Yoder makes a problematic distinction between the "simple meaning" of the biblical texts and the "tradition" that he often thinks obfuscated that simple meaning. He also argues, like Niebuhr, that one of the true markers of the church should be its humility about itself. Ecumenical conversations could proceed more swiftly if the church were more humble. If it "were to receive the grace to say, 'we were wrong,'" Yoder argues, it would provide new opportunities for ecumenical engagement. But this poses two problems.

First, indefectibility is not mere Constantinianism but arises from the biblical witness itself. It is part of the promise Jesus gave to Peter that the power of hell would not prevail against the church (Matt. 16:18). The church can claim *indefectibility* because it is not merely a human social process but has present within it the power of the Holy Spirit to prevent it from falling into complete and inescapable error. The particular form given that indefectibility by Pius IX in the doctrine of infallibility may be objectionable, but even that dogma does not prevent the church from admitting wrong, as John Paul II has amply demonstrated with his willingness to confess the church's wrongs.

Second, Yoder's advocacy for the church to have more humility makes the church too susceptible to modern liberalism. I am not suggesting that Yoder endorsed modern liberalism; he did not. But his vocation to call the church out of Constantinianism did not always recognize that a church mired in modernity is not homologous to a church mired in Christendom. Yoder underestimated liberalism's threat to the church. Like Niebuhr, Yoder seeks a transcendent principle of critique that refuses to concede any particular historical expression as a final authority. Thus he critiques Roman Catholicism for being "its own final authority, it is inconceivable at least in principle, that it converse with anyone."[114] This was written in 1957—prior to Vatican II (although republished in 1994). Yoder opposed any particular tradition from being its own authority and instead suggested, "It is thus only the 'restitutionist' claim, appealing to all of Scripture over the heads of all particular traditions, that can retain the normativeness of the Incarnation over all our efforts to reflect it."[115] But is this restitutionist position "over the heads of all particular traditions," or does it simply privilege a different tradition over all others—the Anabaptist tradition?

For Yoder, authority cannot be located in any historical development. As he notes, "If the locus of our given unity is Jesus Christ, it would seem that the only feasible solution to the problem of authority would be to declare inadmissible the attribution of authoritative character to any particular historical development and to recognize the only legitimate judge Christ himself as he is made known through the Scripture to the congregation of those who call to know him and his will."[116] How is making Christ known through Scripture in the congregation itself not a historical development? Is this not precisely what the dogmatic tradition itself is, making Christ known through the gathered church in councils? Yoder's position does not differ that dramatically from the dogmatic tradition except that he seems to question the diachronic nature of dogma as being able adequately to reflect Christ made known in Scripture. Does this tempt Yoder toward a *progressive* posture that privileges the new, toward the modern?

Yoder does not accept the new as our "fundamental value."[117] He is not a theological liberal who eschews dogma. He recognizes that his own Anabaptist tradition has been tempted toward the rejection of dogma and finds such rejection naive. Moreover, he recognizes that this leads to "theological pluralism or liberalism," and this is not his position. He argues rather for a unity of practice within the Christian church, though he does not correlate that unity with a doctrinal unity. Dogma is inevitable, but it does not have definitive status. Yoder explains, "Others have more soberly argued that there will be many statements of faith but that it is wrong to let any one of them become a final tool to define heresy or to replace the entire body of Scripture as the rule of faith."[118] Yoder is not a modern precisely because his concern is to maintain the authority of Scripture over all historical representations of it. But what Yoder does not seem to account for is that Scripture itself—like the Word made flesh—must be historically represented. And this makes the memory of Jesus something much more than a "continuing critique." It makes it a re-presentation of goodness in historical form. It requires dogma.

Yoder did not reject the christological conclusions of conciliar orthodoxy. He affirmed both Nicea and Chalcedon, but he worried that orthodoxy did not make room for change. Thus Yoder wrote,

> "Orthodoxy" (the word has many meanings) thinks that staying the same is both possible and good. What we call "liberalism" thinks that change is both inevitable and good. And (I suggest) they are both wrong. Change is inevitable so that the orthodox is wrong. But change is not always good, so that the liberal position is questionable. Change is not always in one clear direction, forward, as the liberal tends to think.[119]

But this description of orthodoxy and liberalism caricatures both positions. Liberalism has now become a dogmatic form of orthodoxy incapable of change, and Reinhard Hütter has persuasively argued that theological change cannot occur without a theological attentiveness to the distinction between orthodoxy and heresy. If there is no such distinction, then theology can only be indifferent toward its historical representations. That liberalism assumes that dogma is at most symbolic, reflecting an underlying experience, discloses that change is not possible for it. Only orthodoxy, which assumes that dogmas matter, can incorporate change.

Although Yoder's theology is consistent with the dogmatic tradition of orthodoxy, he worried that reducing Christianity to dogma alone prevented the tradition from embodying Jesus' politics. Yet Yoder's lack of interest in the dogmatic tradition becomes problematic in his sacramental theology. He had little time for discussions as to what happens to the eucharistic elements. Protestant and Catholic debates over the nature of the eucharistic elements, he argued, are "medieval questions [that] have kept us away from the simple meaning of the [biblical] text long enough."[120] In that both the Reformers and Catholics thought they were defending the "simple meaning of the text" in their debates over Jesus' statement, "This is my body," one might have expected Yoder to be a bit more circumspect in appealing to the text's *simple meaning* against them. What can be more simple than to suggest that when Jesus said, "This is my body," he meant *this* is my body? But Yoder believes that the dogmatic tradition misses the heart of the matter and avoids the "simple meaning."

What is this simple meaning Yoder appeals to? "It is that bread is daily sustenance. Bread eaten together is economic sharing. Not merely symbolically, but also in fact, eating together extends to a wider circle the economic solidarity normally obtained in the family."[121] That this is one meaning of the Eucharist is undeniable, but that it is the *simple* meaning is questionable. What makes the Eucharist different from a church's potluck supper? Yoder seems too convinced that practices such as Eucharist and baptism "can be translated into non-religious terms."[122] Of course they can, but should they? What is lost when these practices are explained in terms of social process without also explaining them in the language of the dogmatic tradition?

What is lost is important theological conversations that have taken place since "the original revolution" that began Christianity. For example, in *For the Nations* Yoder stated, "Our history of centuries of speculation and controversy about what happens to bread and wine when a certain special person speaks certain special Latin words over them obscured from our memory for a long time the fact that the primary meaning of the eucharistic gathering in the Gospels and Acts is economic."[123] To accuse both the Reformers and the Catholics of failing to see that the Eucharist is economic misses the significance of those debates. If all our exchanges take their significance from the exchange God makes with us in the Eucharist, then to discuss what occurs in the bread and wine and what occurs in the community of faith is far from obscuring the *economic* significance of the Eucharist.

Yoder uses the term *economic* here in a thoroughly modern sense; it primarily concerns immanent exchanges of everyday substances. He overlooks the more ancient sense of *economic*, where it first denotes God's relationship with the *oikonomia*, the household that is God's creation. Having translated the theology of the Eucharist into "social process terms," Yoder held little place for the role of theological doctrine as that which can render intelligible our immanent exchanges. In other words, without a place for sacred teaching that carefully articulates the transcendent exchange God makes with God's creation, can we articulate well the immanent exchanges that make up everyday life?

On occasion Yoder finds doctrine, creeds, and dogmas to be obfuscations. They represent compromises made during the Constantinian settlement. He stated, "The claims of Mediterranean-European religiosity are not what we should be defending or even redefining."[124] Yoder associates orthodoxy with imperial power. After Constantine's conversion, the development of Christian dogma is tainted because it is associated with the throne. "Henceforth Caesar will not simply support Christianity: he will support orthodoxy and will, therefore, have to have a voice in defining what orthodoxy is."[125] That Caesar sought to do this is certainly true. As is well known, Constantine offered the term *homoousios* to the council that defined the relationship between Jesus' human and divine natures, and it became dogma in the Nicene Creed. But to dismiss orthodoxy because of this would seem to be a species of Donatism. Nor would it fit with the biblical narrative. The God who used Cyrus to free God's people could also use Constantine. Further, to assume that the creeds are somehow "extra-canonical" because they do not use the exact same language as the New Testament begs the question. As David Yeago has argued, "The Nicene *homoousion* is neither imposed on the New Testament texts, nor distantly deduced from the texts, but rather, describes a pattern of judgments present in the texts, in the texture of scriptural discourse concerning Jesus and the God of Israel."[126] Nor did the church simply accept every suggestion Caesar offered.

The church's opposition to Justinian's "three chapters" clearly shows that the post-Constantinian church recognized the problem of Caesaropapism. Yoder sells the dogmatic tradition short when he does not give sufficient testimony to those who defended orthodoxy against Caesar's attempt to define it.

Yoder does not simply dismiss dogma. He is thoroughly orthodox in his theology: incarnation, Trinity, and Christ's two natures are necessary for his work. But he does not show as much interest in the unity of doctrine and worship as he does the unity of ethical commitment. He does not advocate doctrinal pluralism, since he recognizes that pluralism subordinates the church's witness to that of the modern state. Yet oddly enough the Anabaptist Yoder is less opposed to the *modern* democratic nation than either Hauerwas or O'Donovan, both of whom work from within (and react against) thoroughly modern churches. Yoder finds the modern democratic process to be a Christian inheritance. As he puts it, "Dialogue under the Holy Spirit is the ground floor of the notion of democracy."[127] In fact, Yoder assumes the secularization thesis that argues that the true faith can be found in the secular rather than in the church. "The relapse of Christianity into sacerdotal patriarchy led to the loss of this vision as a way of realistically sharing the roles of members in a community, but it has occasionally resurfaced in visions of ministry. Today in fact this vision is more widely operative in the rest of society than in the traditional churches, as the division of labor has enabled the culture of the university or the factory or the city."[128] Can Paul's vision for the new community be so readily equated with the "division of labor" found in modern sociopolitical formations? Here Yoder's opposition to Constantinianism tempts him too much "for the nations."

Jesus, Desire of the Nations

Oliver O'Donovan's defense of liberalism shares Yoder's sentiment that Christ is "for the nations." Yet by defending Christendom O'Donovan finds himself more in opposition to modern political configurations than Yoder. O'Donovan's fascinating work, *The Desire of the Nation: Rediscovering the Roots of Political Theology*, recognizes that subordinating theology to ethics and/or politics results in an unreasonable politics prone to authoritarianism. "The doctrine that we set up political authority, as a device to secure our own essentially private, local and unpolitical purposes, has left the Western democracies in a state of pervasive moral debilitation, which, from time to time, inevitably throws up idolatrous and authoritarian reactions."[129] O'Donovan does not defend religion as a necessary foundation for or contribution to politics, as did Stackhouse, Thiemann, and Garcia. His is a much more radical critique of modern democracies. They are incoherent because they lack an adequate account of authority. But they are more than incoherent; they are prone toward an institutional authoritarianism because they supplant the "human act" as political act with an institutional authority tied to office and structure.[130] O'Donovan's defense of the divine institution of politics does not lessen the importance of human political making; it strengthens it. He argues that the self-contained authority of modern political configurations is responsible for lessening the significance of the human act of politics because it secures itself internally through administrative procedure linked with office and structure. This tends toward political authority grounded in state sovereignty or popular sovereignty. Both forms of sovereignty contain politics within a "self-enclosed field of human endeavour." Such containment sanctions a totality that need not receive anything outside itself to enact political authority. Because it becomes incapable of external contributions, its structures take on authoritarian roles. O'Donovan argues that those who have no possibility of a truth external to their own self-constituted politics are most tempted toward authoritarianism. Politics abandons any possibility for the "theatre of the divine self-disclosure."[131]

As the *desire* of the nations, Jesus makes possible a nonauthoritarian politics opening up authority from its self-enclosure. O'Donovan is willing to grant dogma a definitive status and to show that it does not render Jesus' ethics immaterial. In fact, the key for O'Donovan's political theology is Christology. Political theology must "perform its task Christologically," which means that it makes "its way along the stream which flows from the apostles' proclamation of Christ as 'Lord' to the later, ontologically developed definitions of the ecumenical creeds."[132] O'Donovan defends the "ontologically developed definitions" of orthodox Christology and at the same time explains how these definitions are the result of, and not a retreat from, a political theology: "If Christian theology as a whole has sometimes allowed the careless or skeptical to conclude that the church changed its proclamation from Kingdom to Christ somewhere around A.D. 50, it is the special task of political theology to efface that impression."[133] O'Donovan locates Christology both in the history of Israel and in the production of the church as a *society* where God's rule is *realized*. This history culminates in the confession of Christ's two natures. Christ functions both as "mediator of God's rule" and as "representative individual." But the two are related such that Christ cannot become a mere function of God's rule, a function that could be fulfilled by some other person, movement, or process. Israel, Jesus, and church are not symbols for functions that could be fulfilled by other symbols. There is no place for the secularization thesis in O'Donovan's work. The particular matters.

Whereas Yoder's work tends toward a social cohesion represented by democratic forms of nation-states, O'Donovan's central thesis is that politics needs a fuller account of authority that takes seriously the "idea of political activity as kingly."[134] That a work offering something of a defense for political liberalism begins by appealing to "kingly rule" already lets the reader know that something more than a defense of modern political configurations is occurring. Why does political authority need the idea of *kingship?* O'Donovan answers this in his response to criticisms of his work:

Once we seriously believe in God as agent and author in the realm of politics, we shall always be conscious of the critical question: is this particular instance of human rule that we, he, or she exercises the kind of rule that God has authorized and blessed? Or must it confront God as its judge and destroyer? The most timid and conservative of thinkers in Christendom never forgot that question, which hung like a sword of Damocles over the head of every ruler, however *christianissimus*. If, on the other hand, we don't believe that there is any other solidarity to be had than what we put together for ourselves, no serious challenge to human authority can ever arise.[135]

O'Donovan recognizes that without divine sovereignty, modern political arrangements based on the "will of the people" possess a stronger and more unquestionable account of human sovereignty than the political arrangements present in Christendom. When that sovereignty becomes rooted in formal bureaucratic structures rather than in a human making open to divine self-disclosure, then a critique of sovereignty becomes less possible.[136]

O'Donovan is not advocating a theocracy. He demonstrates that political authority is not self-authenticating. It cannot reasonably be developed out of nature *qua* nature. While he takes the "goods of creation" seriously, he does not interpret them as self-evident. There are not two separate realms: grace and nature, church and politics, where politics can be known *qua* nature alone. He challenges the modern demarcation of a political sphere separate from theology. Thus political authority is not developed under a "natural law" free from divine law. O'Donovan recovers the "lost theological horizon of political authority" and in so doing calls into question the assumption that political authority can be described on its own terms.

But neither does he argue for a seamless theological-political realm. Instead, O'Donovan's political theology is based on the "doctrine of the Two, the core notion of Christendom."[137] This doctrine "supposes the vis-à-vis of church and secular government as distinct structures belonging to distinct societies and, indeed, distinct eras of salvation-history." The relationship between these two societies cannot be explained once and for all; instead, what characterizes the relationship between them is the *mission* of Christ. Even the rulers must become obedient to Christ. The church should accept nothing less than calling for such obedience, even while it recognizes (as did Augustine) that in the king's service to the church "lies greater and more perilous temptation."[138] O'Donovan's "doctrine of the Two" differs from the notion of the separation of church and state enshrined in the United States Constitution, since "the doctrine of the Two" assumes that the church has a mission to replace false rulers with the rule of Christ. Part of the mission of the church is to call the nations to "recognize God's self-disclosure in history." As O'Donovan puts it, "The church's one project is to witness to the Kingdom of God. Christendom is response to mission, and as such a sign that God has blessed it. It is constituted not by the church's seizing alien power, but by alien's power becoming attentive to the church."[139] For O'Donovan, Christendom may have come to an end, but the end (*telos*) of Christendom must remain part of the church's mission. Christ is not merely the desire that orders the church; Christ is the desire that orders the nations.

But how does this happen? How does Christ rule without the church becoming like the rulers? As Arne Rasmussen has noted, the end of Christendom did not occur simply because an alien account of political authority superseded the "doctrine of the Two." Christendom self-destructed because of a particular historical performance of this doctrine. "Christendom," Rasmussen suggests, "killed the rich political theology O'Donovan in many ways so eloquently defends."[140] The modern nation-state system does not develop from a complete rupture with the theological account of political authority that came before it. Somehow it birthed it. Thus, while O'Donovan has helped us recover the theological horizon of political authority, he has not given us enough to explain how the "doctrine of the Two" paved the way for the end of Christendom in events such as the first amendment to the United States Constitution in 1791.[141] Did the "doctrine of the Two" not sow the seeds for its own dissolution long before the full fruit of that dissolution in the eighteenth century? And were some of those seeds an ecclesiology that became too comfortable with its relationship to the *secular* such that it promoted the secular in its own autonomous space? This may be a restatement of O'Donovan's position rather than a criticism of it, but in what follows I hope to develop his orthodox insight that Christ is the desire of the nations along with Yoder's similar conception of Christ's mission for the nations without Yoder's tacit acceptance of the secularization thesis or O'Donovan's inattentiveness to how the authority of the rule of Christ must be different from the rule of the nations if the nations are finally to be ruled by Christ.

Jesus against the Nations

Hauerwas does not deny that Christ is *for* the nations and the *desire* of the nations. But Hauerwas finds O'Donovan's work too hospitable to Christians living among the nations. Thus he and Jim Fodor "differ with O'Donovan to the extent that he thinks resurrection and ascension make it possible for Christians to be more than God's wandering people."[142] Christendom tempts the faithful to settle down and find a secure place among the nations. But O'Donovan's defense of Christendom makes him as uncomfortable among the moderns as is Hauerwas, and even in Babylon God's people were told to build houses and plant gardens. That we do so does not mean we lose our status as "resident aliens" who must be against the nations precisely because Christ is the desire of the nations.

Like Yoder and O'Donovan, Hauerwas affirms orthodoxy. In fact, he argues that change can occur only in the church, where there is orthodoxy. Orthodoxy provides a direction, which is "uncontrolled" and "radically unpredictable" in a way that liberalism is not. Precisely because orthodoxy seeks fidelity to historical enactments it must, of necessity, engage other historical enactments and incorporate them into its ongoing narrative. Orthodoxy is continuously performed. Of necessity it changes because it is not a path a priori scripted, but it nevertheless has a clear direction from incarnation to eschaton. Between these times it negotiates this path, discovering more profoundly what orthodoxy itself is.

Orthodoxy requires traditioning, which entails receiving gifts from the past to live in the present. Only something with profound roots could be capable of incorporating something truly new. But liberalism "renders the past impotent for the ongoing determination of our lives."[143] It assumes the inevitability of progress and the incessant need to be relevant to the *new* such that it becomes thoroughly predictable and thoroughly controlled. It knows only the *new*, and thus the new becomes the norm. It cannot then ever be truly new. There is no path, no direction, only the *point* of the now. Orthodoxy, like a river, is capable of springing forth new movements precisely because it has a direction. Liberalism, like backwater, can only remain stagnant. It loses the ability to discover genuine difference and forces all of history into its homogenous mold of the "new and improved," which become our fate.

Hauerwas recognizes that most of liberal Protestant theology seeks relevance to this controlled and predictable discourse of the new, and thus liberalism becomes more certain and dogmatic than orthodoxy. "Liberals are convinced," writes Hauerwas, "that particular knowledges are certain in a manner that Christian orthodoxy cannot be."[144] Thus liberalism tends to reduce Christianity to "beliefs," that is, beliefs in transcendence, in God's action in history, in the good gift of creation, in progressive revelation—even in a sure and certain belief in ambiguity! But these beliefs do not really matter or make any difference for how one might live within the ever-new that constitutes liberal society. In opposition to the certitude that founds modern liberalism, Hauerwas's work depends upon a historical presentation of Christian orthodoxy, which must be renarrated by every generation of the faithful. Thus, although Hauerwas has not offered sustained reflections on the dogmatic tradition—such as the two-nature doctrine of Christ or the Trinity—all of his work presupposes such dogmas,[145] and his reflections on concrete matters are explications of the practical significance that living one's life within the narrative whole of Christian dogma entails.[146]

While Hauerwas embraces orthodoxy, he opposes understanding Christianity primarily as belief. Reducing dogma to belief is how Christian theologians make peace with the modern and allow for the "democratic policing of Christianity." He notes, "In the process of providing Christian support of democratic social orders, the church became unable to sustain itself—in short, it became a 'knowledge' rather than a church."[147] That is to say, the church *contributes* to society certain beliefs or forms of knowledge—such as the inviolability of the individual, the need for transcendence, an insistence on equality or dignity, or a vague commitment to inclusivity—but the church does not see itself as a society. By reducing Christianity to belief, the church subordinates itself to *society*, which tacitly considers itself to be more normative and central to God's economy than the church itself. Because the preservation of society is located in the nation-state, Hauerwas calls Christians to be "against the nations."

Hauerwas constantly criticizes democratic nation-states, but he has no adequate response to the question, "If you do not like democracy, then what form of government do you think best?"[148] Several considerations seem to drive his unwillingness to answer this question. First, he does not accept the self-description of the liberal democratic nation-state. He notes, "Rather than regulating society into a perpetual state of equilibrium in which individuals find equality and freedom, modern nation-states have developed as ever-increasing power centers sustained by industrialized militarization."[149] He finds the very performance of nation-states to be contradictory. These contingent social formations that pride themselves on freedom and equality have been some of the most warlike social formations yet developed; they incarcerate more people than any previous social formation and make a business out of it. Meanwhile, the churches within those social formations provide apologias for them at the expense of their own theological integrity. This does not mean that Hauerwas seeks to destroy the liberal state. In this sense, Hauerwas is no countercultural revolutionary. In explaining why he is against the nations, he states,

> I hope I have avoided the temptation to attribute to liberalism everything that is wrong with our society. . . .[150] I certainly believe there is much right about our social order. Moreover, I think that liberalism has, sometimes almost in spite of itself, had some beneficial results. It is still unclear if some of those results, such as freedom of religion, can be sustained in a consistently worked out liberal society. For liberalism has been successful partly because it could depend on social structures and habits it did not create and in fact over time undermines. . . . What must be recognized is that liberalism is not simply a theory of government but a theory of society that is imperial in its demands.[151]

Hauerwas is *against* the nations precisely because he is for the nations. If the church does not insist on its own primacy as a social structure, liberalism will not concede it. Its imperial demands seek to incorporate all social formations within its own architechtonic grasp. Liberalism will close down any "complex space" that exists outside of the "simple space" liberalism creates.[152] The church need not destroy liberalism. Hauerwas does not define his work against a social order, assuming that it must be destroyed for the church to be the church. In fact, Hauerwas views his own unwillingness to insist on the direct overthrow of the present social order as consistent with both the strategy of Jesus and the early church:

> There is a continuity between Jesus' refusal to seize power and the early church's refusal to overthrow existing structures. If the church tried to overthrow the existing structures, it would have simply become a parallel structure, a parallel "cause." Instead, the church attempted to create alternative, "local" areas of peace, charity and justice.[153]

Hauerwas's project is *against* the nations only in that it is for the church as the only social formation holding the narrative that can prevent freedom from usurping the good and thus making violence more determinative of our lives than God's peaceable kingdom. The point is not to destroy liberalism but "to help the church recover a sense of its own integrity that it might better be able to make discriminating judgments about the society which we happen to call America."[154] If liberalism is the theory of society under which Christians must live until the eschaton, then the point is to prevent it from realizing its own imperial demands. The church does this by being the church. If another form of society arises, then the church will have to respond to it as well. The response will be different, but Hauerwas follows Yoder in insisting that the response should be one that reflects the "war of the lamb" who refused to seize power and instead endured the cross. Like Yoder, but unlike O'Donovan, Hauerwas disavows Constantianism:

> I would like Christians to recapture the posture of the peasant. The peasant does not seek to become the master but rather she wants to know how to survive under the power of the master. The peasant, of course, has certain advantages since, as Hegel clearly saw, the peasant must understand the master better than the master can understand herself or himself. The problem with Christian justifications of democracy is not that alleged democratic social orders may not have some advantages, but that the Christian fascination with democracy as "our" form of government has rendered us defenseless when, for example, the state goes to war.[155]

The modern nation state is not an unmitigated evil for Hauerwas; it is the church's accommodation to that particular social formation and its tacit subordination of its own social primacy to that of the nation that renders it necessary to speak against the nations.

Yoder, O'Donovan, and Hauerwas relate the church to the nations (and thereby to other social formations as well) while still maintaining the centrality of Christ as Lord. They all offer an alternative to H. Richard Niebuhr's "radical monotheism," which refuses to equate the lordship of Jesus with the lordship of God. For this reason, the theology of Yoder, O'Donovan, and Hauerwas is more political than H. Richard Niebuhr's "enduring problem" of Christ and culture could have countenanced. They recognize that Christian dogma by definition has a social and political face, which must be explicated by each generation of the faithful.

Both Hauerwas and Yoder have a version of O'Donovan's "doctrine of the Two." They all agree that the church does not rule as the secular rulers rule, and they all agree that the church has a mission to bear witness to the state and call the secular rulers themselves to recognize the rule of Christ. They disagree about the historical performance of Christendom in this realization. O'Donovan finds the Christendom project to be more of a faithful fulfillment of this common mission than do Yoder and Hauerwas.[156] But this does not entail that O'Donovan is more susceptible to finding a home in modernity than are Hauerwas and Yoder. In fact, O'Donovan and Hauerwas are less amenable to the secularization thesis than Yoder and thus perhaps less favorable toward the modern nation-state. But what divides them most of all is the crucial question of Christian participation in the state's war-making ability. Yoder and Hauerwas view this as the test case for the church's faithful witness to the modern nation-state; O'Donovan does not. O'Donovan would not thereby condone the methods of warfare used by the modern nation-state. Like Paul Ramsey before him, he recognizes the limits Christian charity places on the prosecution of warfare such that his own defense of the just war may require the production of a Christian difference in the modern era as much as does Yoder's and Hauerwas's pacifism.

The present work has been influenced by Yoder's articulation of the politics of Jesus, Hauerwas's witness against the nations, and O'Donovan's recognition that Christ is the desire of the nations and that this is an integral aspect to the church's mission. This sets the church against the discourse of liberalism, for the church should never seek to make itself relevant to the new and improved. It does not know progress as fate, for in Christ, the end is given in the middle. The church holds forth Christ as the desire of the nations without turning the church into the nations. The church is not merely a voluntary association that contributes to the creation of civil society or civilization. Christ makes the church possible. He is the desire of the nations. Yoder, O'Donovan, and Hauerwas point us to Christ for our theological politics.

THREE

Beyond EVIL through the BEAUTY of HOLINESS: True God, True Humanity

For dogmatics to be ethics, we need a different quest than the Kantian one. The questions that form that quest ended in failure, for they always searched for an abstract freedom. Once it was found, it was incapable of rendering intelligible our everyday desires to be good. A quest for God can help make sense of such everyday desire, for it will not take us beyond sensibility. We do not need to look either above or beneath the physical to find God. God is not for Christians an abstract metaphysical concept.[1] This does not mean that theology must reject metaphysics or falsely assume that it could,[2] but it does imply that *metaphysics* remains only when it is subordinated to theology.

Kant's legacy must be refuted, but not because he assisted the death of the metaphysical god, a god known without theology and sacred doctrine. Kant's legacy must be refuted because he did not kill the metaphysical god sufficiently. Thus, his ethics does not allow the central insight of Christian morality. That insight is simple but profound, and it is the heart of Alasdair MacIntyre's critique of modernist efforts to justify the moral life.[3] Human nature as it is cannot provide the basis for a universal morality. Both Kant's efforts to ground the universal in the postulates of practical reason and Mill's efforts to do so with reference to the increase of pleasure and the diminishment of pain have failed.

They have failed because ethics cannot merely assume human nature as it is. For ethics to make sense, it must have some purpose: to transform our human nature into what it should be. Without such a *telos,* ethics makes no sense. It can only be a soporific appliance.

In Christian theology, Jesus reveals to us not only who God is but also what it means to be *truly human.* This true humanity is not something we achieve on our own; it comes to us as a gift. Only a social ethics that can acknowledge and celebrate this gift can be adequately called Christian. The reception of this gift contains an ineliminable element of mystery that will always require faith. This does not pose an opposition between faith and reason, nor does it assume some leap beyond reason. It suggests that God is not some substance or nature intrinsic to the world that can be assessed and evaluated based on reason's ability to master and control its object. That, of course, is a thoroughly reasonable position. In fact, as Robert Sokolowski has argued, drawing upon the work of Anselm, "Only if the divine is not one of the natures in the world can the incarnation and the salvation it achieved, occur."[4]

The logic of the incarnation requires that the God who becomes flesh is also something other than flesh, or else there is no mystery, no gift. Therefore, a reasonable mystery and givenness is present in theology. But this is not the mystery of a negative theology that ends in silence. This is the mystery of the God who is fully revealed in Jesus Christ. In other words, Christian theology does not assume that God reveals God's self progressively, giving us a glimpse here and a glimpse there. Such a God would not truly be giving himself to us. Rather, at its best Christian theology assumes that in Jesus God is *fully* revealed. The church fathers understood this. If God only gave God's self to us in parts, giving us in the Son a bit of the Godhead and in the Spirit an inferior bit yet, then God's gift would assume *deficiency* and would need to be developed and filled out in history. But this is not consistent with a God who is love and gives himself without reserve.

Thus, when Gregory of Nazianzus explained the Christian doctrine of the Trinity to the faithful, he emphasized that "there was nothing lacking" in this gift. He recognized that "the Son is what the Father is [and] the Spirit is what the Son is." This made the doctrine of the Trinity necessary for the safeguarding of the fullness of God's gift to us in the incarnation.[5] In other words, the Son is everything that the Father is except that the Son is not the Father. This implies that God is not a mystery in the sense that God hides from us. In Jesus, God gives himself to us without reserve. Insofar as God remains mysterious, the mystery is predicated not on God's absence but on God's overwhelming splendor of luminosity that blinds us in its givenness, a givenness that can never be exhausted in Christian dogma but that must have dogma for its representation. Therefore, the articulation of dogma never comes to an end. Progress in theology is possible, but not because we have now received a fuller or further revelation of God. For dogma to bear witness to the mystery that makes it possible, it must stay connected with that original gift. This is not a passive givenness that is only received, as a feeling of absolute dependence would require. It is an active givenness that is made in and through the performance of the church. This account of God is reasonable. It can narrate why good and evil still enchant us even though we cannot account for them via reason alone.

Given the resources of modern ethics, we cannot adequately explain why the terms *good* and *evil* enchant us, yet most of us do not find Nietzsche's alternative compelling. We do not seek to move beyond and cannot do without these terms. Yet philosophy has failed to give us any coherent and compelling justification for their use. Theology finds nothing strange about our reality. The "achievement" of good and avoidance of evil are not possible by reason alone but only through a faith-informed reason, which recognizes that the "achievement" of good and avoidance of evil comes as a gift with which we can at most participate but never create. Freedom does not antedate God in either epistemology or ontology.

God implants in all creatures a basic law of nature whose primary principle is do good and avoid evil. But this principle only sets us in a certain direction. It can never justify morality; it only makes a quest for good central in all human endeavors. No human endeavor, not even that of thievery, can be totally without this quest. Although this quest is often distorted beyond human comprehension, human actions are only intelligible when we assume that they aim at some good. Whether we are building a house, writing a book, rearing a family, preparing meals, or engaging in any other type of human activity, we aim at some good, some end for which the activity makes sense. But the quest for the good does not make us good. There are apparent goods and real goods. The end of that quest must be discovered, and that end must itself be good.

Christian theology assumes that the end toward which we consciously and unconsciously move is the state of blessedness that we receive when we live our lives in cooperation with divine wisdom, which is thoroughly present in the Second Person of the Trinity. He who rules and regulates our hearts toward eternal blessedness gives us a new law. Jesus in his life, teaching, death, resurrection, and ongoing presence in the church in and through the Holy Spirit gives us a new law that orders us toward God. He directs our passions and desires toward that which can finally fulfill them and bring us happiness. This is because he reveals to us what it means to be human. The task of ethics is to assist us in the journey from our human nature as it is—with its inclination toward the good but its lack of substantive content and thus its temptation toward evil—to the concrete, sensuous embodiment of what our human nature should be via the "law of the gospel." The law of the gospel is the ongoing presence of Jesus in the community of faith.

My appeal to the normativity of Jesus does assume some historical claims about who he was and what he did. If these claims are disproven or rejected, this ethics does not work. I am dependent upon Richard Hays's "proposed reconstruction" for the "historical Jesus," which claims that we can know that Jesus was a Jew from Galilee who taught disciples through parables and stories. He did not abrogate the Mosaic law or establish a complete break with Israel but sought to restore Israel through the establishment of a new community, first realized in the twelve disciples. His activity brought him into conflict with the governing authorities such that he was unjustly tried, condemned, and executed. His teachings were embodied in his response to that condemnation; that is, he refused to allow himself or his followers to respond to this injustice with violence. His life was vindicated in the resurrection. This event regathered his disciples and formed them into a community we now call *church*.[6] To these historical claims I would add that we find Jesus' ongoing presence in the life of the church through the gathering of the community of faith, the proclamation of Jesus' words, and the sacramental representation of his body.[7] Christian *morality* seeks to participate in the re-presentation of the life of Jesus through our life together as church. That is how we participate in the good. Such participation is moral and at the same time more than moral. It also requires ritual, atonement, and continual efforts toward reconciliation with God and our neighbor. The resources for the Christian moral life are Scripture, tradition, the sacraments, and concrete practices of the church. As will be evident in the second part of this work, these resources assume law, virtue, gifts, beatitudes, and a particular ordering of social formations. They also assume that true *freedom* is not found in the state, market, or family but only in the church. Within the life of the church, freedom depends on goodness and not a flight from it.

THE REALITY OF EVIL

If God must bow to freedom, evil becomes real. For Augustine and Aquinas, evil had no such status; it was the privation of good.[8] It had no independent existence of its own but arose through efforts to achieve a good that missed the mark. But after Kant, evil took on more of a metaphysical reality. Evil can no longer be the privation of good. Good and evil are determinations of the will. Herein resides a crucial feature of Kant's Copernican revolution. Evil becomes a metaphysical reality, an *arche* against which an alternative *arche*, the "good principle," is set. This opposition of good and evil is illustrated in Kant's interpretation of the fall.

Kant's interpretation of Genesis 3 has a "being of a higher order" who sets himself up as "overlord" and introduces evil into the world. It is "strange" that God does "not avail Himself of His might against this traitor, and prefer to destroy at its inception the kingdom which he had intended to found." But God allows evil to exist because the "Supreme Wisdom" so respects the "principle of freedom." Only through "their consent" do Adam and Eve fall under the spell of the evil principle. Judaism was incapable of remedying this situation because it was concerned only with "external observances" and thus did not address the true problem, "the inner essence of the moral disposition." This resulted in an oppression by a "hierarchical constitution."[9] However, the Greek sage's "doctrine of freedom" prepared the way for a revolution by a truly wise person (Jesus). This wise person did battle with the evil principle not in the realm of nature but in the realm of freedom. He showed that evil is a result of willing it and that one need not will it. This is why Judaism is so unacceptable to Kant. Ritual cannot remedy evil. Only a completely free, internal activity can.

This "wise person" did not introduce any new capacity to will what could not be willed before. He does not redeem us by becoming a ritualized object that orders and reorders our desires. Instead, he reveals the "holiness of this principle [freedom]" present in humanity, and "by example (in and through the moral idea) he opens the portals of freedom to all who, like him, choose to become dead to everything that holds them fettered to life on earth to the detriment of morality." Jesus frees us from the sensual impulses that prevent freedom's moral exercise. He does not conquer the evil principle but only shows what was always present and close at hand, "for the whole world and for all time." Each person possesses a moral faculty by which he or she can defeat the evil *arche*. No external observances can defeat evil; only the free interior exercise of the will can accomplish redemption.[10]

Kant's interpretation of the fall and his remedy set freedom against nature, particularly against any external, sensuous objects existing in *nature*. Such objects confuse the moral agent; freedom overcomes this confusion. For Kant, those who look to nature for moral guidance will falsely assume, like Judaism, that overcoming evil is the result of external activity. Those who look to a freedom that is always already present will realize that evil is overcome only in the noumenal realm of freedom. Thus ritual (like Christology itself) is minimalized. It can have a place in assisting us to own our freedom, but it cannot overcome evil. God's cooperation is not necessary except to guide us to our own freedom. Freedom is the fundamental metaphysical reality; God either refuses or is unable to establish anything different. Once freedom has this fundamental status, the primary form good and evil take depends solely on an interior act of will. The same action can be accomplished using the same means and achieving the same end, but its morality consists in an inner act of will, difficult to name even by the agent herself or himself, for it is grounded in freedom, a supersensible realm, while the agent is grounded in sensible nature. What makes an object good or evil is not the object, per se, but the will's orientation toward it.

This creates a mechanism for a disciplinary society more insidious than the one that created the confessional could ever hope to achieve. One polices one's self. The "introspective consciousness of the West" gives us the freedom to determine the morality of our actions without giving us any knowledge of the good. We can no longer know if what we do is actually good, but we do know we are free and thus should be good. But what it would mean actually to be good remains an elusive and perpetually deferred goal.

For Kant, evil exists through the moral agent's actions. "Hence the source of evil cannot lie in an object determining the will through inclination, nor yet in a natural impulse; it can lie only in a rule made by the will." Evil is radically present within us, in our will. But this evil does not lie in a source outside of us. It is separate from the actual objects we pursue or that pursue us. Nor can the source for the healing of evil lie outside human interiority. This has devastating consequences for the role of Christology in the moral life.

CHRISTOLOGY AS ANTHROPOLOGY

For Kant, Christology is anthropology. Jesus is the archetype of all humanity because he perfectly embodies the perfection of the idea of the moral law. Jesus does this by exercising his freedom, in his humanity, to do his duty without regard to self-interest. The cross is at the heart of Kant's Christology. If it were not for the cross, we would not recognize in Jesus the freedom to subordinate self-love to the demands of the moral law. On the cross Jesus sacrifices his own sensible finitude to the supersensible demands of the moral law. This act allows us to have a "practical faith in this Son of God" that does not conflict with the exercise of our autonomous human freedom. Jesus shows us what lies within us—the ability to overcome the flesh through our supersensible freedom. Such a Christology loses the incarnation and the resurrection but has a central place for the crucifixion as the essence of a moral drama.

A Christology focused on the cross poses no threat to Kant's ethical system, for it does not challenge the *freedom* that Jesus exhibits by his willingness to sacrifice his own sensible interest to a supersensible freedom. However, the incarnation does pose a threat. Kant notes that the incarnation endangers Jesus' role as human archetype if it is viewed as a supernatural event: "The elevation of such a holy person above all the frailties of human nature would rather hinder the adoption of the idea of such a person from our imitation."[11] If the person of Jesus is construed as God assuming flesh, then this threatens Jesus' full participation in our humanity. The "practical validity" of his crucifixion is lost to us because its "analogy to natural existence" is severed. Kant assumes that nature is what is self-evident and that our Christology must be made relevant to it. He does not explicitly reject the incarnation; it simply cannot matter for his christological development. Theology functions for him as a mythical narration of an underlying morality play. Morality does not need Christology, but Christology is unintelligible without morality.[12]

Kant's Christology allows and emphasizes the crucifixion, not as the death of God, but as the human Jesus doing his duty without regard to self-interest. Little or no place exists for the incarnation here; it can at most be tolerated as a speculative dogma that obedience might require for duty's sake. But the incarnation is positively dangerous if it is construed as God actually assuming flesh.

That Jesus is born into a Jewish family is also dangerous to his role as the archetype of humanity. If this universal archetype is too thoroughly tied to Jesus' historical contingencies, then Jesus' life and death will not be construed as consistent with the moral ideal. Jesus would act more as a Jew than as a universal archetype. But for Kant, Jesus' contingent life circumstance poses no threat to his archetypal role because he has a unique ability to transcend such contingencies. Kant wrote, "Would to God that we could be spared the Oriental wisdom. . . . To be sure there was once a wise man who was entirely different from his nation and taught a healthy, practical religion."[13] For Jesus to exercise his role as moral archetype, he must be dissimilar both to his Jewish heritage and to any historical contingency that emanates from him, such as the church.

The incarnation is dangerous to the moral life, however, only because Kant begins with the assumption that he knows what our humanity is and how it must be if we are to be moral, and this he knows solely from the nature of the moral law and what it requires of us. If the benefits of Jesus are to be *for us* (and such benefits are primarily moral), then they must be consonant with us as we already are. Kant's Christology is predicated upon an a priori understanding of anthropology. Thus, to suggest that Christology is anthropology is also to suggest that the secure term in that expression is *anthropology.* We know who we are, and Christology must be made relevant to that a priori knowledge. Consistent with the secure interiority upon which modern ethics is predicated, Kant assumes we have access to our experience as a norm for theological and philosophical reflection, but there is little *ex* to this experience. Perhaps it would be better to call it *in*perience. It is within the context of a secure interior *ex*perience of what it means to be human that Kant interprets the relevance of Christology.

Kant needed the immortality of the soul so that the states of well-being and well-doing could finally be congruent. If morality requires us to do our duty even if it results in something such as the cross, then morality itself cannot ensure happiness. The immortality of the soul and the assumption of a life after death where good actions are rewarded is thus a necessary postulate for a nature in harmony with happiness. But Kant had no place for the resurrection of the body. In fact, he wrote, "Who is so fond of his body that he would wish to drag it about with him through all eternity if he could get on without it."[14] Neither the general resurrection nor Jesus' resurrection matters for Kant's Christology. At most, these dogmas should be believed for the sake of obedience itself and because they are mythical pointers to the necessary postulate of the immortality of the soul.

Kant draws on and even quotes Jesus' teachings but always for the purpose of preserving the central morality play he seeks to retain. So, for instance, he notes Jesus' teaching that his disciples are to look for happiness not on this earth, but in the life to come. Kant also finds evidence for the morality play in biblical statements such as "Rejoice and be exceeding glad: for great is your reward in heaven."[15] While a place exists for Jesus' sayings insofar as they contribute to morality, Kant also allows for the possibility of signs and miracles as natural and rational phenomena prepared from the moment of creation.[16]

The ascension plays no role in Kant's Christology, for it would authorize a privileged witness to the apostles, who are then set apart for a particular service. As has already been noted, Kant thought that the ultimate purpose of the church was to give birth to a universal state, a state previously and inadequately represented and prepared by the visible church.[17] The key political significance of Kant's modern Christology is the subordination of ecclesiology to the politics of the state. This is the result of an ethics that seeks to preserve the freedom of individual dignity against all historical particularity. Like all morality it assumes and perpetuates a social construction; for Kant's morality that social construction is predicated upon the freedom secured by the state. But far from liberating us, it creates a disciplinary society that is difficult to escape because it is difficult to name. We police ourselves, or so it seems.

A CATHOLIC ECCLESIOLOGICAL ALTERNATIVE?

A less disciplinary society can be construed through a thoroughly different account of the moral life as found in John Paul II in his encyclical *Veritatis Splendor*. Here we find both a refutation of and an alternative to the Kantian quest for freedom. For John Paul II, we do not have the complete power of description over our actions. Thus, certain acts are intrinsically evil *ex objectum*. John Paul states, "The primary and decisive element for the moral judgment is the object of the human act."[18]

This encyclical is not merely an authoritative statement of the Roman Catholic magisterium but also a profound articulation of the relationship between Christian theology and the moral life with important practical implications for Catholics and non-Catholics alike. In this encyclical, we discover a close relationship between morality and Christology that could provide the basis for a Protestant and Catholic convergence on the question of moral theology. John Paul II reveals that Karl Barth's concern that Catholic moral theology tends to make the natural law more central than the divine law present in Christ is no longer a reason for protest.

This is not to suggest that all reasons for protest are no longer persuasive. In fact, the extent to which the modern Roman Catholic papacy actually offers an alternative to modern forms of power is an important question.[19] Nevertheless, John Paul II's *moral teachings* set forth an alternative to the dominant moral quest established by the invention of ethics in Kant's ethical revolution against religion. This alternative quest originates because of the pope's christological rendering of freedom. John Paul II's encyclical on moral theology, *Veritatis Splendor*, takes as its starting point the story of the rich young ruler who comes to Jesus and asks what good deed he must do to inherit eternal life

(Matt. 19:16). The rich young ruler poses to Jesus the question of the good, the question of morality. When Jesus tells him to keep the commandments, the ruler confesses that he has done so. But the observance of the law is insufficient; more is required. And the more is *charity.* Jesus said, "If you would be perfect, go, sell what you possess and give to the poor" (Matt. 19:21). The rich young ruler was unwilling to do this, so he went away without having achieved or received the good.

This exchange forms the heart of the encyclical. Good and evil are given a christological determination. "People today need to turn to Christ once again in order to receive from him the answer to their question about what is good and what is evil,"[20] because to ask about the good is ultimately to ask about God.[21] And for Christian theology, to ask about God finds an answer in Jesus. Thus, the moral quest has an end. When we turn to Jesus, his life becomes the object determining our will and eliciting truly human actions. Here Christology is also anthropology but not one a priori known. In Christ we discover what it means to be human, and this is a discovery that never ends. He himself has become the Law that rules our hearts *ex objectum.* While this end includes the observance of the law, the law is not an end in itself; it is a necessary form that points to our true end—this Law that is capable of ruling our hearts.

This Thomistic insight has profound implications for our understanding of morality. As Thomas put it, "Law directs human actions to an appropriate end." Thus the moral life can never be the *mere* observance of the law, for doing one's duty in terms of the law alone does not fulfill the moral life. Law contains purposes, and those purposes are fundamentally expressed in the Second Person of the Trinity, in the revelation of the divine law. As the encyclical states, "Jesus shows that the commands must not be understood as a minimum limit not to be gone beyond, but rather as a path involving a moral and spiritual journey towards perfection at the heart of which is love."[22] Human beings have a "vocation to perfect love" to which the law points if it truly functions as law. The moral life is not first and foremost about following law; it is about following laws that will point us in a specific direction.

This conception of the moral life challenges moral theologians who would reduce it to a minimalist and juridical vocation of assigning certain actions to either prohibitions or permissions based on the law alone. It is a profound critique of the manualist tradition that reigned supreme in Catholic moral theology from the Council of Trent to the Second Vatican Council.[23] Many theologians found this manualist tradition *physicalist* because it seemed to assume that the object of an act alone could define the moral species of an act. In traditional moral theology, object, intention, and circumstance defined the three sources of Christian ethics, and the object gave an act its moral species. Thus the charge brought against the manualists was that they thought one could determine the morality of an act from the physical act itself. However, in trying to overcome the physicalism of the manualist tradition, many modern Catholic moral theologians have simply underwritten the Kantian quest where a subjective disposition becomes the determinative element in the morality of an action.

DOUBLE EFFECT: THE KANTIAN QUEST REVISITED?

Peter Knauer was one such moral theologian. He published a famous essay in 1967 entitled, "The Hermeneutic Function of the Principle of Double Effect." That principle stemmed from the just-war theory and suggested that a person is not morally culpable for the unintended evil of a directly intended act. An example of this would be a military engagement in which the innocent are indirectly killed from an action that directly targeted combatants. The action is morally permissible because the evil that resulted is an indirect effect of a directly intended action. This principle has an ancient lineage, but Knauer did reorder moral theology when he suggested that this principle is not merely a marginal one in the moral life but is the "fundamental principle of all morality." In so arguing, he produced a moral theology known as "proportionalism." It defines moral evil as "the permission or causing of a physical evil which is not justified by a commensurate reason."[24]

The reason Knauer made the principle of double effect so central to the moral life was to overcome any rigid distinction between an external physical act and an inward intention. He suggested,

> This is an arbitrary distinction arising on a Cartesian foundation. Neither the pure external happening nor the psychological intention is morally understandable alone; only the objective relation, in which both have a part, is understandable. This conclusion means that the moral species of the *finis operis* depends on whether this relation is one of correspondence or one of final contradiction, while the *finis operantis* relates to the *finis operis* of another act.[25]

The language of *finis operis* and *finis operantis* is traditional theological language that explains human action. The *finis operis* was understood as the end of the act itself, that is, the external effect that the act created, the object. The *finis operantis* was understood to be the intention of the one acting. But Knauer defined them differently. The *finis operis* is now not merely the external act but the "act which is willed and intended as such." The *finis operantis* for Knauer is not merely the moral intention but the "act towards which the person acting relates his first action."[26] Once a single act is bifurcated in terms of these two ends, then Knauer suggested that the significant moral question is whether these two ends of our actions objectively correspond or contradict each other.

Curiously, in trying to overcome the Cartesian split between thought and *res extensa,* Knauer seems merely to have reproduced it and then collapsed the object into thought, for he argued that the relationship between the two ends of an agent's action cannot be described in terms of direct and indirect physical causality but in terms of commensurate and incommensurate grounds for an action.[27] This means that the actual external object of an action does not define the moral species of the action; rather, an intended thought about that action determines its moral species. If there is a *commensurate* reason for the action based on this intention, the action becomes morally permissible. For example, if my intention (*finis operantis*) in using birth control has a good, moral reason and is not simply to avoid the responsibilities of conception, the fact that the end of my action (*finis operis*) is nonprocreative sex does not alone provide the moral species for my action. A commensurate reason might exist that redefines what that *finis operis* is. This raises the odd circumstance that a moral agent must now know the commensurate reason for the unintended effect of her intention prior to performing it so that she can determine whether the evil that it causes is commensurate to her directly intended action.

Veritatis Splendor finds this form of moral reasoning suspect because it suggests the possibility of doing evil to achieve good. Of course, no modern Catholic moral theologian would explicitly argue that we do evil to achieve good. The central difference between *Veritatis Splendor* and the proportionalists is not merely the relation between good and evil but also what determines the nature of the good. For the proportionalists, good and evil seem to be connected as a necessary antinomy. Thus Richard McCormick suggests, "In nearly all actions a gain is tied to a loss."[28] Similar to modern economists' argument concerning opportunity costs, McCormick and Knauer describe the world in terms of cost-benefit ratios where no good choice can be made without at the same time incurring some loss, some evil. These "disvalues" then must be explained. They cannot be directly intended or we would do evil to achieve good. But because the world is described in this way, what constitutes the object of an act is expanded. When no commensurate reason exists for the evil effect of an action, the act itself constitutes the object and the evil effect would be unwarranted. When a commensurate reason exists for the evil effect, the *finis operis* of the agent is expanded to include the commensurate reason and the evil effect is warranted although not intended.[29]

Like Knauer, McCormick appears to have divided our action into two isolatable elements: the action itself without the evil effect, and the action with the evil effect. Then the central question is whether a commensurate reason exists for viewing the second rather than the first as the object where the evil effect or "disvalue" is warranted based on the commensurate reason that expands the object to include the second account of action.

McCormick gives examples of this by explaining it in terms of "actions independent of the presence of commensurate reason and language describing actions without such reason." Thus we have the action of taking another's property and the descriptive language of theft. We also have the action of killing and the language of murder, of making false statements and lying, of terminating pregnancy and abortion. All these distinctions make sense in terms of the principle of double effect. For example, I could accidentally place my copy of Barth's *Church Dogmatics* on someone's copy of Wittgenstein's *Philosophical Investigations* while visiting in his office, inadvertently pick up both books as I prepared to leave, then walk off with his property without that being a theft. Here we have the traditional use of double effect in its marginal sense. It recognizes an important distinction between taking another's property and stealing. But McCormick and Knauer expand this principle through an appeal to commensurate reason such that it now defines all of morality. Every human action becomes similar to the example of taking versus stealing. We are caught in a world of scarcity where any good action is tied to a necessary loss, an evil that must be accounted for in terms of "commensurate reason."

The all-encompassing role of the principle of double effect results in a too-thorough division between the external effects of our actions and the descriptions we give to those effects. For instance, McCormick suggests that self-stimulation and sperm-testing might provide an occasion for an act to be understood as a single act under this expanded view of the object where a commensurate reason exists to violate the principle against masturbation. Thus the direct intending of an evil is not present. But this is a very odd argument. How can I go into the infertility specialist's private room with cup in hand, self-stimulate, and then suggest that the act itself was not my intention? In this case, is not the bodily act itself constitutive of my intention irrespective of what I say I was doing? Otherwise I inhabit a distinctively bifurcated body where the acts I do in that body are different from the reasons I give for those acts. Not only has Descartes not been overcome, but Kant's pervasive moral distinction between our dispositions and acts remains thoroughly intact.

John Paul II gives a much more embodied account of moral agency when he writes, "By the object of a given moral act, then, one cannot mean a process or an event of the merely physical order, to be assessed on the basis of its ability to bring about a given state of affairs in the outside world. Rather, the object is the proximate end of a deliberate decision which determines the act of willing on the part of the acting person."[30] In this quote we do not have a return to the physicalism of the manualist tradition. Instead, we find a resolution to the mind-body dualism that once plagued philosophies of action. Notice that the encyclical first challenges distinguishing a moral act in dualistic terms. Human action is not to be divided in terms of "a process or an event of the merely physical order" and the descriptive language of that action "assessed on the basis of its ability to bring about a given state of affairs in the outside world." This bifurcation between human action and moral description is what is at stake in the encyclical. Instead of this bifurcation we discover that it is "the proximate end of a deliberate decision which determines the act of willing on the part of the acting person."

Martin Rhonheimer helps us understand the significance of this last phrase by explaining that a "virtue-oriented ethics" is necessary to render it intelligible.[31] The reason is that the objects of our actions are not mere choices of non-moral goods decided upon by value-neutral observers who can then relate these *premoral* actions to their own agency by language descriptions. Rather, the objects of our actions constitute those actions in such a way that they form us into certain kinds of people; they form our moral character. In other words, the moral life is not solely a function of a person's interior disposition (as it was primarily for Kant). Instead, the objects that elicit our will, the objects to which we are inclined, also constitute who we are morally. Without understanding this, suggests Rhonheimer, the encyclical will be misunderstood.

OBJECTS AND INTENTIONS

Richard McCormick finds Rhonheimer's defense of the encyclical unpersuasive. Their debate succinctly clarifies what is at stake in this argument, namely, what constitutes intentionality. Rhonheimer believes intentionality is more directly related to the objects that form the purposes of our deliberations. He finds certain objects to contain within them a stance toward or against the good. McCormick seems to find this alarming and a return to the physicalist ontology of the manualist tradition where an action is understood to be moral fundamentally from its object. Thus, he argues that Rhonheimer is unable to take into account intentionality. That this is true of the manualist tradition, I think, is correct. That John Paul II might be misunderstood as suggesting this is understandable. He suggests, "The morality of the human act depends primarily and fundamentally on the 'object' rationally chosen by the deliberate will." When McCormick reads this he appears to understand it over and against human intentionality. Thus he fears that intentionality is no longer morally relevant. Since Knauer sought to critique the rigid distinction between the internal intention and the external action by means of proportionalism, McCormick fears that the language *ex objectum* will return us to that earlier "Cartesian" separation.

If John Paul II were doing that, McCormick's fears would be warranted. However, as Rhonheimer points out, that is not the case. Instead, intentionality cannot be defined separate from the object, and McCormick himself still functions within the clear distinctions between the sources of morality from the manualist tradition: an object and an intention are two different, unrelated sources until an agent relates them through the will. McCormick differs from the manualists by seeking to make intention rather than the object the fundamentally morally relevant source, but the two sources are still distinct; they are only given different values for the assessment of moral action. For Rhonheimer and the Vatican, these sources effect one another. The object of an act is not merely the external effect but the external effect as it inscribes a reality on our bodily existence. The argument between the proportionalists and the Vatican appears to be over the relationship between an object and an intention.

John Paul II writes, "By the 'object' of a given moral act, then, one cannot mean a process or an event of the merely physical order to be assessed on the basis of its ability to bring about a given state of affairs in the outside world." Where this is discussed in the encyclical, *object* is placed in quotes and an article from Aquinas's *Summa Theologia* is cited.[32] In that article, Aquinas raised the question of "whether an action has the species of good or evil from its end." Aquinas suggested that in a voluntary action, "there is a twofold action, viz., the interior action of the will and the external action: and each of these actions has its object." The interior action of the will gives an external action its form, while the external action is "the species of a human act considered materially with regard to the external action." This division makes possible a misunderstanding, which allows someone to misread him as suggesting a twofold nature to action that would bifurcate the external and internal action, as both Knauer and the manualists did. However, John Paul II reads him differently. The formal and material are intrinsically related. They cannot be separated into the action itself and the moral language describing the actions. John Paul II has not refuted the significance of intention. Instead, he has given us an embodied account of intention.

Only when the importance of an embodied intention is stressed can intrinsic evils make sense. Certain actions are intrinsically evil because those actions, despite all the commensurate reasons for them, cannot orient us toward the good, which is also an orientation toward God. Intrinsic evils are certain *objects* that no commensurate reason can possibly be given to order one's will by pursuing such objects. Whether the Roman Catholic magisterium rightly names all those actions is still a matter of debate and perhaps a reason for protest. However, the nature of the moral argumentation is compelling.

Unfortunately, the debate between the proportionalists and *Veritatis Splendor* seems to have focused on the question of artificial contraception.[33] Other *intrinsically* evil activities quoted in the encyclical from the Second Vatican Council have been largely ignored in the literature.[34] This is particularly the case with regard to the direct and intentional killing of the innocent. Many proportionalists suggest that the Vatican's fears are unwarranted, that proportionalism will not lead to a moral relativism, denial of intrinsic evils, and the bald proposition that we can commit evil to achieve good. But here they are wrong. These concerns are not misplaced fears about the future but were already realized in the proportionalist justification of the horrors of World War II.

Since 1947 some Catholic moral theologians have found a way to use proportionate reason to justify the kind of obliteration bombing that ended in the atomic homicide at Hiroshima and Nagasaki, and this despite Father John C. Ford's prophetic strictures against such a practice.[35] Here is clearly an example of an intrinsic evil, an action so turned against goodness that it could never be directed toward God's good purposes. This does not mean that it cannot be redeemed; in fact, it means it must be redeemed. Any moral justification for the action allows evil too substantive a role in God's economy. Such an action cannot be allowed to stand as justified but needs redemption through repentance and reconciliation, otherwise evil rather than charity will bind us together. Directly killing the innocent can never be legitimate, for it destroys the virtue of charity toward one's neighbor. Yet moral theologians betrayed their own tradition by finding a commensurate reason for this kind of action, which then made possible the utilitarian morality under which humanity was forced to live throughout the Cold War and beyond.

The argument between the Vatican and the proportionalists is not scholastic wrangling over arcane Thomistic distinctions. It concerns the possibility of holding forth a truly good end in a world now defined by the tragic figures of the accountants' cost-benefit ledgers. More important, what is at stake is the efficacy of Christ's redemption for the moral life and thus the subordination of ethics to theology. The second part of *Veritatis Splendor* only makes sense in light of the third part, "Lest the Cross of Christ Be Emptied of Its Power." If our moral agency is bound by a tragic and inescapable cost-benefit analysis, then the efficacy of Christ's atonement is challenged. But John Paul II states, "It is in the saving cross of Jesus, in the gift of the Holy Spirit, in the sacraments which flow forth from the pierced side of the Redeemer that believers find the grace and the strength always to keep God's holy law, even amid the gravest of hardships. . . . If redeemed man still sins, this is not due to an imperfection of Christ's redemptive act, but to man's will not to avail himself of the grace which flows from that act."[36] To preserve a relationship between the moral life and Christology, between ethics and theology, the encyclical must speak against proportionalism. The moral life is not defined solely in terms of ambiguity, where every positive good we do entails some evil. Christ frees us from the necessity of evil, especially lesser evils for the sake of some greater good.[37] Christ both reveals to us what it means to be truly human because he is our proper end and mediates to us through the sacraments and the Holy Spirit the grace by which that end can be achieved. No tragic necessity can then provide us with proportionate reasons for doing less than fulfilling the law of the gospel. If we fail at fulfilling the new law, which is the case for most of us, we must not plead commensurate reason but Christ's mercy, which is available in the sacraments, particularly the sacrament of the Eucharist, where we participate in penance and reconciliation. Evil must never be rationalized; it must be redeemed.

Protestants should take due note of what John Paul II accomplishes by reading the moral life christologically. Here we find no minimalist and juridical conception of the moral life that merely asks what is prohibited and what is permitted. Instead, we find a moral life that can make sense only if Christ is who the church proclaims him to be. As John Paul II stated, "The Crucified Christ reveals the authentic meaning of freedom; he lives it fully in the total gift of himself and calls his disciples to share in his freedom."[38]

The tragic nature of our freedom separate from God is freed in Christ to be something other than what McCormick suggested when he stated, "In nearly all actions a gain is tied to a loss."[39] McCormick suggests a quasi-tragic world. We cannot do good without accomplishing evil so we must have commensurate reasons for both the good we intend and the evil that arises despite our best intentions. But such a world seems alien to the possibility that God was incarnate, that Christ perfectly redeems, and that the Holy Spirit actually sanctifies.

FREEDOM'S JUST ANOTHER WORD FOR NOTHING LEFT TO LOSE

Why do many modern theologians insist on the connection between good and evil, gain and loss? Maurice Blondel can help us make sense of this with his distinction between infinitely willing and willing the Infinite.[40] If we understand freedom as an infinite power to will or as a power to will grounded in infinity, then any choice I actually make will be viewed as a loss, for at the moment of choice I sacrifice this infinite potential for a finite concretization. Thus, the good that I choose comes at the expense of the good I have foregone, a loss. And *freedom* in the modern era is viewed as this infinite desire to choose that can never be satisfied. But if I do not view freedom as infinitely willing but rather to will the Infinite, then once my will wills the Infinite, I incur no loss. I do not then have to speak of the good foregone but of the Good received. As a finite creature, I do not have an intrinsic capacity, of course, to will the Infinite. But in Christ, who is the mediator between God and creatures, possessing both "natures," we can will the infinite without becoming less or more than human creatures. Such a gift makes possible our living the good. Evil, the loss of the good, no longer needs to be that which explains our actions. The good is possible.

We will not always live the good Christ makes possible. Yet even when we fall short of this good, we are not abandoned. There is still a resource to make sense of our failure to avail ourselves of Christ's redeeming power. This resource is found in the sacraments, in that repentance that constantly empowers us to live into our baptism. But the sacraments themselves are intelligible only if we assume that Christ offers to us a substantive good. The Christian moral life is never a capitulation to the reality of evil but a constant turning from evil to live that which is already given to us in our baptism.

Proportionalism seems to assume that good and evil are always a priori connected. If this is true, then we must compare value judgments in nearly every human action. This makes evil too determinative of the moral life. Evil should be nothing but a surd, never explicable and never made palatable by any *commensurate reason.* Any intelligible rendering of evil as necessary for human action will always threaten to make the world unintelligible in terms of Christ's redemptive work. John Paul II helps us overcome the modern anthropology that makes evil radical. For Kant, "man is evil by nature." We can even "find a place for evil at the creation of the world." Thus Kant, like many of the theologians who inherit his anthropology, collapses the fall into creation itself. Evil becomes intelligible, rendered a necessary option for humanity if our freedom is to be real. For Kant, without the ontological possibility of choosing evil, our freedom would only be an illusion.

You Will Be Like Gods, Knowing Good and Evil

One logical outcome of Kant's moral philosophy is Nietzsche's recognition that morality is the will to power. Immanuel Kant was not Nietzsche. He did not will as a maxim the marginalization or even the death of God. In fact, true to his pietist upbringing, he was trying to defend God against the cultured detractors of his age.[41] Yet the birth pangs of postmodernity are present in Kant's definitive statement of a modernist morality. Nietzsche was the midwife.

Kant's practical reason asked us to consider whether an act of violence perpetrated by an individual person could be equated to the violence unearthed by a *natural* force such as a hurricane. At the risk of oversimplifying, Nietzsche deconstructed the modern ethical edifice by suggesting that it was quite possible to consider persons akin to such *natural* forces. In *Thus Spake Zarathustra*, Nietzsche contrasts the "pale criminal" with the "red judge." The pale criminal committed murder, and now the red judge sentences him to death. The red judge seeks an explanation as to why the criminal murdered and thinks his murder must have some causal connection to his desire to steal. But "Zarathustra" gives us a different interpretation.

> But I say unto you: his soul wanted blood, not robbery; he thirsted after the bliss of the knife. His poor reason, however, persuaded him: "What matters blood?" it asked: "don't you want at least to commit a robbery with it? To take revenge?" And he listened to his poor reason: its speech lay upon him like lead; so he robbed when he murdered. He did not want to be ashamed of his madness.

The desire to find some causal explanation for evil is for Nietzsche the true sickness, the sickness of the "good." There is no causal explanation that renders the pale criminal's deed understandable. He *wants* blood; he has a taste for it. He is a "ball of wild snakes," and on the occasion of the murder one snake went into the world to taste its prey. No supersensible freedom is necessary to explain the pale criminal's deed. His passion for blood predominated; that is the only "causal" explanation possible.[42]

Kant's foundation for practical reason in a supersensible realm caught many ethicists on the horns of an unnecessary dilemma. Ethics became trapped by Kant's opposition between freedom and nature. This had political consequences; as a result, we seem to have only two options: liberalism, where freedom is that which we preserve above all other things; or fascism, where some tyrant or tyrannical community imposes her or his account of the good on us all. But Kant's either/or—an either/or that always ensures political liberalism as the only responsible quest reasonable people can pursue—makes little sense once Nietzsche questions whether Kant has *discovered* or merely *invented* this super-sensible freedom. When a free, contentless will is made the basis for the possibility of good and evil, then the options only appear to be *either* a liberalism that does not seek to aim at the good for the sake of freedom *or* a fascism that aims at the good through violence and the coercion of wills. But this is not a true either/or. Both positions assume that politics and morality depend upon the contentless will, a will with no direction other than being pushed by whatever passion or desire predominates. Escaping this illusory either/or is the grave difficulty confronting the (post)modern world.

This either/or does not present us with two distinct alternatives. It is true that liberalism is not fascism. Fascism seeks to incorporate every aspect of human existence within its architectonic system. Thus all social formations that are an alternative to or mediate between the state and the individual are permissible only to the extent that they are "organically" incorporated into the nation's metanarrative. Liberalism seeks to destroy all intermediate and/or alternative social formations that might provide space between the state and the individual. It does this not by incorporating them into some organic wholeness but through dividing and separating individuals from one another and then securing their allegiance to the state through "equality," "rights," and the control of violence to protect and secure those rights. But with either liberalism or fascism, lawlessness and anarchy do not characterize modern political formations. Laws that produce and regulate individual actions characterize them. But these laws have no basis in anything but a contentless freedom and thus appear arbitrary and capricious. Obedience to them can be enforced only through power. They are a-rational. We obey through fear and manipulation, but obey we must. In such a world, to defend *ethics* is dangerous.

Dietrich Bonhoeffer launched an attack on *ethics* that was never completed because of his imprisonment and death during World War II. Bonhoeffer suggested that ethics—the knowledge of good and evil—is "separation from God."[43] His posthumously published *Ethics* began, "The knowledge of good and evil seems to be the aim of all ethical reflection. The first task of Christian ethics is to invalidate this knowledge." This is its first task because "the knowledge of good and evil shows that [the moral agent] is no longer at one with [his or her] origin." Prior to ethics, people knew only God. They were free because God was the object of their will; God was their desire. God is the good; there is no either/or, no choice to be made. They were free because freedom is being turned toward that which is good. Only when this freedom is lost through deception and privation does evil result. Evil arises not from some necessary ontological account of human freedom that requires a tragic dialectic. Evil arises because true human freedom gets lost, and thus we are (partially) deprived of that which is good. Only then can we know evil. To know evil is not a condition for the possibility of freedom; it is the loss of freedom.

The knowledge of good and evil is possible only when we have become the origin of our reason and will, for this is a sign that our desires and our intellect have turned away from God. Bonhoeffer described it as follows:

> Already in the possibility of the knowledge of good and evil Christian ethics discerns a falling away from the origin. Man at his origin knows only one thing: God. It is only in the unity of his knowledge of God that he knows of other men, of things, and of himself. He knows all things only in God, and God in all things.[44]

Bonhoeffer questions the knowledge of good and evil because of his interpretation of the fall in Genesis. His interpretation could be construed as a form of hyper-Protestantism, where grace is so completely alien to nature that no natural knowledge of the good remains. However, this reading of Bonhoeffer would be a mistake. Bonhoeffer's interpretation can be better read as a challenge to "the blasphemy of the *a priori*."[45] This phrase describes the philosophical preoccupation that assumes we can determine the conditions for our knowledge of the good a priori, that is, that we can know the conditions for the possibility of good without actually knowing the good. It calls those conditions *freedom*.

Like John Paul II, Bonhoeffer's interpretation of good and evil resists both the Roman Catholic manualist tradition and certain elements in the Calvinist tradition that reduce the moral life to obedience to commands. Both these traditions regard evil as a free and conscious disobedience of God's law, so the central ethical question is, What is the law and, given the law, what actions are prohibited and permitted? The emphasis on the moral life focuses on the will. Sin is *willful* disobedience where the will is disconnected from the intellect and thus disconnected from our vision of the good. If we assume that a willed transgression of a known law of God constitutes sin, then the problem of evil can be answered in terms of a good will alone. We do not need to know the purpose of the law to fulfill it, simply the law as posited.

In too much of the Roman Catholic manualist tradition and in the Reformed tradition, the focus of the Christian life becomes the servile will. Christian *ethics* concentrates on an ethics of obedience in light of commands. It asks what is permitted and what is prohibited. It also asks what must be restored to the individual moral agent for her or him to be able to *will* the good. The first question becomes the domain of the juridical, legalistic casuist tradition that can be found in the manuals of moral theology and in their successors in the proportionalists. The second question becomes the focus of much of Protestant Christian ethics. Yet this understanding of Christian ethics often perpetuates "the blasphemy of the a priori." It assumes a moral self capable of the knowledge of good and evil separate from the good itself. Thus the individual remains the origin of the moral life, and ethics can only be anthropology; it has little place for theology.

The idea that we are moral selves prior to specifying any content to the good is the connective tissue holding together much of the tradition of Christian ethics. The tradition is held together anthropologically, not christologically. Beach and Niebuhr make this clear in their standard *Christian Ethics:* "the awareness of being a moral self makes the individual contemporaneous with those in the past who have wrestled with their problems and have come to their tentative conclusions."[46] Once the moral self becomes the primary agent in Christian ethics, ethics is understood primarily as obligation. The individual will, now individually graced, must do its duty. Ethics centers on commands and the a priori nature of the individual moral agent by which those commands can be accomplished. An a priori human nature provides continuity diachronically and synchronically so that a tradition and discipline called *ethics* is possible. It is not the quest for what we do not yet have, or have only in part, that makes the moral life possible. It is made possible (and contained by) the reality of what we already possess. The continuity that makes morality possible is anthropological, not christological. Ethics becomes a narcissistic science in which we constantly examine ourselves.

Bonhoeffer questioned the appropriateness of the knowledge of good and evil not because as a Protestant he desired a sharp distinction between grace and nature but because he understood that ethics had made God useless: "Man has become the origin of good and evil. . . . Bearing within himself the knowledge of good and evil, man has become judge over God and men, just as he is judge over himself."[47] Ethics was a discipline of mastery, mastery not only of one's self, but also of God. Bonhoeffer saw what Nietzsche before him had seen. The utter uselessness of God for morality in the modern world made it unimportant whether God lived or died. When, in Nietzsche's *Twilight of the Idols,* the madman announces the death of God, his listeners are silent and astonished. They are not yet ready for this truth. God had become so distant in some noumenal realm that they could not even fathom the need to kill God. Modern ethics finally became so bloodless it did not even need the crucifixion.

Nietzsche realized that "God on the Cross" was a "terribly superlative conception," a "boldness in inversion" that "promised a transvaluation of all ancient values." It went beyond good and evil.[48] It seems he was both sickened by and attracted to this transvaluation of values. If this language of sacrifice was so weak and inoffensive, why did it exercise him so? If God must be killed, how could he account for the sublime terror of this moment in Christianity itself through the ritual celebration of the mass? Nietzsche needed the Christian God to kill God. Only then could he invert the putatively weak and inoffensive Christian morality he found so disturbing. But Christians already offered this sacrifice.

This is not to suggest that Nietzsche was an anonymous Christian. Despite the efforts of certain "death of god" theologies to make Nietzsche's Christology favorable to the true essence of the Christian tradition, Nietzsche's work was and is hostile to Christianity. He gives us not a Christology but an anti-Christology. No place exists in his anti-Christology for the incarnation or the resurrection. That Jesus ends his life on a cross contains no positive import for Nietzsche; it allows him to say that "there was only one true Christian and he died on the cross." Jesus was the only true Christian because he refused to hate his enemies and masquerade such hatred under a false pietistic morality of love. Jesus' actions were not motivated by *ressentiment*. Nevertheless, the idea that Jesus' death represents the death of God seems to be morally repugnant to Nietzsche. It is a sign of the "transvaluation of all values" that Nietzsche found present in Judaism and the ascetic spirit:

> This Jesus of Nazareth, the incarnate gospel of love, this "Redeemer" who brought blessedness and victory to the poor, the sick, and the sinner—was he not this seduction in its most uncanny and irresistible form, a seduction and bypath to precisely those *Jewish* values and new ideals? Did Israel not attain the ultimate goal of its sublime vengefulness precisely through the bypath of this "Redeemer," this ostensible opponent and disintegrator of Israel? . . . And could spiritual subtlety imagine any more dangerous bait than this? Anything to equal the enticing, intoxicating, overwhelming, and undermining power of the symbol of the "holy cross," that ghastly paradox of a "God on the cross," that mystery of an unimagineable ultimate cruelty and self-crucifixion of *God for the salvation of man*? What is certain, at least, is that *sub hoc signo* Israel with its vengefulness and revaluation of all values, has hitherto triumphed again and again over all other ideals, over all *nobler* ideals.[49]

This vengefulness is more present in Christianity than in Judaism precisely because Paul negates the original message of Jesus and puts forward the "lie of the resurrected Jesus."[50] Nietzsche found Jesus' death on the cross heroic and noble inasmuch as Jesus was not God, but the lie of the resurrection created a slave morality built on resentment. It negated the significance of any noble contribution in this world because it established a system of reward and punishment in the afterlife.[51]

That Nietzsche finds Paul and the apostles responsible for the transvaluation of Jesus' original message is, of course, no radical idea; it was consistent with the fashionable biblical scholarship from Wrede to Strauss. Nevertheless, Nietzsche subjected Strauss to scorn in his first "Untimely Meditation." Nietzsche attacked Strauss not because Strauss, like Nietzsche, found Paul and the apostles to be responsible for the loss of Jesus' original message. Rather, Nietzsche objected to Strauss's easy accommodation of the modern spirit in light of the dissolution of Christianity. Strauss's new faith was a mere Christian morality shorn of its theology and made relevant to modernity. Strauss's efforts to maintain a pseudo-Christian morality (under the guise of the modern) while also negating the Christian narrative did not sit well with Nietzsche. What exercised Nietzsche so was that Strauss had made the old Christian morality relevant to modern times without recognizing the banality, insipidity, and "cultural philistinism" of his "timely meditations." For Strauss, everything in Christian theology was denied, but a bourgeois Christian morality remained. Strauss was unwilling to tear down the church and take his Darwinism seriously.

Rather than trying to make a new religion relevant out of the old faith, Nietzsche settled for an alternative: *"unzeitgemässe Betrachtungen"*—unfashionable, untimely, irrelevant, or unmodern reflections. And with that came the need for a different morality, one that went beyond good and evil—and certainly beyond Christianity as well. What Nietzsche recognized, though Strauss and his progeny still have not, is the connection between a theological narration and a morality.[52] If Christian theology is to be denied, so is its morality. One cannot essentialize theological narratives into ethics. This makes Nietzsche a radical alternative to Kant and Strauss. Morality does not stand separate from the theological narrative that renders it intelligible.

The weak and inoffensive Christianized morality against which Nietzsche railed was that which found comfort in Kant's question, "How are synthetic judgments a priori possible?" Such a question merely buttressed a pious morality. But Nietzsche thought this to be no question, for Kant's answer was a mere assertion of a transcendental faculty that was incredible. The delight in this so-called discovery of the moral faculty was only possible because "one could not yet distinguish between finding and inventing." Thus, Nietzsche asked a different question: "Why is belief in such judgments necessary?" He answered his own question: "In effect, it is high time that we should understand that such judgments must be believed to be true for the sake of the preservation of creatures like ourselves; though they still might naturally be false judgments! Or more plainly spoken, and roughly and readily—synthetic judgments a priori should not "be possible" at all; we have no right to them; in our mouths they are nothing but false judgments." They only give comfort to "three-fourth's Christians" who need an "antidote to the sensualism" of the past.[53]

In an ironic twist, Nietzsche exposes the blasphemy of the a priori. As Bonhoeffer suggested, the assumption of a moral faculty a priori capable of distinguishing good and evil opposes Christianity. The first task of the Christian ethicist is to invalidate this kind of knowledge. Christianity presupposes no knowledge of that which is ultimately good original to an individual's moral faculty. This good, and the evil that is its lack, are not found in human nature as it now is. They are objects that determine our will as good when we discover that our will is directed toward them. It is not merely the will that is good; God is good. The will cannot create good but only participate in it. In his criticism of ethics, Bonhoeffer passed on an important interpretation of the Christian story of the fall.

The Fall

No single interpretation of the fall provides a consistent narrative that accounts for evil throughout Christian tradition. No universal metaphysical understanding of "the human condition" is evident in Christian reflection on the fall.[54] Many discussions of the fall replicate Augustine's understanding of the *triplex concupiscentia*. In the *Confessions* Augustine suggested that the fall gives rise to a threefold problem of "the lust of the flesh, the lust of the eye, and the pride of life."[55] In this threefold interpretation of the fall, Augustine read the fall in Genesis 3:4–7 in light of 1 John 2:15–16, which states: "Do not love the world or the things in the world. If any one loves the world, love for the Father is not in him. For all that is in the world, the lust of the flesh and the lust of the eyes and the pride of life, is not of the Father but is of the world." John is obviously interpreting the love of God in contrast to the love of the world through the story of Adam and Eve in Genesis.

In light of Eve's recounting to the serpent the commandment not to eat of the fruit of the tree in the midst of the garden lest she die, Genesis 3:4–7 states:

> But the serpent said to the woman, "You will not die. For God knows that when you eat of it your eyes will be opened, and you will be like God, knowing good and evil." So when the woman saw that the tree was good for food, and that it was a delight to the eyes, and that the tree was to be desired to make one wise, she took of its fruit and ate; and she also gave some to her husband, and he ate. Then the eyes of both were opened, and they knew that they were naked; and they sewed fig leaves together and made themselves aprons.

Augustine's *triplex concupiscentia* emphasizes those portions of Genesis 3 that fit with 1 John 2: "you will be like God" and "desired to make one wise" become "the pride of life"; "the tree was good for food" becomes "lust of the flesh"; and "it was a delight to the eyes" becomes "the lust of the eye." This is a useful and influential account of sin in Christian tradition. But if the doctrine of sin is defined solely by the *triplex concupiscentia*, the Christian moral life can easily become defined by the emphasis on obedience/disobedience to commands. God gives us commands, but our desires prevent us from responding in obedience. Our sensuality prevents the will's free response in obedience. Thus evil becomes obvious: it is pride and sensuality that prevent us from obeying God's self-evident laws. Then Augustine easily becomes criticized for his putative contempt for the body. Augustine is (wrongly) read as a proto-Kantian.

What is neglected in this account of evil is that not only were Adam and Eve not simply disobedient but they had already deceived themselves before they disobeyed. Their evil was not a case of mere disobedience; evil is seldom that obvious. Augustine himself understood this and offered a sophisticated account of evil within which the *triplex concupiscentia* should be understood. He wrote,

The devil, then, would not have ensnared man in the open and manifest sin of doing what God had forbidden, had man not already begun to live for himself. It was this that made him listen with pleasure to the words, "ye shall be as gods," which they would much more readily have accomplished by obediently adhering to their supreme and true end than by proudly living to themselves. For created gods are gods not by virtue of what is in themselves, but by a participation of the true God. By craving to be more, man becomes less; and by aspiring to be self-sufficing, he fell away from Him who truly suffices.[56]

For Augustine, a step is present prior to the possibility of obedience and/or disobedience. Participation in God is necessary for the good and freedom. Evil arises when freedom is lost through turning toward one's own autonomous resources for ethics. The fall does not result from people seeking to be more than they are capable of through pride but from their becoming less than they could be because they separate the knowledge of good from its true end, God, and find themselves self-sufficient.

For Augustine, the serpent's tempting words—"ye shall be as gods"—were not self-evidently problematic. Augustine, like theologians before him, assumed that God became human so that humans could become gods. The words the serpent spoke were neither false nor a temptation to willful disobedience by prideful rebellion in and of themselves. However, the serpent's words make disobedience possible when they tempt us to separate the good from participation in God.[57] Seeking the good through nonparticipation in God, through the "virtue of what was in themselves" makes disobedience possible. The blasphemy of the a priori defines the fall more than simple disobedience to commandments.

For Augustine, there are not two principles, good and evil, that are competing. Evil is only the privation of good. Evil is not necessarily related to good in a tragic dialectical relationship. There is never a *necessary* loss to every gain. Instead, even in a loss, a deprivation, we still bear witness to the centrality of the good. There can be good without evil, but not evil without good. This is clear in Augustine's *On The Trinity*, in a chapter called, "The Likeness of God Is Desired Even in Sins":

In so far, therefore, as anything that is, is good, in so far plainly it has still some likeness of the supreme good, at however, great a distance; and if a natural likeness, then certainly a right and well-ordered one; but if a faulty likeness, then certainly a debased and perverse one. For even souls in their very sins strive after nothing else but some kind of likeness of God, in a proud and preposterous, and so to say, slavish liberty. So neither could our first parents have been persuaded to sin unless it had been said, "Ye shall be as gods." No doubt every thing in the creatures which is in any way like God, is not also to be called His image; but that alone than which He Himself alone is higher. For that only is in all points copied from Him, between which and Himself, no nature is interposed.[58]

Once again, the key to Augustine's description of sin is not first of all a willful obedience/disobedience but the ability to be deceived on the basis of an effort to deny our creatureliness and to seek to be god by some faculty within us rather than seeking the good through our participation in God. The possibility of good and evil does not arise from a contentless will that goes by the name of *freedom*. For Augustine, such a capacity would be already a sign of human fallenness. But Kantian ethics embodies precisely the posture Augustine recognized as the basis for the fall. It seeks to find within creaturely existence a moral faculty that will allow us to know the good separate from knowledge of God. The moral faculty that is *discovered* is grounded in a supersensible realm of freedom that then makes good and evil a matter of willful obedience to a command, the categorical imperative. This is merely another version of all Christian heresy; it stipulates some secure knowledge within the self that knows God without any participation in the knowledge of God mediated through Christ and discovered in the liturgical life of the church. It is a species of Gnosticism.

THE INTERIORITY OF GNOSTIC GOODNESS

Bonhoeffer's criticism of the moral life recovers a neglected dimension of the Augustinian description of evil. It is also consistent with interpretations of the fall by early church fathers such as Irenaeus, Tertullian, Hippolytus, and Origen. They wrote against a Gnostic sect known as the Ophites or Nassenes. This sect was named after either the Greek or Hebrew word for serpent (*ophis, nachash*). According to these early church fathers, this sect viewed the serpent in Genesis as a god greater than the Jewish God, for this god gave humans the knowledge of good and evil.[59]

Irenaeus explained that, for the Ophites, Eve's seduction by the serpent resulted in her knowledge of good and evil. Through this knowledge she and Adam rose above the status of mere creature, "baffling their own creator."[60] Likewise, Tertullian wrote, "those heretics are called ophites for they magnify the serpent to such a degree that they prefer him even to Christ himself; for it was he, they say, who gave us the origin of the knowledge of good and of evil."[61] In challenging the Ophite/Nassene's reading of the fall, Irenaeus and Tertullian do not ask what is permitted and what is prohibited under the laws God gives us. Rather, they ask in what we must participate to know the good. The Gnostics refuse participation in the life of the church in order to serve a god that gives them a secure origin for the good in themselves. They choose a secret interior space within themselves over the public liturgical space that is the church. When this interior space secures knowledge of the good, then the creature is allowed to give moral meaning to the world through judgments of her or his will alone. Obedience to a "good" originating from within the human creature is a threat to knowledge of God.

Kant was not an Ophite, but one of the central theological concerns of Tertullian in his argument against the Ophites is that they deny "the salvation of the flesh."[62] Kant's opposition between nature and freedom is certainly a variation on the Gnostic theme of the denial of the sensual for salvation, as was his denial of the resurrection of the body. Salvation becomes moral, which is grounded in freedom, a supersensible realm. Freedom inserts a new causality within the causal nexus of nature through a secure space in our interior subjectivity. The use of our freedom becomes our salvation.

In opposition to this, Christian theology asserts the significance of the salvation of the flesh. This requires no opposition between freedom and nature. Salvation comes through the sensual mediation of the church's liturgical life, because through it we can participate in the life of God. It is in these "external," "natural," and sensual rites that evil is destroyed. This is not only a moral salvation but a salvation grounded in participation in God. Through the church's ritual we become "partakers of the divine nature."

That evil is privation and defilement remedied through ritual will not be readily accepted. It will appear to many as a residual element of a primitive stage of cultural development. Yet I find this argument convincing precisely because of the persuasive descriptive power it gives us for why good and evil still matter. The modern world can give us psychological and biochemical causes for *evil,* but it has proved incapable of producing a meaningful use of moral language. At the same time, it has been unable to do without moral language. We cannot live with moral language nor can we live without it. We have been unable to determine the conditions for the possibility of these terms by an autonomous use of reason alone. Once we recognize this, we can start out on a different quest. No longer do we need to speak of the conditions for the possibility of goodness; we must begin to speak of goodness itself.

EVIL AS ACCIDENTAL

A quest that begins not by asking "What is prohibited and what is permitted by my will under some categorical imperative?" but rather "What or who is this good I seek and that seeks me?" can give us a better description of what is meant by evil. Evil is accidental, a derivative reality. It is not a substance that exists on its own. It is neither ontological nor intrinsic to human nature. It is an accident of something substantive, a good. Thus evil is a lack.[63] This is not to deny human culpability in evil, that is, "sin." It is to suggest that people seldom aim only to do evil, but in aiming at a perceived good and missing, evil results. Some people may very well seek to do "radical evil," but these are marginal cases. Evil is accidental. Evil is privation. Evil is banal.[64]

Albert Speer, minister of armaments to Hitler, stated that he did not intend to assist in the murder of six million Jews; he only sought to do his job as a good architect in service to the country he loved.[65] Hans Bethe, a scientist who assisted in producing the first atomic bomb, did not intend to facilitate the murder of Japanese civilians. He was only doing his job as a physicist. He once stated,

> I am unhappy to admit that during the war—at least—I did not pay much attention to the moral or humane problems of the atomic bomb. We had a job to do and a very hard one. The first thing we wanted to do was to get the job done. . . . Only when our labors were finally completed when the bomb dropped on Japan, only then or a little before then, maybe, did we first start thinking about the moral implications.[66]

No one said either to Speer or Bethe, "Behold, we set before you this day an unqualified evil; go forth and do it of your own free will." Evil arises from "not paying attention."

Bethe's confession tellingly exposes the inadequacy of the Kantian description of evil (Speer's invocation of the categorical imperative in his defense at the Nuremberg trials only confirms this inadequacy). Our knowledge of good and evil does not arise prior to the objects that claim us, and the objects that claim us always appear to have good purposes. In aiming at those good purposes but missing, or in failing to recognize the deceitful nature of those presumed good purposes, we "back into" evil.

The scientists who created the conditions that made the first atomic mass homicide possible did not directly intend it, if *intention* means the subjective preferences they held as individuals. Many of them had experienced persecution at the hands of the Nazi and fascist regimes and were only trying to protect the civilized world from those regimes.[67] Yet the *object* of their actions was manifest, and it cannot be denied. What constitutes intentions should not be so thoroughly debased that it becomes nothing but subjective preference. If we act as though the object of nuclear homicide did not occur in the bombing of Nagasaki and Hiroshima simply because we cannot find any agent who subjectively preferred mass murder or because we can find a commensurate reason for it, this does not make the object itself go away. The dead are still dead, and the evil still needs to be redeemed. The lingering effects of the object remain with us. Such an object was not the result of a hurricane, tornado, or earthquake. It was the direct result of human actions, even if no metaphysicized freedom can be found to support it.

President Truman and the policymakers around him were aiming at an assumed good in making the decision to drop the bomb. While racist attitudes toward the Japanese (and a legitimate worry about Japanese imperialism) undoubtedly made it easier to drop the bomb, they alone do not account for this evil. According to his memoirs, Truman thought he was aiming at a good, saving half a million lives.[68] Moreover, he invoked the morality of the just war in defense of his actions, arguing that the bombing directly intended to destroy military targets. Although admitting it was tragic, most people in the United

States today would argue that this atomic mass murder was a positive good to preserve freedom. If freedom were the goal of our quest, they might be correct. But what if we live within a moral order where certain things cannot be done without turning away from God, despite the self-descriptions we give those actions? What if directly killing the innocent does deprive us of God, even if it is done out of "good intentions"? What if unredeemed actions prevent us from speaking and thinking about God in an articulate manner? What if unredeemed actions prevent us from living as though God mattered? If there is a moral order such as John Paul II has described it, then we must pass a profoundly negative judgment on the conditions that have ensured our freedom in North American society. But as long as the moral life is based on each person's freedom, this judgment will have a difficult time being heard.

The response to this judgment will be, Who are we to make moral judgments on Truman? the politicians? the physicists? the soldiers? This is not surprising, for the very quest that defines the moral life for us has the odd result that the one prevailing moral judgment by which we live is "Thou shalt not make moral judgments."

Mary Midgley argues in *Can't We Make Moral Judgments?* that two so-called moral insights define modern people, making it increasingly problematic, if not impossible, for us to make moral judgments. These two insights are a "tremendous exaltation of individual freedom" and a "sceptical or incredulous approach to knowledge, designed to weed out all inadequate forms of it in order to make room for modern science."[69] Midgley correlates a dependence upon the will for the ethical life with a diminution of any place for the intellect. We can never know all the pertinent information about a particular action, yet our moral theory often assumes that a person's actions should be judged based on her or his freedom to act one way rather than another. Thus we cannot make reasonable moral judgments, except, of course, for the judgment that we cannot make moral judgments. Moral judgments are no longer possible because of the definitive moral judgment: "Thou shalt not make moral judgments."

REDEEMING EVIL

That evil is accidental does not entail any agreement with the modern assumption that we cannot make moral judgments because we never fully know the interior reasons for our actions. Far from excusing the evil to which we contribute, theological reflections on sin and evil require us continually to describe its "accidental" character in order to lead us to a true and profound confession of the evil that binds us. We are led to confess those sins known and unknown. But the confession of sin assumes that evil can and should be redeemed. It can be redeemed precisely because every act must participate at some level in God's good creation.

FOUR

Christian ETHICS As REPENTANCE

God wills for all creation that good which is God himself. This is enfleshed in the Second Person of the Trinity and mediated to us by the Holy Spirit in and through the church. Through our incorporation into the life of the church in baptism, we are restored to God's goodness and reconciled both with God and with the intended purposes of our own creation. But baptism does not seem to work quite so smoothly. Redemption does not always seem evident. In fact, the baptized sometimes appear to be in a worse state than the unbaptized. This is why Christian ethics must continue to be done. Christian ethics arises because of the tension between what is claimed in baptism and what is celebrated in the Eucharist. In baptism, the new law of the gospel is inscribed in our hearts, and this power heals us such that we can live a good life. We can live into and out of the life of Christ through our incorporation into his new creation discovered in the community of faith. The Eucharist constitutes and is the celebration of that restored community, bearing witness to the reconciliation between God and creation and among God's creatures. But herein resides the problem. What actually takes place at the Eucharist often conflicts with what is claimed at baptism. Baptism reconciles us with God and our neighbor, while the Eucharist celebrates and strengthens that reconciliation by making God himself present in our midst. Yet the participants in these mysteries often do not embody reconciliation. Israel does not seem to be restored. In fact, what baptism and the

Eucharist signify have themselves become sources of division within the church. How can we make sense of this? If these external, perceptible realities transform us into this new creation, why doesn't it seem to work?

We could answer this question by arguing that the expectations are too high. We could argue that baptism does not create a new reality, that Christianity is only about the forgiveness of sins and the imputation of justice, not the actual process of making one good. But that answer assumes that the incarnation of God in Jesus did not create a new reality. To assume that God-made-flesh merely means we will not be judged after death is to miss its central significance. The incarnation is an event that transforms external, sensible realities. If in this event life was not transformed, then the reality and the power of the incarnation must be questioned. For people of Christian faith, such a question can hardly arise. The question is not the efficacy of God's redeeming work but rather the church's failure to embody it. In other words, if in baptism the evangelical law begins to rule our hearts through the power of the Holy Spirit such that we need not sin and are reconciled to our neighbors, and if that power is strengthened and con-firmed in the Eucharist, then why is the reality so often different?

Theologians must not fail to raise this most important question. When the doctrine of sin rather than Christ's redemption begins to define the unity of the church, this question will not arise. When the doctrine that all people sin becomes comforting, the tension between what we should be through our bap-tisms and what we are in practice loses its force. Nothing is more destructive to both the intellectual and practical life of the church. The marks of the church are not "one, catholic, apostolic, and *sinful*," but "one, catholic, apostolic, and *holy*." This does not deny that the church is a hospital for the sick, but we must not forget that the purpose of hospitals is to make people well. That the church is composed of people who are sinful is indisputable. But that sin *characterizes* the body of Christ is scandalous, a repudiation of the truth of Christianity itself.

How, then, are we to make sense of this tension between a church that is sinful and a church that should be holy? Out of this question arises the possi-bility and necessity of Christian ethics. In fact, I would submit, only in answer-ing this question can ethics be Christian, though what is meant by *ethics* here cannot be synonymous with the philosophical discipline that arose after Kant. The tension between what the church should be and what it is in practice gave rise in Christian history to something that resembles ethics.

The history of penance gave rise to Christian ethics. Once Christian ethics seeks to be *ethical* apart from the practice of penance, it ceases to be intimately connected to Christianity. James Dallen has explained the importance of the rite of penance by noting that penance is not a claim for moral superiority but a way for people to be reconciled with the community of faith and thus con-stantly be renewed to their baptismal pledge.[1]

Sin is never merely a private affair; neither is its remedy. Just as sin affects the whole community of faith, likewise its remedy is entrusted to that same body. Paul referred to this when he wrote, "If anyone is detected in a transgression, you [plural] who have received the Spirit should restore such a one in a spirit of gentleness" (Gal. 6:1 NRSV). Restoration is the work of the Spirit. On Pentecost, the Spirit reversed the divisions created by language, restoring unity. Our differences are not transcended through a forged unity. Each still hears in his or her own language, but the divisiveness and violence that accompanied those divisions is redeemed. Through baptism the Spirit maintains "the unity of the [body] in the bond of peace" (Eph. 4:3). Likewise, in repentance the Spirit works to restore sinners to the community of faith and thereby restores the community itself. This work of the Spirit is present in church so that it might discern and heal our sin.

THE MINISTRY OF RESTORATION

Yet the identity of the "you" who have received the Spirit to exercise the ministry of restoration is itself a cause of division within the church. Ironically, nothing has so divided the church as the theological disagreements concerning who exercises the ministry of restoration. The Scriptures themselves seem to complicate our disagreements.

In Matthew 18:15–20 the power of binding and loosing is given to the community of faith to be exercised in an orderly manner. First an individual confronts an offender. If the latter refuses reconciliation, the person confronting takes another believer and confronts the offender again. If the offender still refuses to be restored, then the offense is given over to the entire church. If the offender still refuses to hear, then he or she is to be as a tax collector and Gentile, which implies that the person is once again a subject for conversion. This has provided scriptural warrant for the Anabaptist practice of binding and loosing.[2] But in Matthew 16:19, the keys to the kingdom are given to Peter. He is told that what he looses on earth will be loosed in heaven and what he binds on earth will be bound in heaven. This has provided scriptural warrant for the Roman Catholic position that the bishop first and foremost exercises the ministry of restoration. The divisions that separate Christians from one another are based on our different interpretations about how we exercise the ministry of restoration.

The history of the church's divisions over the ministry of restoration is well known, but its significance for Christian ethics has been overlooked. In the early church, theologians assumed that baptism brought with it a power to live one's life in such a way that one would at least be able to avoid serious wickedness. Lesser sins were to be remedied by daily prayer. Nevertheless, early church theologians seemed genuinely surprised by certain sins after baptism. Although his rigorism may have led him to be surprised by all sin after baptism, Tertullian thought that at least homicide, fornication, adultery, and apostasy should not be found among the baptized. He thought all sins were forms of idolatry and sought to provide the church with guidance as to how those preparing for baptism could be healed from idolatry. He gave us a *culture* that would help us name our idolatry as it is manifested in our everyday activities. Unfortunately, H. Richard Niebuhr's influential *Christ and Culture* has given us an unfavorable view of Tertullian, who is now seen as a sectarian who advocates Christ against culture.

Niebuhr cites Tertullian within the context of the approach that "uncompromisingly affirms the sole authority of Christ over the Christian and resolutely rejects culture's claims to loyalty."[3] This is a most unfortunate definition, because Tertullian's theological critique of the empire bequeathed one of the most profound cultural inheritances in Western society, the idea that the emperor could not claim divinity. In his *Apology* Tertullian argued that he must respect the emperor because God appointed him. In fact, only Christians can rightly understand the limited role the emperor is to play in human affairs; thus, "by putting due limits to the emperor's majesty and subordinating him to God, making him less than divine, I commend him more surely to God to whom alone he is inferior." How this can be viewed as *sectarian* is difficult to understand. Instead, Tertullian reminded the emperor that even in a "triumphal procession" he should hear a voice whispering in his ear, "Look behind you, you are but a man."[4] Far from excluding *culture,* Tertullian engaged and transformed a pagan Roman culture by his loyalty to Christ and his understanding of the faith community as an alternative culture. This concern for the church's holiness produced a profound social ethic.

Tertullian assumed that in the faith community holiness would be practiced such that the idolatry that defined humanity would be overcome. For this reason, he gave guidance to what vocations, actions, and words were appropriate for those seeking reconciliation with the church. As he described it, the church was like the ark, navigating tumultuous waters such that a nonidolatrous life lived in God was now possible: "Amid these reefs and inlets, amid these shallows and straits of idolatry, Faith, her sails filled by the Spirit of God, navigates; safe if cautious, secure if intently watchful. But to such are washed overboard is a deep whence is no outswimming; to such as are run aground is inextricable shipwreck; to such as are engulfed is a whirlpool where there is no breathing."[5]

But not even Tertullian was willing to let the church be shipwrecked without the possibility of rescue. In *On Repentance,* he suggested there was a repentance after baptism called "the second plank." He explained this repentance in terms of "confession" or *exomologesis.* It required certain practices for those who failed to live into their baptisms: a certain dress, diet restrictions, lamentations, prostrations before the presbyters, and kneeling before the faithful.[6] But for Tertullian this repentance was not solely an individual endeavor. The whole church was to be involved because its purpose was to restore the community of faith.

> The body cannot feel gladness at the trouble of any one member, it must necessarily join with one consent in the grief and in laboring for the remedy. In a

company of two is the church, but the church is Christ. When, then, you cast yourself at the brethren's knees, you are handling Christ, you are entreating Christ. In like manner, when they shed tears over you, it is Christ who suffers, Christ who prays the Father for mercy.[7]

Early in the life of the church, the practice of repentance made sense of Christ's ongoing mercy. Repentance aided Christians in living into their baptisms. Tertullian represents that historical period usually described as "ancient penance." Here the church was viewed as an alternative holy community in conflict with the empire that sought to suppress it. The reconciliation that the church offered could bring with it a cross, which some in the age of the martyrs took up. But this reconciliation was communal, as the baptized were reconciled with God and the community of faith. A person could not be reconciled to one without the other. Yet Tertullian is not an unsullied example of the Christian practice of forgiveness. His rigor led him to Montanism and to encourage the faithful to put off baptism until late in life. But his rigor also makes his advocacy of a repentance after baptism all the more remarkable.

CANONICAL PENANCE

In the third century, what constituted sins for which someone must repent and how those sins would be remedied became more systematized. After the Decian persecution (249–250), the rigorists, who wanted to deny the possibility of penance for those who apostatized, were ruled outside the church's practice. The second plank was available to all. Through penance the church made sense of the discrepancy between baptism and everyday life. Although the process could take years, penance sustained the possibility of reconciliation. It functioned almost as a second baptism and became an order of the church.[8]

By the time of Ambrose and Augustine no one was excommunicated from the church except by his or her own confession or by a conviction from a civil or ecclesiastical office. For Augustine, sins were to be forgiven in three ways. The first way was baptism. Augustine still assumed that baptism would effect a change in a person's life and that one's prebaptismal repentance would reflect that change. Thus he wrote, "Of what avail is repentance for dead works, if one persists in adultery and all the other sins with which the love of this world is entangled?"[9] He challenged the idea that one repented only for a "lack of belief" and argued that it was putting off the old and putting on the new.

In his *Enchiridion on Faith, Hope and Love*, Augustine made it clear that the sacrifice of Christ is the remedy for both the evil in the world and for our sins. To achieve good is to be drawn to God, which occurs by our participation in the life of Christ. Christ gives our lives the substance that makes possible our bearing goodness. He is the sacrifice for our sins that we put on at baptism and reenact through the Eucharist.[10] Our will participates freely in the process of baptism, but the freedom to so participate comes solely as gift.[11]

For Augustine, sin was still possible after baptism, but sin could not define the center of the Christian life. For light offenses, which Augustine called *sin,* the Lord's Prayer sufficed as a remedy. For weightier offenses, which he termed *crime,* penance was necessary. Sins, for him, were inevitable, but crimes were not. But even the inevitability of sin was not to be accepted. Sin also needed a constant remedy. The remedy for both sin and crime is found in the church, because the church bears the means by which both sins and crimes can be remedied.[12]

Augustine did not separate the *moral* life from the life of faith. He does not give us an *ethics.* Augustine's treatise, *Of the Morals of the Catholic Church,* has little to do with anything recognizable as *ethical* or *moral* in the modern sense. This treatise is merely a defense of the *mores* (ways of life) of a Catholic against the *mores* of the Manichees, uncompromising rationalists who assumed that religion can be understood via reason alone. But this is false, because "when we learn anything, authority precedes reasoning." Thus, the problem with the Manichees was that they lacked an embodied account of reason that could recognize that any adequate account of *mores* will require obedience to a truthful community.

Augustine's reliance on obedience was not blind and irrational. Reasons could be given for it, and the bulk of his treatise on Catholic morals gave those reasons. Although authority precedes reason, this does not mean that authority as pure power constitutes reason. Reasons are to be given even for the exercise of authority. Augustine agreed with the ancient philosophers that the goal of the moral life was happiness but asked, What constitutes happiness? He answered this by reminding us why we are unhappy. Either we do not possess what we love, or we possess what we love but it is harmful to us, or we possess that which will truly make us happy but do not love it. To be happy, then, is to possess and to love that which can make us happy. Only God can satisfy these requirements. Augustine explained, "Following after God is the desire of happiness, to reach God is happiness itself." But only through obedience to the church can we follow after God. The Manichees falsely assumed that they could think for themselves and find God. Thus Augustine wrote, "It is this presumption which leads the mind to refuse obedience to the laws of God, in the desire to be sovereign as God is."[13]

For Augustine, the Christian life is a journey where we learn obedience. This obedience is a lesson in charity, for charity leads us to God and a happy life. Obedience should be not a coercive act of will but a compelling act of love. God's love draws us to the good, creating in us goodness. The natural virtues are shaped by charity to help us on the journey: "So we may express the definition [of virtue] thus: that temperance is love keeping itself entire and incorrupt for God; fortitude is love bearing everything readily for the sake of God; justice is love serving God only and therefore ruling well all else as subject to man; prudence is love making a right distinction between what helps it toward God and what might hinder it."[14] These virtues cannot be cultivated separate from law: "For the very true beginning of wisdom is the desire of discipline and love is the keeping of her laws." Since the church keeps those laws, Augustine concluded his defense of Catholic morals by urging the Manichees as well as his readers, "[to betake] yourselves bodily to the shelter of the most holy bosom of the Catholic Church."

The Manichees were far from this reality, but they were not without hope. If they repented, they could still regain their true human nature, which had been corrupted by their undue reliance on their own reason. The purpose of penance is not punitive; it is not an arbitrary imposition of law. Penance makes no sense without the virtues toward which the law directs us. Penance is the means of production that gives us a social formation, moving us toward virtues via the laws of God. It is a means known only by the church. Thus, suggested Augustine, the recovery of the Manichee's human nature could not be done separate from the church. Quoting and commenting on Bishop Cyprian's well-known statement, Augustine suggested that "outside the Church sins are not remitted. For the Church alone has received the pledge of the Holy Spirit without which there is no remission of sins."[15]

For Augustine, like Tertullian, the *moral* life and the life of faith lived in and through the church are inseparable. Reason suggests that the end of the moral life is happiness, but this happiness cannot be fully achieved separate from the catholic church—not because of the church's moral superiority but because it alone has been promised the means by which our sins can be remedied. The *moral* life makes no sense without these material means of the reproduction of the journey of charity back to God.

The practice of penance took a new direction when Irish monks began to confess to one another in private. They carried this practice with them on their missionary journeys throughout Europe, and the practice of private confession became the normal social structure within which penance operated. To assist this process, books known as *penitentials* were developed, which listed known sins and what should be done to remedy them. These books, which mixed local customs with the church's discipline, were an early expression of Christian ethics, but they created problems within the church because of their arbitrary nature and lack of systematization. Eventually they were subject to the Carolingian reforms, and then an effort was made to regularize penitential practice in Gratian's *Decretum*. Gratian's *Decretum* was the first effort to systematize the arbitrary and conflicting canons concerning the moral life. This effort eventually led to the development of canon law. Once canon law takes on a life of its own, the Christian moral life can become too thoroughly defined in terms of law and the will's relationship to the law. However, the great moral theologian, Thomas Aquinas, developed an understanding of law that subordinated it to the life of virtue.

PENANCE AS VIRTUE

For Thomas Aquinas, the purpose of law was to direct human actions to virtuous ends. Without those virtuous ends and the virtues that need to be cultivated to achieve those ends, the law makes no sense. For Aquinas, penance was both a sacrament and a virtue. A sacrament is "that which is ordained to signify our sanctification,"[16] that is, it orders us toward God. Sanctification is the heart of the moral life, for it is the process whereby we become what we are intended to be. This process lives out of the central mystery of the church, Christ's passion, and it points to our ultimate end, eternal blessedness.

For Aquinas, all goodness is a participation in God. There are forms of natural goodness, such as building a home, farming a field, rearing a family, that we can achieve without grace, though not without God's assistance. However, to be truly human requires some power more than nature itself can provide: the power of grace that directs all our activities toward God, who is our ultimate good.

The sacraments are ordained to direct us to that ultimate good. Through the sacraments we acquire "knowledge of the intelligible (of the Divine) from the sensible." Thus Aquinas rejects Kant's clear separation between the intelligible and the sensible. This is based not on philosophical argument but on the theological reality of the incarnation and the presence of the sacraments in the church.[17] God speaks a language that we can understand. While Kant was certainly correct that human nature as it is cannot make intelligible transcendental ideas such as God, Aquinas argued that God speaks to us such that God makes himself known. As Aquinas puts it, "The same thing can be signified by diverse signs, yet to determine which sign must be used belongs to the signifier." God signifies the sacraments as the language that unites the intelligible and the sensible for us; the invisible is found in the visible. The reason is that the sacraments are the language of God conveying the Signifier's intention by uniting the *sacramentum tantum* (the sign alone) with the *res tantum* (the reality alone) by means of a *sacramentum et res* (the sign and the reality). Only by divine institution can a sign effect that which it signifies.

As the divine language, the sacraments create a "character" in us, a power in the soul that remedies sin and perfects us. Aquinas describes this character in the same terms as a soldier's brand.[18] The sacraments are "necessary for salvation" because they "unite people together in the name of the one true religion."[19] The first sacrament is baptism. Unlike Tertullian and Augustine, Aquinas did not believe that baptism required an exercise of the church's keys prior to baptism, since "those who are being baptized do not need to be released from their sins by the keys of the Church since all are forgiven them in baptism."[20] Even more so than Tertullian and Augustine, Aquinas emphasized the act of baptism as effecting a new creation. Thus, confession of specific sins is not necessary prior to baptism; only the "inward virtue of penance is required."[21] Confession of sins is rendered necessary after baptism because sin is still possible, though surprising. Because of the discrepancy between what we should be, given our baptism, and what we in fact are, penance is necessary.

As a virtue penance is a species of justice, which is a habit of right reasoning about compensation to be made when an offense is committed. It is also the "door to the other virtues" and thus central to the ethical life. Penance prepares our souls to receive the virtues and at the same time teaches us how to name the evil that prevents us from becoming that which we are intended to be. Penance as a virtue cannot be acquired through some heroic ascent out of the everyday. It is received as a gift through the material means of everyday life. It sets us on a journey that is only complete when the gifts, beatitudes, and theological virtues are found in our character such that we walk no longer by faith but by sight. The vision of God is the journey (and the virtue's) end. Penance is a sacrament of the *new law* that effects what it signifies. As a sacrament, it is instituted in Luke 24 and Matthew 16. Following the earlier work of Tertullian and Jerome, Aquinas also refers to penance as a second plank after shipwreck. The *form* of the sacrament is the priest's administration. Because it effects what it signifies, the priest says, "I absolve thee." God acts through the sensible actions of the priest. The *matter* of the sacrament is the human acts done through satisfaction.

Penance consists of three parts: contrition, confession, and satisfaction. Contrition and confession prepare the person for the substantive matter of the sacrament, acts of satisfaction such as works of charity. Penance has two effects: forgiveness of sins and a return to our former dignity. Through penance we can recover our "principal dignity" as creatures of God. We cannot recover innocence, but because God is merciful, penance is now repeatable as many times as necessary.

Christian ethics arises from and is intelligible in the light of the need for penance. The discrepancy between what we should be and what we are makes the Christian moral life a life lived in repentance. This is not to suggest that it is a life of negation. Nor does a life lived in repentance require an oppressive, introspective conscience. A life lived in repentance is a political form of life that seeks to redeem evil. Repentance is not an inescapable dialectic fluctuating between good and evil, because Christ's presence to us and sacrifice for us creates a new reality. Jesus is the *ought* of the Christian moral life, and this ought implies *can*. As we move from what we are to what we should be, we also gain clearer vision of the ought. But without this *ought* we would not know the *is*. Penance is our social ethic, for it is the constant effort to embody the transformation from what we are to what we should be. In this sense, Luther is correct. Penance can never be separated from baptism. A life of repentance is a life living into our baptism through the repeatable feast of the Eucharist.

The practice of penance assumes laws that will embody concrete descriptions of what is licit or illicit in moving us in the proper direction. Laws such as "Do not kill," "Keep the Sabbath holy," and "Love one another as I have loved you" give a certain shape to the Christian moral life. But the Christian moral life is not merely the observance of laws because they are laws. Those laws must be rendered intelligible by the narrative of God's revelation to us in Jesus. The commands are not arbitrary, and obedience to the law as law is not an end in itself. The commands are reasonable and direct us to appropriate ends. Law serves the purpose of virtue. We could obey the law not to kill our enemies solely out of fear of retribution, but we would then miss the purpose of the law, which is to form our lives christologically. Law is necessary but insufficient. Law truly functions in directing us toward the good when it also contributes to the cultivation of virtue. Virtue gives our lives a christological form. Virtues are those graced habits the Holy Spirit produces in us with our cooperation, although we are often surprised at the production of these virtues in our lives. Thus, these virtues are gifts that cannot lead us to self-sufficiency. Rather, they produce in us a disposition of thankfulness. The theological virtues—faith, hope, and charity—are not achievements of our own; they are never self-possessions. They always come to us as gift. As gifts, they cannot be fully received separate from the sacraments. Penance, then, is necessary for the Christian moral life.

Unfortunately, the very idea of penance as the means that effects our ongoing reconciliation to God and others has been jeopardized within the Christian churches so thoroughly that it calls into question the possibility of a viable Christian ethic. Arguments over how penance should be practiced have always been present in the church. The form of the sacrament has been disputed. Peter Lombard emphasized the contrition of the penitent and placed little emphasis on the role of the priest. Duns Scotus so emphasized the priest's role that he could speak of the sacrament of absolution. The genius of Aquinas was to "combine the contrition of the penitent and the actions of the priest in a causal unity that produced grace and thus made the priest logically indispensable."[22] Aquinas synthesized the intelligible and the sensible such that the concrete material of the church was necessary for efficacious grace. Yet that which was inward and relatively inaccessible, the contrition of the penitent, was also necessary. However, a focus on the matter of the sacrament (the necessary concrete works of "satisfaction") produced a judicial ethic calculating credits and debits. Luther's great gift to the church was to call this reductivistic penitential practice into question, for it could not make sense of the significance of baptism. Unfortunately, in reforming a corrupt practice of satisfaction, Protestantism devolved into a nonconfessional community. Yet without confession, reconciliation is impossible. Grace becomes nothing but acceptance, and Protestantism turns into an antinomian sect.

PROTESTANT LOSS OF PENANCE

With the rise of the Protestant Reformation, the interior disposition of the penitent became the dominant consideration. This has resulted in what Krister

Stendahl once called "the introspective consciousness of the West," where we can never be sure of absolution because our own inner dispositions remain something of a mystery even to ourselves, always subject to further interrogation. Martin Luther can certainly be credited with pointing us in the direction of an ever-vigilant, but never satisfying, introspection, even though it was precisely a "gallow's sorrow" that he rightly protested against.

The Fourth Lateran Council (1215) marked the end of medieval penance and the beginning of modern penance. It made possible a "tariff system" of penance in which penance became an end in itself. No longer was it expected that the social practice of penance would produce virtue; rather, individual auricular confession and the priest's absolution represented a growing cost-benefit analysis of sin and reward in which the Christian moral life was reduced to an accountant's ledger, with sins on one side and penances as payment for those sins on the other. Manuals of confession were produced that focused on those acts alone that violated certain laws and how confessors were to lead those confessing into a thorough examination of conscience and confession. Martin Luther thought that this tariff system resulted in a "gallow's sorrow" that was based on fear rather than the love of God. Thus he protested.

Although Luther protested against a corrupt form of penance that had resulted in a minimalist and juridical conception of the moral life, Protestantism eventually dematerialized the reproduction of holiness in the life of the believer. The extent of Luther's responsibility for this dematerialization of the life of holiness is an open question, but that his protest set us in this direction is not. Alasdair MacIntyre finds an inevitable drift from Luther to Kant. Luther (and Machiavelli) first present the "figure of the individual." For Luther, the transformation of the Christian life becomes "entirely internal."[23] Luther's two-kingdoms doctrine, his emphasis on the freedom of the Christian, his sharp law-gospel distinction, and his invisible church lend themselves to an internal orientation in Christian living that renders the social and material practices of the church irrelevant. The focus on the Christian life becomes an internal disposition separate from outward acts.

But this may be an inadequate reading of Luther. Reinhard Hütter has recently pointed out Luther's emphasis on "holy possessions." They are the works worked (*poiemata*) by the Holy Spirit that constitute the church as church "even in a time of fundamental ecclesiastical conflict."[24] These holy possessions are "the external, orally preached word of God; baptism; the Lord's Supper; the office of the keys as church discipline; ordination and offices; public prayer, praise, thanksgiving, instruction; and discipleship in suffering." As Hütter notes, these holy possessions *mark* the church. These "core church practices" define the work of the Spirit, constitute the church, and render intelligible Luther's distinction between the visible and invisible church. "Precisely the external, visible church is the hidden church, for only faith itself can perceive the externality of the Holy Spirit's activities at issue here; that is, they are to be *believed as works* of the Holy Spirit. As activities of the *Holy Spirit,* precisely their straightforward concrete externality makes them radically "invisible" to unbelief."[25] Hütter's interpretation does not find Luther dematerializing the church into an invisible space. Nor does his worry about reading the gospel in terms of the law require the kind of sharp law-gospel distinction that one finds in a Lutheran theologian such as Althaus.

Hütter recognizes a similarity between Luther's stricture against treating the gospel under the category of law and Thomas Aquinas's analogical use of the term *law* with his new law of the gospel. Hütter explains,

> If one presupposes that the "new law" is for Aquinas the expression of the agent's willing and intending having been drawn—through the infused virtue of charity becoming the form of the cardinal virtues—into the Holy Spirit's willing and intending, then the "new law" cannot be univocally submitted to the etymological definition which Aquinas offers for "law" in the opening Question of his *Treatise on Law*, namely, to have its root in the Latin *ligare* ("to bind"). Rather in the "new law" the *analogical use* of the term *law* becomes fully transparent: the "new law" as the Holy Spirit's external principle of action in the believer is simply true freedom becoming substantive in coinciding with the divine willing and intending.[26]

Perhaps more agreement between Luther and Aquinas is possible than theologians have assumed on both the question of the visibility of the church and the relationship between the law and the gospel. Even Luther's worry about penitential practices did not arise primarily because of an emphasis on the individual Christian's freedom from liturgical practice but because he thought those practices did not do sufficient justice to the liturgical practice of baptism.

When he was reconsidering the sacraments, Luther seemed ambiguous on whether penance should be a sacrament. In 1519 he wrote, "The sacrament of penance renews and points out again the sacrament of baptism."[27] However, Luther rejected the long-standing tradition via Tertullian, Jerome, Augustine, and Aquinas that spoke of penance as a "second plank."[28] Luther thought this diminished the efficacy of baptism. He feared the practice of penance would prevent us from fully trusting in "the first plank, or the ship," baptism. To think that acts of penance restored baptismal grace could too easily make grace dependent upon human works. Because of his emphasis upon the social practice of baptism, Luther avoided emphasizing any individual action as that which merits grace.

For Luther, baptism contained three things: a sign, its significance, and faith. The sign is that act whereby we are thrust into the water in the name of the Father, the Son, and the Holy Spirit. The significance of this sign is "a blessed dying unto sin and a resurrection in the grace of God, so that the old man, conceived and born in sin, is there drowned and a new man born in grace come forth and rises."[29]

However, the rise of this "new man" cannot be complete until death. What is important in baptism is not that the sign effects this reality but that the baptized has the faith to believe the promise that God will do this. The basis for the person's faith should rest on the promise mediated by the church to the baptized, not merely on the individual will's ability to keep some commandment. This places redemption thoroughly within the practices of baptism. Luther emphasized the place of baptism and the promise it held as a sign of God's alliance with human creatures: "You ask, 'How does baptism help me if it does not altogether blot out and remove sin?' This blessed sacrament helps you because in it God allies himself with you and becomes one with you in a gracious covenant of comfort."[30] But Luther could so emphasize the promise present in baptism that the sin that arises after it no longer constituted a central theological problem. So he stated that God does not materially remove sins but "pledges himself not to impute to you the sins which remain in your nature after baptism, neither to take them into account nor to condemn you because of them."[31] God "winks at our sins" and regards us "as if" we were sinless. Sin is so "overruled by our baptism that it does not condemn us and is not harmful to us."[32]

Luther did not argue that we accept our postbaptismal sins. We were to struggle against them, but the struggle would seem futile until we were released from the struggle at death. Luther himself continued to make daily confession to his confessor, Bugenhagen. Despite this, Luther failed to regard as sufficiently serious the problem of the discrepancy between what we should be, given baptism, and what we are. After Luther, Christian ethics as repentance becomes more difficult. The contradiction between baptism and our postbaptismal sin becomes less recognizable.

We should not be surprised, then, that Martin Luther disagreed that the priest exercised the ministry of restoration because of his office. He argued that the keys were given to Peter because of his faith and not because of any position he held. He wrote, "In the place where it says: Whatsoever thou shalt bind, etc., Christ is calling out the faith of the penitent, by giving a certitude based on the words of the promise, that, if he be forgiven as a believer here below, his forgiveness holds good in heaven. This passage makes no mention at all of conferring power, but only deals with the service performed by the administrator promising the words of forgiveness."[33] Luther worried that the corruption of the ministry of restoration both in baptism and in repentance had led people astray, leading them to trust in their own contrition rather than in God's gracious promises. So he instituted new practices. Sins were forgiven through voluntary confession before a brother in private. The keys to the kingdom were given to anyone who had faith in Christ.[34] While this could have led to a more communal practice of repentance, in fact it has had the opposite result. The focus became not a voluntary confession *to another* but a *voluntary* confession. Oddly enough, Luther's new practices led toward the modern practice in which an individual's will, and not the social reality of the church, is the locus for the practice of repentance. Modern Protestantism too often identifies its reform not as a recovery of a communal form of repentance and reconciliation but as a warrant for individual self-assertion. Protestants take from the Reformation the sentiment that we do not need any priest to confess our sins, but neither do we seem to need a community. Although Luther himself practiced regular confession to another, his protest led to confession as a private, individual act of surveillance in which no pronouncement of absolution can be given by another human being.

John Calvin also worried that Christians would fail to trust in the full satisfaction Christ offers and instead trust in their own repentance. He insisted that forgiveness is a gift of sheer liberality (as nearly all earlier theologians did as well). But he opposed the teaching of Aquinas that the *matter* of penance is the believer's own acts. He also disagreed with Augustine that sin after baptism constituted a serious theological problem. Thus he wrote,

> Between Augustine and us we can see that there is this difference of opinion; while he concedes that believers as long as they dwell in mortal bodies are so bound by inordinate desires that they are unable not to desire inordinately, yet he does not call this disease "sin." Content to designate it with the term "weakness" he teaches that it becomes sin only when either act or consent follows the conceiving or apprehension of it, that is, when the will yields to the first strong inclination. We, on the other hand, deem it sin when man is tickled by any desire at all against the law of God. Indeed, we label "sin" that very depravity which begets in us desires of this sort.[35]

This means that postbaptismal sin was less of a problem for Calvin than for Augustine, since the substance of sin is ineradicable. Baptism only releases us from the guilt of sin. Calvin cites Ephesians 5:25–26, "Husbands, love your wives just as Christ loved the church and gave himself up for her, in order to make her holy by cleansing her with the washing of water by the word" (NRSV), then comments, "[In] this statement we refer to the guilt of sin rather than to the very substance of sin."

Sin in Calvin's theology is more a fundamental orientation than any actions that people do. He located sin in desire alone, unlike Augustine, who located it in an action upon an inordinate desire. Thus there is less optimism in Calvin than in either Augustine or Aquinas that sin might actually be conquered or that good can be present without evil. Calvin opposed any account of "satisfaction" in penance and condemned it as a "merit of works."[36] But in doing this, he rejected that exercise of practical wisdom necessary for the Christian life whereby we judge ourselves against the standard of Christ and seek to cultivate those virtues, whose door is penance, that will make us just. Calvin denied this because he thought it threatened the truth that Christ has provided full satisfaction for our sins; it threatened the "sheer liberality" of forgiveness.[37]

Thus, he rejected Aquinas's argument that the human person participated in Christ's passion through the matter of his or her own acts. Calvin wrote,

> On the basis of a saying of Jerome, they [the Schoolmen] torment themselves greatly with a gross error, that repentance is the "second plank after shipwreck." By this they show themselves never to have awakened from their brute stupor to feel a thousandth part, or even less, of their faults. . . . Now set before yourself their pestilent absurdities, that in the first forgiveness of sins only the grace of God operates, but if we have fallen afterward, our works co-operate in obtaining the second pardon.[38]

Though nobly seeking to defend the all-sufficient merit of Christ's passion, Calvin, like Luther, had unwittingly separated the sensible and the intelligible. He did not seem to recognize that our cooperation in penance is necessary after baptism because sin and evil must be not only forgiven but also redeemed. Nor did he seem to recognize that the *second plank* also preserves the sheer liberality of grace. In fact, the second plank is necessary to maintain that grace matters. Penance preserves the gift of grace as a material reality present in sensible, everyday life. Only because earlier theologians held that baptism should constitute a new material reality could they hold forth the need for a second plank. As with Luther, one result of Calvin's analysis was an internalized and individualized exercise of the power of the keys. Lost is the possibility of a liturgical performance whose enactment makes possible a participation in God, creating once again a new material reality of goodness and holiness. But as with Luther, this internalized and individualized exercise comes as a bit of a surprise within Calvinism, for Calvin also emphasized the communal nature of confession and repentance.

For Calvin, the power of the keys was exercised, first, "when the entire church with solemn recognition of its faults implores pardon," that is, general confession. This first exercise makes possible the kind of liturgical correction toward a communal repentance and reconciliation that has disappeared in modern Protestantism. But Calvin's second and third exercises of the keys have worked against such a liturgical performance of repentance and holiness. The second exercise occurs when an individual declares repentance in private, and the third, when an individual discloses weakness to a minister. Thus, for Calvin, the keys to the kingdom are a gate to prayer, both for individuals in private and to all in public.[39]

But with Calvin more so than with Luther, the material means by which virtue was produced were replaced by an inward disposition disconnected from any bodily practice. The Islamic philosopher Talal Asad understands well the predicament this internalization of the ethical life created. He asks, "How did the idea of teaching the body to develop 'virtues' through material means come to be displaced by the idea of separating internal feelings and thoughts . . . from social forms/formulas/formalities?"[40] The preceding narrative has sought to answer how that happened. The result of this process was a dematerialized Christianity in which the intelligible and sensible no longer intermingle except in a person's mind. We are not far from Kant.

Although the Reformers sought to retrieve the ministry of restoration, few churches in Protestant Christianity have viable practices for restoring sinners. The Methodists attempted to do this through class meetings and penitential bands. They initiated a reform movement recovering the ancient practice of penance. They assumed that baptism effected a new way of life, one that could even be characterized by *perfection*. But this was not merely an inward, spiritual reality that happened once. It was a perfection that was to be performed through concrete, social means. The faithful were to gather in small meetings and answer the question, "What known sins have you committed since last we met?" Unfortunately, this remarkable reform of the practice of penance quickly dissolved into a bourgeois, individualized grace through the revivalism fashionable in North America. Now the Wesleyan tradition has no resistance to the internalization of penance produced in the modern era. Repentance is either left solely in the hands of individuals or assumed accomplished by a general confession that does not teach us to name our complicity in evil with any profundity. The law of Christ that requires us to bear each other's burdens has been forfeited. Perhaps this is the consequence of the deep disagreements over how to exercise the keys of the kingdom within the Christian churches. Nevertheless, without the exercise of the keys a Christian social ethics is not possible. The loss of repentance as a social practice reveals Protestantism's greatest failure.

MINIMALISM AND THE MANUALISTS

Unfortunately, the Catholic Counter-Reformation did not return the practice of penance to a quest for virtue and holiness but, through the development of Jesuit casuistry and the manualist tradition in moral theology, developed the juridical and minimalist account of the Christian moral life Luther rightly feared. The focus of this tradition was on permitted and prohibited acts based on law alone. Law did not serve as a means to a virtuous end but became its own end. The tariff system was not overcome. This moral theology has been treated with the contempt it deserved from Pascal and others who told the story of Louis XIV, who would put his mistress away on Thursday, confess to his Jesuit confessor on Friday, go to mass on Sunday, and call her back on Monday. When the question of the moral life becomes reduced to the single question, "Is this act permitted under the law?" then we should expect a truncated account of the moral life.

One of the results of the minimalist and juridical account of the moral life within the manualist tradition was a moral theology known as *probabilism*. This controversial account of the moral life asks whether a given act is licit or illicit under the law. It does not ask whether it is virtuous, nor does it ask, as Aquinas would have, whether the act directs us toward God and the good. Instead, it seeks only to know if something is licit based on the previous precedence of at least five established authorities. In their defense of casuistry, Jonsen and Toulmin explain probabilism as "when the licitness or illicitness of an action is in doubt, one is allowed to follow a probable opinion." If authorities in the life of the church can be found who find a certain action licit, then that opinion can be followed.

This kind of moral theology came under attack by Pascal. In his *Provincial Letters* he satirized the problems with probabilism through a conversation with a fictitious Jesuit. Pascal wrote,

> Reverend father, said I, how happy the world is in having such men as you for its masters! And what blessings are these probabilities! I never knew the reason why you took such pains to establish that a single doctor, if a grave one, might render an opinion probable, and that the contrary might be so too, and that one may choose any side one pleases, even though he does not believe it to be the right side, and all with such a safe conscience, that the confessor who should refuse him absolution on the faith of the casuists would be in a state of damnation. But I see now that a single casuist may make new rules of morality at his discretion, and dispose, according to his fancy, of everything pertaining to the relation of manners. . . . Indeed father! cried I, why on this principle the Church would approve of all the abuses which she tolerates and all the errors in all the books which she does not censure![41]

Probabilism deserved such ire. As Pascal recognized, it truly was a moral theology that assumed moral norms were nothing more than social constructions subject to revision. Nevertheless, the manualist tradition that perpetuated this kind of moral theology still preserved certain elements of the Christian moral life that provided the possibility of a correction. The manuals maintained the importance of the sacraments as the context within which laws were intelligible.

The manualist tradition divided moral theology into three parts: (1) general moral theology, which focused on what constitutes human acts; (2) specific moral theology, which often took the Ten Commandments as its paradigm and discussed specific moral issues; and (3) a discussion of the sacraments. This third part is intriguing because it reminds us that the moral life is inseparable from the sacramental life. However, the lexical ordering of the manuals often subordinated the sacraments to conscience, action, and law, which were so stressed that the virtues and the purposes for which law exists fell into the background. Obedience to the law alone became paramount. Humans were subject to obedience through some innate power of conscience alone or through authority *qua* authority.

This threefold structure can be seen in one of the last great English manuals, Henry Davis's *Moral and Pastoral Theology*. Davis begins his manual by situating actions in terms of a theological "scope" that makes our actions intelligible. He wrote,

> Moral theology is that part of theology which treats of the relation of human acts to eternal salvation. It lays down rules and principles according to which human acts must be performed so that many may, with God's help, attain salvation. Its sources are divine revelation, tradition and the teachings of the Church. It is legalistic; it discovers what the law is and determines how law is to be applied. It is a science of human conduct ruled by law.[42]

Unfortunately, Davis's manual, symptomatic of the manualist tradition, focuses solely on the final two sentences and neglects the weightier purposes of the law. The result is that moral theology appears to be a type of divine-command theory where God gives laws and we obey them solely because God gives them. The priest can too easily become the arbitrary power broker between God's command and the individual conscience, who must accept them without purpose. When moral theology is reduced to this, we lose the heart of a Thomistic ethic in which law is not an end in itself but directs human acts to virtuous ends.

The Christian moral life is best expressed not as an ethics of obligation under law but as an ethics of virtue where law is necessary because it helps direct our actions toward their appropriate ends. Once our actions are so directed, our desires will be rightly ordered, and we will cultivate those virtues that help us in our journey back to God. This means that ethics is grounded not in anything in human nature as it is but in the transition from our human nature in its fallenness to human nature participating in the life of God. Christ is our teacher, example, and source of power for this ethic. He reveals to us what our human nature should be. He also provides the source of healing that transforms us from what we are to what we should be. Repentance and acts consistent with it are necessary for grace to free our lives for God. The ministry of restoration does not just forgive us the guilt of our sin. Rather, we are freed from those disordered desires that keep us from God. Then we are freed for God.

If Christian ethics is inseparable from the social practice of penance, then Christian ethics is not grounded in our human nature as it is. This is not to deny that human beings share commonalities in their nature. Certainly we do. Self-preservation serves us fairly well on our highways. The ability to build bridges, homes, airplanes, bicycles and operate them effectively seems to be fairly universal. So is the ability to reproduce, eat, sleep, enjoy friendships, laugh, and suffer pains. But this common human nature is insufficient to provide the grounds for a Christian moral life because the Christian moral life centers not on what we already are but in what we hope to become, participants in the life of God through Christ in the power of the Spirit. If this is our good end, then the practice of the sacramental movement from baptism to Eucharist through penance will be the pattern for Christian ethics. The social practice of penance makes Christian ethics possible; the absurd discrepancy between what we should be in baptism and what we as church in fact are and have been makes penance necessary.

BUT IS THIS ETHICS?

I could imagine two sorts of criticisms to this Christian ethic. First, theologians such as Thiemann and Stackhouse would see it as too particular and thus leading to exclusive claims for a parochial vision that cannot help but lead to increased conflict and violence in an already overly fragmented world. This criticism must be taken seriously. It is the problem of *sectarian violence*. But in the second half of this work I hope to dislodge this phrase from our vocabulary and thus resituate the question of violence. The phrase *sectarian violence* implies a formal, sociological charge. It assumes that violence results from the sociological form of a community and not the narrative content of its commitments. Thus, uncompromising sects who refuse to cooperate with the dominant society are primarily seen to be responsible for violence.

This analysis of the problem of violence seems to arise from those political philosophies, like Kant and Hegel, that envision the sublimation of particulars into larger communal frameworks as the sign of ethical progress.[43] Hegel's "state" and Kant's "cosmopolis" are not the same communal frameworks, but the journey they mark out tempts us to speak of sectarian violence, because their journey assumes that local, recalcitrant particular communities incapable of incorporation into the larger wholes will prevent the creation of the best possible ethical life. Yet both Hegel and Kant recognize the need for violence against these particular communities for the sake of creating the state or the cosmopolis. We have ample evidence of such violence in the modern era. Thus, perhaps we should speak of *cosmopolitan* violence rather than *sectarian* violence. This is not to say that the violence of some particular communities is not a problem. But it does suggest that their violence is the result not of their sociological form, their *sectarianism,* but of the narrative content that forms their community. Cosmopolitan violence, however, arises precisely because of the sociological form of life it advocates. Democratic nations do not offer a nonviolent alternative, even though they are founded on a so-called cosmopolitan vision. I shall further argue that the substantive content of Jesus' life renders the critique of *sectarian violence* less threatening than the alternative cosmopolitan vision.

A second critique would be to raise the question, If the Christian moral life is movement toward human nature as it should be, who gets to define what this human is? This is an important criticism. If the end is already evident and self-contained, then the temptation will be to impose this certain end on others. It would make possible a *totalizing* of the other into one's own limited narrative. But in naming the resurrected Jesus as this end, this temptation is avoided. God made flesh and re-presented to us through the Holy Spirit is an end that is inexhaustible. It cannot be definitively and securely explained as this end and no other. Rather, as Stanley Hauerwas has noted, "The telos of the Christian life is not a goal that is clearly known prior to the undertaking of the journey, but rather we learn better the nature of the end by being slowly transformed by the means necessary to pursue it."[44] Only by showing how Christ matters in everyday, sensible reality can we begin to glimpse the end of the journey, an end that is definite but nevertheless opens out into a wide expanse that has place for the infinite in its truthful, good, and beautiful forms. To direct us toward this end, the second part of this work will focus on concrete social formations—the family; the market; the nation-state; and the military, police force, and judicial system—to seek to address how we discern the goodness of God, given its revelation in Jesus Christ. By beginning to recognize how Christ orders our desires toward God and how that arranges our participation in various social formations, we can begin to be about the task of Christian ethics, to learn the skills of repentance necessary to live into our baptism and toward the reconciliation embodied in the Eucharist. In these practices, we discover the unsettling and satisfying goodness of God.

the

Church

and

OTHER

SOCIAL

FORMATIONS

FIVE

ECCLESIA: Ordering Desires

If we concede that all moral norms are social constructions, this should be distanced from any intimation that our freedom to will creates the good for us. Instead, the good is a gift, something we find ourselves caught up in and must follow. This does not deny the role of our own freedom in following after this goodness, but it denies understanding our freedom separately from the good that first pursues us. Freedom is not a capacity we can a priori assume; it is a way of life that is elicited by the nature of the good itself. It draws us out of ourselves and draws us toward that which is more than us. In this sense, the good is never our self-possession securely contained within our immanent power. The good eludes our systematizing grasp; it cannot be mastered.

Therefore the Christian life is a constant process of repentance and reformation. It is characterized by baptism, which is only done once as a witness to the complete and all-sufficient goodness by which God redeems the world. In baptism the Holy Spirit actualizes the ministry of restoration as a social reality. But while baptism can only be done once, the Eucharist with its implicit call for repentance and reconciliation is a repeatable feast. By participating in this repeatable feast we live into our baptism and *participate* in the good. It is not something we produce through our own will; it is given to us. Nevertheless, our participation *makes* it real.[1] That is why God needs the church.[2] As Gerhard Lohfink notes, God needs the church because God works through a timeful and concrete people located in a particular time and space. God makes redemption through this social formation. In this sense, and this sense alone, ethics is a social construction. God's goodness is made concrete in time and space through creation, the Jews, and the church. Its concrete timefulness is what allows us to participate in it.

To participate in the good we must be seized by the vision of it found in sensible, material everyday life. That vision is found in Jesus of Nazareth and the stories and traditions that bear his name, which is a vision produced and reproduced in the church. Jesus reveals to us the goodness of God in human flesh. We can now embody that goodness through our participation in Christ's body, the church. The church mediates to us the flesh of Jesus whereby we participate in the life of God. The liturgical performance of his flesh—both in preaching and in the sacrament—continually produces and reproduces a different *city*, which is called church or *ecclesia*. This *alterna civitas* does not have a fixed geographical boundary. It is less a secure place than a time. It is made present wherever its embodiment is realized through liturgical performance and the holiness of life the Spirit calls forth in us through our participation in Christ. The church must have a formal structure related to its apostolic founding, but that formal structure must always be a means to the ordering of the faithful toward holiness and obedience and never become an end in itself.

THE MAKING OF THE TWELVE: A NEW CREATION

The central role for the church in ordering our desires arises first and foremost from the biblical witness. The dominant form of Neo-Protestant theology in the modern era emphasized that the significant contribution Jesus made to ethics was his "absolute individualism." This misreading was based on an argument that Jesus thought the world would soon end and thus taught an otherworldly, individualistic piety. Jesus' *eschatology*, it was argued, rendered his work irrelevant for social and political matters. What truly mattered for Jesus were the individual soul and its relationship to God. Even though nearly every contemporary theologian repudiates this nineteenth-century view of Jesus, few actually replace it with the central biblical insight that what Jesus gives us is the new community called church. Scripture never refers to a truncated, otherworldly view of salvation based on the individual alone. Jesus presents to us not a *new individualism,* but a *new community.*[3]

Gerhard Lohfink draws upon Mark 3:14–16 to explain the significance of this new community for salvation. In that passage Mark tells us that Jesus "created the Twelve." The Greek verb translated "created" is *poieō*, which means "to make, do, or perform." It implies a particular intentionality. Jesus' *making, creating,* or *performing* of the Twelve was not accidental but an essential part of his mission. Thus, at the *beginning* of his ministry "he created the Twelve." In so doing, Jesus was not merely pointing to the future but accomplishing the restoration of Israel in the present. This restoration of Israel does not entail the replacement of Israel; quite the contrary, it requires the permanence of Israel within the Christian narrative.

What Israel and the church have in common is a "quest for the form of the people of God."[4] The history of Israel, like the history of the church, centers on the question as to what *form* the elect people of God should take. This is the key question Scripture seeks to answer. Lohfink examines the biblical answers to this question through the formations God's people assume, such as "the people of God as tribal society without a king." This is the earliest form that God's people took. It distinguished them from the nations around them, but it had a proclivity toward violence. Their distinctiveness was dangerous because it led Israel to insist on its uniqueness at the expense of the other nations. Thus God gave the people a new form, "the people of God as a nation." Here the elect took a form similar to that of other nations: they were given a king. The mixed and contradictory responses to monarchy in 1 Samuel 8–10 reveal that the kingship was also dangerous. Whereas the tribal society was prone to violence because of its distinctiveness, the monarchy tempted the elect to become like the other nations, taking on characteristics such as a standing military and forced labor. Living like other nations, Israel fell like other nations. But they were never abandoned. The elect took another form, "the people of God as a temple community" formed around the Torah. This allowed Israel to survive and maintain the unique identity that was its birthright. Even after the destruction of the temple, the Torah continued to form this missionary community with its distinct service in the divine economy. No longer formed around the temple, the people of God took the form of a "federation of synagogues." Within the Hellenistic-Roman period, this synagogal form allowed the elect people to have their own political existence free from Roman service and "from the imperial cult as well."[5] This synagogal form gave rise to the formation of the early church.

Jesus' actions in the temple can only be rightly understood as a response to the question regarding what form the people of God should take. When he overturns the table and states that he has the authority to do so because he will tear it down and rebuild it in three days, he replaces temple worship with his own body as the form of God's people. The form of the people of God is no longer tied to place. Jesus' body is the house of God. But this house is unlike any other house. As Lohfink puts it: "Here appeared with full clarity what the people of God is: a network of communities spread over the whole earth and yet existing within non-Christian society, so that each person can freely choose whether to be a Christian or not; it is genuine community and yet not constructed on the model of pagan society, a true homeland and yet not a state."[6]

Kant bequeathed to theology the uniqueness of Jesus as someone who rose above his history and revealed a freedom to live according to a universal moral law. Kant's Jesus did not need the church except as an institution transitional to a universal state that would secure individual freedom. But the careful biblical scholarship of Lohfink shows how this reading of Jesus is nothing but a philosophical anachronism. Jesus does not rise above his history; he completes it. In living within the history of the synagogal form, maintaining the distinctiveness of this form within the context of eschatological hope, Jesus forms the church. The church is not a historical accident but "goes back to the actions of Jesus himself."[7] Christians can only view the gathering of the Twelve as the apostolic foundation of a restored community that—like the synagogal form— also mediates to us God's salvation.

Jesus' mission makes no sense separate from the restoration of Israel in the twelve apostles. Their life together is to embody the new community that Jesus envisions. Of course, this new community is not limited to the twelve apostles; there are other disciples who leave everything and follow Jesus. But followers who remain in their communities and support the mission of the Twelve also characterize the new community. Their homes and livelihood provided the means out of which Jesus' mission occurred. In fact, the preaching of the Twelve would not have been possible without other followers, particularly women who "provided for them out of their means" (Luke 8:3). Luke Timothy Johnson notes that this image of the Twelve surrounded by people who share their possessions for the sake of the mission gives us a glimpse of a "picture that foreshadows that of the Galilean community of believers in Acts 1:13–14 and 2:41–47."[8] This image also resonates with the central image that characterizes the people of God—the form of the Twelve with Jesus gathered around the table. As Lohfink notes, "The table around which Jesus gathered with his disciples now became the definitive center of Israel."[9] The Torah remains, but for Christians the table takes precedence over the temple. The cleansing of the temple is the sign by which Jesus inaugurates the form of the eschatological community that will eventually be called church. It is an eschatological gesture with political implications, implications that lead to Jesus' death as a political agitator.

To view Jesus as the restorer of eschatological Israel helps us make better sense of his death. God does not seek Jesus' death because God will not be satisfied without someone's blood. Jesus' death does not reveal to us the nature of a bloodthirsty God. Instead, it reveals to us the fallenness of our own political systems, which are not elect but created through our own will and thus always preserved by requiring sacrifices that allow us to live out the self-deception that our will alone creates social and political formations. As Lohfink explains,

> God's plan is not that Jesus should die. How could God will the death of Jesus? What God wills is the new society, the eschatological Israel. But because Jesus remains true to this divine plan he will die, because people do not will what God wills. Jesus' death on the cross was unavoidable.[10]

Jesus' sacrifice on the cross is not a valorization of sacrifice for its own sake but an "end to sacrifice."[11] It shows us that the sacrifices upon which our politics rely are a sign of fallenness, not divine ordination. Jesus puts an end to the need for such sacrifices by creating the *other city*, the city gathered around the table marked by an "excess of superfluity," not by scarcity. This city has no limited territory it protects against potential invaders. This city refuses to consider others as competitors for scarce resources who threaten our livelihood. This community bears witness to the reality that there is enough for all. In fact, the early apostolic communities are characterized by a *koinonia* in which they share their goods in common to such an extent that no one among them remains "needy."

FAILURE OF THE CHURCH

But even within these early apostolic communities, God's reign is not completely fulfilled. Luke reminds us that some members of these new communities claimed to share their possessions but in fact kept some back. Such is the story of Ananias and Sapphira (Acts 5:1–11), whose sin leads to Peter's judgment upon them, "You have not lied to men but to God." They claimed to be members of the restored community and said they had contributed everything when they had not. In so doing, they brought judgment upon themselves and died. Nowhere in this story does Peter suggest that any form of capital punishment be exercised against Ananias and Sapphira; he never employs violence. That they fall down and expire reveals the "double intentionality" involved in Peter's apostolic administration of this new community. To realize that one has lied to Peter would not cause death, but to discover that one has lied and rebelled against God is to bring death upon oneself. Both Ananias and Sapphira are "carried . . . out," put outside the community. Then we are told, "great fear came upon the whole church."

This is the first time the word *ecclesia* is used in Luke-Acts.[12] The *church* is named in Luke-Acts from the *fear* that comes over it when it realizes what is at stake in responding to the apostolic preaching in order to form the community of faith. The apostles are given a central role in this new community. In fact, the proceeds from the sale of the possessions that are to be shared are laid at their feet, and they are also depicted as exercising a leadership within the community that is the embodiment of God's own discernment. The Twelve who carry on the mission of Jesus are not only given power to exercise their own judgment, but under their judgment God's judgment is also exercised. This is not surprising, because Jesus himself instituted this alternative form of nonviolent discipline when he told the apostles that "the keys of the kingdom of heaven" were given to them and that whatever they bound on earth would be bound in heaven and that whatever they loosed on earth would be loosed in heaven (Matt. 16:19–20). He gave them explicit instructions regarding how this discipline was to be carried out (Matt. 18:15–20). These instructions refused to countenance a violent repulsion of offenders. Instead, one member is first to go to another and confront him or her in private. If that one refuses to listen, then a few others are to be called as witnesses. If no resolution is yet found, then they are to "tell it to the church." If the offender refuses to listen to the entire church, then such a person is to "be to you as a Gentile and a tax collector." This, of course, suggests that the offender is outside the church, but not necessarily permanently. Such a one needs to hear the gospel again. Thus the very discipline instituted by Jesus implies something such as the order of penitents that was developed within the church's tradition.

That Jesus instituted a discipline to discern offenses within this new community is itself intriguing. If his mission was to bear witness to an apocalyptic reality that would break into history solely by God's sovereign deeds, why give instructions for church discipline? That Jesus was an eschatological preacher is undoubtedly true, but that he preached an otherworldly apocalypticism is questionable. That his eschatological teachings ruled out ethics, as Albert Schweitzer suggested, does not make sense of the biblical witness. Schweitzer asserted, "There is for Jesus no ethic of the Kingdom of God, for in the Kingdom of God all natural relationships, even for example the distinction of sex are abolished. Temptation and sin no longer exist."[13] Although Schweitzer can be credited with recovering the eschatological element in Jesus' preaching, the form of that recovery loses the importance of the creation of the Twelve for Jesus' ministry. As with the rest of the nineteenth-century questers for the historical Jesus, Jesus' relation to the creation of this new community played little role in Schweitzer's work. Thus he missed the heart of Jesus' mission and was forced to do what Neo-Protestant theology always does: adopt an ethic from one's own culture and accommodate Jesus to it.[14] In so doing, Jesus' ethic is lost, because it is always related to the apostolic founding of the new community. Because Neo-Protestants can only view the establishment of the church as a fall from Jesus' message, they cannot make sense of his ethics.

To make sense of Jesus' ethic, we must address the question, Why was this discipline necessary within the apostolic community? If Jesus' proclamation of God's reign utterly abolishes all *natural* relationships for an otherworldly apocalypticism, then there is no reason for the church to discipline offenders. All biblical texts that present such a need for discipline will be rendered later accretions. This judgment is not a historical judgment as to the authenticity of these texts but a theological judgment about who Jesus should be, which is then read back into the biblical witness. But if we do not begin by assuming a theological disjunction between Jesus and the community he founds, then Jesus' mission presents us with an *ethics* inextricably connected to the *ecclesia*.

Richard Hays's work has demonstrated this well. He finds the image of "new creation" to be a critical focus through which the New Testament should be read. Such a focus does not separate Jesus from the church nor pit Paul against Jesus. Instead, it helps us recognize why Jesus would both proclaim the inbreaking of God's kingdom and provide the church with a means of disciplining those who are members of the new creation. Hays writes,

> In Christ, we know that the powers of the old age are doomed, and the new creation is already appearing. Yet at the same time, all attempts to assert the unqualified presence of the kingdom of God stand under judgment of the eschatological reservation: not before the time, not yet. Thus, the New Testament's eschatology creates a critical framework that pronounces judgment upon our complacency as well as upon our presumptuous despair. As often as we eat the bread and drink the cup, we proclaim the Lord's death . . . until he comes. Within that anomalous hope-filled interval, all the New Testament writers work out their understandings of God's will for the community.[15]

Not only do the New Testament writers work out their understanding of God's will and reasons for the community within that anomalous hope-filled interval, but every Christian disciple does so as well. And that is what constitutes Christian ethics. Ethics is always subordinated to theology, for it requires us to discern what the church is to be and do as we constantly seek to live into our baptisms through the practices of repentance that lead us into the celebration of the Eucharist.

The church, like the elect people of God, takes different forms in history—some of those forms have been less faithful than others to Jesus' vision. Like the "people of God as a nation," the church has too often brought *throne* and *altar* together and forced people to associate with the community by virtue of race, nation, or geography. In so doing, the church violates the heart of baptism as an *exodus* event. The waters through which Israel passed on its exodus out of Egypt marked a change in rulers. Baptism, a participation in those same waters, is also a "change of rulers."[16] But for it to be a true change, one must express a willingness to take the journey. Unlike national, geographical, cultural, or racial identities that come with rulers to be served, Christ as ruler of the church refuses such coerced forms of citizenship.

THE SCANDAL OF DISUNITY AS A MARK OF THE CHURCH

Nearly all churches recognize the four marks of the church as unity, holiness, catholicity, and apostolicity. This recognition has an ancient lineage dating back to the fourth century and the creed established by ecumenical councils. But precisely how the church maintains continuity with the apostolic witness is itself a source of division among the Christian churches. Roman Catholics and Anglicans find the continuity in the historical apostolic succession mediated through the episcopacy, though only the former privileges the bishop of Rome as the successor to Peter. The Orthodox churches, and to some extent the Reformed churches and Anabaptists, find apostolic continuity not in historical succession but in an eschatological presentation of communion with the apostles through the "convocation of the Church in one place."[17] The Protestant emphasis on Holy Scripture and preaching is likewise a claim for apostolicity. The unmediated witness of the apostles is best mediated to the church not through a historical passing on (tradition) but through the direct hearing of the Scripture in the church.

These different interpretations of apostolicity challenge the church's unity. Many Christians today are unable to recognize the dire threat these divisions produce to the church's mission and witness, a threat akin to that presented by Ananias and Sapphira. Some argue that the diverse churches are simply part of the necessary pluralism of human creation. People need different kinds of worship communities to express their different personality types. Others argue that the church is not that significant for Christian salvation. What matters is the individual's heart, one's "personal relationship" with Jesus, and not which church she belongs to or whether she belongs to a church at all. Unfortunately, many well-intentioned Christians think the church can only be the enemy of the Christian life, something to be avoided because of its hypocrisy. Still others argue that the different churches are epiphenomenal on a more basic and common core religious experience, that is, churches are a human construction that tries, though always inadequately, to give expression to some underlying ineffable experience of divine acceptance. The lack of church unity poses no threat to these understandings of Christian redemption, but such arguments always privilege the individual over the church and are merely the outgrowth of modern societal formations in which people falsely assume that they are individuals separate from social and communal formations. Privileging the individual over the church is always at the same time subordinating the church to the modern nation-state. Believing ourselves to be individuals, we become incapable of recognizing the social formations to which we pledge obedience.

A vivid example of this modern phenomenon can be found in the Monty Python movie, *The Life of Brian*. In that movie the wise men get it wrong. Rather than finding their way to the manger where the incarnate Savior is born, they mistakenly appear at the place where Brian is born. But Brian is no Savior and seeks no followers. Mistake piles upon mistake as throngs of people start to follow Brian. He tries to avoid the crowds, but his opportunistic mother forces him to address his followers. Brian speaks to them and says, "You do not need to follow anybody; you are all individuals." The crowd responds in unison, "We are all individuals." One lone voice retorts, "I'm not," but he is quickly silenced by one of the *individuals* who says, "Hush up, you." Whatever may have been intended by this delightful scene, it nicely depicts the illusory assumption that we can be individuals who are obedient to nothing except a law we give ourselves. The question is not *if* we serve some social formation but *which ones* we serve.

If we recognize that Jesus' fundamental message pertains to the social formation God's people should take, then the question of the unity of the church cannot be avoided. To assume that we can exist as individual Christians without participating in a church marked by unity, apostolicity, catholicity, and holiness is to forego one social formation (an ecclesial one) for another (a thoroughly modern one). Without our participation in the right ordering of social formations, our desires cannot be rightly ordered.

THE RIGHT ORDERING OF SOCIAL FORMATIONS AND THE CHURCH'S NONNECESSITY

The very possibility of church assumes a right ordering of social relations where the central social formation that gives our desires their direction is not the nation-state (*polis*), the market (*agora*), or the familial household (*oikos*) but the church. No individual can exist separate from all these social formations; to a certain extent each requires obedience from us. We are all birthed and sustained by households. We all need the daily exchanges and the orderly activities the *agora* and *polis* make possible.[18] But the church is unique in its nonnecessity, since it is founded not on justice, coercion, violence, or consanguinity but on the gift of charity. The church's nonnecessity is finally most necessary for a good, beautiful, and truthful life.

The church orders our desires according to the gift of charity. It is a nonviolent, nomadic community produced through liturgical performance that should neither bear nor rely upon violence for its possibility. Because it has this *structure*, we should not be surprised that it is often divided against itself. It cannot use force to sustain *spatial* borders that do not exist (though it has often been tempted to do so and succumbed), but this does not legitimate the ecclesial divisions present in the church. It is to suggest that working through those divisions without killing one another is itself a necessary task of being *church*. The discipline it exercises over its members is neither to jail nor kill them but to let them know they have put themselves outside its nonspatial borders. Thus, its discipline at its harshest should be to deny certain persons access to communion. Yet even this is done primarily for the sake of bearing witness to such persons in order that they can be reconciled back to the church.

Because the church is the body of Christ, we participate in the life of God through it. The church has only one head, Jesus Christ. His life, death, and resurrection make possible this community, which continues to make his flesh present in the world. Through the singularity of our baptism we take on his life, and his holiness becomes ours. Through the repetition of the Eucharist we constantly live into that baptism with the purpose of having his life fully formed in us. In baptism we claim that creation is restored and set right according to God's eternal purposes. The repetition of the Eucharist bears witness to that eschatological reality, finding it already present. Because it is already present, it illumines all the ways in which it is not yet here. This makes possible the Christian moral life as a life of repentance where we ceaselessly live into our baptisms through "practicing forgiveness."[19] Only this politics of forgiveness orders our desires to their true end.

Desires are necessary for everyday living. If we do not desire to eat, converse, sleep, wake up, work, or laugh, something is amiss. Without the appropriate desires we cannot achieve our natural ends, nor can we achieve our supernatural ends. However, desire in and of itself is nonexistent. It has no life of its own. Desire is always already connected to some object. It always has a direction toward something, which is either beneficial or harmful to the moral life.

In explaining how our will is moved for our justification, Aquinas described a movement from sin to righteousness. Drawing upon Augustine, he explained it as "a withdrawal or an approach in the motion of the free will according to loathing or desiring."[20] The movement of the moral life is a *recessus* (withdrawal) and an *accessus* (passage or approach) by the free will, which requires both a detestation of our sins and the cultivation of a new desire. The moral life consists in learning to desire what should be desired and despising what should be despised. For Aquinas, this is the reason penance is central to the moral life. We must remember those sins that have bound us in the past so that we can rightly despise them. Forgetfulness is dangerous.

OBEDIENCE AS RIGHT DESIRE, THE SUPERNATURAL VIRTUES

The right order of desire is obedience. For good reasons, obedience is not popular. To obey another is often presented as giving one's will over to another in order to do his, her, or their will instead of one's own. Thus obedience is understood to be coercive, even violent. When the law is undergirded solely by the means of violence, then obedience is forced. In the modern era, law becomes unreasonable because it is primarily invoked for the restraint of will. Law and freedom are set in opposition, not only in theory but also in practice. Contrasting this understanding of law and obedience with that of Thomas Aquinas can help us recognize what we have lost. As Herbert McCabe puts it, given the contemporary dis-ease about the language of law and obedience,

> it comes as a surprise to find St. Thomas Aquinas saying that *imperium*, the act of commanding or ordering is not an act of the will but of the intelligence (though of course it presupposes the will). It is the act of one who understands what is to be done. You must have heard a thousand times that *obedire* [to obey] comes from *ob-audire*, to listen. Even the English phrase, "doing what you are told" conveys, if you think of it, the same notion. To obey is first of all to learn something, to share in another's practical wisdom, *Prudentia* (or Providence).[21]

Understood in this way, obedience can never be "blind," nor can the act of commanding be located in a person's craftiness to get what he or she wants or have the bureaucratic savvy "to always get to yes" or create a "win-win" situation. These modern management techniques are symptoms of the manipulation of the will that occurs when law becomes arbitrary. It then has no purpose but to coerce the other to do my bidding, yet it must exercise that coercion indirectly, making others think they are simply doing what they want. For Aquinas, obedience was not manipulation; it was a function of giving a compelling and beautiful narration of the truth, because for true obedience, there must also be truth-telling.

Once obedience is viewed as a function of a compelling and beautiful narration of the truth, it becomes an aesthetic phenomenon. We become obedient to those beautiful forms that shape our lives. The beautiful, like the good, is obviously present to us; we are moved by it. We cannot do without it, but any philosophical or scientific description of it fails. The beautiful cannot be mastered. That beauty *is* is self-evident; what it is or how we define it is not. Medieval theologians had a way of explaining this phenomenon. Beauty, like truth and goodness, points in itself beyond itself to something that transcends its form, but only through that form. Because of the incarnation, Christian theology can easily make sense of beauty as such a transcendental predicate of something greater than itself. Francesca Murphy develops the theological significance of beauty as such a transcendental.[22] It allows for the singular "fact" that God is found in flesh without losing either the recognition that God is an infinite radiance incapable of being contained or that the flesh, the singular manifestation of a form, matters. In this flesh a form is represented that leads us to see an *object* so beautiful that all other objects receive their beauty from that form. The result is a reordering of desire that finds rest and peace. Far from being coercive, true obedience results in a harmony of reason and desire.

Reordered desire, arising from the vision of Christ as the form of beauty, produces in us the supernatural virtues. Such a production is the work of the Holy Spirit, which is why such virtues are said to be *infused*. In fact, the necessity of the supernatural virtues for human creatures to achieve their true end— friendship with God—and the Spirit's role in infusing these virtues offers the strongest case for the Spirit's *consubstantiality* with the Father and the Son. Yves Congar summarized the church fathers' defense of the Spirit's divinity based on the role the Spirit plays in drawing us into the divine life. As he put it, "If the Spirit is not God in substance, we cannot be truly deified."[23] The Spirit of the Lord is constantly invoked to achieve what we cannot achieve on our own. Only if the Spirit is consubstantial with divinity can it accomplish what our prayers request. The simplest call to prayer embodies this necessary *epiclesis,* for the pastor prays, "The Lord be with you," and the people respond, "And with thy spirit." Even before prayer itself is uttered, a prayer that the Spirit will be present to make our prayer possible is uttered. The fullness of the Spirit makes possible something more than what any immanent human power alone could accomplish. As the Spirit does with prayer, so it does by infusing virtues; the Spirit brings an abundant plenitude to our actions. Thus, the supernatural virtues know no deficiency. They are not a reaction against anything but a singular orientation toward the good, which is God. The good cannot be well spoken of without also speaking of the Holy Spirit.

The supernatural virtues are charity, faith, and hope. Faith is primarily an intellectual virtue. It is not the "courage to be" or affirming one's existence against its threatening dissolution. Instead, faith should be recognized as a virtue of the intellect where we see God's beauty in Christ and recognize it as truth. Faith is an intellectual virtue because it directs our intellect to certain truths. But faith is not an intellectual virtue alone. It is also related to the practical virtues of hope and charity. Hope is the virtue that draws us into God's own life with such joy and delight that we are free from despair or presumption, vices that embrace nothingness and death. Charity is "the perfect love of God for God's sake, which involves the love of others for God's sake."[24] It is a participation in God's love. Although these supernatural virtues know no deficiency, the right order of desire can easily be upset. Such inordinate desire can lead us to turn from God and worship something less than God. Any Christian ethic that seeks to make sense of virtues, laws, and the practice of repentance must be capable of recognizing the dangers inherent in disordered desires.

DEADLY VICES

We can either want inappropriate things or want appropriate things with the wrong intensity. The traditional list of the seven deadly vices helps us name such inordinate desiring. Pride is "the inordinate appetite for one's excellence."[25] Virtue itself is an excellence, so overcoming pride is not found in striving for mediocrity. The key term here, as in all the seven deadly vices, is *inordinate appetite*. Pride despises the good that comes to one's neighbors, friends, and enemies because the prideful person fears that the good given to them will detract from his or her own excellence. The prideful person lives from a sense of scarcity and operates out of a sense of entitlement. He fears that if the good comes to others there will no longer be sufficient good for him. He wants it all.

Pride has a distant cousin in covetousness, "the inordinate love of temporal things." Like the prideful person, the covetous person fears loss, though here the loss is not one of status but one of temporal goods. He is so led by this fear that he lives a life of deceit, doing everything possible to ensure his own security against that of his neighbors.

Related to covetousness is lust, "the inordinate appetite for sexual pleasure." It should not be equated with sexual desire itself. Lust is a vice that leads one to dominate, consume, and destroy another for one's own gratification. Such a disordered desire keeps one from the true things of God, from the peaceful desire of prayer and worship.

Gluttony (and drunkenness) is "inordinate indulgence in food or drink." It is the desire to eat all the time and never know satisfaction. To lack all desire to eat is likewise disordered. Either gluttony as excess or the sloth that lacks sufficient desire is deadly precisely because, like lust and the other deadly vices, it keeps one from performing his or her proper role in the community of faith.

Anger is "the inordinate inclination to take revenge." To desire the death of our enemies is the vice of anger that always leads to vengeance. To lack all desire to stand up against injustice is cowardice, which is no virtue, but to be angered to such an extent that one seeks the death of one's enemies is a sin against charity.

Envy, the "willful sadness on account of the good of another, whether temporal or spiritual, regarded as diminishing one's own good," bears a striking resemblance to pride and covetousness. This works against charity because it implicitly wills evil for one's neighbors, friends, and enemies. It inevitably leads to hatred because of the *ressentiment* one experiences for the good that God shows to all God's creatures.

Sloth is that "cultured despair" all too common to modern people, an "oppressive sorrow" that causes one to despair and to refuse to live a virtuous life because it does not seem to make a difference. It is that inactivity that arises in a person's life because she is convinced that all others are hypocrites lacking in righteousness.

These vices are deadly because they lead to an embrace of death. In fact, they are neither only *personal* nor *social* but both at the same time. These vices destroy communities, but they are also related to the formation of particular forms of community that dominate our lives. Lack, fear of insufficiency, and scarcity are often heralded by some as being able to construct desires that assist in efficient economic exchanges. These vices are recognized as constitutive of community. Both vices and virtues are only possible because of social formations, and both perpetuate social formations. But communities based on vice will always embrace death as the true answer to life, for the deadly vices all work from that sense of scarcity that death falsely bears witness to as our final reality.

Even virtues can be understood in a dialectical relationship to the vices, such that virtues require vices for their own exercise. When that occurs, vices define the moral life just as much as do virtues. But the virtues are not *necessarily* related to vices, which are simply the insufficient actualization of a virtue. Thus, they are not a thing against which one should react. Instead, they are the lack of God's goodness found in faith, hope, and charity. Insofar as one's life begins to embody these deadly sins, one's life is reduced to nothingness. The remedy for such nothingness is not to struggle against these vices, for the damnable force of vice is that the more we focus on overcoming it, the more it captures our imagination and binds us to it. Rather than a struggle against vice, the focus of the Christian life is to have one's life reordered toward God's gifts of faith, hope, and charity. The practice of repentance is the means by which our lives are reordered.

GIFTS AND BEATITUDES

Along with the theological virtues of faith, hope, and charity and the warning to guard against the seven deadly sins, the Christian moral life also entails receiving the gifts and beatitudes Jesus gave us in the Sermon on the Mount. That the moral life is found in gifts and beatitudes has a long history within Christian tradition from Augustine through Aquinas and reaching even to a post-Reformation theologian like John Wesley. It was Thomas Aquinas, however, who had to explain the role of these gifts and beatitudes in light of their oddness within an Aristotelian framework.

Like Aristotle, Aquinas stated, "Everything someone desires, he desires for an ultimate end." This is because all desire falls under the character of the good and the ultimate end moves the appetite toward itself (Ia IIae Q. 1, art. 6). This is not to say that all our actions are good. Of course they are not. But our will desires under the character of the good even if those goods are apparent rather than real. The good here signifies, as Ralph McInerny notes, "something like perfective of or fulfilling of the agent."[26] This naturally leads to virtue because it is a power to make actual a potential intrinsic to human nature. It is at this point that virtue theory can mislead the theologian, for it can too easily suggest that the goal of the Christian life is to acquire virtue by cultivating a power intrinsic to human nature. Theological works on the virtues that can rest content with explicating the four cardinal virtues and their subvirtues with only passing reference to the theological virtues miss the heart of Aquinas's moral theology. Such works fail not only to realize how central the theological virtues are for human action, but they also lead to a failure to take note of the other elements of human action that are central to a Thomistic account of the Christian moral life. These elements are the theological virtues, the gifts, beatitudes, and fruits of the Spirit. Aristotle had no need for such elements. He and Aquinas did not share a similar ultimate end and, without such an end, there can be little commonalty in the development of human action—which does not deny that there is nevertheless some commonalty in their development of human action.

For Thomas Aquinas, our ultimate end is beatitude based on the vision of God. This is a moral and theological claim. As with Aristotle, Aquinas rejected the idea that happiness or blessedness is to be found in wealth, honor, glory, power, pleasure, or in any bodily good. Unlike Aristotle, Aquinas found happiness in a beatitude that is a vision of the essence of God. Beatitude for the human creature "is something created existing in him" and thus it is an "activity" (*operatio*) because "insofar as something is perfect it is actual; for potential without actuality is imperfect." But only God is *"beatitudinem per essen-*

tiam" because God's being is itself God's work" (Ia IIae q. 3 art. 2 resp.). Our beatitude is a participation in God's own life, for our nature is not *"beatitudinem per essentiam."*

That our beatitude is found in God who alone is blessedness in his essence means that Aquinas must incorporate theological virtues, gifts, beatitudes, and the fruits of the Spirit in a way that could not have occurred to Aristotle. We see these elements incorporated in the important shift that occurs in question 62 of the *prima secundae* from a discourse on moral virtues to one that concerns theological virtues. In question 62, Aquinas begins to explain why the natural virtues are insufficient for the moral life. He then explains the reason for theological virtues, as well as the need for gifts, beatitudes, and fruits of the Spirit. But an obvious objection to the possibility of any theological virtue arises.

Aquinas has already explained, following Aristotle, that "virtue is the disposition of a perfect thing to which is best." Such a perfective disposition assumes that virtue perfects something's intrinsic nature. Theological virtues, however, are divine and this is above human nature. Therefore, how can theological virtues be attributed to human nature? They cannot. Yet because friendship with God constitutes human happiness, and virtue directs us toward happiness, human creatures cannot be truly blessed without the theological virtues. We need theological virtues that perfect a nature that is not our nature. If it were not for Scripture, Aquinas could not find an answer to our dilemma. He finds it on the basis of 2 Peter 1:4. It states, "Thus God has given us, though these things, his precious and very great promises, so that through them you may escape from the corruption that is in the world because of lust, and may become participants of the divine nature." Because virtue perfects a nature, theological virtue is only possible if we participate in the divine nature. It is not that the divine nature needs perfection; of course it does not. But "by Christ," according to Aquinas, human nature can participate in the divine nature and be perfected. Human nature cannot be attributed with the divine nature essentially, but it can through participation, and because of this participation in the divine nature, theological virtues are possible.

Participation in the life of God is the determining theological consideration for reflection on the moral life. To participate in the divine nature is to participate in beatitude, and this is the ultimate end of human action. But if participation in this beatitude is our ultimate end, it cannot be an achievement on the basis of natural virtue alone. This argument initiated in question 62 was anticipated in the very beginning of the *prima secundae*. It helps us read Aquinas's use of Aristotle christologically.

This move also produces problems for moral action that could never have arisen for Aristotle. Like Aristotle, Aquinas suggested that the beatitude we seek consists of an *"operatio intellectus speculativi"* (activity of the speculative intellect). This is because the contemplative life is that which is highest in the human creature, for it is done for its own sake whereas the practical or active life is done for the sake of something else. This is an important point because Aquinas does not argue that a passive contemplation is preferable to an active life of justice. His argument is that the *operatio* involved in contemplation is an end in itself and thus is more encompassing of lesser ends such as the ends involved in the political pursuit of justice. But unlike Aristotle, this creates a problem for Aquinas because "the contemplation of the speculative sciences is not able to extend beyond as the cognition of the sense is able to lead." So he states, "Hence it is necessary that the ultimate perfection of the human creature occurs throughout the cognition of some thing which is beyond the human intellect," and this cannot be obtained through our senses alone.[27] Then we are told that ultimate and perfect beatitude exists in nothing less than the vision of the divine essence.[28] Here the difficulty in being ordered toward our ultimate good is exacerbated because the ability to see God is not naturally given. How then can we speak properly of virtue as the actualization of a natural potential to achieve its end? One way Aquinas answers this is with his distinction between imperfect beatitude, which is found in this life and requires a body and a society of friends; and perfect beatitude, which is not found in this life and doesn't require a body or a society of friends. But the more profound way he answers this difficulty is through the theological virtues.

Beginning with his articulation of Aristotle's teleological account of the moral life, and with the end as given in the revelation of Christ, Aquinas was logically led to insist on the theological virtues as a way to save Aristotle in light of Christ. He did then argue in a rather convoluted way that there can be acquired virtues separate from the infused virtues, but the acquired virtues are not virtues "simpliciter." Rather, they are "virtues in a restricted sense." He maintains the separation between the acquired and infused virtues not as a way of protecting the natural against incursion from the supernatural, but to point out the limitations to the natural virtues. "It is therefore clear from what has been said that only the infused virtues are perfect, and deserve to be called virtues simply: since they direct man well to the ultimate end. But the other virtues, those, namely, that are acquired are virtues in a restricted sense, but not simply, for they direct man well in respect of the last end in some particular genus of action, but not in respect of the last end simply."[29]

The infused virtues are similar to the gifts, and the beatitudes are assigned to the gifts. Aquinas distinguishes between the gifts and the virtues in the following manner:

> There are three kinds of virtues: for some are theological, some intellectual, and some moral. The theological virtues are those whereby man's mind is united to God; the intellectual virtues are those whereby reason itself is perfected; and the moral virtues are those which perfect the power of appetite in obedience to the reason. On the other hand the gifts of the Holy Spirit dispose all the powers of the soul to be amenable to the divine motion. Accordingly the gifts seem to be

compared to the theological virtues, by which man is united to the Holy Spirit, his Mover, in the same way as the moral virtues are compared to the intellectual virtues, which perfect the reason, the moving principle of the moral virtues.[30]

For Aquinas, the beatitudes differ from the gifts not "as habit from habit" but "as act from habit." The gifts, like the infused virtues, lead us to our true end because we get caught up into God's own life. As Aquinas puts it, "the Holy Spirit" perfects us "with His gifts that we may obey and follow Him." The beatitudes are not habits other than the gifts, but they are the actualization of the gift in the believer ordering her desires toward beatitude, our true happiness. For instance, when the gift of humility (or fear) is actualized in the believer, the result will be the *blessedness of poverty of spirit.* In other words, the beatitude—poverty of spirit—is no longer a struggle to master a chaotic pride. Instead, it is the logical result of a gift that comes from being caught up in the movement of the Holy Spirit. The beatitude brings joy, not struggle. The interplay between the theological virtues, gifts, and beatitudes is the "performance" in the believer of the Holy Spirit's movement. The believer is caught up in the life of the Trinity and finds his or her nature harmoniously satisfied. Fear or humility arises out of the appropriate reverence that recognizes the moral life is not a result of our own essential nature, but of our participation in something beyond us in which we find ourselves "caught up."

Augustine, Thomas Aquinas, and John Wesley all envisioned the moral life as a moving interplay between beatitudes, gifts, and virtues (Wesley called them holy tempers). Precisely because this interplay reflects the movement within the divine life itself, the relationship between the beatitudes, gifts, and virtues cannot be spelled out neatly in a logical system where every beatitude can be construed as the actualization of one gift correlated to a single virtue. If moral theology were capable of creating such a complete and tidy system, it would obviously not reflect the movement of the infinite and inexhaustible God. Nevertheless, we can see how these theologians related the beatitudes, gifts, and virtues with a remarkable similarity.

Augustine, Aquinas, and John Wesley correlated the seven gifts from Isaiah 11 with the eight beatitudes from the Sermon on the Mount, though the correlation is not always as direct with Aquinas and Wesley. Still, they all found the beatitudes to be related to the gifts. The gifts in Isaiah are fear, piety, knowledge, fortitude, counsel, understanding, and wisdom. The eight beatitudes are poverty of spirit, meekness, mourning, righteousness, mercifulness, purity of heart, peaceableness, and persecution for righteousness' sake. The eighth beatitude is viewed as the culmination of all the gifts and beatitudes.[31] These beatitudes are the activity of the gifts in the believer, which are infused by the Holy Spirit. The result is that our life will be rightly ordered and we will be happy.

The beatitude of *meekness* stems from the gift of a true piety where a love-informed knowledge is not capable of allowing one's baser passions, such as vengeance, to rule one's actions. Instead, this true piety prompts an ordered response to such passions. The beatitude of meekness and the gift of piety correlate well with the virtue of temperance. The beatitude of *mourning* is the actualization of the gift of what could best be called a joyful sorrow that arises from the knowledge of the loss of those things that can only produce a false happiness.

While *mourning* is a joyful sorrow over the loss of inordinate appetites, *righteousness* is the proper distribution of ordinate appetites. It renders to each what is her or his due. It is the matter of the active life and is associated with the virtue of justice. Because it distributes ordinate desires, it is itself a gift of "ardent desire." Yet, as John Wesley noted, this righteousness can never be truly satisfied if it remains content only with regulating one's relations with one's neighbors. To achieve its full potential, it must also find "fellowship with the Father and the Son."[32] An ordinate appetite is discovered in the desire for participation in the divine life.

The *merciful* find blessedness because of the wise counsel mercy entails. This is an interesting correlation, for it assumes that mercy is not simply some irrational act of forgiveness; mercy is thoroughly reasonable. Mercy arises from a practical wisdom that recognizes that mercy, liberality, forgiveness, and forbearance are not the exceptions but the norms in human exchanges, for we are created in the image of God and God is merciful. The very act of our creation occurs only through the mercy another shows to us in birthing us. To deny the beatitude of mercy is to fail to recognize the practical wisdom that makes our lives possible in the first place.

Purity of heart is the blessedness that makes possible the vision of God. Therefore, it arises from contemplation and understanding, but it does not do so at the expense of the active life. In fact, purity of heart is generated out of understanding that all things reflect the goodness of God. To see all things in God with a simplicity and unitary vision is to be blessed with purity of heart.

The gift of wisdom generates the beatitude of *peaceableness*. This is a blessing that comes from the active life with its quest for justice and righteousness. The end of the active life is not the accumulation of power but the harmony and order that abhors and refuses to participate in strife. Peace finds no joy in the violence and conflict that all too often characterize the active, political life. Of course, such a beatitude can easily make one prey to *persecution*. The actualization entailed in being caught up in the movement of all the gifts of the Holy Spirit can lead to the culminating beatitude: persecution for righteousness' sake. This is not something one should seek; that would be masochistic and a counsel of despair, not a beatitude or gift. But the joy found in the movement of the Spirit is so profound that true blessedness knows no *ressentiment*. It does not seek vengeance, not because it is weak and ineffectual, but because the overwhelming joy itself is satisfying.

THE SOCIAL FORMATION OF GIFTS

The moral life requires, then, the right ordering of desire. A right ordering of desire is not a matter of reason alone but a matter of a faith-informed reason that requires our participation in certain social formations. Desires rightly ordered require appropriate positioning within social formations. This is a positioning we are to cooperate in; we even help *construct* it. But we cannot construct it by ourselves. Only our participation in something that is more than our actions alone frees us to *construct* such social formations. Like the gifts and beatitudes, our participation in social formations comes not from our own secure self-possessions but from God's gifts.

The right ordering of desires requires a hierarchy of social institutions that recognizes the preeminent role of the church. This is necessary because only the church bears the divine law that directs us toward our supernatural end. Without such an ordering, our natural ends cannot themselves be maintained within their appropriate limits. If the market becomes more central to our lives than the church, then our desires can only be disordered and unsatisfying, since the market produces in us what Leo Tolstoy once described as "the gnawing agony of desire."

If the nation-state becomes more central than the church, our lives will also be disordered. The state can serve only limited "natural" goods; it knows nothing of those supernatural virtues that direct our desires to their appropriate end. This is not to suggest that a realm of politics based on "pure nature" exists. Quite the contrary: the state must be divinely ordered, which means that the state must never be allowed to be self-interpreting. The church must constantly subject it to critique to remind it of its limits. Such a critique does not occur from some secure, transcendent realm where the definitive account of the relationship between the church and the state can be given. Instead, it occurs within the nomadic community that the church is.

This does not in any sense entail a theocracy, only that the justice and power of the state cannot be exercised based on the interests of the state alone. Otherwise, it will be disordered (as it inevitably seems to be). A disordered state is characterized by reliance on the military, police, and judicial systems to secure its borders both internally and externally. The state (or revolutionary parties who seek to create a new state) will use violence "by any means necessary" to achieve political ends. Warfare will become merely political, where *political* means the effort to compel someone to submit to a stronger will. The practitioners of warfare will shun theological limitations on their activities. Selective conscientious objection will not be tolerated because the war-making power of the state is forced on individuals despite the dictates of conscience. Policing will know no mercy, and capital punishment will become routine. For the church to *divinely order* the state is not for the church to rule or even legitimate the state. Instead, the *divine order* the church gives to the state is for the church to be the church and not look to the state for its intelligibility. The conditions that make the church possible are not the freedom the state secures through violent means but the freedom that comes through the cross and resurrection.

The family can also exceed its limits. This occurs when the modern category of race, based on an evolutionary scheme, becomes more determinative of one's identity than baptism. It also occurs when gender becomes the criterion by which faithful theology is measured. If parents find their future in their progeny rather than in Christ, the family exceeds its due limits as well.

Social formations must know their limits. They also must know their appropriate ends. The state cannot define marriage, and the church cannot mandate the use of violence. The church certainly has an obligation to discern and pronounce judgment on the justness of wars. The church has an obligation to call all Christians, not just the clergy, to live as befits a people who celebrate the Eucharist together. But the church does not bear the sword, nor should it ask its members to do so.

COMMANDING DESIRES

The right ordering of desires assumes a hierarchy of social institutions where each knows its appropriate ends. These appropriate ends, and the underlying social institutions that serve them, are best revealed to us in the moral wisdom shared by Jews and Christians known as the Ten Commandments. They are a political economy, that is, they contain regulations of social formations and human authority that order desires to their true, good, and beautiful ends.

Commandments are not ends in themselves but necessary rules that direct us to our appropriate ends. Commandments are signs that point us in a certain direction. They cannot be intelligible without the virtues, gifts, and beatitudes to which they point. The virtues, gifts, and beatitudes are the *substance* of the moral life, making possible our understanding of the commandments as they let us know why we must worship God, honor our elders, not cheat our neighbor, and so on. We cannot be oriented toward God's goodness without the commands, but the mere observance of them does not ensure that we will be appropriately directed. For instance, we can obey the command against adultery through sheer force of will without cultivating the virtue of fidelity. Simply refraining from adultery does not ensure that we achieve the good of marriage, although the good of marriage cannot be achieved without refraining from adultery.

The commandments assume both virtues and social institutions. For instance, the commandment against adultery assumes the social institution of marriage.[33] If no practice of faithful, monogamous marriage is present within a community, the command makes little sense. The command assumes a way of life that gives us a concrete, material presentation so that we can know what the commandment means. Without such concrete, material practices, commands would become mere regulative ideals that have little function in every-day life. What is true of the sixth commandment is likewise true of every commandment. Thus, we can order the commandments according to the social formations that render them intelligible.

The Ten Commandments give to us the *order of charity*. This order assumes a role for various social formations to direct us toward certain ends. Without these underlying social institutions, the commands will be reduced to the divine-command theory, where we obey them arbitrarily without recognizing their reasonableness in producing charity and justice. If no church, family, neighborhood, or market exists, the commandments make no sense. The commandments are signs of these underlying social institutions, and to participate well in those institutions requires that a person respect the appropriate order. The Ten Commandments assume the following social institutions:

COMMANDMENTS:	SOCIAL INSTITUTION:
1. I am the Lord your God; you shall not have strange gods before me.	church or synagogue
2. You shall not take the name of the Lord your God in vain.	church or synagogue
3. Remember to keep holy the Lord's Day.	church or synagogue
4. Honor your father and mother.	family
5. You shall not kill.	neighborhoods, the state and its "security" systems
6. You shall not commit adultery.	marriage
7. You shall not steal.	neighborhood, market, police
8. You shall not bear false witness against your neighbor.	neighborhood
9. You shall not covet your neighbor's wife or husband.	neighborhood, marriage
10. You shall not covet your neighbor's goods.	neighborhood, market

All ten commands do not produce the same virtues. The first three are necessary for the theological virtues of faith, hope, and charity. These virtues cannot be achieved through human effort alone, but the commands point us in a direction that opens us up to receive them from God. The commands do not ensure the reception of the theological virtues, but the virtues cannot be adequately received and cultivated without obeying the commands. Likewise, the commands cannot be adequately kept without the infusion of the theological virtues, which requires the centrality of the church. Neither the market, the state, nor the family can direct us toward the theological virtues, for they do not order our desires toward God. Because theological virtues are necessary for us to achieve our true humanity, a right social ordering cannot exist without the central role of the church.

Certain social practices, such as prayer, sacrifice, the performance of religious vows, and the duty of worship, are necessary for the reception and cultivation of theological virtues. Whenever the market, state, or family attempts to be the social context where these practices reside and these virtues are cultivated, the *order of charity* is disrupted. The result is an aberration in our politics, morality, and theology.

The church is the only social institution that can legitimately claim divine origin and substance, for it alone can be called "the body of Christ." Neither the family, a racial group, the neighborhood, the state, the military, nor the market can make such a claim. In a very real sense, only when the church claims its own proper due can these other institutions/formations know their limits. Without this, there can be no true justice, for there is no true charity.

To understand the role of other social formations within God's economy, we must first understand Israel, the church, and their common history. In fact, the ordering of desire in God's economy is a social ordering embodied in the law given to Moses, which prioritizes church (and synagogue) over all other social formations. This means that a good ordering of desire is not primarily to be discovered in the nature of things *qua* things. It cannot be generated out of utility or rights alone. Nor can it be discovered through a phenomenology of desire, love, law, need, being, and the like. A good social ordering of desire arises through the contingent movement of history, which also generates nature and the possibility of phenomenology. Although this good ordering of desire given in and through history is not primarily generated out of nature *qua* nature or a phenomenology of being, it does not conflict with nature or being. We discover what our being is after discovering a gift not contained within our nature. That gift is the law given by God to Moses. It properly orders our desires through the hierarchy of social formations it assumes. Without this law, our desires cannot be properly ordered.

THE FIRST THREE COMMANDMENTS: CHURCH LIFE

The early church theologian Tertullian understood the political implications of the first commandment. In *On Idolatry,* he suggested that idolatry is the fundamental form of sin. All other sins participate, at some level, with idolatry. This led him to produce a social ethic that brought the church into conversation with other social institutions. The question he posed was, How can we be the church and participate in these other social institutions? He gave us one of the most profound social ethics of all times, for no social institution was exempt from his careful analysis of its relationship to the church.

Tertullian carefully examined a number of social practices of his time to determine their compatibility with the central role of the church. He delineated what prevented Christians from the true ordering of desire, which is justice. The second and third commands teach us this justice, and, for Tertullian, we keep these commands by learning forms of disobedience to other social institutions' unwarranted claims on our lives. So, he argued, Christians cannot participate in any professions that make idols, even if they are doing it merely for the sake of gain and do not believe those idols are real (ch. 6). Likewise, they cannot traffic in the production and selling of idols. All trades are not unlawful to Christians, but those trades that assume idolatry, fornication, murder, covetousness, and mendacity are illegitimate. Each trade must be examined before Christians participate in it (ch. 11). If schoolmasters are required to recite and honor the gods of the nation, then this profession is ruled out (ch. 10). Likewise, military service is illegitimate because Christ has taken the sword away from Peter (ch. 19).

Tertullian's method should become the standard for Christian social ethics in our post-Christendom era. His social ethic had profound implications not only for the Christian church but also for all the citizens of the Roman Empire, for Tertullian's social ethic assisted the de-divinization of the emperor, a task that must be repeated in every generation, since the state is constantly tempted to set itself up as an idolatrous power. The state tries to teach us that it gives us the *right* to worship; it secures our freedom to serve our God, and its sacrifices are how we keep the Lord's Day holy. But this is false. The state may have a limited role to play in God's order of charity, but that role cannot make possible observance of the first three commands. It can never be the precondition for the possibility of freedom of worship. Only Christ's sacrifice for us can do that.

In his novel, *A Canticle for Leibowitz*, Walter M. Miller portrays how the church must be vigilant against the state's ever-recurring claims to divinity. His novel begins and ends with a nuclear holocaust. During the three thousand years that separate these atrocities, a religious order preserves their tradition within the closed confines of their monastery. Outsiders see these monks as irrelevant and backward, but the Enlightenment figure Thon Taddeo (*thanatos deo?*) discovers they have preserved the knowledge to make light, and he is scandalized that they have cloistered such knowledge away. He believes it should be shared with the world for the betterment of all humankind. But the monks recognize something Taddeo does not. Knowledge is not an unmitigated good. Knowledge that should be bound by one social formation and its narratives of the good becomes demonic when it falls in the hands of another bound only by efficiency. Taddeo takes their knowledge and resituates it. No longer is this knowledge confined by the monks' religious tradition. Taddeo "liberates" the knowledge for a new tradition, a tradition of political utilitarianism ruled by a tyrant king named Hannegan. The result is that the knowledge serves new interests and results in a second nuclear apocalypse. After this occurs, the abbot of the monastery surveys the damage and laments,

That's where all of us are standing now, he thought. On the fat kindling of past sins. And some of them are mine. Mine, Adam's Herod's Judas's Hannegan's mine. Everybody's. Always culminates in the colossus of the State, somehow, drawing about itself the mantle of godhood, being struck down by wrath of Heaven. Why? We shouted it loudly enough—God's to be obeyed by nations as by men. Caesar's to be God's policeman, not His plenipotentiary successor, nor His heir. To all ages, all people—"Whoever exalts a race or a State or a particular form of State or the depositories of power . . . whoever raises these notions above their standard value and divinizes them to an idolatrous level, distorts and perverts an order of the world planned and created by God . . ." Where had that come from? Eleventh Pius, he thought. But when Caesar got the means to destroy the world, wasn't he already divinized? Only by the consent of the people—same rabble that shouted: *"Non habemus regem nisi caesarem,"* when confronted by Him—God Incarnate, mocked and spat upon. Caesar's divinity is showing itself again.[34]

Miller's novel illustrates well Tertullian's social ethic. The role of the church in divinely *ordaining* the state is neither to rule over it as if it were another state nor to bless its activities. The church *orders* the state simply by being the church and refusing to concede to the state the mantle of divinity it explicitly and implicitly claims. Only someone who does not understand the virtue of justice as the right ordering of desire could possibly construe either the monks in Miller's novel or Tertullian's theology as *sectarian*. This social ethic does not imply that we neglect the world, nor need it imply that the world is not within each of us. We make alliances and work where we can, but we also recognize that the fragile social existence we have on this planet requires a community in-formed by God that directs our desires to the good.

Tertullian's analysis is not far from St. Augustine's. Augustine also subjected the social institution of the state to a searing critique in his *City of God.* Tertullian said,

> We do not forget the debt of gratitude we owe to God, our Lord and Creator; we reject no creature of His hands, though certainly we exercise restraint upon ourselves, lest of any gift of His we make an immoderate or sinful use. So we sojourn with you in the world, abjuring neither forum, nor shambles, nor bath, nor booth, nor workshop, nor inn, nor weekly market, nor any other places of commerce. We sail with you and fight with you, and till the ground with you; and in like manner we unite with you in your traffickings—even in the various arts we made public property of our works for your benefit. How it is we seem useless in your ordinary business, living with you and by you as we do, I am not able to understand.[35]

Augustine described the relationship between the church and the world quite similarly when he stated,

> The heavenly city while it sojourns on earth. . . , not scrupling about diversities in the manners, laws, and institutions whereby earthly peace is secured and main-

tained, but recognizing that, however various these are, they all tend to one and the same end of earthly peace . . . is so far from rescinding and abolishing these diversities, that it even preserves and adopts them so long only as no hindrance to the worship of the one supreme and true God is thus introduced. Even the heavenly city, therefore, while in its state of pilgrimage avails itself of the peace of the earth and so far as it can without injuring faith and godliness, desires and maintains a common agreement among men regarding the acquisition of the necessities of life.[36]

Augustine's reflections on church and state did not assume an inevitable cooperation between the two. Rather, he assumed that they could cooperate only insofar as the state did not hinder worship.

FOURTH AND SIXTH COMMANDMENTS: FAMILY LIFE

The first three commands direct us to our supernatural end, the worship and adoration of God. The fourth and sixth direct us to a natural good, family life. The family is an ancient social institution, older than the state. It cannot be a salvific institution, but it can be a *domestic church.* This phrase assumes that the family is rendered intelligible by its connection to the church. The family is not the church; it can at most be a domestic ordering in service to the church.

This understanding of the family assumes marriage and children. Marriage is not a legal arrangement based on rights or what Kant described as "contracting for one another's genitals."[37] Instead, marriage is a sacrament best understood in terms of a theological description rather than a description based on its "natural use." Family serves a natural end, but this end cannot be separated from our supernatural end. The sacrament of marriage creates the family, and thus the family originates out of the church's life. Family is to be understood in terms of the church's mission. The church births families. In turn, families are open to birthing children.

Married life is not necessary for human fulfillment, but marriage is a holy vocation where our desires can be ordered to produce the virtue of chastity. This virtue can also be learned through celibacy and friendships. Thus, the church recognizes other social arrangements that serve a similar function as does marriage. This reminds us of two things. First, every Christian need not enter into marriage. Second, marriage is not a private contract free from public accountability; it receives its integrity from its situatedness within the church.

If the family becomes more central to our lives than the church, our lives will also be disordered. The family is an ancient and honorable institution that deserves our respect. Yet the family is not salvific, and when it is turned into the social institution that gives us our only identity, the family cannot help but become what Sartre defined as "the hell-hole of togetherness." Likewise, when the family is reduced to an instrumental status in service to the state, it will lose its honor and respect. The family lives out of the life of the church, not out of the state. The family is sustained through the church, since baptism and the Eucharist provide a source of accountability for the family.

Mary Daly has critiqued this idea. Finding the church to be a central institution in the perpetuation of patriarchy, she describes the church hierarchy as follows:

> Graciously they lifted from women the onerous power of childbirth, christening it "baptism." Thus they brought the lowly material function of birth, incompetently and even grudgingly performed by females, to a higher and more spiritual level in which they alone had competence. Feeding was elevated to Holy Communion. Washing achieved dignity in Baptism and Penance. Strengthening became known as Confirmation, and the function of consolation, which the unstable nature of females caused them to perform so inadequately, was raised to a spiritual level and called Extreme Unction. In order to stress the obvious fact that all females are innately disqualified from joining the Sacred Men's Club, the Looking Glass priests made it a rule that their members should wear skirts. To make the point clearer, they reserved special occasions when additional Men's Club attire should be worn. These necessary accoutrements included delicate white lace tops and millinery of prescribed shapes and colors. The leaders were required to wear silk hose, pointed hats, crimson dresses and ermine capes, thereby stressing detachment from lowly material things and dedication to the exercise of spiritual talent. They thus became revered models of spiritual transsexualism.[38]

This is a witty criticism, and in place of Christianity as an irredeemable patriarchal institution with its male savior, Daly sets forth the idea of woman as the final cause. But Daly misses the heart of the matter. No one in Christian tradition has explicitly argued that maleness is salvific. That Christ is male is not redemptive, but that he was Jewish is. Just as *maleness* cannot be salvific, neither can femaleness. It is not the final cause, but when it is made such we are bound to create one more idolatry. If Christian worship conveys the idea that maleness redeems, then such an idol should be destroyed. It should not be replaced with femaleness, whether that femaleness is understood in terms of feminism or the philosopher's "Eternal Feminine."

Jean Bethke Elshtain finds the language of Christianity more liberatory for women than does Daly. Elshtain suggested this in *Public Man/Private Woman* (1981) and elaborated on it in her 1995 work, *Augustine and the Limits of Politics*. She stated,

> What I am clearer on now is the appeal of what I called "the language of Christianity" to women in the late antique world, because the things Christ held dear and cherished—forgiveness, succor, devotion—helped to forge the terms of their own lives, that and the fact that the Christian rhetoric that Augustine at first

found inelegant and even vulgar was simple and direct—told in the language of the people, cast in the forms of everyday speech, speech that communicated, speech with a liberatory moment that reached out to incorporate into a new community—the *koinonia*—those who were severed from the classical *polis*, women and the poor.[39]

Gerhard Lohfink views the demands of baptism similarly to Elshtain when he writes that Jesus' disciples are not to call anyone father, "for they will find everything again in the new family of God, brothers and sisters, mothers and children; but they will find fathers no longer. Patriarchal domination is no longer permissible in the new family, but only motherliness, fraternity and childlikeness before God the Father."[40] Family situated within the broader context of church need not stifle feminist criticisms of patriarchy. It should strengthen them.

As a social institution the church contains important implications for addressing feminist criticisms of contemporary social relations. Many feminists have suggested that the locus of patriarchal power occurs through the institution of the heterosexual family. Indeed, the family can be a source of patriarchy, particularly when it is defined primarily in terms of *fatherhood*. For instance, the Catholic *Catechism* suggests, "The divine fatherhood is the source of human fatherhood; this is the foundation of the honor owed to parents."[41] The difficulty with this statement is that it assumes a univocal relationship between God the Father and human fathers, and the family is then defined in terms of this relationship. But God as Father is not male, and any suggestion to the contrary violates orthodox Christian doctrine, because it suggests that God has body, parts, or passion. Christianity has never advocated a pagan worship of the phallus. (Nor should it worship the womb. Christianity is not a fertility cult.) That such a heretical interpretation of Christianity may have been implied by some is probably true, but the tradition itself cannot be judged as intentionally advocating this. Still, even the implicit suggestion that such pagan rituals are present in Christianity should cause us to be vigilant against such a suggestion. The relationship between God as Father and human fathers can only be one of analogy (Luke 11:11–13).

The church certainly stands guilty of promoting patriarchy, but current discussions too often reduce the power of women to the woman as one more autonomous consumer who *chooses* what happens to her own body. Feminism becomes co-opted by the market, to the forces of capitalist society. But women are no more autonomous moral actors than are men. In an era marked by the dominance of technology, we are all *nodal points* in communication networks. The illusion of autonomy prevents us from recognizing our social position. All moral actions assume a sociology. The predominance of the global market in all our lives continues to define too much of contemporary feminist thought. The church's teachings are a better alternative.

The purpose of marriage is not merely to produce the virtue of fidelity and to reproduce socially; it is also to restrain domination. Therefore, the family must arise out of and live from the broader community of the church. The church's emphasis on openness to procreation as a central good for marriage is profoundly anti-Gnostic. Procreation as a necessary good for marriage is an embodied account of a social ethic, for it assumes that neither *mind* nor *spirit* nor subjective wishes alone can determine our social ethic. Our bodies are already inscribed into a moral order that contains purposes. The social institution of marriage should embody those purposes.

COMMANDMENTS SEVEN THROUGH TEN: LOVING NEIGHBORS

After the social institutions of church and family, the commands imply institutions such as neighborhoods, markets, and governing authorities with the power to prevent violations of the commands.

Apart from the church, the family, and a limited role for the state, the Ten Commandments assume a central role for neighborhoods. God directs us not toward citizens or comrades in our relations with our neighbors. The social institution of a neighborhood is third in rank only to that of the church and family. Jesus' summary of the law in terms of loving God and one's neighbor assumes, first, an institution that will assist us in charity toward God, which can only be the church or synagogue, then charity toward our neighbors, which assumes something like neighborhoods.

Neighborhoods have been vastly diminished because of the hegemonic power of the nation-state and the global market in all our lives. Michael Ignatieff has noted this in his compelling critique of the welfare state, *The Needs of Strangers*. Ignatieff describes how the welfare state mediates goods to the needy and turns "relationships" into contractual transactions among strangers. He writes,

> The mediated quality of our relationship seems necessary to both of us. [The needy] are dependent upon the state, not upon me, and we are both glad of it. Yet I am also aware of how this mediation walls us off from each other. We are responsible for each other, but we are not responsible to each other. My responsibilities towards them are mediated through a vast division of labour. In my name a social worker climbs the stairs to their rooms and makes sure they are as warm and as clean as they can be persuaded to be. . . . It is this solidarity among strangers, this transformation through the division of labour of needs into rights and rights into care that gives us whatever fragile basis we have for saying that we live in a moral community.[42]

Citizens as strangers are indeed a fragile basis for moral community. This may be preferable to strangers competing for basic goods that the so-called free-market state seeks to produce, but to imagine that the disorder created by the welfare state is the only alternative to the greater disorder of a state-instituted, deregulated market is merely to accept one state of disorder over a greater one.

Both the welfare state and the free-market state destroy neighborhoods, and corporations are the central actors in both. Malls can be built, incinerators established, educational institutions closed or consolidated—and neighbors have little recourse. Public education seeks parents to participate in the school system only through bake sales and fundraisers. We are constantly alienated and isolated from the tasks of everyday life, which are given over to the professionals and experts. The only control remaining is the occasional vote for who will rule us. How can we fulfill the command to love our neighbors when we are no longer neighbors but strangers?

"Public" theologians and political philosophers seek to combat this increasing alienation and isolation. Jean Bethke Elshtain attempts to resurrect the idea of the *citizen* as necessary to preserve democracy. However, her usual considerable insights fail here, as she finds herself arguing for the church as a "civil site."[43] A certain forgetfulness seems to be present here. Such experiments have been tried in the past, and they often required the imposition of national identities over religious ones such that clergy were required to take oaths to the state and forswear allegiance to a catholic church.

For a Christian social ethic, the concept of neighbor is much preferable to the controversial category of *citizen*. Neighbors are not mere citizens, for the concept of citizenship requires a sameness, a commonalty, a catholicity that the state should never seek to forge. Nor should theologians contribute to a public consensus or public philosophy. Such social practices as oaths of allegiance and the effort to establish a common identity through hymns, prayers, and adoration to the state is an inappropriate end for theologians to pursue. Rather, the state should be fragmented, for it is nothing but a communal effort to negotiate our different identities with as little violence as possible. The church serves the state by helping to fragment it. When the state superimposes another identity over these others, it usurps the more important identities for idolatrous purposes. Neighborhoods are where we learn to negotiate these differences, not as citizens or comrades, but as people who need one another to fix leaky faucets, watch children, bake and clean in times of crisis, and discuss and argue about things that matter—politics, faith, morality, and whether the local woods will be turned into one more strip mall.

Only when we have recovered a sense of neighborhoods can we fulfill the seventh through the tenth commandments. The command against stealing implies a certain form of private property, but one vastly different from our contemporary understanding. Because law directs us to an appropriate end (charity), private property within Christian tradition is warranted only on the assumption that we must be free to use our property for the sake of others to cultivate and receive the virtue of charity. Private property is not a *right* the state gives; it is necessary only for the exercise of charity. Thus Thomas Aquinas argued,

> Things which are of human right cannot derogate from natural right or Divine right. Now according to the natural order established by Divine Providence,

183

inferior things are ordained for the purpose of succoring man's needs by their means. Wherefore the division and appropriation of things which are based on human law do not preclude the fact that man's needs have to be remedied by means of these very things. Hence whatever certain people have in superabundance is due, by natural law, to the purpose of succoring the poor.[44]

Aquinas's understanding of property conflicts vastly with modern property rights. They are based upon the individual as citizen who is given rights by the state, which rights are protected and defended by the state's security apparatus. Thus, individual property rights take precedence over neighborhood concerns. The result is a market that does not function to promote charity but inhibits a life of virtue for the vice of greed.

Adultery, bearing false witness against a neighbor, coveting a neighbor's spouse or goods—all these commandments assume the concrete material that constitutes daily living within neighborhoods. Here is the place where discipleship is ordinarily exercised. The commands point us to the virtues of temperance, justice, and prudence. By learning not to desire that which is my neighbor's, I learn to rejoice with him in his good fortune without resentment, cunning, or duplicity. We learn to look upon our neighbor's spouse not as something to be obtained for our own desire. Thus, we respect our neighbors' relationship and do not turn it into one more property transaction to be consumed. We learn to be a neighbor, and then we can honor the commandment to love our neighbors as ourselves.

FIFTH COMMANDMENT: THE MEANS OF VIOLENCE

Social formations most dependent upon the cooperation that meekness requires—family and neighborhoods—can only function when the command not to kill forms their relationships. In families and neighborhoods we recognize that our lives and their sustenance occur through the gifts of others. If we react against those gifts through envy, covetousness, pride, and gluttony, we will be tempted to violence; we will be ordered toward the death of those who threaten our self-sufficiency. Only when family and neighborhoods have broken down do we need to raise the possibility of some supervening social formation that helps restore the nonviolence that makes our everyday lives possible. Recognizing the possibility of this supervening authority is a great temptation to God's order of charity. Does God's economy have a place for the state with its coercive institutions of justice, police, and military? Can these be recognized without inevitably subordinating the church to their hard-to-contain power?

Only after discussing the church, the family, and the neighborhood can we begin to discuss the institution of the state. Curiously, a command that begins by prohibiting a certain activity has prompted the church to defend the state's control of the means of violence. For the Roman Catholic Church this stems out of the duty to love one's own life, which is called a "fundamental principle of morality." The Church defends the legitimacy of self-defense on the basis of the principle of double effect: "The act of self-defense can have a double effect: the preservation of one's own life; and the killing of the aggressor. . . . The one is intended, the other is not."[45] As we have seen, Knauer and the proportionalists made this principle the defining principle of all morality, which led to a disembodied account of the moral life that allows a subjective intention to define the moral species of our actions. The *Catechism of the Catholic Church* borders on this same mistake here. Because the order of charity requires us to love and preserve our own life more than that of another, legitimate defense is not merely a right but a "grave duty." We should not use more violence than is necessary to deter an aggressor, and our use of violence should fall within the criteria of the just-war tradition. Still, the *Catechism's* advocacy of the means of violence as a grave duty conflicts with its teachings on "the witness of sacred history," as articulated in the paragraph preceding the discussion of this legitimate defense:

> In the Sermon on the Mount, the Lord recalls the commandment, "you shall not kill," and he adds to it the proscription of anger, hatred and vengeance. Going further, Christ asks his disciples to turn the other cheek, to love their enemies. He did not defend himself and told Peter to leave his sword in its sheath.[46]

Here the Church's teaching contradicts itself. If legitimate defense is not merely a right but a duty for one's self and for the common good, and if Jesus refused to defend himself, then the logical conclusion is that Jesus' actions in the garden were unjust. Jesus' actions become an exception to the rule rather than the basis for our actions to be human. Jesus' life, teaching, death, and resurrection no longer define what our human nature should be.

The Catholic Church's teachings on war likewise involve a contradiction. What we learn from Jesus' actions and what we learn from the natural law conflict. But this cannot be, because grace perfects, not contradicts, nature. Despite this contradiction, the Church is one of the most vocal opponents of unlimited warfare. It also teaches, "The fifth commandment forbids the intentional destruction of human life. Because of the evils and injustices that accompany all war, the Church insistently urges everyone to prayer and to action so that the divine Goodness may free us from the ancient bondage of war."[47] Thus, the Church, unlike political realists and other tragedians, does not teach that war is inevitable. Peace is possible because Christ has been found in human form.[48]

Despite its teachings that limit the state's employment of the means of violence, one wonders if the Catholic Church has gone far enough in challenging the emperor's sword. Has it (like Protestantism) grown too accustomed to making alliances with state power such that it lacks theological courage? Thomas Aquinas called the clergy to embody this form of theological courage when he responded negatively to the question of whether it was legitimate for clerics and bishops to fight. He stated,

> All the clerical Orders are directed to the ministry of the altar, on which the Passion of Christ is represented sacramentally. . . . Wherefore it is unbecoming for them to slay or shed blood, and it is more fitting that they should be ready to shed their own blood for Christ, so as to imitate in deed what they portray in their ministry. . . . Now no man who has a certain duty to perform, can lawfully do that which renders him unfit for that duty.[49]

If those who preside at the celebration of the Eucharist have a duty to refrain from shedding blood, then has the time not come to recognize that those who participate in that celebration should equally be bound by this same duty? In principle, Protestantism contributes to the Catholic Church the principle that all persons—clergy and lay—are to embody the holiness of the Christian life, which was once called "the counsels of perfection." These are not only for persons in religious orders but now belong to the whole church. Of all the Christian communities, the Wesleyan tradition has recognized this and offers it as a gift to the Catholic Church. We are all called to go on to perfection and live as persons who have a duty to represent the passion of Christ in our lives. This is the true "priesthood of all believers." It is not that anyone should be able to represent this life sacramentally but that everyone should represent it in his or her daily living. The traditional Catholic distinction between counsels of perfection for those in religious orders and ordinary precepts for other believers no longer holds. But this should not lead to a reduction of Christian living to the precepts; it should have the opposite effect. All are called to live more like the counsels of perfection.[50] This would be a Reformation worthy of the name.

The church has a long and equivocal tradition in pronouncing judgment on the state's use of the sword. However, we must recognize that modern accounts of warfare are no longer theological matters. Perhaps the transition to modern warfare occurred when Clausewitz sought to do to warfare what Kant had done to reason: to give us an account of war in terms of reason alone. He argued that "war is the continuation of politics by other means."[51] For us, warfare is political, where politics is understood primarily in the modern terms of the assertion of power. Thus, warfare is solely entrusted to the state. War is neither cultural nor religious. This has its advantages. We no longer explicitly offer up our victims as worthy sacrifices to God. Still, the reduction of warfare to politics alone also contains disadvantages, which were most visible in the twentieth century. Once war becomes bound only by political purposes, then the state is given the ability to do whatever it must to break the will of the enemy. In 1945 this new tradition bore "fruit" and determined our lives for the rest of the century. We lived as if "God were dead and we had killed him." Given our politics, how can anyone be surprised at the nihilism of our age? We now live in a transitional age. We do not know what will come next. If the forces of modernity let loose on Hiroshima and Nagasaki are not brought to bay, then our lives can only remain fundamentally disordered. Perhaps the church can yet recover its own theological courage and remind us all that charity is the right order of our desires. This order requires a church that overcomes the pathos of humility characteristic of modern theology and owns the fact that it is itself a social ethic.

To obey the commandments is not an end in itself. To obey the commandments in order to have our lives directed to God is an end in itself. Such an ordering provides infused virtues, gifts, and beatitudes because it is a participation in God's own life. Such an ordering only occurs when our lives are formed by a particular ordering of social formations. Thus, all moral norms are social constructions, where the church gives to all other formations their intelligibility and proper due. Only when the *ecclesia* is recognized as a social institution unlike any other can we then recognize a just ordering of institutions like family, market, and state.

OIKOS

"Honor your father and your mother, that your days may be long in the land which the LORD your God gives you." Exodus 20:12

"If any one comes to me and does not hate his own father and mother and wife and children and brothers and sisters, yes, and even his own life, he cannot be my disciple." Luke 14:26

The fourth commandment opens into what is known as the second table of the Ten Commandments. Whereas the first table orders our actions toward God and thus requires the theological virtues of charity, faith, and hope for its fulfillment, the second orders our life toward our neighbors. Such a life also presupposes the *supernatural* virtues to fulfill and make sense of the *natural* virtues. A true love of neighbor can occur only within the context of love of God. Thus, the order of the Ten gives us an order to our lives, including an ordering of social institutions. The first three commandments presuppose the institution of the church (or synagogue) for their fulfillment. The fourth commandment assumes the family, which is second in rank to the church. But although the family is a necessary and natural social institution, what it *is* is not self-evident. The presence of the church illumines the character of the family and not vice versa. This is why the church makes marriage possible.

ECCLESIAL SOCIAL REPRODUCTION

The family is not a self-sufficient institution. In fact, within Christian tradition, the family is no longer understood as the primary social context within which social reproduction takes place. The "new birth" makes Christians, not biological birth alone. This is clear from Jesus' teaching. When his mother and brothers came to find him, Jesus redefined the family: "Whoever does the will of God is my brother, and sister, and mother" (Mark 3:35). This seems consistent with other claims Jesus made about the family. He claimed that he would bring division within the family (Luke 12:51–53) and went so far as to proclaim, "If any one comes to me and does not hate his own father and mother and wife and children and brothers and sisters, yes, and even his own life, he cannot be my disciple" (Luke 14:26). Jesus refused to allow a potential follower to bury his father before he followed him, stating, "Let the dead bury their dead." At the same time, Jesus claimed that a family forsaken would be returned to his followers "a hundredfold" (Mark 10:29–31). The loss of family in Christianity is no heroic sacrifice. We do not need to abandon family and rise above particular achievements to achieve some cosmopolitan harmony. Any loss of family in Christianity is made for the sake of a greater return: a new family is created. Nevertheless, this creation of a new family does not permit a thorough dissolution of the biological family. Jesus strengthened the prohibition of divorce (Mark 10:2–9) and ensured that John would make a place for his mother at his death (John 19:26–27). Theologians should avoid either valorizing the family into a salvific institution or demonizing the family as the origin of all human evil.

The new birth is not possible without biological birth, so the church cannot do without families. This is an exemplification of Thomas Aquinas's famous saying, "Grace perfects and presupposes nature." But this theological truism should not be used to sanctify the biological family. The direction in which *grace* and *nature* work in this phrase is significant for recognizing God's goodness. Grace is not added to nature merely because nature has been corrupted. In fact, the corruption of nature is found in the assumption that it is self-interpreting, that we can know nature separate from grace. Therefore, a proper understanding of Aquinas's statement recognizes that the family does not make the church possible; the church makes the family possible.

Karl Barth noted that Aquinas's "dangerous" saying has a proper place in church dogmatics when it is taken to be a statement of God's patience.[1] That grace presupposes nature signifies that God does not impatiently destroy that which is not yet perfected within God's order. Instead, God is patient with us, offering us the chance to bring our "nature" into concert with God's grace. Only then do we discover our true nature.

Thus the family needs the church for it to attain its own nature. The family is both an instrumental good and a good in itself. But its own goodness cannot reside in some autonomous realm where the family is free from ecclesial interference. What purpose does the family serve within the politics of the church? The family is a "common venture" where persons are bound together to learn how to live in charity in everyday life.[2] The family is where we are trained to be forgiven and to offer forgiveness. This occurs through the practices of everyday life as we seek to be just and charitable in preparing and enjoying meals, playing, working, resting, arguing, and mediating the many conflicts that arise. This training is possible only through the patient endurance that makes the family. For the family to achieve its proper end, it must have timefulness. The "common venture" of the family takes place over lifetimes. In fact, its "common venture" does not come to an end but is ceaselessly reproduced. The family bears the memory of those who came before us, reminding us that our lives are not possible without theirs, reminding us of redemption and of the need for redemption. Without those memories no one could receive God's goodness.

Because of this understanding of the family as a "common venture," Christian tradition came to recognize three ends to marriage: fidelity, the restraint of lust, and procreation. These three ends are not unique to the Christian tradition. Ancient Roman society emphasized both procreation and marriage as friendship.[3] Procreation was understood primarily as a civic obligation but also as a religious duty.[4] Thus the Stoic Musonius Rufus argued that any form of contraceptive practice opposed "Zeus protector of the family, who watches for sins against the family: and he who sins against the gods is impious."[5] Ancient Roman society did not distinguish between *civic* and *religious* duties. Marriage, procreation, and family were all part of a sacred cosmos where familial actions participated in civic and religious realities. If Christianity brought anything unique to this understanding of marriage, it was the fact that marriage was unnecessary. Celibacy was now a possibility. This could be taken too far, as it was in many Gnostic sects, which denied the goodness of marriage altogether. Gnostics severed the relationship between marriage and childbearing, either making the goodness of the sexual relationship between persons a function of some secret form of knowledge separate from the physical act of sex itself or denying that sex could ever have good purposes and thus shunning it.[6] The former position assumed that trapping the "light of divinity" (found in the sperm) within a body was immoral and taught that sexual intercourse was permissible only for nonprocreative purposes. Nonprocreative sex was legitimate; procreative sex could only be accidental. The latter position assumed that sexual intercourse should be foregone, not because pleasure per se was wrong but because celibacy would avoid procreation.[7]

In opposing the Gnostic view of sex, many of the church fathers negotiated between the Stoic insistence on procreation and the superiority or possibility of celibacy as a faithful Christian response. In so doing they proclaimed "the goodness of marriage."

THE GOODNESS OF MARRIAGE

Why were the Gnostics wrong? What constituted the goodness of marriage? While an emphasis on procreation opposed the Gnostic myth, the goodness of marriage was not to be found in procreation alone. The biblical command to be fruitful and multiply (Gen. 1:28) was not the primary source for many church fathers' understanding of marriage, for they assumed that this command had been fulfilled. That this command was given to Adam and Eve implied, for Tertullian, that we are to have one marriage partner. What, then, do we do with the polygamy of the patriarchs? It was permitted so the seed could be broadly sown, the Holy Family born, and from them the Messiah could come. Now the Messiah was here. The command to be fruitful and multiply was placed into a new political and social context. Thus, a theologian such as Tertullian did not argue for the goodness of marriage based on Genesis 1:28, for it had been superseded by 1 Corinthians 7:29—"the appointed time has grown very short; from now on, let those who have wives live as though they had none." Marriage and procreation were no longer necessary; they had been replaced by the eschatological urgency of the gospel. Why, then, not forego marriage altogether? Even an eschatologically-driven theologian like Tertullian still found a purpose for marriage. He read Genesis 2:24 ("Therefore a man leaves his father and his mother and cleaves to his wife, and they become one flesh") in light of the Christian mission and commented, "Where there is one flesh, there is also one spirit. Together they pray, together they prostrate themselves, together they fast, teaching each other, exhorting each other, supporting each other."[8] Marriage serves the end of the common mission of the church.

Tertullian still maintained the superiority of celibacy. Like many of the church fathers, he read 1 Corinthians 7:1 ("It is well for a man not to touch a woman") not as an erroneous Corinthian position that Paul was correcting but as a position that Paul advocated.[9] Tertullian himself had leanings toward such an eschatological interpretation of the gospel such that he may have finally lost any place for marriage within the Christian dispensation and joined the Gnostics himself.

Although many church fathers found little use for marital sexual intercourse other than procreation, that still constitutes a higher view of the goodness of sex than is found among the Gnostics. For instance, in the *Acts of Thomas,* Jesus encourages us to "refrain from filthy intercourse" and is quoted as saying, "If you produce many children, you will become greedy and avaricious because of them, robbing orphans and defrauding widows."[10] In this Gnostic text children are viewed as a threat to just distribution. People with children defraud the poor to care for their own children. Oddly enough, this sounds strikingly similar to liberal political economists who suggested that the only way to achieve a just political distribution consistent with economic necessities was by curtailing procreation. Both conservative Christian theoreticians such as Malthus and philosophical radicals such as J. S. Mill found procreation to be the major constraint in producing a just distribution of goods. Both their positions reduce to an oxymoron: the problem with human existence is human existence. If we had fewer people, we would have fewer problems. This is, in fact, a dangerous argument, for it asserts that the answer to the problem of human existence is either to limit or do away with it. This does not rule out the need for prudence in maintaining one's family, but to make the reception of children the fundamental problem of human existence can only lead to frightening solutions.

One source for a defense of procreation within marriage against both the Gnostic denigration of it and its modern-day variation among economists comes from Clement of Alexandria. Clement explicitly rejected the argument of some Gnostics that bearing children only increased death and misery. They mistakenly read creation itself as evil and thus rejected the goodness of the body. Clement was one of the earliest church fathers to argue that every act of sexual intercourse should intend procreation. Otherwise, he asserted, we violate nature. Unlike Tertullian, Clement did not adequately see the purpose of marriage as pointing to the Christian mission. Nevertheless, he did suggest, "Just like celibacy, marriage has its own distinctive services and ministries for the Lord: I refer to the care of one's children and wife."[11]

The purpose of marriage was not only procreation and the care of family but also the restraint of lust and domination. For example, Lactantius wrote, "If someone cannot restrain these impulses, he should control them within the prescribed limits of a legitimate marriage." This most antiromantic view of marriage had political significance, for Lactantius went on to state, "God does not want the body to be divided and torn apart."[12] That is to say, God does not intend for persons to indiscriminately engage in sexual intercourse and thus disorder the body—individually and socially—for common bonds cannot be formed through indiscriminate sexual practices.

In a culture such as ours, formed by the "myth of repression," the fathers' teachings on the need to control desire through discipline, order, and marriage can only be viewed as psychologically damaging. As John Updike noted regarding the church's teachings against lust, "How strangely on modern ears falls the notion that lust—sexual desire that wells up in us as involuntarily as saliva—in itself is wicked."[13] The teaching of the church fathers that we should strive for *apathy* in sexual matters is so strange to generations formed by modern psychology (and its progeny in the advertising industry) that we cannot even understand what they were advocating. We falsely accuse them of denigrating the body while we starve, pierce, tattoo, and finally kill it. For too long, theologians have falsely viewed *apatheia* as a Hellenistic importation into the biblical narrative. *Apatheia* is assumed to be a Greek effort to control the threatening chaos of the body's desires, an impossible discipline of human mastery that can end only in some kind of pathology. Today some theologians and clergy speak of a "right" to sexual pleasure.[14] What could this possibly mean, except that these religious leaders are bound by the modern myth of repression, which assumes that, if one does not receive sexual pleasure, if one lives a life of *apatheia,* it could only be a form of immaturity and repression? Bound to the dogmas of modernity, such religious leaders not only appeal to the state to secure sexual pleasure through the language of right but obviously find the Christian tradition of *apatheia* to be a source of oppression.

John Milbank explains that, far from denigrating the body and its passions, a church father such as Gregory of Nyssa "stresses *apatheia* even more strongly than his pagan predecessors and near-contemporaries, precisely *because* he thinks this is demanded by the deliverances of revelation and by categories of gift rather than being."[15] Gregory's *apatheia* is precisely a challenge to the assumption that the Christian life requires the self-sufficiency and self-containment *apatheia* conjures up in modern ears. Instead, his *apatheia* allows us to be receptive to God and at the same time active so that our activity is not ruled by arbitrary and unsatisfying passions—unsatisfying precisely because they are all too momentarily satisfying. As Gregory puts it,

> This truly is the vision of God: never to be satisfied in the desire to see him. But one must always, by looking at what he can see, rekindle his desire to see more. Thus, no limit would interrupt growth in the ascent to God, since no limit to the Good can be found nor is the increasing of desire for the Good brought to an end because it is satisfied.[16]

The modern myth of repression has advocated an indiscriminate capitulation to desire because it suggests that the repression of the sexual impulse has led to disastrous social and political consequences.

The myth of repression is precisely that, a myth. The proliferation of sexual desire as the *secret* that will unlock human flourishing has been present in Western culture for some time. As Michel Foucault taught us, "since the end of the 16th century, the 'putting into discourse of sex' far from undergoing a process of restriction, on the contrary has been subjected to a mechanism of increasing incitement."[17] For Foucault, sexuality is disciplined in Western culture not through silence and repression but through its very public presentations in all kinds of discourses from penitential to psychotherapeutic to modern advertising practices. Making sex public through incessant speech promised "healing" because sex held some secret to our innermost being. This public discourse, this incitement to speak about "it," is the mechanism by which sexuality is disciplined to serve the interests of the market and the state (Foucault would add church). To assume that the problem with contemporary sexuality is its repression is to avoid the public social and political manipulation sexuality has undergone in Western culture. The reading of the church fathers as producing a discourse of repression from which the modern era delivers us is part of that avoidance. And of course, Augustine is misunderstood most of all.

Augustine's teaching on marriage participates in an ongoing argument between positions put forth by Jovinian, Pelagius, and the Manichees. The Manichees had condemned marriage altogether. Jovinian established marriage on an equal footing with celibacy. Pelagius opposed Jovinian's view and found celibacy superior to marriage. Yet even Pelagius tells the matron Celantia that her vow of chastity cannot be fulfilled if she took it without her husband's consent. Pelagius advises her,

> The rule of apostolic teaching does not with Jovinian, equate the works of marriage with continence, nor does it with Manichaeus, condemn marriage. The chosen vessel and apostle thus takes a moderate and middle position between the two, so that he allows a remedy for incontinence, while he calls forth continence to the reward. His whole purpose is this: to propose chastity when both partners agree to it, or at least for both partners to pay the common debt.[18]

Pelagius allows for the possibility of marriage, but he clearly struggles to explain why it might be good. It only seems to serve the purpose of giving an outlet for those who are weak until they can become stronger. Thus Celantia must submit to her husband's sexual needs until he might become continent himself. It is against this understanding that Augustine explains the good of marriage.

In *The Good of Marriage,* Augustine explains both why Christians should still marry and why they should have only one spouse. The latter explanation is particularly important, for the church's Scriptures put forth polygamous patriarchs as examples to be emulated. Augustine argues that the patriarchs were under the command to be fruitful and multiply. They held several wives not because of any promiscuity but because of the promise. The seed had to be widely sown, which made possible the birth of the Holy Family. Thus, the marriage of Abraham, like the celibacy of John the Baptist, "did service for Christ in accord with the needs of the time."[19] Now that the fullness of time has come, the command to multiply is no longer to be understood primarily as biological. In fact, Augustine challenged the Roman understanding of procreation in order to serve the empire. Augustine stated, "Indeed in the marriage of our women the sanctity of the sacrament is of more importance than the fecundity of the womb."[20] Sexual intercourse no longer serves the primary end of procreation. Instead, Augustine argues, marriage "does not seem to me to be a good solely because of the procreation of children, but also because of the natural companionship between the sexes." Marriage makes possible the gift of friendship.

Augustine identified three ends that marriage serves: offspring, fidelity, and sacrament. These are the goods of marriage. Children are to be welcomed as the gifts God offers us. Fidelity is to be observed, for it is more important than health. Augustine finds fidelity so important that he was willing to state that an adulterer faithful to his adulterous partner is "less wicked" than an adulterer who lacks even this fidelity.[21] The sacrament is found in marital fidelity.

Augustine likened marriage to ordination. An ordained person may show up to gather the people, but the people might not assemble. This does not void the sacrament of orders. The priest does not cease being a priest because the people of God refuse to gather. Likewise, the marital bond participates in the same sense of sacrament. The bond is discovered not in the strength of the partner's wills but in the relationship that makes the sacrament possible. Marriage is indissoluble because Christ's reconciliation with us is indissoluble.

As a sacrament, marriage should produce the virtue of chastity, a form of charity whereby we learn to be a "witness to our neighbor of God's fidelity and loving kindness."[22] Chastity is the basis for friendship, and only chastity can create the friendships that build good neighborhoods. Concupiscence destroys friendship because it is the desire to have the other solely for one's own pleasure; it treats the other as a commodity. This cannot produce friendship, for it only leads to conflict, conquest, and vanquishing the other. Chastity, on the other hand, orders one's desires such that the desire to dominate itself is subdued. Neighbors need not fear one another. The intimacy of marital life will not be trespassed by usurpation, which can only be a form of domination. It can only be domination because that which opposes chastity—lust, masturbation, fornication, pornography, prostitution, and rape—is sexual intercourse that refuses to be part of a larger project or common mission. The other partner must eventually be put away. Sex loses its timefulness.

WHICH MASTER SHALL WE SERVE?

Sexuality is inextricably related to the goods of the church, the neighborhood, the market, and the state. It always serves the politics of some community. Any person who thinks that his or her sexual practices are nonpolitical, arising from autonomous decision-making, lives an utter illusion. As Stanley Hauerwas and Michel Foucault remind us, sex is always public, always political.

The anti-Christian philosopher Bertrand Russell understood that sexual practices both presuppose and foster some politics. His controversial 1929 book, *Marriage and Morals,* set forth the program of the sexual revolution that seems to have become commonplace in the twentieth century. Russell argued that Christianity had destroyed marriage because it required all sexual intercourse to take place within a monogamous, lifelong commitment, primarily for the restraint of sin. Thus Christianity fostered a negative view of sexuality. In response, Russell advocated the need for a new sexual ethic that would "cleanse sex from the filth with which it has been covered by Christian moralists."[23] This new sexual ethic would view sex as a natural, biological instinct that should be basically unrestricted in people's private lives. It should be left free. "If marriage is to achieve its possibilities, husbands and wives must learn to understand that whatever the law may say, in their private lives they must be free. . . . Love can flourish only as long as it is free and spontaneous; it tends to be killed by the thought it is a duty."[24] In 1929 Russell's sexual ethic was scandalous, but not so at the beginning of the twenty-first century. The belief that sexual practices are private matters that should remain unregulated as long as they do not harm others has become the norm. What is interesting about Russell's "new" sexual ethic is that he recognized there were political dimensions to this ethic.

Russell recognized that marriage and family provided some resistance to the power of the nation-state. Marriage was bound up with the "intimate texture of society" and had a "social purpose." Marriages were necessary for the procreation and education of children. Thus, although one need not be monogamous in one's sexual practices, marriages should stay together until the children were reared. Of course, marital infidelity often destroys marriages (as it did with Russell) and thus removes any power that the family had against the state. Once the timefulness of the family is interrupted, some other social formation—the state—must take up its social tasks. Russell believed, however, that the substitution of the state for the father was, on the whole, an advance, though it had certain pitfalls:

> The substitution of the State for the father, so far as it has gone in the West, is in the main a great advance. It has immensely improved the health of the community, and the general level of education. It has diminished cruelty to children, and has made impossible such sufferings as those of David Copperfield. It may be expected to continue to raise the general level of physical health and intellectual attainment, especially by preventing the worst evils resulting from the family system where it goes wrong. There are, however, very grave dangers in the substitution of the State for the family. Parents as a rule, are fond of their children, and do not regard them merely as material for political schemes. The State cannot be expected to have this attitude.[25]

The state as superparent results in the loss of the family as a form of resistance against the incursions of the state. Children become projects to serve the state's interests. Parents and children are treated as equal individuals, given rights by the state, which also has the sole power to protect and determine those rights. Once the state usurps the role of parents, only a centralized power—and individuals who receive and call on that central power—remains.

Russell recognized that the loss of marriage and family would increase the power of the state. Moreover, the relations between elders and children would no longer be defined in terms of bonds of affection, but in terms of a larger political project. Children would be formed and fashioned with the primary identity of *citizen*. Their lives would become increasingly regulated and choreographed so that they would take their place as individual citizens before they would see themselves as sons and daughters of a particular family, or baptized members of the people of God. This poses a threat not only to the stability of the family but even more to the possibility that our children will see themselves as inheritors of a sacred and holy mission to be the people of God. The formative pressure to have their lives envisioned solely as individuals ordered by the state too easily leads them to prefer the disordered desires of the state and market to their vocation in the common mission of the church. Every parent loses his or her children to the market.

The family should not strive to be a private institution free from state and market. That would be neither welcome nor possible. The family should not seek to consolidate its power of resistance by a retrenchment into the patriarchal family, where the husband has control over the household such that, as English common law once suggested, he can beat his wife with a branch smaller than his thumb. Rather, the family must reclaim its proper place in God's economy, as the "common venture" where people learn how to enact the theological virtues in everyday life. In order to do this, as well as to avoid the past problems of patriarchy and domination, family life must be held accountable to a community greater than itself, to the church.

FAMILY AS SOURCE OF IDOLATRY AND DIVISION: THE INVENTION OF RACE

Family is an ancient institution, older than the state. The second table of the Ten Commandments assumes its presence in some form for us to live as God intends. But family can also be the source of our greatest evils. Until we recognize that the evils of war, racism, and conquest do not arise simply because of an unmitigated radical evil that tempts people to be wicked for wickedness' sake, we will not begin to address the self-deception of our lives. (We can never address this fully; that is the nature of self-deception. We must always confess and find forgiveness for sins known and unknown.) War, racism, and conquest arise as much from our loves as from our hatreds; that is their true pathos. In his essay, "Hating Mothers As the Way to Peace," Stanley Hauerwas addresses this reality and finds Jesus' harsh sayings against the family to be a sign of the new age Jesus inaugurates. Jesus proclaimed hatred of family for the sake of discipleship (Luke 14:26). How can we make sense of such a radical proclamation? Hauerwas writes,

> It is surely absurd to think we can follow Jesus while clinging to the attachments of the old age. Rather to be his disciple means that all our pasts and all our loves (the loves of our mothers, our fathers, our wives, our husbands, and children) are now made part of a new order. We have become part of a new kingdom that makes it possible for our loves to be the basis of peace rather than the source of violence. For now in this New Age, we love, knowing that our security is in God who has redeemed us through the establishment of his kingdom in Jesus. Now we need not desperately try to ensure the survival of those we love, as we can

now love them with the security of the conviction that God's kingdom is surely here. In short, Jesus brought the end-time so that now we have the time to love without that love becoming the source of our violence.[26]

Love of family is often the source of oppression, not because we actually live in scarcity where the love of our family entails that we cannot love others, but because the love of our family tempts us to think that love, like other commodities, is scarce. Therefore, the love of our family must come at the expense of others. This idolatrous love of family has a diabolical influence in the modern era, for a byproduct of the love of family is the love of race.

In 1939 the various branches of the Methodist Church that had split over the question of slavery (the Methodist Episcopal Church, the Methodist Episcopal Church South, and the Methodist Protestant Church) sought merger. Like other Protestant churches in North America, the Methodists had split along racial lines during and after the Civil War. The merger that came in 1939 did not challenge that division but perpetuated it through what was known as the "Central Jurisdiction." The three churches to be merged were divided into five jurisdictions based on geography. But the Central Jurisdiction was based not on geography but solely on race. All Black Methodists were separated out of their geographical jurisdiction and placed in the Central Jurisdiction. This compromise made merger possible, but it was a compromise that prevented the Methodists from embodying the catholic unity that should characterize the church. After this compromise, Roy Wilkins of the NAACP stated,

> We hope God has the Methodists in mind and that He will give compassionate attention to their special needs. They separated a hundred years ago over slavery. Now they have got back together again with old wounds fairly well healed, and with the persistent black man roped off into a separate conference where he will be happy riding to Glory on a sort of Jim Crow car. We trust that if heaven is truly one great unsegregated family, God will not induct the American Methodists in too great numbers, or too rapidly, into a society that would shock them, perhaps, beyond hope of salvation.[27]

Racism was by no means a peculiar trait of Methodism; nearly every Protestant and Catholic church went through a similar period of infidelity. I tell the story of Methodism to exemplify how family can tempt us to heresy. Wilkins's prophetic utterance bears witness to the insidious fact that biology became more determinative for Methodist identity than baptism. In short, the *natural* family supplanted the *supernatural* one. For white Methodists to challenge this identity was to challenge family. White racism arose as much from a love of one's biological family as it did from an irrational hatred of another race. That is what makes racism so insidious; it arises not out of some obvious and irrational hatred but from love grounded in disordered social formations. Its consequences distort the politics of the new age.

Roy Wilkins named the racism present in the churches not primarily as a discourse about civil rights, human rights, or social inclusion; it is a soteriological matter that calls into question the new age, the family that Jesus inaugurates. Segregation and racism privilege the old family over the new; it is a sign that the church clings to the old aeon, to the biological family.

Racism represents the sinfulness of clinging to the old aeon even when the *old* aeon is a modern invention. The reality of cultural differences leading to violence against others is ancient, but the racism that privileges biology over baptism is a peculiarly modern heresy. Perhaps this is due to the rise of the empirical sciences, with their dependence upon the brute facticity of nature as providing the narrative descriptions that render our lives intelligible. Once *nature* appears to us as self-evident and "on the surface," the category *race* arises. The cultural differences that separated persons are no longer viewed as *cultural* differences. In other words, Athenians, Spartans, and Ethiopians no longer oppose each other because they are Athenians, Spartans, and Ethiopians. Instead, differences of *race* are given a universal basis that sublimates the cultural differences behind the legitimating discourse of science. Consequently, the brute fact of biology becomes more determinative over our lives precisely because we no longer recognize differences as *cultural* and subject to revision, conversion, and defense.

In his essay, "Genealogy of Modern Racism," Cornel West argues that modern racism has an insidious hold on Western culture and philosophy because its basis is recognized not primarily in terms of cultural differences but in terms of a universal science:

> I will try to show that the idea of white supremacy emerges partly because of the powers within the structure of modern discourse—powers to produce and prohibit, develop and delimit, forms of rationality and scientificity and objectivity which set perimeters and draw boundaries for the intelligibility, availability and legitimacy of certain ideas.[28]

For West, racism is not merely the result of an obvious wickedness to which the uneducated and uncultured were primarily receptive. It was produced along with some of the greatest achievements of Western culture, its science and philosophy. For example, Linnaeus, Hume, Jefferson, Kant, and Montesquieu did not "put forward their own arguments to justify racism" but simply held to racist beliefs and assumed they were evident by the authority of "naturalists, anthropologists, physiognomists, and phrenologists."[29] In other words, *race*-ism is not possible without the authority of science assuming a normative white culture that can no longer recognize that it posits itself as normative. It is the self-deception present in the modern that renders racism so insidious and difficult to address. A society based on individual freedom and equality cannot recognize that that very language privileges one culture over another, for the language itself is one culture's imposition over others. It creates a putative universal culture, but it is actually a sinister form of imperialism that subjects other cultures to its own hegemony. This is the tragic pathos of liberalism; it is a hegemonic discourse that cannot recognize itself as such.[30]

The pathos of liberalism results in an inability to address the question of racism. This is in part due to the inability to describe and confess the sin of *racism* well. What is racism? The witness of Malcolm X can help us understand. He argued that the language of "civil rights" distorted the political and historical character of black oppression by subordinating it to an "internal United States issue."[31] This subordination produced an irresolvable antinomy, because once black suffering was construed as an internal political matter, it was addressed primarily in terms of the politics available within the United States. But the liberalism upon which America is predicated instantiates a doctrine of white supremacy. Therefore, its language of freedom, inclusivity, and equality cannot seriously address the history and politics of race. Such language assumes a norm (whiteness) against which terms such as *inclusivity* and *equality* can work. *Those terms cannot be used without the assumption of such a norm.* That is why they will always fail as an effort to address the sin of racism.

For Malcolm X, resolving the political history of racism required a privileging of African history and culture. African-Americans did not need to seek inclusion but to produce a space for a different norm within a dominant culture that makes whiteness normative. Thus, he called for black schools, businesses, and organizations. In this sense, the political strategy he advocated can perhaps be best understood by comparing it to the experience of another "minority" group in the United States, Roman Catholics. They also discovered that, despite America's putative language of freedom and equality, it had made normative a Protestant culture that threatened the viability of Catholicism. In response, they created an alternative culture within the dominant culture primarily through a unique system of education. Unfortunately, Catholics in America soon discovered that they had a unique advantage over African-Americans: they were predominantly white. Thus, Catholics have long since made peace with America such that Catholic parochial schools have now proved to be more nationalistic than America's public schools; the Pledge of Allegiance is more central to their daily functioning than the Nicene Creed.

The pathos of modern liberalism is that the *language* of equality and freedom cannot address the *history* of slavery, segregation, and racism that modernity itself "secreted." This leads to an inability to tell the truth. Stanley Hauerwas illustrates how this creates "the politics of the lie":

> For example, when George Bush nominated Justice Clarence Thomas for the Supreme Court, he had to say that Judge Thomas was the most qualified justice

he could find. We know that is the politics of the lie. Someone like Justice Thomas should have been nominated for the Supreme Court because the United States is and continues to be a racist society. George Bush could not tell Americans that we need African Americans in such offices so that they might use their power to protect their people in this racist society. He could not say that, because Americans do not want to acknowledge that this is a racist society. We have not the skill to know how to live truthfully with such sin.[32]

But what might it matter that we confess truthfully the sin of the particular racist history in which some of us as Christians find ourselves ensconced?

ONE, HOLY, CATHOLIC, APOSTOLIC, BLACK OR WHITE CHURCH?

If the church is, rather than has, a social ethic, then its separated histories into black and white churches betoken at most a temporary moment necessary for preserving Christian faithfulness by black Christians who needed a separate tradition to exercise faithfulness under conditions of oppression. This is not to suggest that a time will come when the black churches should be dissolved into the predominantly white churches; such a desire for *inclusion* merely reflects the politics of the United States. The traditions of the black church will be with us, just as we hope the traditions of Irish Catholicism, Wesleyan Methodism, and British Anglicanism will remain with us, contributing to the catholic church. The tradition of the black church and black theology provides an important mission calling all Christians to be faithful.

The very fact that we understand the designation *white church* reveals perhaps the most significant impact black theology has had on the church. I was neither reared nor baptized into any institution explicitly named "the white church," yet through the work of a theologian such as James Cone that designation has been disclosed. Ecclesial divisions that were more familiar, Catholic/Protestant, low church/high church, established church/free church, were further complicated by a more pervasive North American political distinction black/white. Cone told us not only that there were *white* churches but that those churches were species of heresy where baptism introduced us more into a cultural discourse (whiteness) than a redeemed, messianic community. To accomplish this, he spoke and wrote with a bluntness and a theological particularity that ensured that the point could not easily be missed.

Cone's work is significant precisely because he breaks through the bourgeois sentimentality that too often masquerades in the (white-dominated) language of contemporary theological education, the language of pluralism, inclusion, diversity, and dialogue. Cone transgresses the boundaries this language establishes, boundaries that seem to invite the production of a civic and civil theology. In the midst of that language Cone tells us,

The time has come for white America to be silent and listen to black people. . . .

All white men are responsible for white oppression. . . .

Theologically, Malcolm X was not far wrong when he called the white man "the devil.". . . .

To love the white man means the black man confronts him as a thou without any intentions of giving ground by becoming an it. . . .

Any advice from whites to blacks on how to deal with white oppression is automatically under suspicion as a clever device to further enslavement. . . .

The task of black theology is to take Christian tradition that is so white and make it black, by showing that whites do not really know what they are saying when they affirm Jesus as the Christ.[33]

Cone's work is neither sentimental invitation for dialogue nor liberal pleading for inclusivity. For those of us in the white church, there is no way out of the judgment these quotes render. The liberal move of inclusivity does not work; one cannot incorporate Cone's work into some generic cosmopolitanism. One cannot co-opt it through some vague call for an invitation to dialogue. And although I assume most of us understand the sentiment put forth so charitably by Rodney King ("Can't we all get along?"), the reality of the black/white division seems to be so pervasive that such sentiments detract from a proper social analysis of the conditions that make black suffering normative in the United States. Cone confronts us with this reality and gives us no room to affirm his work and avoid that reality. In fact, Cone lets us know that, far from seeking reconciliation, establishing community, or working on a common project, the relationship between blacks and whites in America can best be described as a low-intensity conflict. He boldly states, "The asserting of black freedom in America has always meant war. . . . there is no place for the white liberal in this war of survival."[34] There may be particular truces where blacks and whites work together without violence, but in North America the political and cultural narrative that perpetuates this low-intensity conflict seems always to be present. Any appeal to the one, holy, catholic, and apostolic church that overlooks this low-intensity conflict will ring as hollow as asserting a unified church in Northern Ireland.

When reading Cone's work, white folk seem caught on the horns of an uncomfortable dilemma: either liberal self-loathing or conservative denial. This dilemma finds expression in such statements as either "Yes, my white ancestors and I are personally responsible for the untold misery of black suffering" or "Why bring that history up to me? I didn't own any slaves." Even though there is partial truth in both responses, neither is satisfying. The first response can still be a veiled way for white culture to control the situation: look at what *we* did; now *we* must fix it. The second is simply to live from amnesia, some-thing quite possible in the modern era but not a viable option for the baptized who are sustained only through remembrance.

The problem with both liberal self-loathing and conservative denial is that they leave the power asymmetry unchanged. White folk still get to control the discourse. By coupling black theology with the black power movement, Cone left no place for such control. As he put it, "Religiously or philosophically Black Power means an inner sense of freedom from the structures of white society which builds its economy on the labor of poor blacks and whites."[35] At one level, the status of the white church in Cone's work is that of spectator; we are positioned such that we must listen and discover what it means to be out of control. It is a position to which the white church is unaccustomed.

The status of spectator to which black theology positions the white church could tempt it to misunderstand its role, imagining it has no place in the con-versation.[36] It can too easily lead to the sentiment that it is a black thing we cannot understand; therefore, we can affirm it, but we need not listen. This leads to an indifference toward black theology on behalf of white theologians, an indifference that occurs when white theologians refuse to engage black theo-logy either through a patronizing affirmation or through a not-so-benign neg-lect. But even though black theology places white responses under suspicion, it still recognizes that our fates are inextricably linked. As Cone noted, "When blacks assert their freedom in self-determination, whites too are liberated."[37]

Black theology should not be read such that it tempts the white church toward a paternal or malignant indifference. Instead, it discloses how the health and salvation of our communities are necessarily linked. This also seems to be a les-son Cone teaches, for even when he tells us that "all white men are responsible for white oppression," he seeks to expose white supremacy not for the purpose of condemnation alone but to issue a prophetic call. He goes on to say, "Inso-far as white do-gooders tolerate and sponsor racism in their educational insti-tutions, their political, economic and social structures, their churches, and in every aspect of American life, they are directly responsible for racism."[38] The phrase that begins Cone's sentence comes as a challenge and not merely a uni-versal indictment. "Insofar as" we merely look the other way, refuse to speak, then, says Cone, to that extent we are responsible. And those of us who are white know that it is almost impossible at some moment in our lives not to have looked the other way, to refuse to speak. Cone tells us what is at stake: "Racism is pos-sible because whites are indifferent to suffering and patient with cruelty."[39]

On the one hand, Cone's theology is not intended for a white audience, at least not one prepared to do anything other than listen. On the other hand, Cone's work demands a white audience. He has done something revealing; he has broken the silence that exists between the black and white communities in the United States by saying in public what often is said, or assumed, in private. That is a risky venture, which finally can have been motivated only by a severe charity. Insofar as black theology (like Irish Catholicism, Wesleyan Method-ism, liberal Protestantism, etc.) does not set itself apart as the only true form of Christianity and perpetuate a form of donatism, it contributes to the faith-fulness of the catholic church. It teaches us to confess our sin well not so that we might be able to control or engineer a different future but so that we might be able to discover what it would mean to redeem a history we cannot change.

ALTERNATIVE FAMILY LIFESTYLES

Family life is not a self-interpreting institution. Within Christian theology the significance of the family grows out of the mission of the church. This means that the family cannot be explained in biological terms alone. Once the family is defined in terms of a brute facticity of nature, it can take on demonic propor-tions. The mere *fact* of race becomes its own legitimization for an unwarranted superiority. That *race* is embedded in a cultural discourse and social formation—that it is a "moral norm" arising from a "social construction" and subject to revi-sion—disappears behind the authority of science. Because family is not a self-interpreting institution, the mission of the church offers it the gift of a particular vocation that provides it with limits. Marriage is not a brute biological fact but an adventure, which like all journeys needs something other than itself for its own mission. Eugene Rogers has given us a profound theology of marriage. Mar-riage is a form of asceticism that assists our sanctification. It does this by order-ing our desires toward another as they should be ordered toward God. Marriage becomes an analogy of the Triune Life in our everyday life.

In one sense, family life in the church already is an *alternative lifestyle,* which is why we call one another brother and sister and recognize a place for celibacy and singleness. After all, celibacy itself is a gift of the Christian moral life. Sin-gleness is not to be regarded as an insufficient or unfulfilled expression of our humanity. Instead, singleness and celibacy can be a superior form of life that embodies the kind of *apatheia* Gregory of Nyssa described, a form of life that does not oppose desire but helps the church discover desires that it might not otherwise know.

Assuming that the family is self-interpreting, that it can be explained in terms of a brute biology, tempted the church to make the biology of race more central to its life than the new age inaugurated by baptism. Is the church com-mitting the same error with regard to same-sex marriages in this postmodern era? Does the created distinction between male and female have a privileged role in marriage, or does the new age require, as Eugene Rogers has argued, even this "overturning of nature"?

The question of gay marriage has dominated contemporary theological debates as no other issue has, threatening to divide the churches yet again. Cer-tain forms of the debate are not worth pursuing. A few on the pro-gay side argue that this is an issue of civil rights. What someone does with her or his body is fundamentally the concern of that individual and not of the church. Each person should be granted the freedom and protection to exercise his or her sexuality as long as it does not entail coercive or manipulative behavior. This legalistic account of sexuality assumes that *consent* gives sexuality its moral bearing. Sexual intercourse, like other forms of exchange, becomes grounded in *values* based on human willing. This argument is dangerous precisely because it leads to the further dissolution of the church into the state and market. The rights-based argument for gay and lesbian marriage rips the family from its context in the church and resituates it within the state. The state becomes the condition for the possibility of our sexual practices because it grants and protects the *rights* that render such practices intelligible.

The opposite side can also further dissolve the church into the state by opposing homosexuality because of its potentially detrimental influence on heterosexual marriage, which is viewed as necessary for the civil order.[40] But how would this argument not also work against the alternative family relationship known as celibacy within the church? Would the toleration of gay unions have any more or less deleterious impact than celibacy? Why should *civil society* be the privileged social formation that allows Christians to think and act faithfully in their sexual practices? Precisely how homosexuality harms the civic order is not well spelled out, but this argument seems to suggest that the productive capacity of the heterosexual family is essential for a strong civic realm. Homosexuality is viewed as a threat to heterosexual stability. This is an odd argument. Its basis lies in an irrational fear that, once society opens the door to homosexuality, some will throw off their heterosexuality and embrace homosexuality. Such an argument has the same devastating consequences for the positioning of the family within a charitable social order as the argument for rights. Once again, the family is ripped out of the social context that makes it theologically intelligible and placed within a different social context—it is subordinated to "civil society."

LOYAL OPPOSITIONISTS

Liberal Protestant theology is particularly prone toward making the nation-state the primary social formation within which we think about sexuality. This inevitably results in the defense and toleration of a bourgeois decadence. The collection of essays put forth by a number of United Methodist theologians, laypersons, and clergy, *The Loyal Opposition: Struggling with the Church on Homosexuality*, is a prime example of this. The collection was born out of the hegemonic liberalism characteristic of mainline Protestantism that eschews difference and neglects substantive theological reflection, all in the name of inclusivity.[41] The official dogma that generates such a collection is the need to follow Jesus in welcoming the outcast and lifting up the downtrodden. This, of course, is nonnegotiable for Christian discipleship. Tex Sample persuasively argues that the church's vocation to lift up the downtrodden means that it must resist accommodating its life to the dominant culture, which "victimizes people who live on the margins of society."[42] But is the dualism of oppressor/oppressed so easily appealed to in the case of the church's stance against gay unions? Is there a single dominant culture in North America that informs our understanding of sexuality and that is repressive toward alternative lifestyles? Or do not those who advocate gay and lesbian unions need to recognize that they too resemble a dominant North American culture of sexuality?

The easy acceptance of a victim/victimizer dualism in works such as *The Loyal Opposition* does not contribute toward a substantive theological discussion. In fact, this dualism works as a form of power and coercion, for a discussion framed in terms of the oppressors and the oppressed is already over. If adopting the traditional teaching of the Christian churches on sexuality is a priori scripted as a form of oppression, no conversation can take place. All that can be done is for the oppressed to throw off the mantle of the oppressors through any means necessary.

The difficulty posed by the loyal oppositionists is not *that* they appeal to the church to reconsider its traditional sexual ethics but that they *base* this appeal on an inadequate theological foundation. Their advocacy for gay unions within Protestant churches involves much more than issues of equal rights, inclusivity, and the alleviation of suffering. It represents a particular theological dogmatics that privileges the modern over Scripture, a creation spirituality that functions as a new form of natural theology, a law/gospel distinction that borders on anti-Judaism, and a commitment to "progressive revelation" where some theologians proclaim with a thoroughgoing certitude what God is doing in the world today and how it differs with what God was thought to have worked in previous times.

For example, when he explains the relationship between the loyal opposition and Scripture, Victor Paul Furnish asserts, "Every one of the specific moral rules and teachings of Scripture is time bound and culturally conditioned."[43] Furnish tells us not to be dismayed by this revelation because what is distinctive about the Scriptures is not their moral rules but their understanding of God. Evidently, although the biblical writers were "time bound and culturally conditioned" when they offered teachings on moral matters, they were not so when they wrote of the "boundless grace of God." But how can Furnish so easily distinguish between the timeliness of biblical moral teaching and the timelessness of biblical theology? In fact, that moral teachings (and theological utterances) are "time bound and culturally conditioned" is a truism. To write, speak, or communicate in any form is by definition to be "time bound and culturally conditioned." Thus, the question is not *if* we can find some teaching that is not "time bound and culturally conditioned" but *which* time and what culture binds and conditions our teachings and readings.

Furnish seeks to locate the time-boundedness of Paul's teachings in order to demonstrate their inapplicability. Then he privileges modern science as providing us with the instrument by which Paul's time and culture should be measured. "None of the presuppositions reflected in Paul's statement" on homosexuality, Furnish writes, "can be allowed to stand unchallenged, given what the best of modern research is teaching us about human sexuality."[44] But once we begin to locate a teaching in its time-boundedness in order to dismiss its applicability to our time, we are headed for a *reductio ad absurdum*, for what Furnish says about Paul can equally be said about Furnish, particularly with regard to *his* embeddedness in the time of modernity and its culture of technology. None of Furnish's statements on homosexuality can be allowed to stand unchallenged until we have interrogated *their* timefulness. None of the results of modern technology can stand unchallenged until the newer, more modern technological forms interrogate them. That is the nature of modern technology: progress becomes our fate, and nothing ever stands. This is the modern problem of the legitimation of scientific knowledge that Furnish never addresses. But only someone who still assumes he inhabits a transcendental place capable of surveying the whole and distinguishing between historical relativity and transcendent ideals could make these kinds of arguments.

Perhaps Furnish sees what he sees not because modern science gives us some uncontestable facts, but because he lives in a culture marked by late capitalism with assumptions about values and exchange. For instance, in such a cultural system, a thing's "value" is a product not of what it "is," but of the preference or orientation one has toward it. Thus value—economic and moral—is a function of the will's exercise in effecting exchanges and not a feature of a created order independent of a combination of human wills. The time and culture of late capitalism could as easily affect Furnish's reading of Paul as Paul's time and culture affected his moral teachings. His apologia for gay unions is easily construed as reflecting the dominance of exchange values in late capitalist culture, where what a thing is (male or female body) has no bearing on its "values," but how it is exchanged through what the will wants (orientation or preference) gives it its value.

Where does this *reductio ad absurdum* lead us, except to charges and countercharges about which culture and time renders our teachings intelligible? Even so, if it leads us to this recognition, it will have done us a great service. This recognition takes away the primary strategy of rendering the biblical teaching inadmissible as is found in the loyal oppositionists. For if we recognize that *all* moral and theological teachings are "time bound and culturally conditioned," this should prevent us from dismissing them simply because their teachings are "time bound" and instead ask in which time and culture we discover the good.

Like many other moderns, Furnish has discovered a timeless ideal that relativizes any historical presentation of Christian teaching on political and moral issues. Furnish's absolute and unchanging norm is that God's grace is boundless. Evidently that means that no law can ever be adequate to the gospel. Instead, "what the church teaches always stands under the judgment of the gospel, and has to be constantly reconceived and reformulated to take account of ever new realities, deeper insights, and an enlarging vision."[45] Here grace is the new and improved; grace is progress. Such a view can only conflict with the ancient church teaching that recognized Jesus himself as the new law of the gospel, for such a modern understanding cannot make sense of the logic of the incarnation. It perpetuates a subtle form of the christological heresy known as Nestorianism, where Christ's two natures remain forever disunited. The ideal is never found in the historical; God is not discovered in flesh or in Judaism. Rather, God and God's grace are only discovered when we abstract from history and flesh, when we *negate* them for the sake of the new. To receive *grace*, we abstract from and destroy our laws, virtues, histories, traditions—even our bodies. This view of grace as the new set against all forms of law is present throughout the loyal oppositionists. In fact, it borders on anti-Judaism. Jews, it is implied, are tempted toward a legalism that maintains their identity at the expense of others. Their "tribal loyalty" prevents their vocation toward the establishment of an international community.[46] When the church makes legislation on moral matters, it falls into the same temptation of Judaism. Thus, the story of grace is the story of a "universalizing message" versus a "legalistic faction."[47]

The universalizing impulse present in the loyal oppositionists also produces a neonatural theology. This is an odd development, since homosexual activity has been traditionally viewed as incompatible with Christian teaching on the basis of a *natural* theology. Because same-sex body parts do not naturally work toward procreation, homosexual activity was viewed as contrary to nature. It was not part of God's created order but a consequence of human rebellion against God. Such an argument treats nature as self-interpreting and thus does not need the church and sacraments to render nature intelligible. Nature has a brute facticity to it that can be known through the sciences and their reliance on technological means. Although the appeal to a natural theology has traditionally been a "conservative" strategy to oppose homosexual activity, modern Protestants have developed a natural theology that finds the *natural* to be self-interpreting in order to affirm homosexual activity.

The natural theology used by the loyal oppositionists assumes that our sexual orientation is self-evidently good because it *is* our sexual orientation. Thus another one of the loyal oppositionists writes, "Asking God to alter someone's sexual orientation is asking God as Savior in Jesus Christ to contradict the work of God the Source or Creator."[48] The writer could not have meant this sentence to say what it actually says, for there are many sexual orientations (toward multiple partners, to oneself) that he would not affirm as beyond the transformation that should take place in baptism. But here the writer finds an orientation we do not choose to be a sign of God's good creation not subject to the fallenness that characterizes human existence. In this view, the only moral culpability one has is the *integrity* by which one lives in concert with one's orientation. This affirmation is also thoroughly modern in that it assumes that not to be true to one's orientation through sexual repression will result in pathologies. Orientations may very well be *given,* but to assume that a given orientation is an *essential* ontological ingredient poses serious theological problems. It traps us within a posited ontology that can only lead to the demise of any meaningful use of the terms *good* and *evil.* Our *authentic* being becomes a function of discovering and living in continuity with some pregiven natural code.

The creation spirituality and natural theology that inform the position of the loyal oppositionists fails on at least two accounts. First, like the more conservative natural-theology strategy, it has no place for baptism and the practices of the new age in order to understand sexuality. Sexual practices are to be read off the empirical evidence of our sexual orientations. Little place exists for a baptismal practice that invites one to renew and rediscover one's nature through a life of obedience. Within the practices of this neonatural theology, baptism can at most, be an affirmation of what we already are and a call to learn to accept with integrity the orientation we already possess.

But even the loyal oppositionists do not consistently make this argument. They remain sufficiently traditional and *legalistic* such that they continue to make judgments on others' sexual habits. Thus Dale Dunlap refers to "the promiscuity of saunas and bathhouses and the Playboy culture that we decry."[49] Dunlap raises a significant theological issue, which unfortunately the loyal oppositionists have not given us the resources to answer. If the church is to sanction and bless gay unions, then why should persons (straight or gay) oriented toward the promiscuity of bathhouse sex and a Playboy culture not also be included? Why do they still subject these persons to the legalistic judgment of being "incompatible" with Christian teaching? Why do they assume that this form of sexuality is not an "authentic" expression of one's pregiven orientation? Their laws seem arbitrary. The loyal oppositionists have not given us significant theological resources to explain why they still make judgments on such people. Perhaps their only basis is the certitude they have that progressive revelation gives them a positive summary judgment.

Another central dogma for the loyal oppositionists is progressive revelation, the claim that God progressively reveals God's self to the loyal oppositionists with such certitude that they can be loyal to God in the present moment without necessarily discerning what Scripture or tradition says. While hermeneutics was once understood as the discipline of discerning the significance of Scripture and tradition for the present, it now becomes a discipline that dispenses with the exegetical task altogether. With God's progressive revelation, even what the text *meant* is irrelevant. What it means for me in my experience becomes the norm.

The certitude with which some proclaim God's "new surprises" contains profound theological problems. The wisdom of the church fathers that the Son reveals everything that the Father is, except that the Son is not the Father, is rendered moot. The fathers recognized that, without this, God would seem arbitrary and subject to capricious acts of disclosure to special in-groups who would not be accountable to the community and its traditions. This resembles the heresy of Gnosticism. In opposition to this, the fathers confessed that God is *completely* disclosed in the Son. Thus, no further revelation is needed, and no secret knowledge has been or can be revealed to a private group unaccountable to the fullness of God's disclosure in Christ. Otherwise, God appears to be doing something of a striptease act, giving us a bit here and a bit there, but withholding God's self for a more felicitous occasion. Such a God does not seem to be as trustworthy as the God of Christian orthodoxy. This God actually *gives* himself to his creation, as true lovers should. Of course, that it is *God* who gives himself completely means that we can never take it all in. That the Son reveals all that the Father is does not mean that we have exhausted God's fullness. Time continues even into eternity precisely because we can never exhaust the mystery. Dogma is irreversible, but it is never exhaustive. It must always be developed. Further theological work on dogma is always necessary precisely because the Son reveals *all* that the Father is and the Spirit leads us into that truth. But we need not adopt the capricious Gnosticism of a progressive revelation to recognize that the God who gives himself fully to us comes as an inexhaustible mystery.

That God gives himself to us also implies that we are not *already* in a relation with God as God sees fit. Otherwise, what is the need for the gift? The natural theology of both the conservatives and the loyal oppositionists renders the Christian journey for the good unnecessary because it assumes that we have all we need through our nature *qua* nature. We need no supplement to a *fallen* nature, such as is found in baptism. The Christian journey toward the good assumes that we need to be caught up in a narrative grander than the narrative of our own choosing. In that sense, it is a *supernatural* narrative. Likewise, our complicity in evil is not fundamentally a *choice* but an inheritance over which we do not have complete control. The loyal oppositionists neglect the biblical narrative of the fall. But as Richard Hays puts it, such a neglect cannot make sense of a biblical anthropology:

> The Bible's sober anthropology rejects the apparently commonsense assumption that only freely chosen acts are morally culpable. Quite the reverse: the very nature of sin is that it is *not* freely chosen. That is what it means to live "in the flesh" in a fallen creation. We are in bondage to sin but still accountable to God's righteous judgment of our actions. In light of this theological anthropology, it cannot be maintained that a homosexual orientation is morally neutral because it is involuntary.[50]

The journey toward the good is not a journey I make through what my own will chooses or values; it is a journey where we get caught up and are moved by a vision larger than our individual volitional and affectional capacities alone can provide. Such a vision comes to us through communal mediation. If the church does not set before us an *object* of desire worthy of a journey toward God, we will seldom get caught up in anything other than a journey of our own making.

The "loyal oppositionists" are also on a traditioned journey. In fact, more than the issue of gay and lesbian unions, what divides the contemporary churches is the understanding of tradition that informs moral and political deliberations. As Ignacio Castuera states, one narrative of Protestantism is that it is a tradition of dissent, a tradition characterized by the dialectic "loyal-opposition." He views Luther and Wesley as "loyal oppositionists" who stood against the church's corrupt rules by practicing ecclesial disobedience. Thus they set forth a tradition whereby faithfulness requires ongoing dissent. This is merely the repetition of the (so-called) Protestant principle that assumes the dialectic of "permanent revolution." Although this does characterize modern Protestantism, particularly Protestantism as practiced in North America, this reading of the Protestant churches limits its narrative to Protestantism as a modern project. Neither Luther, Calvin, nor Wesley rejected the dogmas of the ecumenical councils. As Reinhard Hütter has shown, Luther did not simply privilege protest for the sake of protest itself; he identified core ecclesial practices, which Luther termed "holy possessions," where one can "justifiably speak of 'church.'"[51] Far from a permanent revolution based on a "tradition" of dissenting from tradition, Luther identified key characteristics of the church that give it continuity through time. Characterizing Protestantism as "loyal opposition" misses this continuity. It fits nicely within modern socio-political formations. In passing, Castuera notes that ecclesial dissenters found shelter in America. This causes him no pause, but it raises for me a lingering question that I already put to Furnish's reading of Paul. Do the loyal oppositionists ask us to exchange the time of the church for the time and space of America?

Loyal oppositionists develop rigid confessions and dogmas that cannot be scrutinized because they cannot be recognized. As a result, they lose the ability to confess the contradictions of their position and to see how their movement is more inflexibly dogmatic than orthodoxy itself. Their confessions and dogmas arise from the now. This is a thoroughgoing "*neo*orthodoxy," where the eternal now that never comes is privileged as the true, but traditional orthodoxy is assumed false because it was presented in history. This new dogmatic tradition, as the loyal oppositionists recognize, is the dominant consensus in mainline Protestant seminaries. Our dogma, our fate, is to be permanently progressive.

The loyal oppositionists are not the only voice speaking for gay and lesbian unions in the life of the church. Much more substantive theological apologias do exist. But *how* one argues for or against gay and lesbian unions is as significant in our quest for the good as the resolution advocated. As we have seen with the loyal oppositionists, advocacy for gay unions can come with a broader theological dogmatics that dissolves the time of the church into modern time.

Likewise, opposition to gay unions can occur through arguments that privilege the *civic* order to the exclusion of God's charitable economy.

CIVIL OPPOSITION

Some oppose gay marriage on the basis that it will do harm to the civic order. This is an ancient argument based on an imperial misreading of the story of Sodom and Gomorrah. In the fifth century the emperor Justinian outlawed homosexuality on the basis that it jeopardized the civic order, causing as it did, "famine, earthquakes and pestilence."[52] Justinian, deducing a political theology directly from the story of Sodom and Gomorrah, thought that God brought such plagues on the civic realm when it tolerated homosexuals; thus, he imagined himself under obligation for the sake of the civic good to root out all "sodomy." Enshrining this prejudice and perceived threat to the public order in Western law, Justinian made homosexuality a capital offense. This is beyond unfortunate and a reading of the story unsupported by Genesis 19:1–29, which does not designate the sin of Sodom as any kind of sexual misconduct. In fact, when Scripture does speak of the sin of Sodom, it states, "this was the guilt of your sister Sodom: she and her daughters had pride, surfeit of food, and prosperous ease, but did not aid the poor and needy" (Ezek. 16:49).[53]

Is continued opposition to gay and lesbian unions within Western politics a residual element of this oppressive and misinformed reading of the story of Sodom? Following Justinian, Christendom certainly suppressed homosexuality, but the repression of homosexuality cannot be attributed solely to Christendom. Communist politics once viewed homosexuality as bourgeois decadence. Confucianist cultures see it as a Western cultural practice that promotes self-interest over communal goods. Is defense of homosexuality a Western cultural product? Far from being only in opposition to Western culture, homosexuality once had a rather central place in Greco-Roman culture. Its current resurgence as a legitimate alternative lifestyle in which opposition to it is a priori denounced as "heterosexism" is certainly new, but this resurgence also bears resemblances to that pre-Christian Hellenistic era before the political dominance of Christianity. One question that cannot be avoided for a Christian social ethics is whether Western culture's return to normative homosexual relationships brings with it a return to that period of time Christians referred to as *paganism,* a return that we should refer to as a "re-Hellenization" of Western culture.

RE-HELLENIZING THE GOSPEL

Any re-paganization of Western culture will be precisely that: a *re*-paganization. Thus it is not a mere return to that which cannot be returned. Nietzsche found in Greek tragedy the possibility of a new myth to guide the West after the defeat of the Christian and Jewish revolt against Greek honor. Central to this myth was the assumption that "nature" does not "surrender her secrets" unless she is forced to "by victoriously opposing her by means of the Unnatural."[54] Knowledge only comes to the initiate who follows the passions to that place beyond, to that place of excess. This excess does not bring freedom; it brings discovery. It is a discovery of *will*, not a longing and desire for *something* but longing and desire *qua* longing and desire. Such a discovery is no more freeing than a Dionysian revelry, which culminates in horrifying excess. While discovery cannot take place without initiation into excess, such excess must be tamed through aesthetic production. It must be made beautiful. This myth is embodied in modern therapeutic practices, where the posited *unconscious* conceals from view our excessive sexual desires. Not able to confront these desires, we repress them. Such repressed excess, however, will always emerge into some pathology if we do not carefully bring the repressed to consciousness. This myth is not responsible for the renormalization of homosexuality in the West, but it certainly has become a dominant myth informing Western sexual practices. Contemporary homosexual practices can participate in this myth just as much as heterosexual practices already do. Once this myth gains normativity, celibacy and fidelity become, at best, signs of immaturity and, at worst, pathologies. In a reversal so profound it must be admired, *deviant* and *normal* sexual practice exchange places after Christendom.

Is this reversal a resurfacing of the suppressed, which is to be expected after the decline of the influence of Jewish and Christian narratives on sexual practices in the West? Did Nietzsche foresee it? If at the end of Christendom we are living through antiquity's resurgence against its repression, the church's response should not be to recover the Caesaropapism of Justinian and impose a sexual ethic through rule and domination. It should be to recognize our changed context and rediscover again what it means to live not as "Gentiles of the flesh" but as those who "have been brought near in the blood of Christ" (Eph. 2:11, 13–16).

What does it mean to be *Gentile?* Paul associated it with all kinds of sexual immorality, including homosexuality. In Romans 1:18–32, Paul establishes, as Dale Martin notes, "a sting operation." He draws upon a common Jewish reading of Gentile culture, that its fall from worshiping one God into idolatry resulted in *unnatural* sex (Rom. 1:26). Jews appear to have viewed homosexual activity as a peculiarly Gentile practice. Although Richard Hays finds Paul's listing of sexual "depravities" to be the consequence of "rebellious humanity rather as the plagues were visited upon the Egyptians in Exodus," Dale Martin finds that too encompassing. For Martin, Romans 1 refers not to the fall but to the origin of idolatry. Martin finds this distinction significant because it implies that Paul condemns Gentile polytheism rather than offering a "general condemnation of perverse human nature."[55] By reading Romans 1 as concerned with Jewish prejudices about purity rather than with universal accounts of unnatural desire, Martin suggests that Romans 1 can be read against the "heterosexist purposes" to which scholars like Hays put it. If Paul's primary concern was idolatry, and Gentile homosexuality was a consequence of idolatry, then we would expect that "the abolition of idolatrous cults and polytheism would spell the end of homosexuality."[56] Since the end of idolatrous cults did not spell the end of homosexuality, we must recognize either that Paul was wrong about the consequences of idolatry or did not understand homosexuality as we do today. In either case, Romans 1 should no longer be used to explain homosexual desire.

Martin argues that Romans 1 does not offer a critique of homosexual desire at all because the ancients did not distinguish between homosexual and heterosexual desire; they only had desire. To be "contrary to nature" was to have not a "disoriented desire" but an "inordinate desire."[57] Just as gluttony was "too much eating," so homosexuality resulted from "too much sex." Martin is not arguing that Paul would have advocated homosexuality in moderation. Rather, Martin argues that Paul, like many if not all ancients, thought that homosexuality was generated out of an insatiable sex drive that went beyond heterosexual intercourse in order to find new and more exciting forms of sex. The fact that not all homosexuality can be explained in terms of this inordinate desire renders Paul's teachings irrelevant for modern knowledge about homosexual orientation.

The key difference between Hays's and Martin's interpretations of Romans 1 is their understanding of *kata physin* ("according to nature"). Martin denies that Paul distinguished between heterosexual and homosexual desire. For Martin, Paul did not oppose homosexual desire because it was unnatural; he opposed all desire. Thus, he saw heterosexual marriage as a remedy for desire, because it allowed for sexual intercourse without desire. This is based on Paul's teaching that "it is better to marry than to burn." Martin does not concede that satisfying desires within heterosexual marriage is any more "ordered" by biblical teaching than is satisfying homosexual desire; he makes no distinction between lust and desire. He finds Paul opposed to all desire. However, Martin never explains to us how Paul thought that we could engage in sexual intercourse in marriage without desire. Was biology that significantly different in Paul's generation? One is left wondering why Paul argued against the Corinthians' suggestion that Christians should refrain from marriage altogether. If Paul opposed desire *qua* desire, how could he tolerate marriage at all?

Richard Hays, however, argues that Paul found homosexuality to be "unnatural." This is not based upon some necessary distinction between homosexual and heterosexual desire, for Paul would find many expressions of heterosexual desire *unnatural* as well. The distinction between *natural* and *unnatural* is not a function of orientation but a function of creation's purposes. By "nature," Hays suggests, Paul intends "created order," which does "not rest on empirical observation of what actually exists; instead, it appeals to a conception of what ought to be, of the world as designed by God and revealed through the stories and laws of Scripture."[58]

What constitutes *nature* is not to be read off someone's empirical orientation, whether that orientation be hetero or homo. For Hays, neither the biological necessity of male-femaleness in procreation nor some genetically predisposed orientation gives us access to *nature*. Instead, what is natural is discovered through and in the biblical narratives, which are univocally opposed to same-sex intercourse. That is what makes it "unnatural." Hays also notes that wealth, violence, and lack of concern for the poor are more often pronounced "unnatural," in contrast to the few biblical references to same-sex intercourse, yet his reading of Scripture differs significantly from Martin's in its political consequences for the church's relationship to the recovery of normative homosexuality in Western culture. For Hays, the church should stand against same-sex intercourse *and* these other "unnatural" practices even while it pleads God's mercy in Christ and recognizes our complicity in all of them.

RE-EVANGELIZING HELLENISM?

One of the more theologically compelling arguments for same-sex marriage within the church is made by Eugene Rogers, who argues that, as Gentiles were incorporated into the Jewish covenant in an "excess of nature" (branches grafted on to a root), so same-sex marriages can be included in the Christian covenant through a similar excess of nature. Rogers does not begin with the question of rights, biology, orientation, or fears about the consequences of homosexuality to the civic order. His reflections on homosexual marriage begin theologically, in terms of ecclesiology.[59] He develops his position by reading marriage within the relationship between Christ and the church.

Rogers avoids the all-too-common temptation to put the debate in terms where all persons who oppose homosexual marriage are homophobic and all who favor it are sexually promiscuous. Instead, he gives these debates an ecclesial orientation. Sexuality finds it place within "the politics of the people of God," which entails a theological rendering of marriage. "Marriage is peculiarly suited to teaching God's desire for human beings," Rogers writes, "because it mirrors God's choosing of human beings for God's own."[60] Rogers recognizes that Christian marriage is a participation in God's economy. It is an ascetic practice where we discover the *apatheia* necessary for chastity. There is no celebration of sexual activity for its own sake in his Christian apology for gay marriage. He does not "establish sex as a privileged spiritual access route."[61]

Rogers finds the grafting in of Gentiles into God's covenant with the Jews precedence for the Spirit's work in the church to bring faithful gay marriages within its common life. This is not an argument for *homosexuality* any more than the church has ever defended *heterosexuality*. Rather, he focuses on holiness, which, unlike *rights,* is something in which the church has a stake. He helps us address the question, What does it mean to be the people of God in the midst of a "pagan" culture that seeks to define our sexuality? God does not leave a "pagan" culture to its own devices. Instead, God seeks to graft it into God's own life. So Rogers argues that just as God elected the Gentiles through an "overturning of nature to graft wild olives onto a domestic tree," so God may be "overturning nature" to bring faithful gay marriages into the life of the church. To deny gays access to the common life because it is "contrary to nature" would be to deny the election of the Gentiles.

Rogers's argument does raise questions. Does God "overturn nature" in grafting us Gentiles into the Jewish covenant? What in our "Gentile nature" should be overturned? Bernd Wannenwetsch reminds us that the grafting of Gentiles into the Jewish covenant no longer asked of them circumcision, but they still had to obey Torah.[62] What is it about being Gentile that needs to be redeemed before we are grafted into the covenant? Is it our *nature* that must be overturned? If so, what does that do to the relationship between nature and grace? Will we still be able to make sense of Aquinas's statement that grace does not contradict but perfects nature? For instance, in Rogers's argument, childlessness almost becomes a norm of Christian sexuality because it witnesses to the resurrection more than does biological childbirth.

For Rogers, adoption approaches a preferred method of reproduction because it signifies a grafting into the family similar to the inclusion of the Gentiles. This argument is unpersuasive, for even adopted children must be given biological birth. Granted, biology is not a self-evident science but belongs, as René Girard has explained, entirely to culture.[63] Still, that does not make it arbitrary. It also fits with God's economy such that *male* and *female* are part of the created order. What will it mean to lose this? Will we still be able to recognize our very existence, our births, as gifts of labor? Or will we lose something decisive and begin to live out the myth of autochthony in Plato's *The Republic,* where for the sake of "egalitarianism" the guardians are told that they were born without mothers and fathers? The theological narrative that praises the arduous and noble task of giving birth, which assumes male-female normativity, still has a legitimate place in the church. Unfortunately, Rogers's appeal to the sacramental practices of the new age tempts us to forget the original gift that makes our lives possible.

Wannenwetsch writes, "When the sacramental reality is invoked to transcend the meaning which the Creator has written into our bodies so as to make it irrelevant for Christian ethics, something else must be wrong."[64] He sees in Rogers's argument a kind of anthropological Docetism. The human body loses the significance of its concrete form, its physicality. Rogers disagrees and responds, "Why is it that when a man has a bodily (emotional, affectional and physiological) reaction to a woman, it's real, but when a woman has similar bodily reactions to a woman it's mere appearance? Or why is it that the shape of the body counts as real, but the reaction of the body counts as mere appearance."[65]

This response is unfortunate, because it introduces what Rogers has been careful to avoid, an argument for gay unions based on affectional orientation. Rogers must show us he can respond to Wannenwetsch's critique from the perspective of ecclesial mission if his own dogmatics is to succeed.

To his credit, Rogers locates sexual desire within the life of the church and its politics. It is not rendered intelligible by the state or the market. The dominance of the latter over our lives makes chastity a countercultural virtue. While the church continues to respond to the question of the place of gay and lesbian marriage within its common life, it can only do so with a concern for the virtue of chastity. Still, too many questions remain for the church to act hastily at this point in time. For example, why is the argument for gay and lesbian inclusion in the church primarily a North American and European phenomenon? Is it one more sign of our imperialism that assumes that the church in Africa, Asia, and Latin America is still not as progressive or developed as we are? Or does this question arise as an outgrowth of the hegemony of capitalist "values" over all our sexual practices?[66] Does the assumption that one's sexual orientation legitimates one's sexual practices arise because we assume that *preference* or *will* gives the world its value? In other words, *male* and *female* no longer signify anything normative in God's created purposes because we know that what gives the world *value* is not our embodiedness but our will or affectional orientation. This argument is the logical conclusion of Western philosophy's mind/body dualism and would be consistent with the cultural discourse of capitalism.

Moreover, must one accept the "creation spirituality" that dominates mainline Protestant seminaries to affirm the inclusion of homosexual practice? Nearly every theological apologia for homosexual practice argues for it on the basis that our *sexual orientation* is a gift God gives us at our birth. When we exercise it, we become more whole. Since when has nature as biological orientation provided the basis for Christian sexual ethics? Has this will to overcome any limits of creation become itself a kind of modern natural theology? Does this argument finally reduce baptism to an affirmation of who we already are? Does it make baptism unnecessary?

Is it adequate to analogize the issue of homosexuality to the church's exclusion of women, defense of slavery, segregation, and the like? I am not sure. Here the argument for the inclusion of gay marriage in the church's practice contains compelling power. We do not want to repeat the sins of the past. Yet in both tradition and Scripture an argument for the inclusion of women as priests and opposition to slavery existed along with the arguments that were used to exclude women and defend slavery. Thus, one could appeal to portions of Scripture and tradition against other portions of Scripture and tradition. I do not think this has yet been done with respect to the inclusivity of gay practice. Both Scripture and tradition seem to be clearer on this, although Rogers's argument for the inclusion of certain Gentile practices must be taken seriously.

The question that his argument begs concerns which Gentile practices are included and which are not in our call to be obedient to Torah.

What shall we do with Scripture? We should not use Scripture only by finding in it propositions for ethical guidance, but this does not mean propositions are irrelevant. The Levitical proposition that a man lying with a man as with a woman is to be stoned cannot be a decisive argument against gay unions. It advocates capital punishment for homosexuality, which is not a *proposition* anyone should set forth today. But this does not imply that the Leviticus passage has no significance for our theological reflections. This passage comes in that portion of the Holiness Code that legislates against incest, and no Christian should dismiss this proposition. Simply to dismiss the purity laws in their totality because they are purity laws is to separate Jesus from Judaism, to perpetuate a subtle kind of anti-Judaism, and once again to privilege the modern over our legacy as a sect within Judaism. It is a subtle form of Marcionism. One cannot be a Christian, which is to be in a sect within Judaism, without concern for holiness and purity.

The pressing theological problem we confront is how to be faithful friends to gay and lesbian Christians in our company. Some have made sacramental vows to one another. Even if we disapprove of such vows, undoing them is no small matter. Other gay and lesbian Christians are not asking us to bless their unions, for that leaves them in practices with which they are uncomfortable. Is it sufficient to dismiss such persons as suffering from internalized homophobia? Is it sufficient to ask all faithful gay and lesbian couples to forsake relationships grounded in fidelity? Can we accept gay unions without demeaning the significance of the creation of male and female for the purpose of creation? David McCarthy has suggested that we think of gay unions as we do infertility, a "natural anomaly" for which the church can find a place without valorizing it as the normative vocation we call marriage. Just as Augustine recognized that an adulterer faithful to his adulterous partner is preferable to an indiscriminate and promiscuous adulterer, the church should at least argue that a faithful gay couple is preferable to the indiscriminate and promiscuous consumer sexuality that pervades both hetero- and homosexuality at present. The real problem challenging the church's holiness is not so much homosexual promiscuity as heterosexual promiscuity. Such a form of "social reproduction" inevitably serves the interests of the market. The market's global power, and its formation of our sexual activities, is testified to in the practice of abortion; it is its sacrament.

ABORTION: THE COMMODIFICATION OF HUMAN FLESH

When it comes to abortion, the question of our culture is, "Are you pro-life or pro-choice?" But this is not the right question, because it neglects to place abortion within a social and political context. It assumes abortion is a momentary decision without a history, without a context. Abortion becomes a function of the individual, which neglects that the *individual* is already a social and political creation. Abortion is then considered to be either an arbitrary decision by a callous woman who could do otherwise or a decision forced upon a woman by her circumstances. Once we are forced into this either-or, we are also forced into assuming that the other side argues either out of bad faith or ignorance. Those who assume abortion is a callous choice are either misogynists or unaware of the vulnerable conditions biological reproduction faces. Those who assume women cannot choose otherwise either hold a callous disregard for life or are so comfortable in the modern world that they are unwilling to consider alternative political possibilities. Many pro-lifers believe that pro-choice is a euphemism for anti-life. Many pro-choicers believe pro-life is a euphemism for misogyny. The apparently deep disagreements between these two groups have led to vicious confrontations between them and curious alliances within them. Evangelicals and Roman Catholics, long-time enemies, have joined together to practice civil disobedience in the Operation Rescue movement. Civil disobedience was once the tactic of the cultural left, but now the left has invoked the power of the state (previously a tactic of the cultural right) against those practicing civil disobedience. Has the defense of pro-choice led the left into a politics of the right, where it makes alliances with the security apparatus of the state? Has the civil disobedience of Protestant evangelicals and Roman Catholics moved them toward the political left, where they find themselves at odds with the modern nation-state? Perhaps *left* and *right* no longer make sense. Space and time are indeed out of joint. These spatial categories will no longer do. They are now mired in confusion.

Despite the apparent deep differences between these two groups, they share a great deal in common. The pro-life position argues that an unborn should be considered an individual. As an individual, the unborn is then entitled to rights, including the right to life. This positions the question of abortion primarily in terms of the state and its power. The pro-choice position argues that the pregnant woman should likewise be considered an individual who has rights, this time the right to choose what will happen within her body. This also positions abortion primarily in terms of the state and its power. Thus, the social formation the argument assumes on both sides is basically the same. Likewise, the form of their moral argument is quite similar: individuals have rights that should not be violated.

What the public debate over abortion reveals is that no moral argument can make sense when the only language we have available is that individuals are rights-bearing creatures. Because pro-lifers and pro-choicers share this basic fundamental assumption, the current debate is really not a debate at all, at least not a debate over the political and cultural philosophy that undergirds America. There is no *culture war*, since there is only one culture, the culture of economic liberalism with its reduction of all human life to rights-bearing individuals and value preferences. The only conflict that exists is how this underlying culture is to be applied to the question of abortion. Because this culture knows only power, it is incapable of adjudicating differences without coercion and/or violence. North American culture provides no way to adjudicate between the two applications of its common culture other than through sheer power and violence. Can we think about abortion differently?

ABORTION: STATECRAFT OR ECCLESIAL POLITICS?

Abortion has been practiced since the earliest times of Greek and Roman society. It occurred through the introduction of pessaries into the birth canal that either caused the fetus to abort or destroyed it, through mechanical techniques such as striking the fetus, through oral drugs, and through delicate surgical operations. Such techniques were obviously harmful to the mother, sometimes fatal. Yet many people mistakenly think that abortion was an accepted practice in these early societies and that only the influence of Christianity mitigated against it. The Hippocratic Oath shows this to be not quite the full story:

> I swear by Apollo Physician, by Asclepius, by Health, by Panacea and by all the gods and goddesses, making them my witnesses, that I will carry out, according to my ability and judgment, this oath and this indenture. . . . I will use treatment to help the sick according to my ability and judgment, but never with a view to injury and wrong-doing. Neither will I administer a poison to anybody when asked to do so, nor will I suggest such a course. Similarly, I will not give to a woman a pessary to cause abortion.[67]

People in power in Greco-Roman society opposed abortion. The reason for doing so was that the unborn was the property of the father and of the state. The state should protect the man's right to his wife and his offspring. Cicero even calls for capital punishment for a woman who aborts on the supposition that she has done injury to the father, the family's inheritance rights, the human race, and the state. The prohibition against abortion served the power of patriarchy.

Many early Christians opposed abortion, but not on the same grounds. In the *Didache*, an early Christian manual thought to be a first-century document, abortion was expressly forbidden among the faithful. Likewise, Tertullian wrote around the year 197 that

> in our case, murder being once for all forbidden, we may not destroy even the fetus in the womb, while as yet the human being derives blood from other parts of the body for its sustenance. To hinder a birth is merely a speedier man-killing, nor does it matter whether you take away a life that is born, or destroy one that is coming to the birth. That is a man which is going to be one; you have the fruit already in its seed.[68]

For Tertullian, the argument against abortion is not based on paternal property rights but on the premise that the Christian community is bound by a law that expresses the life of its gentle Savior. Origen worked from a similar basis when he stated,

> If a revolt had been the cause of the Christians existing as a separate group, the lawgiver of the Christians would not have forbidden entirely the taking of human life. He taught that it was never right for his disciples to go so far against a man, even if he should be very wicked; for he did not consider it compatible with his inspired legislation to allow the taking of human life in any form at all. Moreover, if Christians had originated from a revolt, they would not have submitted to laws that were so gentle which caused them to be killed as sheep and made then unable even to defend themselves against their persecutors.[69]

For the Christian community, abortion is neither a question of individual rights nor of the sacredness of human life. Rather, it is a question of how our communal politics are consistent with their origin in Jesus' life, teachings, death, and resurrection. Origen points out that his opposition to a Christian's taking life is based on the need for continuity with the originating act that gives rise to the politics of the church. This leads to an understanding of the politics of the church that runs counter to other originating political myths.

Most societies are predicated upon a myth of originary violence, which they then celebrate annually, such as the Fourth of July in the United States. If this were our politics, abortion and war would make sense. They would reconstitute the identity of a people who know that their identity is originally constituted by violence against enemies and all who threaten them. However, the political society we call the church was not founded upon a violence committed. The cross and resurrection are the originating factors of our politics. Therefore, we cannot condone abortion as the norm within the community of faith, even though we recognize that, given the politics of this world and the pervasive power of patriarchy, some women have no choice. If a woman has no choice but to have an abortion, this is most likely the responsibility of the community of faith, who was unable to provide for her an alternative where such a *choice* would not be countenanced. Abortion arises as a choice because the church fails to offer the hospitality it is called to give.

In the United States, abortion is allowed under the constitutional right of privacy. *Choice* is the key word by which abortion is permissible. Whether or not this defense of abortion has given women more control over their sexuality is itself a contested issue among feminists. Catharine MacKinnon recognizes the economic and cultural conditions that made abortion possible in the United States when she writes,

So long as women do not control access to our sexuality, abortion facilitates women's heterosexual availability. In other words, under conditions of gender inequality, sexual liberation in this sense does not free women; it frees male sexual aggression. The availability of abortion removes the one remaining legitimized reason that women have had for refusing sex besides the headache. As Andrea Dworkin put it, analyzing male ideology on abortion, "Getting laid was at stake." The Playboy Foundation has supported abortion rights from day one; it continues to, even with shrinking disposable funds, on a level of priority comparable to that of its opposition to censorship.[70]

Abortion is *legal* under the right to privacy, but it is defended on the basis of a cultural understanding of morality that makes *values* the heart of the moral life.

The political context that makes abortion possible assumes (and therefore constitutes) it as a matter of private choice. Even though certain persons may find it objectionable and may seek to persuade people against exercising this choice, certain things are private and are finally left up to a person's individual judgment. They are called *values*, and morality is thought to be a matter of values. Of course, morality as values arises when the market has so thoroughly invaded the moral life that people cling to the false assumption that what constitutes morality is the individual will's preferences. Choice is the quintessential capitalist value. The purpose of the free-enterprise system is to allow for as many private choices as possible without governmental interference. As a practice, abortion is the commodification of human flesh left up to the individual consumer's choice, providing economic resources for entrepreneurial physicians and others who assist them. Abortion as a practice is in obvious continuity with the philosophers of economic liberalism and their insistence on human control of reproduction to serve economic ends. To think otherwise is to avoid the social and political conditions that make abortion possible in our society.

Since the rise of the study of economics, one of the factors present in making nations wealthier has been the need to regulate population. This was evident in Parson Malthus's wrong predictions about the future shock involved in the rising exponential rate of population. Other early economists (who were all philosophers of human action) joined him in explicitly linking the development of a capitalist economics with control of human reproduction. In his *Principles of Political Economy*, published in 1817, David Ricardo argued that when the market price of labor went below its natural price (the price necessary for laborers to subsist), the market price would once again rise to meet the natural price only after their privations had reduced their number.[71] The poor have always been expendable when labor is cheap in a capitalist society, and abortion is one option to keep the market price of labor close to its natural price. The language of choice makes the economic necessity appear moral.

Within Christian tradition, abortion is understood as an *intrinsically* evil act. That is, it can never be justified under any circumstances; the *act* itself is always wrong. The Christian morality of acts is classified on the basis of act, object, and circumstance. These three things—the act itself, the circumstances that made the act possible or necessary, and the purpose for which the act was done—formed the mitigating factors for assessing whether acts were good or evil. However, many modern Christians deny the possibility of any act being intrinsically good or evil. Instead, acts are always judged on the basis of the circumstances that give rise to this act and by cost-benefit ratios. Still, it is quite licit to argue that an act is intrinsically evil, such as abortion, without arguing that the major culpability resides with the woman who has had the abortion. In fact, in his encyclical, *Evangelium Vitae,* Pope John Paul II states something quite similar to this when he calls abortion a structure of sin and suggests that the moral culpability for its powerful presence in Western society is not so much that of the mother as it is of fathers, doctors, nurses, legislators, and hospital administrators.[72]

Abortion is an economic reality in capitalist societies. The first question for Christians should not be whether we advocate choice or a right to life but whether our churches can be places that welcome and care for the children in their midst and the women who bear those children. Can we form men and women who will be responsible for their progeny and responsible in their sexual practices? Can we offer an economic alternative to the commodification of human flesh? Whenever an abortion occurs within the life of the Christian faithful, we are all culpable. We should all confess and seek to live so that such violent forms of life are no longer necessary among us.

DYING WELL

While the Christian community must be a place that welcomes life and does not embrace death as the answer to life, it must also be a place where we learn how to die. How shall we assist ourselves, others, and particularly our elders in dying well? When we answer this question, we will also know how to live well, because living a good life includes learning to die well. Such an art has become a neglected and forgotten theme in Christian theology. This was not always the case. Works such as Jeremy Taylor's *Holy Living and Dying* recall a time when theologians put forth obligations to prepare the faithful for death. The "art" of "dying well," suggested the Anglican divine, required daily practices of general preparation. For Taylor, this general preparation was based on three precepts. First, the person who would die well "must always look for death every day knocking at the gates of the grave; and then the gates of the grave shall never prevail upon him to do him mischief." Second, "he that would die well must all the days of his life, lay up against the day of his death." The necessary provisions, stated Taylor, were "faith and patience." Third, to die well required a life that eschewed "softness, delicacy and voluptuousness" in favor of "a life severe, holy and under the discipline of the cross." Taylor then suggested daily activities that would assist us in this general preparation for death, such as examination of conscience and the exercise of charity.[73]

Jeremy Taylor put forward these duties in the mid-seventeenth century, but they still provide a context within which we think about not only our own deaths but also the deaths of our elders.[74] To honor one's elders would be to help them complete life with a holy death. But now, more than two centuries later, Taylor's general precepts seem alien, if not morbid, to us. We focus our attention not on death itself but on that period prior to death known as "retirement" or the "third age."[75] We speak of *aging* rather than *dying*. We still possess preparatory duties for death, but these duties take as their primary purpose a comfortable retirement before death so that we will be the least burdensome on our relatives, friends, and enemies. Such duties can easily conflict with prior theological duties to prepare daily for death at all ages through a severe and holy discipline. The language of dying is no longer cloaked in garments such as fasting, prayer, and preparation for suffering. Instead, it is dressed up with retirement, pensions, and security.

This change in dress has some distinct advantages that reflect positive social changes since Taylor's time: we bury our children less, our parents and grandparents live longer and healthier lives, and we suffer less from diseases and poor health. These changes have resulted in a new language. We now speak of a "third age," a stage in life where we must learn to adjust to the process of aging, adjustments our forbears had little opportunity or necessity to make. Only a masochist could find in these new developments something to bemoan, for no one should seek suffering and an early death for their own sake. Yet the difficulty with acknowledging the positive gains of these changes is the social and political narrative that is often given credit for them. That narrative suggests that these gains were realized primarily by the creation of the free market as a neutral, technical instrument that allocates scarce resources in the most efficient way possible, thus diminishing pain and suffering and furthering life and prosperity.

This narrative creates two problems. First, viewing the market as a neutral, technical instrument removes from analysis or consideration the social, political, and theological conditions that make such a market possible and that such a market produces.[76] Second, once this narrative is conceded as the source of this best-of-all-possible worlds we now live in, then the dominant language available to think and speak about aging and death is the language of the economists. That language will always find preparatory duties such as Taylor's alien. It will also produce false contexts within which people of faith can easily be misled in their good intentions to fulfill religious obligations such as honoring one's elders.

Perhaps the reason we find terms such as *fasting, severe discipline,* and *preparation for suffering* strange, and yet are comfortable with the language of *retirement, pensions,* and *security,* is precisely because our dying is defined more by considerations of *economics* than by moral and theological ones. Our language of aging and dying has implicitly and explicitly become defined by the "burden of dependency," which is given definition by economists: "From an economic point of view, a person who has retired from the labor market is a 'burden' on society in the specific sense that his current consumption expenditure outweighs his current contribution to the total marketable output."[77] This technical definition of retired persons is not intended to imply a value judgment; it supposedly reflects nothing but a necessary presupposition for the economic analysis of intergenerational resource distribution. Nevertheless, such language does produce different moral considerations for the process of aging and dying than did language such as Taylor's obligations to honor one's elders. It prompts us to secure our future aging so that we will be the least burdensome on others. Our preparatory duties for death include securing our future not only against want but also against any dependence on the charity of others. But these preparatory duties are not the result of some natural desire for autonomy; they arise from the demands of a particular sociopolitical order, one that was given shape by the marginalist revolution.

SPEAKING OF AGING AS THE OPTIMAL ALLOCATION OF SCARCE RESOURCES: THE LANGUAGE OF ECONOMICS

Economists describe the relation between the elderly and the young in terms of the marginalist rationality (or neoclassical liberalism) that revolutionized economics in the latter part of the nineteenth century.[78] This rationality assumes that the starting point for economic analysis is individuals who must make choices concerning exchanges in conditions of scarcity.[79] The market is a neutral, value-free, technical instrument to effect these exchanges in the most efficient and rational way possible. Such reasoning abstracts both from the social conditions within which these individuals are situated and from conditions of accumulation by assuming that "the initial allocation of goods is taken as given historically and so is no matter for the economist to investigate."[80] The task of the economist is to optimize efficiency with the social and political conditions assumed as given.

Marginalist rationality does not describe something that is natural (the way things are) but assumes the normativity of a social order (capitalist society). It seldom acknowledges this social order, because economics presents itself as something of a natural science. This is important for intergenerational economic analyses, since marginalist rationality also assumes a *natural* conflict of interest between the generations. In fact, some economists believe we will face an economic crisis because of our aging population. As one economics textbook puts it, "Is a $20,000 hip replacement for a ninety-year-old with a life expectancy of a few years the most valuable use of society's resources? These are difficult and unpleasant questions, but as long as society as a whole bears the brunt of these costs through its Medicare and Medicaid programs, there is no way of avoiding them."[81] This question seems *natural* enough. We have a straightforward and stark choice that we cannot avoid. Either we expend "society's resources" on a ninety-year-old individual's hip replacement, or we expend these resources on something else more valuable. The mathematics is simple. We have X amount of resources. Y equals the value of a ninety-year-old individual's hip replacement. Z equals other "more valuable uses of society's resources." The result is an obvious equation: $X = Y + Z$. If we increase expenditures on Y, we decrease possible expenditures for Z. But with a little reflection, this apparently natural choice disappears and we see how misleading and abstract it is, since it hides its politics behind a putatively *natural* choice.

The first abstraction we encounter is in the terms of the comparison itself: a ninety-year-old individual's hip replacements versus more valuable uses of resources. But the comparison assumes all ninety-year-olds in need of hip replacements share a similar socioeconomic status. This is simply false. Some ninety-year-olds will have access to resources other than federal expenditures for health care. All such people should be exempted from the comparison. Then we realize that the comparison works only between those who depend on federal expenditures for their health care (the poor) and other, more "valuable" uses of resources. Yet what are these more valuable uses of resources? What does Z represent: nuclear armaments? tobacco subsidies? bicycle trails? enterprise zones for inner cities? expenditures for special prosecutors? Until we know what we are comparing, we simply are incapable of exercising any practical judgment.

This brings us to the second abstraction with which *we* meet. Who is the *we* that is assumed to make these practical determinations about the allocation of "society's resources"? We are asked which use of society's resources is more advantageous, as if *we* had some direct political mechanism to make this determination, as if *we* had a coherent society. But of course *we* do not, and marginalism works on the assumption that we *should* not. No political mechanism should exist other than the choices of individual consumers. Choice is exercised by individuals who each determines for herself what she wants. The market merely acts as a neutral instrument to index those preferences by matching wants with products and services. Thus, if either the elderly or those concerned about them find it useful to employ their resources for hip replacements, the market will provide. The market will provide such services until the marginal utility of such an employment of resources is no longer viable, that is, until individual consumers determine that the employment of their limited resources for other services or products is of more use to them than hip replacements for ninety-year-olds.

These collected and indexed preferences are all that the marginalist economists can mean by "society's resources." Politically, the logic of their position entails that institutions refrain from social constraints on the market; otherwise, the *rationality* of marginal utility would be adversely affected. If the government or some other entity subsidizes hip replacements, then I as a consumer might be able to employ my resources for both my grandmother's hip replacement and my son's college education, not realizing that this is an *irrational* employment of resources because the costs are hidden in such a way that I am not forced to allocate my own resources in the most efficient way possible. So, to use the expression "society as a whole bears" within a marginalist analysis is both abstract and misleading. Few, if any, *social* resources exist, and *we* have no political mechanism to make judgments about the control of such resources other than as individual consumers (which is what voting represents).[82]

Of course, X in the equation above (the amount of resources available at a given time) is not fixed indefinitely. It may be fixed momentarily at the point where I must choose between utilizing my resources on hip replacements or on a child's education, but it is not fixed over time. The only possible alternative to difficult decisions between competing values is to increase X as much as possible. In this view, the best possible answer to our social problems is always increased economic growth. But here we see a contradiction. The very same economists who argue that in the long term we must increase growth and that the advantage of capitalist society is that it is the most efficient form of wealth production also tell us that the means to achieve this most efficient form of production is by recognizing that we must choose in the present between our elders' hip replacements and our children's education or other more "valuable" uses of resources.

So we are confronted with the economist's abstract logic, "These are difficult and unpleasant questions but as long as society as a whole bears the brunt of these costs . . . there is no way of avoiding them." But we do not have a society that bears the brunt of these costs, and economics works to prevent us from any *communal* discernment about uses of resources. It permits us the privilege of avoiding social and political questions about the allocation of scarce resources. The purpose of the economist's question is not to exercise practical judgment about the expenditures of social resources; the question functions merely as a way to legitimate the economist's social and political starting point: we are all individuals who must make choices about scarce resources, and the most efficient way to do this is to leave it to the "neutral" working of the market.

The market decides, and we must realize that the market is the most rational form of life available. We have no politics available to us that would allow us to live otherwise, for such a politics would have to answer questions such as, "What is a good use of our resources?" *Good* would have to be more determinative of our society than freedom and choice. We would need some common conception of a good life for which people should aim. *Good* would be intelligible. But this is precisely what our democratic process protects against.[83] Thus, the market is our only politics; it has become our fate.

Once the market has become our politics, then we should not be surprised that we begin to speak of the elderly, aging, and death in terms intelligible within the market. To honor our elders is to submit them to the logic of the economist's rationality. We must now think of our elders as economic burdens whose care should be subject to the conditions of marginal utility. This is not because health care is *by nature* a scarce resource whereby choices must inevitably be made between hip replacements and children's education. This is a feature of our particular social order.

DYING AS A PARTICIPATION IN CHARITY:
THE LANGUAGE OF THEOLOGY

How can we relate theology to this socioeconomic analysis? The question is improperly stated. Economics is supposedly a technical science, much like auto mechanics, gall-bladder surgery, or housing construction. Because these are neutral, technical disciplines, we do not need to relate theology to them, nor should they encroach upon theological language. While this may be the case with carburetor adjustments, economics constantly surpasses its proper limits and imposes its logic on all aspects of human life. But theology must refuse to concede any intellectual space free from its own intrinsic logic. This is a necessary feature of Christian theology because it is a *metadiscourse* that positions all other discourses within its own narrative order of creation and redemption. Any Christian theology that refuses to do this will cease to express adequately its own internal logic and become dependent upon other discourses for its intelligibility.[84] Theologians on both the political left and right have denied this claim by making space for economics or social analysis as an autonomous sphere. But such concessions inevitably reduce theology to the status of the irrational, cultural, or valuational over against the factual.

Christian theology cannot concede an autonomous space to other intellectual disciplines because the logic of theology arises from a universal metaclaim (always mediated historically) that Christ is Lord and that such lordship cannot be superseded. The strength of a theological analysis of aging is that it explicitly gives us what economics conceals: a common conception of a good life for which people should aim and to which judgments about good uses of resources can and should be subordinate. This is because no higher authority exists than that of Christ's. Thus no intellectual discourse can position theology within some authoritative structure other than the logic of Christ's sacrifice. As Karl Barth put it,

> We are told in Jn. 19[28] concerning the crucified Jesus that He knew that now all things were finished (*tetelestai*). And His last word when He died was "it is finished" (*tetelestai*) (Jn. 19[30]). Jesus knew what God knew in the taking place of His sacrifice. And Jesus said what God said: that what took place was not something provisional, but that which suffices to fulfil the divine will, that which

is entire and perfect, that which cannot and need not be continued or repeated or added to or superseded, the new thing which was the end of the old but which will itself never become old, which can only be there and continue and shine out and have force and power as that which is new and eternal.[85]

In the all-sufficient, unsurpassable sacrifice of Christ, Christian theology suggests that *all things* are completed. Nothing escapes the force of the *all things* here; all things have received their proper end. Christ's sacrifice is the "perfect redemption."[86] The logic of this perfect redemption is such that all other intellectual discourses must be positioned in terms of its truth and never vice versa.

While theological engagement with other intellectual discourses must position all other discourses within its own internal logic, it must also reflect the nature of its own logic and not become a form of tyranny. This internal logic is the charity that defines God's being. This must be embodied in the politics of the new creation; if not, it will be tempted toward fascism. A metanarrative need not be fascist, although it could always be tempted toward it. What prevents it from being fascist is precisely the *content* of the narrative. As Milbank reminds us, "There is a continuity between Jesus' refusal of any seizure of power and the early church's refusal to overthrow existing structures, in favor of the attempt to create alternative ones, as local areas of relative peace, charity and justice."[87] This continuity should not only exist between Jesus and the early church but also be a permanent feature of the church's life, for it is intrinsic to the logic of the gospel. The task of relating theology to economics is not, then, to overthrow the existing structures in some cataclysmic revolutionary act. We are not waiting for the proletariat to rise up and seize control of the means of production any more than we are waiting for the free market to work its miracle and provide its always-not-yet achieved wealth of nations. Neither are we waiting for the imposition of some "righteous" theocracy. Instead, the theological task is to create space for faithful Christian practice wherever that space can be found. For this reason, a theology of dying need not begin by responding to the economic and sociological analysis. Economics and sociology should seek to be relevant to theology and never vice versa.

Christian theological reflection does not begin with the allocation of scarce resources among individuals but with the appropriate distribution of the fullness of life Christ offers in his cross and resurrection. This claim must be something more than pious sentiment if theology is to matter substantively. By beginning with the fullness of life Christ offers, I am not denying the possibility of tragic conflicts; we still might need to tell ninety-year-olds that hip replacements are not the appropriate use of our resources. Yet such judgments will be based on an understanding of an ecclesial mission subject to Christ's authority and not simply on the abstract calculations of marginal utility, which always hide politics behind "usefulness." We assume our elders are free not to cling desperately to life because death is not the ultimate scarcity; life returns in the resurrection.

Jesus' fullness of life breaks the boundaries of race, class, family, and nation to produce a new form of social reproduction that we call church. The church is the visible inauguration of God's reign, which is both founded by Jesus in his teachings, death, and resurrection and endowed with certain sacramental structures by which all people are called to Jesus' ongoing mission through participation in his life. Jesus' actions reveal to us the role our elders have within the new community he has established. They provide the context within which we can faithfully honor our elders. Jesus provides this by fulfilling the law revealed to Moses on Mount Sinai.

When Jesus tells us that the entirety of the law is fulfilled in the commandment to love God and our neighbor, he is directing us to the realization of the Torah revealed at Sinai to Moses and now fulfilled in him.[88] This does not constitute a decisive break with Israel but retells the story from the perspective of Christ as the one who decisively brings and enacts God's reign.[89] All social, political, and economic institutions are now subjected to the authority of Christ. We can begin to see how this works for the family, and for the care of the elderly, by observing the odd way Christ fulfills the fourth commandment: "honor your father and mother."

HONORING OUR ELDERS

Law is never an end in itself. If it were, obedience would be arbitrary, the mere observance of commands. Law directs human actions to virtuous ends; it assumes a virtuous life as the context for its intelligibility. Law without virtue is capricious; virtue without law lacks direction. Jesus presents to Christians the social and political life that directs our actions toward virtuous ends. When we examine the fourth commandment, however, the social life Jesus presents to us seems to contradict rather than complete the commandment. His treatment of his elders appears dishonorable.

Luke tells the story of Jesus' disappearance from his parents' care for three days to spend time in the temple. When Mary finds him and asks why he disappeared, Jesus responds, "How is it that you sought me? Did you not know that I must be in my Father's house?" (Luke 2:49). Jesus dismisses his parents' anxiety as unwarranted. This is not the only occasion Jesus seems dismissive of his family. Mark records Jesus' response to the announcement that his mother and brothers are waiting for him as "Who are my mother and my brothers? . . . Here are my mother and my brothers! Whoever does the will of God is my brother, and sister, and mother" (Mark 3:33–35). Although Matthew and Luke seem to soften this encounter (Matt. 12:46–50; Luke 8:19–21), both record a statement of Jesus against the family that Mark does not have. Luke puts it in its starkest form: "If any one comes to me and does not hate his own father and mother and wife and children and brothers and sisters, yes, and even his own life, he cannot be my disciple" (Luke 14:26; Matt. 10:37–39). Such statements do not seem to hold forth much promise in any attempt to develop a theology of aging and dying. John's Gospel likewise recounts a shocking statement of Jesus to his mother when she tells him that the wine has run out at a marriage feast. Jesus says, "O woman, what have you to do with me? My hour has not yet come" (John 2:4). So we find in Scripture multiple attestations from diverse sources that Jesus acted almost dishonorably toward his own elders. The urgency of his mission seemed to leave little room for a theology focused on the needs and concerns of the elderly, including the needs of his own parents.

However, Jesus' harsh actions toward his elders need to be supplemented with the poignant scene in John's Gospel when Jesus, suffering on the cross, saw his mother and John standing nearby and said to Mary, "Woman, behold, your son!" and to John, "Behold, your mother!" (John 19:26–27). This agonizing scene does not contradict the harsh ones mentioned earlier. Rather, it sets them in an appropriate order. In fact, this scene occurs right before Jesus remarks, "It is finished" (*tetelestai*). The bequeathment of his mother to the disciple participates in Jesus' completion of all things. From this we learn that the family has been restructured and brought into submission to the authority of Christ. Beneath the suffering of the cross, John receives Jesus' mother and provides a space for her in his own home.

This scene can serve us well in our efforts to think about an appropriate theology of aging and death. Raniero Cantalamessa explains this scene well: "Beneath the cross, Mary therefore appears as the daughter of Zion, who after the death and loss of her sons received a new and more numerous family from God, but by the Spirit and not the flesh."[90] The fourth commandment is fulfilled not by dishonoring the family but by restructuring it. Just as there is no longer male nor female, Jew nor Gentile, slave nor free in the community of faith, so there is also neither parent nor child. As Jesus commanded, all the faithful are to be brothers, sisters, and mothers to one another. This commandment assumes the virtues of charity and hope. Charity is present because we must take others into our homes and provide for them out of our resources, as John did Mary. Hope is present because death will not leave the widowed and orphaned abandoned. Within the church, they are to find new homes. Our use of resources must bear witness to this new reality that is made present beneath the cross.

That we are to be brothers and sisters to one another is easily explained, but that we are to be mothers is certainly surprising. This surprised Augustine such that he wrote, "I understand that we are Christ's brethren and that the holy and faithful women are Christ's sisters. But how can we be mothers of Christ?" Augustine did not let his puzzlement prevent him from using the expression, which he explained ecclesiologically:

Who gave you birth? I hear the voice of your hearts answering "Mother Church!" This holy and honored mother, like Mary, gave birth and is virgin. . . . The members of Christ give birth, therefore, in the Spirit, just as the Virgin Mary gave birth to Christ in her womb: in this way you will be mothers of Christ. This is not something that is out of your reach; it is not beyond you, it is not incompatible with you; you have become children, be mothers as well.[91]

Augustine also finds in Jesus' bequeathment of John and Mary to each other evidence of his humanity and divinity. The harsh sayings of Jesus toward his elders represent Jesus' divinity, since they reveal that Jesus is not bound by biological ties to the family. However, Jesus' bequeathment evidences his humanity: "Then it was, as a man on the cross, that He acknowledged His human mother and commended her in a most human fashion to the Apostle he loved most."[92] The love for his mother was natural but also supernatural and thus grounded in grace, in his freedom to love through and beyond the biological ties of family. It was not necessary; it was gift.

The bequeathment of Mary and John to one another occurs prior to Jesus' proclamation, "It is finished." The all-sufficient sacrifice on the cross includes Christ's restructuring of the family so that our duties toward the elderly are no longer obligations merely to biological family. Instead, the family is expanded. To honor one's parents is for John to take Mary into his home now that she has lost her son. To honor one's parents is also to honor those who are parents to us in the faith. Our obligations to our parents include being not only children to them but parents as well. Conversely, parental obligation to our children includes not only the role of parenting but also a readiness to allow our children to be mothers to us, to birth in us faith. This does not imply any disrespect for our own parents, for by his actions on the cross Jesus teaches us that disciples are to prepare such a place for their own parents within the community of faith.[93] Nor does this imply that *Mary* stands as some symbol for the *elderly*, per se, for Mary is "a type of the Church in the order of faith, charity and perfect union with Christ. . . . The Church indeed, contemplating her hidden sanctity, imitating her charity and faithfully fulfilling the Father's will, by receiving the word of God in faith becomes herself a mother."[94] By her faithfulness, Mary is mother to us all. She is the symbol of the church and a symbol of the restructuring of family bonds.

The way we think, speak, and act concerning our aging, and the aging of our elders as well, should reflect that the family has now been restructured and subordinated to the authority of Christ. The well-known description of Mary as the "daughter of her son" reflects the completed ordering of the family. This restructuring of the family should become our politics and provide us with the language we use in preparing our elders, and ourselves, to die.

SEVEN

AGORA

You shall not commit adultery.
You shall not steal.
You shall not bear false witness against your neighbor. Exodus 20:14–16

You shall not covet your neighbor's wife or husband.
You shall not covet your neighbor's goods. Exodus 20:17

Lend, expecting nothing in return. Luke 6:35

People cannot live without economic exchanges. Unlike the church, the *agora* (or market) is a necessary institution. The question is not *if* we live within the necessary exchanges that constitute the market but *how* we do so. However, the word *market* here is not intended the capitalist market as it currently exists. That particular social formation is not necessary; it is merely one specific version of an *agora* that is constantly shifting and changing. Because the goodness of God is known by the right ordering of desires, which the Ten Commandments and the virtues form in us, the reasonableness of the market cannot be evaluated on its own terms. It is only within the overall harmony of a vision of the good life ordered in God that the legitimate role of the market can be discovered.

Two points must be made immediately about the market's role within social formations. First, the contemporary mechanism of the market plays a more central role in our lives than in any previous historical period. Second, the Christian faith is inextricably connected with economic matters. Evidence that these two points should be relatively noncontroversial can be found in the very term *economics*. Although it now designates a specialized, autonomous discipline that studies the mechanism of market exchanges, the word itself has an ancient lineage with a more encompassing significance. The term comes from two Greek words, *oikos* (house) and *nomos* (law). In its more ancient and encompassing sense, economics concerns that structure or regulations of a household, where *household* is intended in the broadest sense possible. In fact, the term can refer to God's economy, designating God's creative and redemptive activity upon which all being depends.

When the term *economy* is understood in this more encompassing sense, its relationship to theology becomes noncontroversial. Theology does not provide the *values* that form the basis for an independent economic realm; theology offers the signs within which our necessary exchanges can become faithful.

JESUS AS SIGNIFYING EXCHANGE

The life of Jesus is the sign within which all exchanges should be understood. That life is primarily attested to in the apostolic witness that is present in the Scriptures and the ongoing life of the worshiping community. When considering economic matters, Luke-Acts is the most useful witness the church has as to how we should engage in exchanges with one another and with the world. Yet what should we look for in Luke to help us with these necessary exchanges? Should we look for a specific code of conduct with well-formed regulations? Medieval moral theology found just that in Jesus' admonition, "Lend, expecting nothing in return" (Luke 6:35). This admonition fit well the ancient prohibition of usury found both in the Old Testament and in the ancient Greeks. Usury was the practice where lenders received interest for money lent. For most of the church's history, it has been prohibited. But this prohibition never implied that all profit on one's investment was immoral. It suggested, rather, that exchanges should have a public character to them, where what was being exchanged and how it was being exchanged should be regulated by a common life; exchanges should serve the ends of justice and charity and never the vice of greed.

Few biblical scholars, theologians, or ecclesial leaders would now draw upon Luke 6:35 as a specific rule forbidding all interest. In fact, few biblical scholars, theologians, or ecclesial leaders find in the Scriptures specific regulations that are binding upon the faithful when it comes to economic exchanges. Instead, they generally relate Christianity to economic life through more general principles such as love or justice. But the fact that theologians appeal to these principles and arrive at opposite conclusions demonstrates the uselessness of this approach. Modern Christian ethics has been indiscriminate in that it uses formal principles abstracted from Scripture in an effort to give guidance and direction to the faithful, but this method of ethical thought has abandoned the faithful to the contemporary polarization of the dominant culture's moral alternatives. Thus, even though they appeal to a common moral language, the language does not matter; it does not accomplish anything.

If the Scriptures do not give us a specific rule to be followed, and if the modern method of a formal general principle has outlived its usefulness, what should we expect? Perhaps the Scriptures give us a specific political and economic platform that is not necessarily a specific rule to be followed. This is the argument put forward by John Howard Yoder in *Politics of Jesus*. Yoder suggested that Jesus' ministry presented neither a politics in general nor an apolitical principle but "one particular social-political-ethical option."[1] This particular option includes not only the politics of nonviolence but also a Jubilee economics. Yoder characterizes this type of economics as a periodic redistribution of capital where all things are made new as a witness to that day when God will be all in all. It is to be a permanent witness to the restoration of all things that comes about in Jesus' ministry. The biblical warrant for such an economics is found in Jesus' teaching in Luke 4:18–19. "The Spirit of the Lord is upon me, because he has anointed me to preach good news to the poor. He has sent me to proclaim release to the captives and recovering of sight to the blind, to set at liberty those who are oppressed, to proclaim the acceptable year of the Lord." This passage is actually a quotation from Isaiah 61:1–2. What constitutes Jesus' teaching is his proclamation after the reading of this passage in the synagogue, when he states, "Today this scripture has been fulfilled in your hearing." How is it *fulfilled?* Following the work of André Trocmé, Yoder suggests that Jesus' proclamation would have been understood as something like the fulfillment of the Jubilee year in Leviticus 25. The Jubilee year was the restoration of the people's relationship to God, each other, and creation. Slaves were set free, property was redistributed, and any who had lost home, land, and family had them restored. Yoder never argued that Isaiah 61 was a specific reference to the Jubilee, only that the Jubilee year would have provided a cultural context within which Jesus' message would have been intelligible.[2]

That Jesus' proclamation was understood as something such as Yoder suggests is borne out in the response to Peter's preaching in Acts. On two different occasions, the response to the apostles' preaching resulted precisely in the redistributive witness Yoder notes as a Jubilee economics:

> And fear came upon every soul; and many wonders and signs were done through the apostles. And all who believed were together and had all things in common; and they sold their possessions and goods and distributed them to all, as any had need (Acts 2:43–45).

Now the company of those who believed were of one heart and soul, and no one said that any of the things which he possessed was his own, but they had everything in common. And with great power the apostles gave their testimony to the resurrection of the Lord Jesus, and great grace was upon them all. There was not a needy person among them, for as many as were possessors of lands or houses sold them, and brought the proceeds of what was sold and laid it at the apostles' feet; and distribution was made to each as any had need (Acts 4:32–35).

Is this how Jesus' proclamation in Luke 4 is fulfilled? The biblical witness is clear that a faithful response to Jesus' proclamation is the restoration of all things, including the redistribution of material goods. The church cannot be the church without embodying this witness in its life.

At some basic level, the church cannot but embody this redistributive Jubilee economics when it celebrates the Eucharist. Even if this is all the church ever "accomplishes" in its life, this is sufficient as evidence of its divine institution, for this is the sign the world needs to be turned toward God and God's goodness. This is not to argue that the Eucharist has instrumental value to teach us an economic ethics. That would subordinate theology to ethics. Rather, it is the sign that gives all other signs their significance because it is the repetition of the moment of *ultimate exchange* between God and humanity that Christians cannot but claim to be the basis for all other exchanges.[3] The church is made in the celebration of the Eucharist. Without this celebration, the church cannot be.

ACCOMPLISHING EUCHARIST

That the church *accomplishes* the Eucharist is never, however, mere ritual. The accomplishment of the Eucharist entails a divine-human exchange, which at the same time will affect other human exchanges. Such an effect can come in the form of fulfillment of the divine goodness, as occurred in Acts 2 and 4, or it can come in the form of judgment, as is found in Acts 5:1–11 and in Paul's judgment on the Corinthian Christians for their partaking of the Lord's Supper unworthily (1 Cor. 11:27–32).

In Acts 5 Ananias and Sapphira seek to participate in the redistributive economic Jubilee by giving half of their possessions and withholding the other half. Peter reminds them that they were not forced to participate in this restoration, and thus by withholding their goods and seeking to deceive others about it, they place themselves outside the community of faith. They die. Peter's response to Ananias and Sapphira was not a Stalinist purge that forced them to part with their property, for not an enforced justice but a gifted charity is the basis for this restoration. But treating it as if it were a coercive law rather than a gift, they hid from it. Peter does not condemn them to death (Acts 5 provides no justification for capital punishment), but the consequence of their activity was death.

Similarly in 1 Corinthians 11, the apostle Paul states that the reason some of the Corinthian Christians are sick and some have died is because they eat and drink at the Lord's Supper without "discerning the body." What does it mean to discern the body? Paul has given us the answer to this by reprimanding the Corinthian Christians for the way in which they gather to eat this meal: "each one goes ahead with his own meal" (1 Cor. 11:21).

The term used for "his own meal" is *to idion deipnon.* This is an interesting expression, for the faithful response to Peter's preaching in Acts 4 contrasted a faithful life where "they had everything in common" (*ēn autois panta koina*) with the life that is left behind, where each treated his property as if it were his own (*ti tōn hyparchontōn autō elegen idion einai*). A faithful response to God's good news results in believers holding their property *koina* (in common) rather than as *idion* (one's own). The latter ends in death. The very presence of the church in the world requires one of these two realities: hold our property in common and find life and goodness or hold our property as our own and embrace death. One or the other of these realities will be fulfilled in the life of the church. Either way, the Eucharist will be accomplished: it will bring life or judgment.

This theme of fulfillment is the heart of Luke's witness to us. In his prologue he tells us that, just as others "have undertaken to compile a narrative of the things which have been accomplished among us," so he too will write an "orderly account." The seemingly innocuous phrase, "the things which have been accomplished among us" (*tōn peplērophorēmenōn . . . pragmatōn*), is in fact theologically significant. This is not just a claim for some objective narration of the "facts." It is a theological claim about what has been fulfilled, particularly how the Old Testament vision of God's people is fulfilled in Jesus' restoration of that community.[4]

The restoration of God's people is central to the gospel's witness. As Luke Timothy Johnson notes, "In Luke-Acts, the Twelve play a particularly important symbolic role as the basis and leadership of the restored Israel called by the prophet."[5] The restoration theme is also closely related to economic matters. John the Baptist witnesses to this when his message of repentance culminates in inquiries from the people as to what they should do and he responds that they should share their clothes and their food (Luke 3:11). The key themes for Jesus' ministry are also prophesied in the songs of Mary and Zechariah. Jesus will exalt those of low degree, fill the hungry with good things, put down the mighty from their thrones, send the rich away empty-handed, forgive sins, and bring peace (Luke 1:51–55, 78–79). Jesus accomplishes this ministry with the Twelve and some women who are with him (Luke 8:1–3). The women provide for them "out of their means." If not for their willingness to hold things *in common,* Jesus' ministry would not have been possible. The Twelve are given "power and authority over all demons and to cure diseases" (Luke 9:1). They assist Jesus at the feeding of the five thousand (Luke 9:11–17), but they also often fail at performing the ministry Jesus himself performed (Luke 9:40). The Twelve expands. Seventy others are appointed to carry on this ministry (Luke 10:1). This is also symbolic of the restoration theme, for it was seventy elders who were picked by Moses to assist him in ministry (Exod. 24:1, 9–14; Num. 11:16–17). The promise is that this restored community will grow such that it is not bound by any geographical borders (Luke 13:29), but a sign of this catholic community will also be the reversal of roles Mary prophesied when she sang that Jesus would fill the hungry with good things but send the rich away empty.

REVERSAL OF ROLES

The gathered catholic community will be characterized by the fact that "some are last who will be first, and some are first who will be last" (Luke 13:30). This is given vivid illustration in three stories found in Luke 18–21.

First, we find the story of the rich young ruler who comes to Jesus and asks what he must do to be saved. Jesus tells him to keep the commandments, and these he believes he has kept. But to keep them well Jesus suggests that he lacks only one thing, "Sell all that you have and distribute to the poor . . . and come, follow me" (Luke 18:22). The ruler could not do this because "he was very rich" (Luke 18:23), so he went away empty-handed. The prophecy is fulfilled: the rich are sent away empty; the first are made last.

Then comes the story of Zacchaeus. Unlike the rich young ruler, Zacchaeus is not so bold as to ask Jesus what he must do to be saved. Instead, he offers him a proposition, "Behold, Lord, the half of my goods I give to the poor; and if I have defrauded any one of anything, I restore it fourfold." This seemed to be acceptable to Jesus, for he replied, "Today salvation has come to this house" (Luke 19:8–9).

This startling reversal is made complete when we move from the rich young ruler who was sent away empty-handed through Zacchaeus who received salvation to the poor widow who put two coins into the treasury. Her example is the one lifted up as central to the kingdom of God, for she gave "out of her poverty" (Luke 21:4). The catholic community of faith Jesus restores and ceaselessly reconstitutes is built by such acts, not by rich young rulers with large endowments.

But this catholic community does not progress by "natural" means. Jesus prepares the Twelve for his death (Luke 18:31–34), which they were unable to understand. One of the Twelve betrayed him, and even Peter refused to acknowledge him on the day of his arrest. This is done even though Jesus promised that they would be given thrones to judge the twelve tribes of Israel (Luke 22:30). The Twelve (now eleven) are reconstituted by Jesus' appearances after the resurrection. He is made known to two of them in the breaking of the bread on the way to Emmaus. As these two tell the others, Jesus appears bodily and eats with them again (Luke 24:34–43). The gospel is not just the restoration of the Jubilee community with its redistributive practices. The gospel is the restoration of this community in and through the body and blood of Jesus. As

Luke Timothy Johnson puts it, "The restoration of Israel by the prophet Jesus is equally sealed by sacrificial blood. But now the blood is not of animals, but of the Prophet himself. It is by the giving of his life in sacrifice—donation to God for the sake of others—that a regeneration of the people can take place."[6]

This salvation is a politics because its repetition constantly reconstitutes the people of God. The liturgical enactment of this exchange renders all other sacrificial forms of life, including capital punishment, war, abortion, and the necessary sacrifices present in the laws of capitalism, as clearly opposed to God's reign. Capital punishment assumes that through the sacrifice of the offender we can secure civil society. War assumes that through the deaths of our enemies we can secure the body politic. Abortion assumes that through the sacrifice of the unwanted unborn we can secure the best harmony for family and economic life. Capitalism assumes that through its periodic sacrifices of workers to the laws of supply and demand it can secure the best possible economic order. All such sacrifices are idolatrous because they cannot secure anything but death. Such sacrifices exchange the goodness of God for the security of death. It becomes the "reality" that renders our lives secure. The liturgical enactment of Jesus' all-sufficient sacrifice for us renders these other sacrifices demonic. Insofar as they define our civil, political, family, or economic lives, we are serving the principalities and powers of this world.

COMMON OWNERSHIP?

Jesus' sacrifice, witnessed to in the Eucharist, is the only event that can constitute the church. It alone is sufficient to order our life toward God's goodness. But what is the relationship between Jesus' sacrifice and our ownership of goods? If the church is to embody a redistributive Jubilee economics, does that entail that *common ownership* is a norm for Christian faith? To this question the Roman Catholic tradition has said a clear no. Beginning with Pope Leo XIII's famous 1891 encyclical, *Rerum Novarum,* the official teaching of the Catholic Church has been that the state should use the power of the law to safeguard private property.[7] No papal encyclical has ever abrogated this teaching. Private ownership is not an inalienable right within the Catholic tradition, since with it come duties to acquire and hold property consistent with the requirements of justice and charity. Nevertheless, common ownership of property is not a goal to be achieved within the world in the Catholic tradition. Nor has common ownership been a *status confessioni* in the Protestant, Orthodox, or Anabaptist traditions. A number of communal forms of Christian living have developed and flourished in each of these traditions, but none has been taken as the norm for the entire church to embody.

A 1923 Sobor of the Russian Orthodox Church, led by the Archpriest A. Vvedensky, did issue the following pronouncement, which is the closest proclamation we have of common ownership as a *status confessioni:*

> Having heard the report of Archpriest A. Vvedensky, the All-Russian Local Sobor of the Orthodox Church witnesses before the church and before all mankind that at present the world has become divided into two classes: capitalists-exploiters, and the proletariat, by whose toil and blood the capitalistic world builds its prosperity. No one in the world but the Soviet government of Russia has undertaken a struggle against this social evil. Christians cannot remain indifferent spectators of that struggle. The Sobor declares capitalism to be a mortal sin, and the fight against it to be sacred for Christians. . . . the Sobor calls attention to the fact that the Soviet authority is the only one throughout the world which will realize, by governmental methods, the ideals of the Kingdom of God.[8]

But one would hardly accuse the twentieth-century Orthodox Church of embodying some radical vision of communal ownership based on Acts 2 and 4. In fact, the 1923 statement by the Sobor is consistent with an impulse within the Orthodox Church to find in the powers of the state the central means by which the ideals of the gospel are to be mediated to the wider world.[9]

On the whole, Christian tradition has not taken Acts 2 and 4 as authorizing a necessary communal ownership of goods as a sign of Christian discipleship. Is this a falling away from the demands of the gospel? Luke Timothy Johnson thinks not. He argues that Acts 2 and 4 were not intended as a specific practice of communal ownership of possessions but as an apology for the Christian community within Greek culture. The portrayal of the Acts community embodies the kind of friendship held up as ideal in Greek culture, where friends held things in common not for their own sake but for the good of the friend.[10] But Johnson seems to see this apologetic strategy of Luke's as a mistake. Thus he argues, "I consider it past time to renounce our long romantic attachment to the community of possessions and to look more deeply into that part of our tradition which flourished in Judaism to our own day but which is equally part of our Christian heritage—almsgiving."[11] This is an odd argument. It first suggests that Luke depicted the early Christian communities as embodying the ideal of friendship because they embodied what the Greeks thought was most noble: a community of possessions. But if Luke's primary intention was to use the Greek ideal of friendship apologetically, why did he include the story of Ananias and Sapphira, which disclosed the opposite of the intended strategy? And does not Johnson's argument assume the nineteenth-century position of biblical critics who claimed to be able to distinguish the Jewish from the Hellenistic influences in the gospel, which sent us on a quest for the true Jewish Jesus? This is the very kind of distinction that Johnson has rightly and persuasively taken the Jesus Seminar to task for in *The Real Jesus.*

If Luke found the early Christian communities to be an embodiment of the Greek ideal of friendship, that does not weaken, but strengthens, the argument found in John Howard Yoder, who suggested that Jesus drew upon a Jubilee tradition within Judaism in his proclamation of the acceptable year of the Lord. Yoder assumes that this Jubilee tradition is proclaimed by someone who is true God and true humanity and thus the archetype of humanity and creation. That the Greeks discovered via reason a similar archetypal reality does nothing to challenge the authenticity of that proclamation.

One reason biblical scholars and theologians are cautious about using Acts 2 and 4 as a pattern for an ecclesial economics—even in the ideal—is because of the failures of scientific socialism in the twentieth century. One could be forgiven for a romantic attachment to this kind of political society in the 1920s, as the Russian Orthodox Sobor was and a number of Christian theologians and pastors in the United States were. But after Stalin, one cannot be so romantic. It is not merely a *counterrevolutionary* reaction to begin to wonder if common ownership has the implications that Plato thought necessary to pull it off: everyone over ten years of age had to be eliminated.[12] But we should not read Acts 2 and 4 through the early twentieth-century question of either capitalism or scientific socialism. The early Christian communities did not seek to address that question, nor does Christian tradition.

INTERROGATING TRADITION

We do find evidence of the importance of how we hold our property in Christian tradition. The *Didache*, an early Christian teaching (dated anywhere from A.D. 60 to 125) on the way of life and the way of death, stated that if the faithful are deprived of their property, they are not to ask for it back (Luke 6:35). The *Didache* explains the theological reason for this. "For the Father wants his own gifts to be universally shared. Happy is the man who gives as the commandment bids him, for he is guiltless." But the *Didache* gives guidance not only to those who give (it does not assume that the primary problem for the Christian life will be how the church gives away its surplus) but also to those who receive: "But alas for the man who receives! If he receives because he is in need, he will be guiltless. But if he is not in need he will have to stand trial why he received and for what purpose." Those who receive are not to receive for inappropriate purposes. Those who give likewise assume responsibility to ensure that their gifts are received for the appropriate purposes. Therefore, the *Didache* suggests, "Let your donation sweat in your hands until you know to whom to give it." We have an obligation to know those in need in order to ensure that our gifts are gifts of charity and not burdens based on deceit.

The *Didache* counseled Christians to give to everyone who asked and to ask only out of a true need. To be in a position to give assumes the power of disposal of property, but to give without asking for a return assumes that the power of disposal of property is relative and limited. Moreover, the *Didache* assumes that those in need of goods are present within the community of faith. The *Didache* is suspicious about wealth, for the "way of death" is characterized as those "who look for profit, have no pity for the poor, do not exert themselves for the oppressed . . . turn their back on the needy, oppress the afflicted, defend the rich, unjustly condemn the poor and are thoroughly wicked." Such a way of "life" embraces death.

If we are called to give to everyone who asks, then a kind of communal ownership of goods is already present among the faithful. In fact, some evidence exists that one reason the Christians were viewed as a threat to emperors such as Diocletian and Galerius was their greater allegiance to their community because of the "retirement and funeral insurance companies" that they operated for one another. It was under the auspices of such cooperatives that the early Christians may have sought legitimacy under Roman law.[13]

That Christians are called to give to everyone who asks is a common theme in Christian tradition, as is the principle that they cannot ask for a return. But a vexing question was, How much are they called to give? Are all Christians called to give everything, as Jesus commanded the rich young ruler?

Irenaeus (130–200) was one of many early Christian theologians to address this question. Why was the rich young ruler, but not others, asked to give all? Why not Zacchaeus? Irenaeus's answer became a standard response within Christian tradition as to the relationship between faith and money. He suggested that the particular sin of the rich young ruler was covetousness and that as a healing for his particular sin Jesus offered him the possibility of almsgiving. Almsgiving as a cure for the sin of greed and covetousness is a consistent theme in Christian tradition. It is based on the assumption that all wealth arises from unrighteousness, even though goods in and of themselves are not unrighteous. The test of whether or not one holds goods righteously or unrighteously is found in one's willingness to give them away to those in need.

If Irenaeus assumed the problem was not wealth, per se, but one's attachment to it, Clement of Alexandria (150–215) made that assumption explicit. As Justo Gonzalez notes, Clement's *Can a Rich Man Be Saved?* is "the first attempt at a systematic discussion of the relationship between faith and wealth."[14] Clement argued that, if the story of the rich young ruler were lived out by every Christian, the faithful would have no goods to give and thus the command to do so could not be fulfilled: "Those who have nothing cannot feed the hungry or clothe the naked." He read the story of the rich young ruler as an allegory in which the "selling of all possessions" is equivalent to "ridding the soul of passions."[15] Inasmuch as Clement used the story of the rich young ruler only as a spiritual allegory about the soul's passions, he represented a decisive *spiritualizing* of Jesus' Jubilee economics. But inasmuch as Clement still recognized a connection between one's inordinate passions and one's possessions, he is far from guilty of such spiritualizing.

After Clement was forced to flee Alexandria, Origen (185–254) became his successor. We have already seen how he defended Christianity against Celsus's charges that it was a threat to public order. Origen's argument was that the Christians were an alternative city to that of Rome, a true city founded not on violence but on the demands of a peaceful and gentle savior. He gave a similar defense concerning the generosity of the Christian community: "How can a people with a wicked mind practice temperance and self-control or generosity and sharing (*koinonikón*)?"[16] This appears to be evidence, as Gonzalez suggests, that the communal practice of *koinonia* was used as a witness for the goodness of the Christian community against the charges brought against it by the Roman authorities.

As the school of Alexandria exercised influence on the church in the Greek-speaking East, the theologian Tertullian exercised influence in the Latin-speaking West. He also used the sharing of Christians at their love feasts as an apology for the goodness of this way of life.[17] In *On Idolatry* Tertullian argued that all sin can be traced back to idolatry. Central to his argument was the notion of "fraud." To defraud another is to refuse to give to her her rightful due. Thus it is to dishonor her. Likewise, idolatry is to refuse to give God God's due honor. But God's due honor includes much more than spiritual worship. Thus concupiscence, lasciviousness, drunkenness, vanity, and mendacity are all species of idolatry.[18] Tertullian took great pains to explain how certain occupations should be avoided because they could not but order one's actions to idolatrous practices. He asked whether "trade" entailed covetousness: "Is trade adapted for a servant of God? But, covetousness apart, what is the motive for acquiring?" He then answered his question with some care, not assuming that all trade and business arise only from covetousness. He rejected forms of trade and business that were particularly culpable of covetousness but nevertheless suggested, "Let none contend that, in this way, exception may be taken to all trades."[19] Few of us have to worry today about the specific trades that troubled Tertullian, but his work bore witness to the important relationship between one's occupation and one's faith. For him, this relationship had to be assessed before persons were admitted to baptism.

Although no single socioeconomic reality bound all Christians together in the early church, the theologians mentioned above assumed that the sharing of possessions was both a sign of the Christian community's faithfulness and a form of witness to the world. Throughout this history of struggle and accommodation between the church and the empire, the Catholic tradition formulated some basic principles that were to guide the faithful in their use of money. Three themes gradually emerged. First, all property is a gift from God and therefore should be held for the good of all. Second, usury or an unjust taking of profit/interest is a faithless performance of the Christian life. Third, a just wage should be paid to workers. It should be sufficient to support them and their families and have enough surplus to be able to contribute to a common good. Charity should not be hoarded by the rich.

Consistent with the theme of sharing one's possessions, Catholic tradition came to speak of the "universal destination" of all our goods. This supports a legitimate form of private-property ownership but suggests that the true end of all such ownership must be for the good of all, particularly the needy. Such a view hearkens back to Bishop Cyprian's recognition that the church has a special obligation to the poor and needy. The church (including the faithful within it) should hold its property for the poor. If it does not do so, it violates the "universal destination" of all our goods.

That this conflicts with contemporary understandings of property rights can be seen in Thomas Aquinas's explanation of the command against stealing. Stealing is not simply taking something from another. If one is destitute to the point of being unable to sustain the life of his or her family, then one does not steal in taking from a wealthy person, even if the latter refuses to give. For his property, like all property, is a patrimony to be used for the good of all.

Because all our property is a gift from God, not only must we use it in accordance with its proper end (its "universal destination"), but the faithful must also abide by the prohibition against usury, for to use our money to gain money is to fail to live by the charity we are to have toward our neighbor. The prohibition against usury has an ancient lineage. It was based upon the assumption that money stored value in order to facilitate exchange. Therefore, to use money to make more money was viewed as a form of disordered desire, particularly greed. But it was not simply because usury was prohibited by the ancient Greeks and Romans that the church forbade it. More important, it was condemned in Scripture. "You shall not charge interest on loans to another Israelite, interest on money, interest on provisions, interest on anything that is lent. On loans to a foreigner you may charge interest, but on loans to another Israelite you may not charge interest" (Deut. 23:19–20 NRSV; see also Exod. 22:25; Ps. 15:1, 5). Jerome argued that because the Gentiles had now been incorporated into the *ecclesia,* there were no "foreigners." Therefore, the prohibition against usury was strengthened in the early church.

As previously noted, Luke 6:35 was also appealed to for the prohibition against usury, but that did not become a standard argument until Pope Urban III reaffirmed the Church's stance against usury in 1187. Yet as early as the Council of Nicea (325) usury was prohibited among the clergy:

> Many clerics, motivated by greed and a desire for gain, have forgotten the scriptural injunction, "He does not put out his money at interest," and instead demand a monthly rate of one per cent on loans they make. . . . they shall be deposed.

Pope Leo the Great also condemned the practice of usury, calling the gain that came from it *turpe lucrum* (shameful gain). This became the vice by which the practice of usury was named. And although it was always condemned in the church and among the clergy, it was also condemned in the empire under Charlemagne (742–814). In 850 the synod of Pavia excommunicated lay usurers.

The nature of the sin of usury was a contested matter. Anselm of Canterbury (1033–1109) argued it was a sin against justice, while Albert the Great (1200–1280) argued it was a sin against charity. His pupil, Thomas Aquinas, seems to argue that it bore within it a sin against both. It was a sin against justice because it did not seek what was due but asked for more. It was a sin against charity because it failed to treat every person "as our neighbor and brother, especially in the state of the Gospel whereunto we are called." Usury was condemned by Aquinas because it sold something nonexistent, the "use" of a thing rather than the thing itself, but a thing and its use are inseparable in consumable exchanges. For example, to sell someone a consumable good such as a meal and then charge for the *use* of it would be usury. Aquinas also recognized vendible exchanges where use and consumption were independent of each other, as in renting a home. For Aquinas, money could only be a consumable good. It basically functioned as a store of value to facilitate exchanges. Thus, to enter into an exchange with someone where the giver charges for the money and its use is a sin against justice.[20]

Late nineteenth- and early twentieth-century economists argued that Aquinas, like Aristotle, misunderstood the way money worked. They suggested that the ancients had a *zero sum* view of economy and thus did not realize that money could, in fact, make money. All loans where interest is taken are not necessarily oppressive. From Aristotle to Aquinas, it was also assumed that money was barren, that it did not fructify. Capitalist economists view this as irrational; money does produce more money. But the economists' critique of the ancient prohibition mischaracterizes it.

Aquinas did recognize that money could be employed in profitable enterprises and more money would result. He wrote, "A lender may without sin enter into an agreement with the borrower for compensation for the loss he incurs of something he ought to have, for this is not to sell the use of money but to avoid a loss."[21] For instance, if a lender has a sum of money that she could employ in a productive enterprise, such as purchase a pear orchard, she would be entitled to the profit she could have received from the employment of such money if, instead of purchasing the pear orchard, she lent it to someone else to employ in a productive enterprise. If she charges a profit on the money she loaned consistent with what she could have earned by employing it herself in the productive enterprise, she does not commit usury. Her loan is not contrary to justice; she does not seek more than she should.

This principle extends to the formation of a "society," where someone enters into a communal arrangement and entrusts his money to the society without thereby transferring ownership of it. As Aquinas explained,

He that entrusts his money to a merchant or craftsman so as to form a kind of society, does not transfer the ownership of his money to them, for it remains his, so that at his risk the merchant speculates with it, or the craftsman uses it for his craft, and consequently he may lawfully demand as something belonging to him part of the profits derived from his money.[22]

Far from failing to realize that money can be employed to make more money, Aquinas both recognized and permitted it. The question of usury was not a question of profit, per se. All profit is not illegitimate. However, Aquinas found it necessary to describe how those exchanges occur so that faithful forms of exchange (profit) could be distinguished from faithless ones (usury). When modern economists assume that money generates more money without any careful analysis of how this works, they are the ones with a simplistic narration of exchanges that prevent us from knowing whence comes our daily bread and what practices make it possible.

The ancient prohibition against usury was not overturned at some singular point in time. In fact, it was seldom sustained by the force of law. Even Thomas Aquinas allowed the faithful to profit from a usurer. He stated, "It is by no means lawful to induce a man to sin, yet it is lawful to make use of another's sin for a good end, since even God uses all sin for some good since He draws some good from every evil as stated in the *Enchiridion*." Therefore, it was illicit for the faithful to induce someone into usury, but it was licit to borrow money from a professional usurer.[23] This seems to be a distinction without a difference, but it shows that the usury prohibition did not function as a state-enforced law imposed upon a superstitious society by religious zealots.

The idea that the church used authoritative coercion to impose an irrational economics upon a benighted public was a narrative created by economists such as Eugene Böhm-Bawerk in their apologetic for capitalism. Robert Heilbronner's *The Worldly Philosophers* uses the same argument. He suggests that society can organize its economics on the basis of the "whip of authoritarian rule" grounded in tradition or on a more rational basis. The former organization characterized the Middle Ages; the latter, modern capitalist formations. Only as society begins to organize around the basic rule of capitalist economics ("each should do what was to his best monetary advantage") does the authoritarian nature of society based on tradition give way to a more free and rational order.[24] But Heilbronner's narrative is a retelling of a tradition originating with Max Weber.

Weber popularized this notion of medieval economics when he defended the "rational" way of life of Calvinism as opposed to Catholicism. Weber explained the difference as follows:

The normal mediaeval Catholic layman lived ethically, so to speak, from hand to mouth. In the first place he conscientiously fulfilled his traditional duties. But beyond that minimum his good works did not necessarily form a connected, or at least not a rationalized, system of life, but rather remained a succession of individual acts. . . . To the Catholic the absolution of the Church was a compensation for his own imperfection. The priest was a magician who performed the miracle of transubstantiation, and who held the key to eternal life in his hand. . . . The God of Calvinism demanded of his believers not single good works, but a life of good works combined into a unified system. There was no place for the very human Catholic cycle of sin, repentance, release, followed by renewed sin.[25]

But this understanding of medieval economics has been decisively rejected in current historical examinations. Medieval Catholicism was not the romanticized, enchanted world Weber assumed. Priests did not control economics through superstition and cyclical rituals.

For instance, Sandra Cavallo has debunked the notion that a major shift occurred in the sixteenth century, where the economic administration of poor relief was taken over by secular authorities because of the ineptitude of the priests. The notion of a priestly administered economics that eventually gave way to a more rational secular economics cannot be sustained.[26]

In fact, the priest's role was far from that of mere magician who held the people in check through the power of superstitious tradition. The role of the priest was contained within a lay-constituted and -enacted social order where the ritual act both produced and lived from a social harmony. To violate that liturgical enactment could be viewed as a violation of a charitable social economy. Eamon Duffy provides an example in the story of John "Kareles," who took more than his share of the eucharistic host. He was "denounced to the Archdeacon of Lincoln by his neighbours in 1518 for taking too large a piece of the holy loaf, so that other parishioners were bilked of their share." "Kareles," Duffy argues, was accused not of "gluttony" but "of pride, of usurping the principal place in the community."[27] To the people of Lincoln, the Eucharist produced not a punctiliar magic show but a social harmony that had expectations beyond the mere act of the ritual itself. Likewise, John Bossy has argued that the parson's list of vices, such as usury and the refusal of wages and alms, depended upon maintaining a social order that privileged a life of charity above all other virtues.[28] The vices do not make sense without the social order that sustains the virtues.

Weber misreads and misunderstands Catholicism. This is due to his understanding of *rational* as nontraditional and noncommunal. For Weber, what counts as rational is individual self-interest, which produces a *rational spirit* despite the intentions of the individual actors. He borrowed this understanding of rational from marginalist economics and found its closest approximation in Calvinism, not because Calvinism directly intended to produce a social order based on such marginalist principles, but because it produced such an order unwittingly, by tearing "the individual away from the closed ties with which he is bound to this world."[29] But this is an inadequate reading of Calvinism that neglects the fact that Calvin's teaching on economics was much more closely aligned to that of Aquinas than to that of Böhm-Bawerk or Friedrich Hayek.

Although Calvin's literal interpretation of Scripture led him to deny the use of Luke 6:35 as a direct command from Jesus to prohibit usury, he maintained Aquinas's teaching. Calvin argued that lending money as a potential risk to help the poor was a legitimate endeavor. All usury need not be forbidden, but Aquinas allowed for this same possibility. The key difference between Aquinas and Calvin was that Calvin did not have the subtlety of argument that one finds in Aquinas, such that he does not maintain the distinction between usury and profit. Still, Calvin, like Aquinas, was prudent when it came to a place for usurers in society, stating that "it would be desirable if usurers were chased from every country, even if the practice were unknown. But since this is impossible, we ought at least to use it for the common good."[30] Unfortunately, the slight differences between Calvin and Aquinas on economics have been exaggerated and used both as a polemic and an apologetic for the superior rationality of Calvinism against Catholicism. Some Calvinist theologians, accepting Weber's interpretation, find in Calvin a superior form of ethical reflection because his work supposedly lends itself more readily to incorporate theology and the church into modern capitalist society. Unfortunately, some Catholic theologians are beginning to use a similar apologetic strategy to find in Catholicism the same spirit of democratic capitalism. But, of course, neither Calvin nor Aquinas was interested in such a social order, and one cannot help but think that both would be utterly scandalized by the dominance of a utilitarian ethic in such a social order rather than a social order that seeks to instill into its members the life of charity.

Even Calvin's argument to tolerate some "usury" remains far from the kinds of arguments later found in someone like Jeremy Bentham, who argued that no constraints should be placed upon an individual in his pursuit of what he deems best suited to his own interests. Calvin, on the other hand, argued that "we ought not to consider only the private advantage of those with whom we deal but should keep in mind what is best for the common good. For it is quite obvious that the interest a merchant pays is a public fee. Thus we should see that the contract will benefit all rather than hurt."[31] Calvin thought this possible; few economists would find it a possibility in the real world. The difference is that for Calvin, like Thomas, the real world was not defined in terms of an immanent, self-enclosed totality.

CAPITALISM'S CHOREOGRAPHY

For theologians, the real world cannot be understood in terms of a social order defined only by individuals acting within self-contained purposes such as utility, but that "real" world defines the capitalist order. As Catherine Pickstock has argued, modern liberalism and capitalism produce an "immanentist city" where citizens are reduced to the status of individuals and then regulated visibly through military force or invisibly through some written contract. This regulation occurs "invisibly through the 'dissemination' of unquestioned assumptions regarding the nature of reality and the human subject." The result is that the immanent city "eradicates the unknown" and "choreographs spontaneity," but beneath its regulations lurks a nihilism that embraces death as the only true certainty capable of establishing the borders of the immanent city.[32] Capitalist economics is based on the death of God. This is no secret revelation; some of the key architects of capitalist economics fully understood this and stated it publicly.[33] To question and name the assumptions of the immanent city at least poses a challenge to its self-containment. It is an act of charity.

The conflict between the immanent city of capitalism and the other city, which the church represents, crystallizes on the question of the just wage. While the usury prohibition has so many qualifications that it can readily be conceded as not fundamentally challenging the capitalist social order, the just wage cannot so easily be construed. The just wage assumes that it is *intrinsically evil* for an employer to pay a wage less than what is necessary to sustain workers and allow them to make their own contributions to the common good. That latter qualification is important because it shows how the practice of the just wage assumes the priority of a charitable social order. Not only the wealthy are to be the benefactors of the common good; all who work should be able to have sufficient resources that they can likewise be benefactors. Such a charitable social order prevents the unjust hierarchy that gives undue power to those with wealth simply because they have wealth rather than wisdom or virtue to give away. By not paying a just wage, employers can amass large endowments for themselves by which they can hoard the practice of charity. But to hoard the practice of charity is to violate it at the same time.

Capitalist economics can only find practices such as the just wage to be a utopian rule put forward by people who do not understand the real world of economics. Although economics as a discipline is as riddled with conflict and division as is theology, economists are perhaps more unified around some basic principles. One of those principles is that wages must be determined by what the market will allow and not by the intrusion of *political* authority. Thus, most economists argue against the state fixing a minimum wage, let alone a just wage, because the establishment of such a wage will produce unemployment and low productivity. A minimum wage is permissible only insofar as it is less than what the market would actually bear if left to itself. But here is where the social order that theology assumes conflicts with that assumed by the economists.

John Milbank has argued that "the secular culture of modernity squeezes out" the economic sphere of charity between an ethics of "the integrity of the private will respecting the freedom of others" and a politics based on a Machiavellian rationality, that is, a politics that is nothing but a formal orientation to power that can never be justified on the basis of substantive claims about truth or goodness. Thus, no distinction exists between coercive and noncoercive rules. All rules are mere orientations of formal interests by which some seek to coerce others.[34] The political structure that would render something like the just wage possible can never be enacted in modern secular society precisely because the rule of the just wage assumes a substantive good to which all exchanges should bear witness. And it assumes that such a rule is not merely an arbitrary convention by which someone's interest rules the interests of others. It assumes that economic exchanges should produce more (not less) than wealth alone; they should also orient our actions toward virtuous ends. Without those ends, the rule makes no sense. Why should an employer never pay an employee less than a just wage? Because such an action cannot be oriented to the good of charity, which is God's essence as revealed in Christ. Such an action cannot be brought into God's economy, which is defined by the central sign of Christ, who is God's exchange with us.

The only question raised by the ethics of modern secularism is that of *pluralism* or a heterogeneity of ends. Not all people share a substantive common good grounded in charity. Shall we impose our vision of the good upon others? Once this question is raised, and it always is, then we are once again trapped in the immanent city with its choreographed spontaneity. Everything remains the same even while *difference* is putatively affirmed.

But an economics of charity cannot be imposed upon a people. That would obviously be uncharitable. A theological ethic of charity is not intended for an empire, to be coercively imposed even by the coercive power of amassing sufficient votes to carry the day. It is an ethic that finds the church to be the social institution within which it primarily, but not exclusively, resides. The first question for an ethics of charity is not how we can structure a global market to allocate scarce resources in the most efficient way possible. That question will inevitably end in the adoption of the modern ethics of secularity that eschews any substantive good. The first question is, How can we participate in the life of God, a triune life characterized by a giving that is charity and goodness? This does not entail that we live without prudence, but it does assume that the rules handed down to us can be ignored only to the peril of the virtues to which they point: a life of charity. To ignore those rules and neglect the virtues to which they point us will result in our lives being defined more by the false catholicity of the market than the true catholicity of the church. Exchanges assume some social formation. Thus the church must ask: Which social formation renders intelligible our daily exchanges? Is it primarily the global market or the catholic church?

THE CATHOLIC CHURCH/THE CATHOLIC MARKET

Several years ago, I lived among the Guarifuna people of Central and South America, an African people displaced to Central America during the Middle Passage.[35] One evening I was invited to witness their traditional African dances, passed on from generation to generation despite their displacement. They instructed me to go to a meeting place some distance from their village late in the evening. As I walked toward the place, anticipating a "cross-cultural experience," I noticed a familiar rhythm. Coming closer, the rhythm became more obvious. I arrived to discover that the Guarifuna youth had assembled but were not dancing the traditional dances I came to "observe." They were dancing to Michael Jackson's "Beat It."

The story of the Guarifuna youth signifies the dominance of the catholic market over local traditions. For four hundred years local African customs were preserved in spite of an oppression that sought to annihilate them. What this oppression could not accomplish, the global market did: the dissolution of local African customs into a larger cultural accommodation. Why should anyone be troubled that some Guarifuna forsake long-standing tradition in favor of global cultural products? Perhaps, some might argue, no one but the Guarifuna have the right to pass judgment upon their own cultural traditions, whether they be rejected or maintained. The right of self-determination should allow them to determine the music to which they dance. If Guarifuna youth choose to dance to this particular music, they should be granted the freedom to do so. But this begs the question. It assumes something to be a normal state of affairs that might not be so—that the Guarifuna are free to choose which cultural products they consume.

Do the Guarifuna youth in any sense determine which cultural products they consume? Or are their "choices" limited from the outset such that *self-determination* no longer refers to any empirical reality (if it ever did)? Guarifuna culture has never been marketed through global cultural industries, nor could it be. The means for its preservation have been embodied—in words, gestures, dance, and stories—and passed on within a community. These means conflict with the technological resources by which global cultural products are marketed. Guarifuna cultural mediation cannot occur through such technological means. They would alter and shift the content of the culture, for these technological means cannot include the sense of touch, smell, and locality that Guarifuna culture required. Thus, arguments for Guarifuna self-determination only further impose a particular global cultural product: the *right* of self-determination, which can be mediated through technological means. *Rights* have a formal and disembodied nature that easily allow such technological incorporation.

Guarifuna consumption of global cultural products can only falsely be defined as a free act of will. Granted, the Guarifuna are not violently coerced to buy and consume global cultural products, but a coercion does exist. The center of Guarifuna life is neither the church nor the village assembly; the center is the shrimp and lobster plant that operates outside the village square. This plant takes the lobster and shrimp from the waters off Punta Gorda where the Guarifuna live, processes them, and ships them to the United States for fast-food consumption. The Guarifuna men provide the hands for the lobstering and shrimping; the women prepare the product for consumption—but the end product is unaffordable to the majority of the Guarifuna. However, their low wages and erratic employment keep the price low enough that lobster and shrimp can be consumed by landlocked people who eat this produce as a hobby.

The women were paid a wage of seventy cents an hour, and they worked as long as shrimp and lobster needed preparation. When the work was done, they waited until it became available again. Sometimes there would be no work for days; other times they would work ten to twelve hours a day. The wages they were paid were insufficient to purchase the product they prepared, yet other cultural products were made available. The shrimp and lobster plant made possible an "exchange" of essential nutritional elements in return for access to global culture. Thus, the incorporation of Guarifuna culture into an increasingly homogeneous world economy occurs through a complex system of exchange where *lobster* and *shrimp* no longer refer to basic food stuff. Instead, they become infinitely interchangeable with soft drinks, VCRs, professional wrestling mementos, and, on rare occasions, vaccinations. Insofar as the Guarifuna participated in this exchange process, their lives became increasingly grafted into the global market, which possesses its own rites of initiation (working for the plant) and creates a catholic unity. These people's lives directly make possible the consumptive habits of others, and the consumptive habits of others make these people's labor possible.

This complex system of exchange is, in many ways, *postmodern.* By using that term I am not suggesting a radical break between modernity and postmodernity. Modernity can be marked by the dominance of exchange values over use values. That is, rather than necessary exchanges occurring on a proportional basis determined by use according to standards of some particular social institution (a *polis* or a church), the middle term in the exchange becomes an end in itself determining its conditions and possibilities. Neither the Roman Catholic Church, where many Guarifuna worship, nor the local assembly has any say in the price of the exchange between lobster and shrimp and other commodities. Everything is given a formal equivalence in terms of *value,* where the only determining factor in the exchanges is what people want to pay to consume lobster in the North American market. The usefulness of lobster and shrimp to the Guarifuna people has no bearing on the social formation that makes the exchange possible. Money as the means of people's preferences alone determines exchange. Postmodernity intensifies the process whereby the terms of exchange (money) have no reference other than to individual preference. Thus, products can be rapidly and almost instantaneously *re*signified or *ex*changed. This process is assisted by new technological forms that accelerate the process.

THE CULTURAL LOGIC OF A CATHOLIC ECONOMY

This process leads to a political irrealism where almost anything can signify anything else. This exchange system is real, but its reality has no center to arbitrate conflicts. Reinhold Niebuhr wrote, "There must be an organizing center within a given field of social vitalities. This center must arbitrate conflicts from a more impartial perspective than is available to any party of a given conflict."[36] Political irrealism finds such descriptions of realism inadequate because they assume the normative status of the state as the center. No such center exists today. It cannot be found in the state, nor can it be found in the corporation. Transnational corporation power is not a center that gives political and social life coherence and concretization; it is more like a flux that dissolves every *real* into the possibility of a power for exchange, which is not even controlled by the corporations themselves.

While postmodernity does not represent a decisive break with modernity, it does betray a shift in the hierarchy of social formations. Transnational corporations have become dominant social formations because of the tension between the two times in which we live, characterized as modern/postmodern, liberal/postliberal, or centralized/segmented.[37] The earlier time was dominated by the nation-state, the latter by the multinational corporation. But both times were shaped to a large extent by the cultural logic of the global economy.

The cultural logic of the global economy had two dominant manifestations: the modernist era with the deconstruction of world empires and the construction of central core nation-states;[38] and the postmodern era with the dominance of transnational corporations and the breakdown of national sovereignties.

Immanuel Wallerstein argued that the rise of a global economy assisted the development of strong nation-states and the devolution of long-standing world empires.[39] For example, a smaller state like Portugal was more entrepreneurial and could more readily negotiate newly developing trade routes within the global economy than could an empire like Spain. Portugal did not need to focus its attention on internal strife and maintaining the borders of an empire. Spain was not as flexible.

As long as production depended on raw materials, nation-states retained a central role in the global economy since they secured the necessary raw materials and created *stable environments* for production. In high modernism, oil became the central raw material.[40] Thus, with Fordism as the dominant mode of production, oil as the necessary raw material, and Americanism as the cultural analogue, the United States embarked on a new form of imperialism where the social institutions of corporation, state, and military worked together to create high modernity. But even this was not to last.

A global economy is a persistent threat to the nation and its cultural logic, modernism. Nations can negotiate the global circuitry to some extent, but they are not as flexible as corporations, much as empires were not as flexible as nations. Though boundaries shift, nations are grounded to geographical areas and usually cannot relocate to a different location without the use of the military. Corporations can. They do not operate with the same modernist discourse of an objective ground but within language such as *difference* and *the other.* The corporation thus thrives in a postmodern culture. This is due to its transnational character, its dominance over communication networks, and the rapidity with which it can separate signs from references. The transnational character of corporations means that they are no longer dependent upon any single nation as a particular grounding. Global sourcing and the mobility of capital allow corporations to shift from one cultural location to another almost instantaneously. In addition, the success of certain chain discount mega-stores and its devastating impact upon local business is a result not of the superior production of a good but of a highly-skilled communication network utilizing satellites to "have instant access to inventories, delivery schedules, and other data."[41] Finally, marketing and its infinite flexibility of signs, not production, defines transnational corporation power.

Of course, this affects other social institutions as well. For example, the relation between the state and the military shifts significantly. Anthony Giddens argues that as long as the state controls the means of violence, the social dominance of the transnational corporations will face certain limitations.[42] But if the global economy conditions the political possibilities of the nation-state, then the corporation possesses at least the possibility of indirect control over the means of violence as well. The rise of low-intensity warfare, where the military is used to keep certain geographical regions open for the *world market,* and the similarity between the advertising industry and military psychological operations suggest that corporations control more of the means of violence than Giddens allows. This was certainly the case in El Salvador, where corporate advertising techniques were used as part of a psychological "assault."[43] The rise of low-intensity warfare, where advertising firms are used in cooperation with military means to secure stable environments for the market to function, suggests an important shift in the purpose of the military, which both uses and is used by transnational corporation power.

The hope that the state would place limitations on corporate power received its finest articulation by Hegel. For Hegel, the state with its war-making power preserves the ethical life because it prevents civil society from deteriorating into the mere security of "individual life and property."[44] Drawing upon classical sources, Hegel had a vision of what the good life should be and understood that bourgeois society was incapable of creating it. Bourgeois society leads to the "bog of humanity" where the virtuous life suffers because vice, greed, and addiction prevent the cultivation of courage.[45] The state, however, actualizes universal principles of freedom and rationality in its particularity. And through the exercise of its war-making power, it prevents the dominance of corporation power. Only the totalizing power of the state could contain bourgeois values.

If Hegel were correct about the need for the state and its war-making power to preserve the ethical life from the threat of bourgeois society, then his project failed miserably. As A. Sivanandan suggests, trade does not follow the flag; the flag follows trade.[46] Likewise, Ross and Trachte point out that the new "global mobility of capital disciplines both labor and state decisionmakers, who lose discretionary power over some major matters . . . lest investment decline within their area of jurisdiction."[47] The global mobility of capital makes impossible the existence of a strong state capable of creating virtue. States cannot control the means of production, so they control the means of violence for limited purposes defined by the corporation. States are useful in the global economy only in that they continue to create stable market environments.

Marx's critique of the liberal state is more persuasive than Hegel's. He argued that the liberal state developed not as a way to preserve the ethical life but as a precondition for capitalist modes of production. Capitalists required the abolition of older forms of social production, such as feudalism and slavery, because the laborer must own her or his "capacity for labor." The worker must be a rights-bearing individual equal to all other rights-bearing individuals.

For Marx, modernist discourse, with its emphasis on "freedom, equality, property and Bentham," makes capitalist modes of production possible. But these putatively universal moral concepts actually hide the "secret of profit making."[48] The liberal state does not preserve the ethical life but actually makes possible the corporation's control over the global economy and the production of its cultural "values." Thus the nation-state seldom offers true resistance to the corporation. The cultural logic of the nation-state—its language of freedom and democracy—provides the conditions for capital to work without governmental interference. For the state to be an alternative to the global economy, it would have to embody the ethical life as Hegel suggested. This would require a totalizing use of force and coercion, which offers no hope.

THE CHURCH

Unlike social institutions such as the transnational corporation, the state, or the military, the church is seldom understood as a significant political actor. In truth, the church as a social institution has largely been incorporated into the cultural logic of the nation-state. In the United States and Western Europe, Liberal Protestant Christianity and much of post–Vatican II Roman Catholicism adopted the cultural logic of the modern state with little critique. Moreover, the current dominance of the church-growth movement and the unabashed adoption of corporate organizational theories for clergy and churches attest to the church's increasing incorporation into the cultural logic of the transnational corporation. Yet political theorist Michael Budde argues in *The Two Churches: Catholicism and Capitalism in the World System* that the church is one social institution that possesses an intrinsic resistance to the encroaching power of the global economy. A catholic church may be the last source of resistance to the false salvation put forward by a globalizing market. Such resistance has been long in the making.

In *Whose Justice? Which Rationality?* Alasdair MacIntyre has argued that the papacy of Gregory VII provided an important framework that resists the pretensions of empires and states. Such a political theology also resists the universal pretensions of the market. For MacIntyre, Gregory VII "supplies a continuation of Augustine's thought in which the relationship of the two cities in a Christian society is understood in terms of the difference in both function and origin of the papacy and of ecclesiastical institutions generally from secular sovereignties."[49] Secular sovereignties such as empires, states, and global markets do not possess the same origins as the church. This difference in origin implies different functions. The state and the market can serve only limited ends. This necessitates some *other* social formation that is incapable of being totalized within the state or market and that reminds states and markets of their limits. This is the role of the church. Only when it owns its proper origin and function can these other social institutions know their place. Therefore, the *Dictatus Papae* of Gregory VII may not be the mad ramblings of an autocrat but a right ordering of social institutions based on their different origins. Notice the implication of Gregory VII's defense of the papacy and how his dictates order the *polis,* setting limits to its pretensions. In *Dictatus Papae,* he promulgated the following laws:

1. That the Roman Church was founded by God alone.
7. That the Roman Pontiff alone is rightly to be called universal.
8. That he alone may use the imperial insignia.
9. That the pope is the only one whose feet are to be kissed by all princes.
10. That his name alone is to be recited in churches.
11. That his title is unique in the world.
12. That he may depose Emperors.[50]

These assertions defend the universality of the church against other false catholicities, particularly the false catholicity of empire. The critique of the empire that began with theologians such as Tertullian reminding the emperor that he is but a man gives rise to the papacy reminding would-be emperors that they can never oversee true universal communities. The ends they should serve are more limited. What it means for other social institutions to be divinely ordained is that they are ordered to their proper ends by the Church.

ECCLESIAL MARKS AND AGORA SCARS

The traditional marks of the church are that it is one, holy, catholic, and apostolic. The significance of the catholicity of the church has caused popes and theologians to stress that only the church can be universal; neither the empire, the state, nor the market can claim that role. Yet the new *global* village has at its center not a church but a market. The global market threatens the church's catholicity with a competing catholicity.

The global market has been a reality at least since the fifteenth century. Perhaps it began in 1415 when the Portuguese seized the Muslim port of Ceuta on the African side of the Straits of Gibraltar. This opened up the Atlantic Ocean to the Portuguese and allowed them access to India. The Portuguese established ports in West Africa and in 1500 crossed the Atlantic to Brazil. Although global links had already been established to the East through the Crusades, new global links were now produced, links that brought the world closer together and made possible the new form of slave-trafficking. The Portuguese were the first to begin this trade, first enslaving the white inhabitants of the Canary Islands, the Guanache. The trade made possible was not yet the slaves themselves; they were the means for trading in other "goods." But when Sao Tome and Principe were found to be uninhabited and ideal for growing sugar, a new form of agriculture emerged that created the conditions for the slave trade to grow. It is estimated that from 1451 to 1600 approximately 275,000 slaves were sent to America and Europe. From 1600 to 1700, 1,341,000 were sent to run sugar and tobacco plantations in the Americas. By 1660 the English established the Royal Africa Company, and from 1700 on the English dominated the slave trade. From 1700 to 1800, over 6,000,000 slaves were sent. In 1807 Britain abolished the slave trade, yet 2,000,000 more slaves were transported between 1810 to 1870. That means that 80 percent of all slaves taken to the New World were transported between 1701 and 1850.[51] The estimates on the number of people who died in the slave ships and the number of native peoples who died through violence, slaughter, and enslavement are notoriously difficult to make. Some estimate the number as high as seventy million.

Slavery, of course, was not new. But for the first time it was based on the "scientific" category of race and was occasioned by a global market system. The church was complicit in this, yet voices did cry out against the practice. Although his eleventh remedy led to the increased production of the African slave trade, Friar Bartolomé de Las Casas recorded the words of the Dominican Anton Montesino, who preached against those responsible for the conquest:

> You are all in mortal sin! You live in it and you die in it! Why? Because of the cruelty and tyranny you use with these innocent people. Tell me, with what right, with what justice, do you hold these Indians in such cruel and horrible servitude? . . . How is it that you hold them so crushed and exhausted, giving them nothing to eat, nor any treatment for their diseases, which you cause them to be infected with through the surfeit of their toils, so that they "die on you"— you mean, you kill them—mining gold for you day after day: And what care do you take that anyone catechize them . . . Are you not obligated to love them as you love yourselves?[52]

The conquest of the Americas; the slave trade; the introduction of spices, coffee, cocoa, and sugar—all these both made possible and resulted from new trade routes that increasingly linked the world into a single market. As Montesino proclaimed, such links were not forged out of charity. This process has continued and intensified over time. It now poses a threat to the catholicity of the Christian church much as the divinity of the emperor threatened it in the age of the martyrs and Caesaropapism endangered it in the age of the church's accommodation to the empire. It raises the question whether our participation in its daily exchanges can be directed toward the charity that should define our lives. The global market is a serious threat to the church's claim that it is the primary social formation that mediates the peaceable reign of God because it is Christ's body in the world.

Some economists have gone so far as to argue that the global market has now replaced the church as the institution we should look to for hope. But the global market is not a sign of the rule of God; it is a competing salvific institution whose spokespersons claim it can offer what the church cannot. When we accept this rhetoric, we are held captive to an idol.

The global market is present to us as a text. We gain access to it through the daily reading and devotion it asks of us. The ability to read, interpret, and translate it both creates the *market* and sustains the power that moves it. As a text, it trades on an infinite play of signs where the ultimate interpretive condition that makes this constant deconstruction and resignification possible is indefinitely deferred. An ultimate interpretive condition that renders it intelligible is not permitted; it can always be deferred.

Such an ultimate interpretive condition for reading a text was traditionally called its "anagogical interpretation." In the words of Frederick Jameson, this is where "the text undergoes its ultimate rewriting in terms of the destiny of the human race as a whole."[53] Because the global market works at the interpretive level of constant deconstruction and resignification, an ultimate referent cannot easily be found. The global market feeds on an infinite desire that should never be satisfied; it needs lack. But here we find the global market's anagogical interpretation. Unbounded and unsatisfied desire itself becomes the destiny of humanity. However, the church cannot long remain the church without acknowledging a different anagoge. Our desires are not to be unbounded but are to be satisfied by being ordered to the Word spoken by the Father eternally in the power of the Spirit. The Word functions as an anagogical referent that is necessary for the ultimate writing of humanity's destiny.

In his disturbing book *Reaching for Heaven on Earth,* Robert Nelson suggests that the market mechanism has supplanted the medieval church as that which, in practice, offers people their salvation. What is disturbing is not that Nelson is wrong but that he persuasively argues that the dominant social practices forming our exchanges and any remaining quest for salvation in the contemporary period are not those of the church but of the market. Nelson understands that the market creates and thrives off of a postmodern culture where geographical grounding is no longer important. The world market becomes itself a kind of text that we daily read and meditate upon, much as earlier generations practiced morning and evening prayer. That text is presented to us through new technological means. Social scientists and economists have become priests who now interpret this new text and thus provide us with our future security and give our lives their ultimate meaning.

Nelson argues that the market can provide what the church tried but failed to provide. The market will provide the maximization of individual liberty, the annihilation of all coercive uses of power, the realization of all relationships based on voluntary consent, the achievement of perfect harmony, and the equality of all humanity throughout the world.[54] This market-driven vision replaces the vision that once went by the name the kingdom of God. Yet Nelson does not want to dismiss god, who is still present in bringing about this new kingdom. But god only has a bit part, grounding certain laws of nature that ensure the realization of this other kingdom if we leave the market alone and allow it to work freely. However, this god is not the God of Christian revelation. Atheism is a necessary Christian posture before this god, for this is the god of a peculiar form of providence to which natural theologians always appeal to justify a particular set of rules under the legitimizing claim that they are "natural."

According to Nelson, the natural laws this god secures are as follows:

1. The pursuit of self-interest is inherently good.
2. To be rational is to be "efficient."
3. The goal of communal life is increased productivity.
4. A select group of persons, economists, and social scientists, who now form a new priesthood, are to be the privileged interpreters of the market.[55]

Nelson's argument is instructive because it explicitly offers a comprehensive and coherent description of salvation within which the market is intelligible; he gives the market an anagogical interpretation. The transnational corporation becomes the social institution that makes this form of salvation possible. Theology is now based on the presupposition of the normalcy of the current economic state of affairs. Theology that contributes to this new salvation is acceptable; all else is illicit.

This demonstrates with stark clarity that the global market is in competition with the church for people's souls. It offers an overarching view of salvation that promises the alleviation of suffering based on the inherent rationality of the market and the ability to discover and manage that rationality accordingly. This overarching view of salvation is theological and not accidental to the global market; it has even become an acceptable way to market the church. Thus, even the language of the church is now used to seduce us into this other catholicity. Yet the theological claims implicit and explicit in the global market are heretical, a false salvation. They enclose our existence within the immanent city that defines capitalism and keeps us from that other city.

The market as salvific institution is and must be heretical. All orthodox Christians should recognize its deceitful power and oppose it. The church can oppose the catholic market because it cannot long ignore the Word that calls it into being, a Word that breaks the bonds of the immanent city. The unity we share is a unity in the body of Christ; separate from this unity we can live only in Babel. As Christ gave himself for us, so we participate in his sacrifice every time we worship. The true Word calls into question the false word of the market. The true Word is found in the church's liturgy.

In collecting tithes the church claims that we do not own our productive capacity as an inherent right. Even if such productivity is responsible for great financial benefits, to produce without regard for the Giver of all gifts leads to unrighteousness. The task of our economic life is not to produce efficiently but to serve God. Thus, we try to honor the Sabbath and keep it holy with few exceptions allowed, even though honoring the Sabbath is obviously inefficient and a threat to increased productivity.

In the Eucharist we discover how God deals with us and thus how we are to deal with one another. The Eucharist utilizes the basic elements of life, and God transforms them into God's own self. This gift is given to us upon our repentance and baptism. What would happen if during the Eucharist one person seized the entire host and ate it in front of the others? Would we not recognize such a person as violating the sacredness of the sacrament? But what happens when we come to the table with some who possess an immense amount of this world's goods who are unwilling to share with others who do not? Is it not an analogous situation? Have we not likewise violated the sacredness of the sacrament? Can we keep the Lord's Day holy when such a reality defines our lives? We cannot.

The market is a subtle tempter offering quick and big results. But such results are illusory, the result of human hands alone. The new priests Robert Nelson mentions, the economists who can read market trends and have the flexible capacity to adjust accordingly, usurp traditional priests' role of the redistribution of material elements through the ordering of the faithful by word and sacrament. Our task as Christians is not to bow the knee to the false salvation of the global market.

EIGHT

POLIS

You shall not kill. Exodus 20:13

Love your enemies and pray for those who persecute you. Matthew 5:44

In the Gospel of John, the last utterance the chief priests put forward before Jesus is crucified is, "We have no king but Caesar." This is the ultimate betrayal, not only of Jesus, but of Judaism itself. Of the reasons given in the Gospels as to why Pilate yielded to the cry to crucify Jesus, Raymond Brown suggests that the argument made by the crowd and by the chief priests, namely, that "Pilate worried about what might be said at Rome," is most historically credible.[1] For the sake of remaining in patronage to Rome, Pilate acquiesces to the crowd and the chief priests.

Such worry inevitably results in the betrayal of Judaism and Christianity. Jesus' mission, like Israel's, was born in the conflict between loyalty to Caesar and loyalty to God. This was not the conflict of the avant garde who seek to be against the system because it is always fashionable to be so. This conflict was not precipitated by revolutionaries whose first concern was the overthrow of the existing political order. In fact, in reading through the sources one cannot help but realize that the greatest of all revolutions—the de-divinization of the emperor—was spearheaded by reluctant revolutionaries who were more intent on serving the God whom they knew to be good than the emperor about whom they were unsure. They were unconcerned with any *overcoming*, with any permanent revolution. Thus, a key text the early church fathers appealed to in order to explain both why they were not a threat to a good political order and why they could not participate in civic festivities was Matthew 22:15–22, which records Jesus' teaching, "Render therefore to Caesar the things that are Caesar's, and to God the things that are God's."

Justin Martyr, in commenting on this passage, told the authorities, "We adore only God, but in other things we gladly serve you, acknowledging you as emperor and sovereign."[2] However, for Caesar this was an insufficient acknowledgement of his authority. Justin Martyr was finally denounced as a Christian and beheaded when he refused to offer sacrifices to the Roman gods. The authority of the emperor and the cult of the empire were closely associated. To challenge the latter was to challenge the former.

DE-DIVINIZING EMPERORS

Justin Martyr was not alone in posing the Christian challenge to the emperor. Theophilus of Antioch explained why he did not worship the emperor by confessing, "Because he is made not to be worshiped but to be reverenced with due honor, for he is not god, but a man appointed by God not to be worshipped but to judge justly." Although Theophilus's statement, like the other apologists, is in the context of loyalty and due honor given to the emperor, it also brings with it resistance: a constant need to check Caesar's pretension to divinity against the true divinity revealed in Jesus Christ. In fact, Tertullian suggested that Christians alone can truly claim the emperor as theirs "because our God appointed him," and they alone can truly give him his due honor "by putting limits to the emperor's majesty and subordinating him to God, making him less than divine." Thus, the due honor the Christian gives to the emperor is by reminding him, when he passes in triumphal procession, "Look behind you, you are but a man."[3]

Likewise Hippolytus (170–236) explained that the example of Daniel in Daniel 6 fulfilled the intent of Jesus' words in Matthew 22:21. Just as Daniel refused to bend the knee to another god or king, Hippolytus reminds us, "Who bows to another becomes his slave." His point is not that we should be free and no one's slave but that we have already bowed the knee to Jesus and are his servants alone. To bow the knee to the emperor would be an act of injustice, for it would give to Caesar what belongs only to God, and would lack charity because it would be deceitful; it would not order our actions to their true end but would participate in a false performance of true worship. The early Christian revolution appears to have occurred through the refusal to participate in mundane everyday practices as a sign of true obedience. Wearing the color purple, refusing to wear a crown, standing while others bend the knee—all these simple practices brought down the empire. No wonder that great commentator on this period of history, Friedrich Nietzsche, was so exercised by what the

Christians had done. Such apparent weakness transvalues the ancient values of nobility and strength and issues in the "slave revolt in morality." People who call themselves *slaves* attain a moral victory over that free noble spirit that is willing to take to itself even the divine ascription. By the time the Christian revolution was finished, the emperor could no longer seize for himself such a noble title. A new strategy would have to be pursued to legitimate the divine authority of the emperor. This, of course, took place with the Constantinian shift and the new problem of Caesaropapism.

DIVINITY RE-EMERGES: CAESAROPAPISM

The problem of Caesaropapism arises most vividly with the emperor Justinian. Whereas prior to Constantine Christians could expect sporadic and local persecution, after Constantine, as Hugo Rahner explains, the way was prepared that led to Justinian, who took it upon himself to act as bishop. In the eyes of many Western Christians, Justinian sought to use his authority to overturn conciliar decisions. This is Rahner's charge against Eastern Christianity. The creation of an imperial church led to the subordination of the church to the emperor rather than to the bishop of Rome. Without the "guiding role of the papacy," suggests Rahner, the church became vulnerable to the power of the state: "All the Churches who wish to withdraw from the unity of the Church dogmatically first of all seek refuge with the state but soon are absorbed by the state and fall with it."[4]

This, of course, is not the whole story. One can hardly affirm Roman Catholicism for its ability to keep itself disentangled from imperial power. Nevertheless, Rahner's point is significant, for while many periods in history demonstrate the relationship between the papacy and certain *national* regimes, the papacy itself has remained an office of unity that cannot by its very nature explicitly subordinate itself to any imperial structures. Only the Orthodox, the Church of England, and various Protestant bodies have developed an apologetic that subordinates the church to a national body. That is why these bodies cannot do without Catholicism even when they seek to reform it (and themselves as well).

Once the emperor becomes a Christian, he cannot claim the mantle of divinity but can only claim to be in service to it. But not even this source of allegiance would stand forever. It was slowly called into question, and a new strategy was devised: the strategy of investing "the people" as a whole with divine authority and viewing their collective will as that which gives divine values. That strategy is now coming to an end—the end of modernity. But that modern strategy, the strategy of the divine right of the people, was just another variation of the call by the people in the Gospel of John to be the judge of God rather than be judged by God. Moreover, just as the church originally fostered a revolution that de-divinized the emperor, so the church must call into question any deification of human willing, even when it is the people as a whole that is constructed as the subject of such a will.

Jean Bethke Elshtain explains the original Christian revolution in her book, *Public Man, Private Woman*. Elshtain suggests that Christianity "ushered a moral revolution into the world which dramatically, and for the better, transformed the prevailing images of male and female, public and private." It did this by transvaluing the ancient pagan virtues of courage and justice, which were centered in the life of the *polis*. As Elshtain noted, Christianity turned "Aristotle on his head."[5] The *polis*, suggests Elshtain, was created as a domain of male power to free men from the power of the *oikos*, the home.[6] This resulted in the silencing of women by rendering the home as private, as an apolitical realm contrasted with the public *polis*, the place where the business of the real world occurred. The original Christian revolution was that "Christianity challenged the primacy of politics."[7]

Although a number of church fathers and mothers—one thinks of Monica, who saved her son Augustine, and Macrina, who saved her brother Basil of Caesarea, from a life associated with imperial politics—could be identified as sponsoring this alternative to the *polis* as an ecclesial site for the political, none did so more persuasively than Augustine. As John Milbank notes, Augustine identified the violence that is at the heart of the *polis* and countered it with an alternative city based on the "ontological priority of peaceableness."[8] This *other city* finds its home in the pilgrim people we call church. This *civitas Dei* sets forth a universal standard of justice, rooted in charity, whose requirements, suggests Alasdair MacIntyre, "have from time to time been discovered to have yet further and more radical application throughout the subsequent history of the church."[9] One of those revolutionary applications is found in the papacy of Gregory VII (1073–1085).

To call Gregory VII a *revolutionary* is, of course, odd. If revolution implies throwing off the power of the old for the sake of the new, Gregory VII could hardly be so described. Instead, he revived the ancient laws of the church and sought to ensure that conciliar decrees were in fact honored by clergy and laity alike. But this was not how the imperial powers viewed Gregory's reforms. When Henry IV repudiated Gregory, he appealed to the Gelasian doctrine of the two swords. Henry sought to argue that his kingship was ordained by God as a distinct and separate means by which God ordered the world. "[T]he kingship and the priesthood should remain," Henry wrote, "not as one entity, but as two."[10] But Gregory was unwilling to concede any autonomous territory to the *polis*. Instead, he gave "institutional and political form [to] St. Augustine's theology of the two cities."[11] While the church was to remain free from interference by the earthly *polis*, the earthly *polis* could never be free from the claims of the *ecclesia*. The *polis* was not merely to enforce a negative conception of justice because of the threat of original sin. The *polis* was also divinely ordained. This did not mean (contra Henry IV) that it could be independent of the church but rather that without the church, the state could not know what justice is.

Justice was for Augustine, as for Plato, a transcendent universal separate from sense-experience. But it was also more than that. After Augustine, justice was not a self-evident virtue. It required something more than knowledge of its own universal form for its intelligibility. It required charity as defined by Jesus. In *The Trinity* Augustine spoke of this something more: "Thus in that realm of eternal truth from which all things temporal were made, we behold with our mind's eye the pattern upon which our being is ordered, and which rules all to which we give effect with truth and reason, in ourselves or in the outer world."

Just as the pattern by which all is made is the Word spoken from all eternity, so the truthfulness of our knowledge of things also depends upon a "kind of word." Truthful knowledge exists in us as a "kind of word," a word that we "apply" in service to others through speech and other signs. Such service renders possible true ethical judgments, but this "kind of word" that we offer is conceived by charity, and the service we render will be intelligible only in terms of this charity. The charity that prompts this service is both love of God and love of neighbor. The latter can be had only within the context of the former. Only this allows us the true enjoyments of this life, a life of necessity lived in relationship with neighbors.[12]

What has this to do with the *polis?* As Gregory VII recognized, the polis can never be self-interpreting. It does not possess the codes that render it capable of the true enjoyment of our neighbors. Of course, to insist that the church bears the codes that makes life truly enjoyable will be viewed by the *polis* as a threat to its sovereignty, as it was for Henry IV and is for contemporary democratic regimes. This places the church always in a precarious position before the *polis*. It must remind the *polis* that only the church is to be called universal; the state can never usurp that title, for only the church truly possesses the word of charity. But this is something that emperors—in antiquity and in modernity—do not want to hear. The church's role in relation to the *polis* is doubly precarious, for not only does the *polis* consistently refuse to hear this charitable word but the *polis,* unlike the church, holds a power of coercion over its citizens to create an endurable order in the time between the times. This is a power the church oversees without itself possessing. But how can this work? As Stalin said of the pope and as Henry IV demonstrated, the church has too few troops to impose its will.[13]

THE POWER OF THE SWORD

What role does the sword have within the church? On the night he was betrayed, Jesus told his disciples that, whereas he sent them out earlier without purse, bag, or sandals, they should now buy a bag and even a sword. The disciples (who were evidently already prepared with swords) said, "Look, Lord, here are two swords." Jesus responded, "It is enough." Although most biblical scholars would interpret Jesus' statement as something like "stop this silliness," the medieval church interpreted it in terms of the doctrine of the two. This led to the Gelasian doctrine of the two swords, which suggested that God rules the world through both a secular and a spiritual sword. The church holds the spiritual sword, and the ruler/state the secular sword. The church cannot exercise the secular sword itself, but it has the power to call upon the ruler/state to use the secular sword. But here the church's tradition needs correction by the rest of the biblical story, for the tradition embodies the very misunderstanding the disciples themselves embodied. As Luke Timothy Johnson notes, the disciples' misunderstanding "reveals just how 'unready' the disciples are to follow where Jesus must go." They later use the sword in the garden, to which Jesus responds, "No more of this!" (Luke 22:51).

A theologian such as Tertullian interpreted Jesus' statement in Luke 22:51 as a universal command binding upon all Christians. In answering the question whether Christians can participate in military service, he stated,

> There is no agreement between the divine and the human sacrament, the standard of Christ and the standard of the devil, the camp of light and the camp of darkness. One soul cannot be due to two masters—God and Caesar. And yet Moses carried a rod, and Aaron wore a buckle, and John the son of Nun leads a line of march; and the People warred: if it pleases you to sport with the subject. But how will a Christian man war, nay, how will he serve even in peace, without a sword, which the Lord has taken away? For albeit soldiers had come unto John and had received the formula of their rule; albeit likewise a centurion had believed; still the Lord afterward, in disarming Peter, unbelted every soldier.[14]

Tertullian did not argue that Christians were prohibited from military service because of the sacrifices offered to the Roman gods. He clearly argued that such prohibition was grounded in the different allegiance Christians had to a Savior who had taken away the sword. The *sacrament* or loyalty oath one takes to God in Christ conflicts with the *sacrament* or loyalty oath Caesar or any ruler requests. Tertullian must have received queries about this prohibition because of the warfare present in the Old Testament. He did not discount those queries but situated them within the master narrative he read in Jesus' action in the garden.

GOD AND VIOLENCE

Can Tertullian and the early church's nonviolence be so easily defended against the warfare both God and the people waged in the Old Testament? Is such an interpretation a species of heresy, a proto-Marcionism that reads the New Testament God against the Old Testament God and thus begins the long, tortured history of anti-Judaism within Christianity? Does the necessity of reading the old and new covenants as covenants with the same God entail the assumption that God is violent? Christians are not the first to raise these questions. Shalom Spiegel put the question to Christians. He saw the Akedah (Genesis 22, where Abraham is prevented from sacrificing Isaac) as a "historical remembrance of the transition to animal sacrifice from human sacrifice. This was a religious achievement which in the folk memory was associated with Abraham; namely, the father of the new faith and the first of the upright in the Lord's way."[15] The Akedah was an end to human sacrifice. Far from the problem of violence being the difficulty of the Old Testament God supposedly needing blood sacrifice, Spiegel argues that Israel's God revealed the end of any such human sacrifice. He then raises the question whether Christianity assumes a pagan conception of human sacrifice and undoes what the Akedah accomplished. Does the sacrifice of Jesus as the propitiation for sin return us to the age of human sacrifice? Does it make God violent? Does God seek human blood as some form of appeasement that makes God turn from wrath? And is our warring a part of a blood ritual that satisfies God's justice?

Such questions about Christianity's relationship to violence are not only a Jewish critique of Christianity; they have also been raised by Christian feminist theologians. For instance, Joanne Carlson Brown and Rebecca Parker find Anselm's "satisfaction" theory of the atonement a sanction for suffering and violence. It makes God a tyrant who uses coercion and violence against the innocent to work his will. This is based on their argument that Anselm taught that God "desired the death of the Son." They quote from *Cur Deus Homo,* "The Father desired the death of the Son, because he was not willing that the world should be saved in any other way."[16] But this is not the full quote Anselm wrote, and what is left out significantly challenges their reading. Before this statement Anselm wrote, "In this sense, then, the Father willed the Son's death." The phrase "in this sense" qualifies Brown and Parker's interpretation of Anselm. Far from insisting that God was a tyrant who willed the death of the innocent, Anselm has a lengthy discussion where he addresses this specific objection to the sacrifice of Christ. B questions Anselm, "For what justice is there in giving up the most just man of all to death on behalf of the sinner?" Anselm responds, "For God did not force him to die or allow him to be slain against his will; on the contrary, he himself readily endured death in order to save men." Why did he die? Not because God directly willed his death but because of his obedience. As Anselm put it, "Therefore God did not compel Christ to die, when there was no sin in him, but Christ himself freely underwent death, not by yielding up his life as an act of obedience, but on account of his obedience in maintaining justice, because he so steadfastly persevered in it that he brought death on himself."[17] In other words, Anselm does not locate Christ's *obedience* in his willingness to die for the sake of sacrifice itself. Anselm locates Christ's *death* as a result of his obedience to God's righteousness in a world where that righteousness is unwelcome. What redeems is Christ's obedience even in the face of death, his unwillingness to turn from God's righteousness. Only insofar as such obedience will lead to death because of humanity's warring madness, which God knows beforehand, only "in that sense" is it appropriate to say, "God desired the death of the Son."

Far from setting forth the kind of bloodthirsty sacrifice Brown and Parker attribute to Anselm and other doctrines of Christ's sacrifice for us as redemptive, Anselm argues that only when we understand that Christ's death came as a byproduct of his obedience to the goodness and beauty that God is—restoring that order in its proper harmony—can we dare to say, "In this sense, the Father willed the Son's death." Like Anselm's interlocutor in *Cur Deus Homo*, who misunderstands this, Brown and Parker also fail to read Anselm's sacrifice as a theological aesthetics that does not valorize suffering and sacrifice. What Anselm says to B could equally be said to Brown and Parker, "you fail to distinguish what he did as the requirement of obedience from what he endured, apart from any requirement of obedience, simply because he maintained his obedience."[18] Anselm clearly held that "God did not compel Christ to die," nor did "the Father prefer the death of his Son to his life."[19] Christ's sacrifice does not appease a wrathful God; it restores the "beauty" of God's created order in a way that is "fitting" to God's "kindness." It permits no act in God that is "unseemly to God."[20] What, then, causes contemporary critics of Christ's sacrifice to so misunderstand it that they seek to develop Christian theology without this essential element to the Christian narrative? Perhaps it is the commitment such critics have to the modern discipline of psychology.

Theologies based on modern psychological theories, like those found in the book *Christianity, Patriarchy and Abuse*, are unable to understand the significance of sacrifice. They are incapable of understanding it because, as René Girard has so compellingly argued, the relationship between violence and sacrifice is deceptive. Far from valorizing violence and setting it forth as something to emulate, sacrifice "serves to protect the entire community from its own violence. . . . The purpose of the sacrifice is to restore harmony to the community, to reinforce the social fabric."[21] For Girard, sacrifice restores harmony by ending the cycle of violence and retribution that are an ever-present threat in primitive societies without a strong centralized judicial system. If those of us in modern societies do not understand the economy of sacrifice and reduce it to psychological considerations, it is because our judicial system rationalizes the vengeance that threatened primitive societies. "Primitive societies do not have built into their structure an automatic brake against violence; but we do, in the form of powerful institutions whose grip grows progressively tighter as their role grows progressively less apparent."[22] Because tightly controlled and policed modern societies cannot recognize their practices that rationalize vengeance, they psychologize earlier forms of sacrifice as forms of repression that the modern discards. This is precisely what the contributors to *Christianity,*

Patriarchy and Abuse do in their critique of Christ's sacrifice. They read it as a psychological motivation for abuse and fail to offer a detailed analysis of the real threat of violence as a social reality. Thus, far from moving us beyond a sacrificial economy, they valorize suffering and make it the ontological key to understanding life. Brown and Parker reject Jesus as an "acceptable sacrifice" and argue instead that

> suffering is never redemptive, and suffering cannot be redeemed. The cross is a sign of tragedy. God's grief is revealed there and everywhere and every time life is thwarted by violence. God's grief is as ultimate as God's love. Every tragedy eternally remains and is eternally mourned. Eternally the murdered scream.[23]

A god who so thoroughly allows evil to triumph, who allows it to constitute an eternal ontology, would be a tyrant not worthy of our worship. In fact this god is not new; it is the god of Greek tragedy, a god against whom we must secure ourselves precisely because, as Nietzsche recognized, for this god grief is as eternal as joy, evil as eternal as good. Brown and Parker's argument is merely one more sign of the re-Hellenization of Western culture. That it should make such inroads into Christian theology is worrisome. Anselm's God is so much more worthy of worship precisely because he knows beauty without the possibility of eternal torment. He refuses the eternal valorization of suffering Brown and Parker insist is necessary for our "liberation."

If suffering cannot be redeemed, Christianity is false, and we should create new festivals to the ancient Greek gods that recognize tragedy as our only "redemption." Such *new festivals* will help us secure our lives against a god who allows the cries of torment to have an eternal existence. Modernity is itself such a new festival. The assertion of will that characterizes it arises in response to the arbitrariness of the nominalist's portrayal of God, who seems to act solely on the basis of freedom and not on the true, good, or beautiful. Brown and Parker repeat the strategy of modernity. Their quest for goodness requires an eternal grief. Otherwise, we betray past victims and diminish the hope of any future liberation. For their sake we refuse to acknowledge the possibility of any redemption of evil. But the preservation of memory as nonredemptive for the sake of liberation offers no resistance to modern political and social formations, for they are also based on such a sacrificial economy. John Milbank has argued that this sacrificial economy defines both the modern state and the exchanges present in capitalism.

> There is a notion here of loss without return, save for the posthumous praise of celebration of one's austerity or bravery. A return of the living self is not involved, save in rather shadowy intimations of an after-life. . . . Such a logic elevates an abstract space, the notion of the perpetually abiding city which outlasts the lives of its citizens and is elevated in value over the lives of individual humans, even

where this is disguised in the form of the notion of "sacrifice for future generations." For since every generation should logically be subject to the same imperative, consummation is forever postponed, and indeed morality itself is defined
as perpetual postponement or else as self-sacrifice.

Milbank argues that the "perpetual postponement" of any possible redemption
of evil is itself the necessity of a sacrificial economy. This sacrificial economy is
not only the logic of the modern, where morality is defined in terms of "surrender of the self for the future, for science, and for the State," but also the logic
behind the postmodern, where "thinkers discover the good, or the moral act or
self-giving sacrifice to be perpetual postponement." Both are "simply perfect-
ing this cruel and annihilating logic under whose tyranny we all now live."[24]

Milbank finds Christianity an alternative to this sacrificial economy because
it does not eternally ontologize evil, loss, and grief. Drawing on the apostle
Paul, Milbank finds in Christianity an "offering of passion" that differs from
the sacrificial economy because "Paul is talking about an offering of self (soul
and body) to a personal God which implicitly involves a trust in a return of
self as a more abundant living soul and body."[25] Far from ontologizing evil and
making tragedy the eternal word, this offering of passion looks for the redemption of evil and the restoration of all things in God. We see this now such that
the sacrificial economy must not be valorized even in our current politics and
economics. This is the Christian interpretation of the Akedah in the book of
Hebrews. Abraham looked to the other *city* whose foundation is God (Heb.
11:10). This gaze frees us from the "fear of death" and the "lifelong bondage"
of the fleshly city (Heb. 2:15). It does so because of the promised return, a
promise given to Abraham and Sarah, so that Abraham could in faith offer up
Isaac. This *offering of passion* was not a valorization of sacrifice or the assumption that life is composed of eternal grief and joy. Abraham's offering was based
on his consideration that God was able to raise humans even from the dead.
It could only be done because of the promise of return, a return that undoes
the sacrificial economy precisely because no single other can stand as my *sacrifice*. This promised return, this resurrection, is the end of sacrifice.

WAR AS DEVOTIONAL PRACTICE

Shalom Spiegel criticized Christianity for valorizing human sacrifice, which
the Torah had overcome in God's great generosity. But Christianity stands with
Spiegel in recognizing that the biblical narratives put an end to human sacrifice
as necessary for the identity of God's people. Perhaps this is the key to understanding the violence in our sacred Scriptures. What do we do with the biblical
command to offer human sacrifices in the *herem,* the ban that requires putting
everything to death as a sacrifice to God in thanksgiving for victory? How do we

understand Leviticus 27:29, which commands, "No one devoted, who is to be utterly destroyed from among men, shall be ransomed; he shall be put to death"? Such a ban was commanded of Joshua, "All that is within [Jericho] shall be devoted to the LORD" (Josh. 6:17). But this "sacrifice" does not seem to be an expiation for sins, nor can it be dismissed as "ethnic cleansing," something moderns produced. It is an offering of "devoted things," things that are already holy to God. As Susan Niditch has argued, the ban is not exercised because "human life was given little value" but because it had such "high value." It was the greatest of God's works and thus could be offered back to God as a return to God that would not entail loss.[26] To suggest this is not to defend an ancient practice that moderns assume is no longer present among civilized people.

We do not view our sacrifices as devotional practices, but we continue to sacrifice others through war, the judicial system, a sacrificial economics, and abortion. Perhaps to recognize that the ones we sacrifice are the highest form of life—"devoted things" that give us our identity—would be preferable to our disregard for them and consequent self-deception about our own sacrifices. If we blessed them as devoted things before sacrificing them, then we might have some fear that their sacrifices would one day cry out for vindication. Perhaps it is we who value life so little that we think it can be permanently lost and thus incapable of crying out for a redemption that might not be perpetually postponed. It may take more courage to believe in a return of life where injustice must be redeemed than a nihilistic end to life where injustice and justice, grief and joy, remain perpetually mixed. This is not to suggest that we valorize human sacrifice as redemptive. But perhaps Scripture could bear witness to the end of sacrifice in the Akedah because God's people knew the temptation of the ban; they knew that life was a "devoted thing" to the Lord so that sacrificing it involved them in contradictions. The ban is not to be emulated. It is to help us make a realistic examination of our own complicity in a sacrificial economy.

More troubling than the ancient witness of the ban as sacrifice may be the rationalization of the sacrifice in the Deuteronomic History, when the ban becomes a practice of God's justice. Now the vanquished are offered to God not so much as an offering but as condemned sinners. Could this be a sign that our forefathers and mothers have become like the other nations, living from a sacrificial economy? Perhaps such stories should be read with the same ambiguity with which Scripture presents to us the monarchy and the building of the temple (1 Samuel 8–9; 2 Samuel 7). The point is not to rationalize or emulate them but to see the consequences when the *other city* founded by God becomes like the nations. In fact, Scripture does not present any single legitimation of or practice for war. Different kinds of warfare are present.

Along with the ban as sacrifice and as God's justice, Niditch identifies the priestly ideology of war in Numbers 31, the bardic tradition that glorifies heroic deeds, the tricksterism used by the powerless to vanquish the powerful, the ideology of expediency by which even the powerful in Israel dispatch their enemies, and the ideology of nonparticipation (Judges 7; Joshua 6; 2 Chronicles 20; the exodus). The Old Testament does not give us a singular moral or political treatise on war. As Ben Ollenburger has noted, "There is no limit in principle on the form that God's action can take, and there is no systematic correlation or disjunction between God's action and human military participation. There is, however, a strict disjunction in the order of necessity between trust in God and military means."[27] As the psalmists put it many times, it is not by the strength of the horse that God's city triumphs over the other city; it is only by faith in the Lord. The Old Testament simply does not offer a rationalization of warfare; the modern era provided that.

FROM SPARTA TO CLAUSEWITZ

What is war? In his *On War*, where he tried to do to war what Kant had done to reason, Clausewitz gives us the definitive modern understanding of war: "War is the continuation of politics by other means." For us, war is simply a continuation of politics; it is its outside limit that constitutes political identity itself. It constitutes *political* identity because politics has become thoroughly defined in terms of will, power, and freedom. War is the ultimate act of getting some other entity to do one's will. That is usually accomplished by other means in everyday political interactions, but war is consistent with those other means. War is the continuation of everyday politics by means that are always present but not always used, for what can count as politics in the modern era is the *will* of the people to pursue their own goods. War, both *ad intra* and *ad extra,* negotiates the conflicts such an account of politics necessarily entails. We moderns do not assume our warring is a religious or cultural form of life; it has been rationalized as a distinct form of politics. But war has not always been so understood. If we asked an ancient Spartan why he warred, he might have found the question puzzling and simply responded, "Because I am a Spartan; that's what Spartans do." To be a Spartan was to be a warrior. War was not just the continuation of politics; it was a culture, a way of life, a matter of honor.

War is also a *religious* duty, where the term *religion* is used not in the modern sense of an ineffable realm of private experience separate from politics and social concerns but in the medieval sense of *piety.* Religion is devotion. The *herem* in Deuteronomy 13:12–18 explains war in these terms. Likewise the Islamic Jihad is a "war" that does not seek a calculation of ends but is a faithful exercise of a religious duty during a time of severe testing.

In the Greco-Roman world, war and its preparations were a natural part of social, religious, and political life. Plato recognized that justice must be more than mere violence, but it could easily degenerate into nothing but "the advantage of the stronger." A just city requires guardians who will be entrusted with the means of violence against internal and external enemies, but entrusting these guardians with violence is a precarious venture, for who will keep the guardians from using this power to secure their own advantage at the expense of the city? To accomplish this, Plato assumed drastic measures were necessary. A "noble lie" had to be perpetuated on the guardians, a religious myth that told them they had sprung from the earth and had no biological parentage. This noble lie was necessary because the partiality that threatened the city was the partiality of family. If the guardians were too attached to their families, they would be tempted to use the power the city gave them to their family's advantage and not to the city's. Religion served the city by making citizens more loyal to it than their families.

Aristotle also viewed warfare as an essential ingredient of a well-formed city. In his view, the city was a "partnership of similar persons for the sake of a life that is the best possible," namely, happiness. Such a city required the performance of certain tasks—sustenance, arts, arms, funding for sustenance and arms, divine superintendence, and judicial and political deliberations—which were performed by the four key parts of the city: merchants, farmers, the military, and the deliberative part. The latter two were the *political* parts of the city: the military represented the *power* present in the younger members, and the deliberative function represented the practical wisdom present in the older members. A well-formed *polis* would subordinate the younger to the elder, the power function to the deliberative. When these differences were not honored, the city became tyrannical and ruled by uncontrolled violence.

Both Plato and Aristotle viewed warfare as a political and religious duty, as part of a well-ordered city. It was a form of piety and, like all things divine, could easily become excessive and destructive. Thus warfare was both necessary and dangerous, needing to be contained. Subordinating familial interests to those of the *polis* contained the violence. Cicero also recognized that warfare originated from filial piety. He saw its origin in two seeds nature implanted within us: self-preservation and the tender love of offspring. We war against others out of our loves: for ourselves and for our families. Because nature implants these sentiments within us, the one who does not use violence against the unjust who threaten his life or the life of his family or neighbors is as guilty as the unjust themselves.[28] Our love of self, family, and neighbors leads to the necessity of war; it also places limitations on it. War should not be mere vengeance. We owe duties even to enemies. Cicero stated, "It is sufficient that the aggressor should be brought to repent of his wrong-doing, in order that he may not repeat the offence and that others may be deterred from doing wrong."[29] War cannot be "by any means necessary" if that implies the warrior knows no limits in putting an end to injustice and to his enemies. War arises out of love, but it can quickly degenerate into an uncontrolled violence that knows no distinction worthy of the love out of which it arises. To treat the enemies' loves as if they could be legitimate targets of violence would be to violate the natural duties that generate war in the first place.

This brief discussion of *war* reveals that the term does not designate a single social formation that the church is either for or against. War as a cultural and religious form of life is not identical with the modern rationalization of warfare as the continuation of politics by other means. The church's posture toward the city militia of Athens, the ancient vocation to *herem*, Islamic Jihad, or the rationalized violence of the modern nation-state will not be the same. Still, a consistent theme in the church's political theology has been that Christianity does not assume that violence and warfare constitute the true *polis*. Thus, warfare does not signify a truly human nature; it does not constitute politics. At most, war signifies fallen nature. Warfare is not natural when *natural* means consistent with God's created purposes. As Augustine put it, there can be peace without war, but there cannot be war without peace. War and violence are no longer the *bene esse* of politics.

Augustine is often credited (or blamed) for a change in political theology that moved the church from its early radical resistance to the empire to the establishment of a responsible ethic that assumed the need for the church to cooperate with and accommodate to the imperial culture. For instance, in their opposition to historians who find in the early church a "pacifist" ethic that was then lost with the Constantinian shift, Helgeland, Daly, and Burns see a progressive evolution from Jesus to Augustine where the church struggled from an insignificant Jewish sect to its rightful place of imperial responsibility. They divide this evolution into four periods. First is the apostolic age where a new community struggles "to grow out of its Jewish background" and grow into "the much broader Greco-Roman context." Second is the patristic age where Christianity is an "insignificant and powerless minority struggling to establish its identity" against an inhospitable and hostile world. Third is the age of persecution from the emperor Gallienus in 250 to the persecution by Diocletian in 299. This marks a time when church and empire test each other and Christians begin moving into public office. Fourth is the period of Constantine and Eusebius, a time of "accommodation and cooperation" between church and empire. Helgeland, Daly, and Burns see this as a "logical extension" of the early church's argument that Christians were no threat to the empire. Thus, the early opposition of the empire to Christianity was not because of anything intrinsic to Christianity but because of the empire's own mistaken perception of the church. With Constantine and Augustine, this mistaken perception is overcome, and Christians can take their rightful place as soldiers, senators, and leaders of the empire with responsibility for the world.[30]

Not only those who defend Christian participation in warfare tell this story, but also those who do not. Roland Bainton also reads Augustine as developing a responsibility ethic that "assigned to the Church a larger role in the fashioning of society, because the duration of that society was extended by the projection of the Lord's return into an indefinite future."[31] Bainton, like the others, subordinates Augustine's political theology to an overarching concept, *society*.

This is a quintessentially modern argument that assumes a single system of (political) truth and measures everything by its relationship to that single system. Thus, political theology is defined by what theology contributes to *society*. But this is precisely what Augustine rejected, arguing that empires were but "large-scale criminal syndicates." His work cannot function to legitimate Christianity's contribution to some overarching, singular political concept called *society* because he had no such conception. He recognized the "other city" that positions other societies by its (ideal) peace; he did not recognize an entity larger than this "other city" that could position it or to which it must accommodate itself.

Augustine's vision of this other city was consistent with the early church's witness to it. Thus, Helgeland, Daly, and Burns are correct to argue that Augustine's theology did not represent a rupture within Christian tradition, though for the wrong reason. Augustine's political theology did not seek to make contributions to *society* or *civilization* or *culture*. Like Tertullian and others before him, he sought faithfulness in the time between the times when the church had to bear witness to the other city while the logic of the empire still ruled. In this sense, the development of the just-war theory by Ambrose and Augustine did not signal a decisive rupture within Christian tradition. Continuities remain between the pre-Constantinian Christian refusal to serve in the military and a post-Constantinian theologian such as Augustine's use of Cicero's just-war obligations. The continuity is not, however, that both share a "presumption against violence." That allows both the early church's refusal and the post-Constantinian church's permission to participate in warfare to be defined in terms of what they are reacting against. Neither position can be adequately understood in its opposition for or against something called *war*, but both are "for the church" as an alternative political order that assumes violence does not constitute true, *natural* politics. Just war, like pacifism, assumes that no single political structure can determine a Christian's allegiance other than the church and its teachings. The faithful have duties that the state may not know, and as loyal members of such states, the faithful must let others know of these duties. They must bear witness in word and deed to God's goodness, which stands over and against any human presumption to constitute politics through a will to power by its own construction of political and moral norms. Whenever pacifist or just-war arguments become mere codifications of rules to contain violence through the power of the state, they lose this continuity with Christian tradition. They lose the vision of the other city and are falsely led into thinking that a single political system is present to which the church must accommodate itself. Pacifism and just war are not *against war;* they are *for* a different kind of politics, a different kind of war—the war of the Lamb.

Augustine's departure from Greco-Roman political formations can be rightly understood in all its radicalness when we realize that his criticism only made sense in terms of a more credible *theological* politics. As Oliver O'Donovan explains,

Augustine was in a position to belittle the political culture of antiquity; he could dismiss its achievements as "the fragile splendour of a glass which one fears may shatter any moment"; he could do this without turning his back on society as the Cynics did, simply because he could point to a divine authority and a more lasting social order (*City of God* 4.3,4). Unmasking supposes a theological point of vantage, essentially an eschatological one. Christ has led captivity captive; he has disarmed the principalities and powers; the Kingdom of Heaven is at hand. When we claim to have seen through the appearances of political power, we act, as King Lear says, "as if we were God's spies."[32]

Only because we glimpse the other city can theology properly order the city still bound to violence. Does this mean that the church concedes a proper power of coercion to that earthly city?

VIOLENT CONCESSIONS?

The church cannot *concede* a power of coercion to the state; that would assume the church rules like a state dispensing power rather than charity, faith, hope, truth, goodness, and beauty. The latter constitute *church*. Power seems to constitute *state*. Every state seems to take for itself this power of coercion and fears any questioning of it. Why this fear? The state, and especially those who rule it and claim to have a *mandate* to do so, desires to constitute itself as an autonomous society. If certain persons are conceded a power of coercion—the police, the justice system, the national guard—then this power must be subordinated to good and truthful ends. Otherwise, the power can only be arbitrarily exercised. The problem is that the *polis* neither contains nor (in its modern variation) knows how to honor the true end(s) of human existence. The church cannot ask the state to impose the church's true end by force, but neither can the church disregard this true end and posit some putatively universal, "public" space called society where this true end must be bracketed for the sake of freedom. Perhaps the least the church can do is recognize the inadequacy of political existence in this age and seek to ensure that the state's use of coercive power does not degenerate into an arbitrary exercise of violence that only serves the interests of the state. But, given the constitution of the modern state, can its use of violence be other than arbitrary? The church can "order" the state *only* through the means appropriate to it: the proclamation of a compelling vision of an alternative politics to that of the state and the faithful witnessing to this alternative through proclamation, sacrament, and holiness of life.

Oddly enough, this brings us back to the vision of Gregory VII and his Augustinian theology of the state. He recognized that the church is the true universal city and for this reason imposed reforms against simony and upheld episcopal authority over that of the secular power. This entailed that the concord of the city of God be a hierarchical ordering where we recognize that more honor is owed to the church than to secular rulers. To uphold this hierarchy is to uphold the virtue of charity that makes justice something other than vengeance, power, and the need for sacrifice. Secular government is divinely ordained, but that means that secular government can never be conceded an autonomous power to define itself apart from the rhetorical judgment the church must always offer to and against it. The secular always stands under divine judgment, under the rule of the church. But the rule of the church cannot, by definition, be imposed through the power of a violent coercion. The church must rule from below by following the true King, not allowing any usurpers to define its life. To that extent, the church cannot be the church without the desire to embody a universal form beyond national boundaries that is patterned after its gentle Savior.

Only one such universal form has had an effective presence in the modern era: that embodied in the papacy. All other conciliar efforts to produce such a universal form have failed. Is it time to abandon them and recognize that the church cannot be catholic without the papacy? Is Hugo Rahner's judgment correct? "All the churches who wish to withdraw from the unity of the Church dogmatically first of all seek refuge within the state but soon are absorbed by the state and fall with it." Therefore, concludes Rahner, "the guiding role of the papacy is needed."[33] If we Protestants have no other response to this than that Catholicism has subordinated itself to the *polis* just as we have, then we have no reason to maintain the protest. Only by repenting of our own complicity in the subordination of the life of the church to that of the *polis* can we finish the work entrusted to us: to reform Catholicism such that the impulse present in leaders such as Gregory VII will divinely order the state through means other than what the state itself recognizes. Our protest should be directed against Catholicism's temptation to rule like a state.

When Martin Luther began his protest, the Catholic Church had claimed the power to call on secular authorities to wield the sword for its sake against the "Turks" for over four centuries. Luther was viewed as being in error by some precisely because he denied papal jurisdiction over the physical wielding of the sword, particularly against the Muslims. Thus the Catholic theologian Vitoria wrote, "Of course, despite the agreement of all Catholics on this point (that wars are in many cases lawful), we find if we investigate the question that Martin Luther, who has left no nook untainted with his heresies, denies that Christians may lawfully take up arms, even against the Turks."[34] That Vitoria misunderstood Luther's position is revealing; it shows that some Catholic theologians thought Luther's theology would lead to the loss of the Church's temporal political jurisdiction *and* that it would do so by Luther's refusal to allow Christians to bear the sword.

That Luther's theology led to the former is undoubtedly true. In some sense, Luther's sharp distinction between the two kingdoms led to the depoliticization of the church and the privatization of Christianity. This is to be decried.

That this depoliticization was associated with a *pacifist* Luther is, of course, simply a misunderstanding. Luther's political theology was much more nuanced than that. He did deny that Christians within the "Christian estate and God's Kingdom" could use the sword. No place existed for it. However, the sword was still necessary within the secular realm. While Christians *as Christians* could not use the sword, Christians as members of the secular order were under obligation to use it for the good of another. In reversal of long-standing Catholic tradition, Luther argued that it was not contrary to the calling of Christ for the ordained to use the sword.[35] Thus the exemption that Augustine and others had wrestled from the empire that those in holy orders should not stain their hands with blood was undone. This was Luther's way of undoing the Catholic distinction between precepts and counsels, but it was undone in the wrong direction. Rather than pointing in a direction where all the faithful were to live by the divine counsels, Luther's theology points in two different directions at the same time. Everyone is to live by the counsels in one sphere of life and by the precepts in another. The call of the ordained is not above that of the laity; both are called to the same holiness and ministry. If one can legitimately bear the sword within God's secular economy, so can the other.

That Luther insisted that the church should not use the sword is a biblical insight worthy of the Reformation. That he posited two realms of God's activity and failed to connect them adequately is problematic. He failed to recognize Augustine's key insight that the state is *divinely* ordained. This does not mean that the state represents some hidden work of God about which the church has nothing to say or no authority to bear. This seems to approximate Luther's position when he writes, "We must firmly establish secular law and the sword, that no one may doubt that it is in the world by God's will and ordinance."[36] This ordinance is given primarily a negative reading: in order to "restrain the wicked doers, murderers should be slain." The role of the secular authority is primarily to implement the law in its negative impact on the will of another.

Luther argued that no person could truly lead another in theological matters because "the thoughts and intents of the heart can be known to no one but God."[37] Seeking forcibly to compel someone to believe is "useless and impossible." This kind of compulsion impinges only on external realities, not the inner reality of the heart. The secular authority can compel, but only with respect to these external realities. In cases of the inner reality of the heart, no compulsion is possible. The result is the loss of "outward authority" in theological matters within the life of the church. But this, contra Vitoria, did not result in the loss of the power to compel and coerce by force. That is still safely preserved in the secular realm, but now the church has no jurisdiction over it. Far from lessening the power of the secular over us, Luther's reforms led to its increased control and power, a power that is not reasonable but purely volitional.

By making the power of the law a function of the will and by conceding the power of coercing the will primarily to an independent secular authority, Luther loses the Augustinian insight that the state should be divinely ordered. He undoes the ecclesial revolution of Gregory VII and makes space for the emergence of a nontheological, secular realm. Gregory's revolution viewed the state as a temporary but necessary institution for the purpose of restraining evil. Luther agreed. But Gregory also recognized that the state should submit to the church's authority. No independent space is possible where the state can claim to be ordained of God and yet free of the church.

Thomas Aquinas provides a development of this theological understanding of politics through his hierarchical structure of the law. For Aquinas, the power of the law resides primarily not in the will but in the intellect. Therefore, its purpose is not merely to restrain someone's will in order to protect a good but to direct people to the appropriate ends for which they should act. Thus, the power of the law is always dependent on a prior good. Without the articulation of those prior goods, the law is arbitrary at best and tyrannical at worst.

RELIGIOUS LIBERTY AS STATE PROJECT

Aquinas's political theology worries us today. On whose prior good is the law predicated? The assumption of a good as the basis for political society has been so problematized that we can hardly think it possible. If we think the good, we think of it primarily as someone's assertion of an interest over others. Even the term *politics* primarily signifies power and manipulation. We seek a public square neutral toward any substantive good. Michael Sandel has recognized that, far from producing the "neutrality" that we seek, this strategy supports and encourages a particular politics that cannot be subject to critical investigation. This particular politics invades religion, establishing and defining its limits. He describes this as the "voluntarist conception of religious liberty." In other words, "religious liberty" is ensured a place in modern political arrangements only insofar as religious adherents recognize a more basic political stance that makes their religion possible. For instance, Supreme Court Justice John Paul Stevens defended religious liberty in 1985 through the following argument: "The Court has unambiguously concluded that the individual freedom of conscience protected by the First Amendment embraces the right to select any religious faith or none at all. This conclusion derives support not only from the interest in respecting the individual's freedom of conscience, but also from the conviction that religious beliefs worthy of respect are the product of free and voluntary choice by the faithful."[38] This defense of religious liberty privileges the *polis* over the *ecclesia* precisely because the justices usurp the authority to determine the *worth* of religious belief. Embodied in this defense is a normative *theological* judgment about what constitutes a worthy faith. To concede that the state gives "religious liberty" on these grounds is to privilege the *polis* over the *ecclesia*. To accept this concession means that the order of charity cannot be adequately adhered to and that the goodness of God cannot be fulfilled in our community life.

Christians cannot avoid the clear biblical teaching that the state is divinely ordained; they cannot leave the state to its own devices. But neither must they be tempted to rule like a state. For the state to be divinely ordered signifies that everyday life, even within a nation, cannot be separated from theological claims about God's creating and redeeming purposes. The God who *orders* creation orders all its aspects. The task of the church in *ordering* the state is not to claim power over others but to remind the state that it does not know the good and thus should not impose its apparent goods on our lives. The church orders the state by refusing to recognize its power as the ultimate form of politics. Only by such a word of witness can the divine ordering be faithfully fulfilled. Each generation is called to work out this order with fear and trembling.

For this reason, the ancient prohibition against clergy taking up arms must be upheld whether the state concedes the *right* or not. Luther's innovations against this ancient tradition should be rejected.[39] However, Luther's rejection of the Catholic distinction between counsels and precepts is to be affirmed. The clergy are not to embody one form of discipleship and the laity another. Both are called to be the one body of Christ and to seek to "be perfect."

If Luther's reforms are taken to extend the counsels to all the faithful, Protestantism might still have a necessary vocation within the Catholic Church. The purpose of Protestantism was to undo any two-tiered call to Christian discipleship, which assumed that Jesus' teachings were different for laity and clergy and religious orders. Protestantism challenges the division that clergy and the religious are to live under counsels and laity under precepts. But this should not have led to the antinomian tolerance found in Neo-Protestantism.

Protestantism's vocation should be the *extension* of the counsels (with celibacy understood as chastity) to all the followers of Christ. But insofar as Protestantism has simply allowed the faithful to disappear into the overarching secular nation-state, the only protest that makes sense is a protest against Protestantism, for Protestantism has undoubtedly led to the subordination of the church to the state. The Protestant churches have become so cautious and filled with a bad conscience about their witness to the gospel that they have unwittingly privileged the violence of the nation-state to their own priority of peaceableness in their gentle Savior.

This, of course, is not done explicitly. It is accomplished by accepting a false narrative: that prior to the modern era religious people irrationally waged war on one another because they held religious doctrines to be true and good. Modern secular political arrangements supposedly secured peace through a "voluntary" conception of neutrality by refusing to grant any truth content to these irrational religious people. Only by privileging freedom and rights over any good, so this false narrative goes, can *peace* prevail. This standard defense for the modern nation-state arose after the wars of religion to prevent fanatical religious persons from killing one another over doctrine.

William Cavanaugh lodges a compelling criticism of this defense, demonstrating that the "wars of religion" language is an anachronism that reads the sixteenth- and seventeenth-century conflicts from the perspective of the modern nation-state as a soteriological social formation, that is, the nation is savior on the assumption that history reveals that religious people irrationally kill one another over apolitical doctrinal beliefs. The nation-state then emerges as the neutral mechanism that ensures peace by limiting the influence of religion to its proper private place. *Religion* is private. The secular nation, which privileges freedom, is *public*. But this myth overlooks the fact that the wars of religion were not fought between easily defined, doctrinally driven, religious sects. It was not just Protestants versus Catholics or Protestant sects against one another. The so-called wars of religion were primarily waged by *politiques* who had a stake in telling the story of the "wars of religion" so they could privatize religion, thereby depoliticizing it and then asserting their own uncontested sovereignty over newly formed nation-states. Far from being the saviors from the savagery of the wars of religion, argues Cavanaugh, the rulers and architects who formed the secular nation-state legitimated it by first developing the category *religion* as "privately held beliefs without direct political relevance" and then depicting the state as necessary "to secure absolute sovereignty over its subjects." What characterizes these wars is not primarily doctrinal disputes but the consolidation and centralization of power by these *politiques*, who, as John Figgis argues, replaced the religion of the church with the religion of the state.[40] The purpose of the narrative of the so-called wars of religion is to position the secular nation-state as the true harbinger of peace over and against the church. But this narrative simply does not work. Not only is it a selective historical reading of the sixteenth and seventeenth centuries, but, if this narrative were true, one would have expected the modern state to bring peace. In fact, the unparalleled violence of the twentieth century, when these states dominated global politics, reveals the illusion behind this narrative.

MODERN WAR

In *Religion in Public Life,* Ronald Thiemann gives us yet another version of the myth of the nation-state as the harbinger of peace. Liberal democratic nations are superior political arrangements, he argues, because they are less bellicose than the alternatives. But is this claim warranted? How can it overlook the fact that democratic nations warred with such ferocity in both the nineteenth and twentieth centuries? To put it in other words, what made the "enlightenment" of Hiroshima possible? A conventional, modern answer can be found in the film *All Quiet on the Western Front.* As German soldiers enjoy a respite from their labors on the frontline, they discuss the causes of war.

One soldier asks the question, "How do they start a war?" The following dialogue ensues:

"One country offends another."
"You mean a mountain in France offends a field in Germany?"
"No, one people offends another."
"I'm not offended."
"Then who wanted this war?"
"Maybe the English, but I don't want to shoot an Englishman."

Later in the film, a German soldier hides in a foxhole during the heat of battle. When a British soldier jumps into the foxhole, the German stabs him with his bayonet. The German soldier must then watch as his enemy dies. "When you jumped in here," he says, "you were my enemy and I killed you, but now I see *you are a man just like me.* We only wanted to live, you and I. Why do they throw us out to die? You will have to forgive me."

All Quiet on the Western Front conveys the message that war results from a denial of our common humanity through irrational commitments to our particularities. But, of course, this is just one more version of the myth of the wars of religion and the emergence of the secular state as the harbinger of peace. The power this myth has over our interpretations of violence helps explain why many people will find my Christian ethic objectionable. Emphasizing theological particularity tempts us toward violence because it diverts our gaze from the only thing that modern humanism thought could save us: our common humanity. We neglect the lesson learned by the German solider, which leads to an increase in strife, acts of violence, and even war. Once this is the diagnosis for war, then its appropriate remedy is the promotion of a common humanity and a chastened humility about our particular loyalties. Because war arises from our attachment to particular groups—such as family, nation, or religious community— the appropriate remedy is an epistemological humility concerning any truth claim grounded in a local, historical community.

Of course, I am not the first to proclaim that this humanism is dead. Postmodern philosophers have recognized this without drawing on theological sources. Just as Nietzsche proclaimed the death of God, so Michel Foucault proclaimed "the death of man." By that he recognized that the humanistic replacement of God in the modern era was no longer sustainable. This should have led to a more substantive challenge to the analysis of violence as an irrational commitment to particularity and its remedy in the logic of humility and assertion of a common humanity. I want to challenge the adequacy of this analysis and its remedy from a theological perspective, and I will do so in three steps. First, I will set forth the logic of humility as a remedy for war. Second, by drawing upon the work of the Islamic philosopher Talal Asad, I hope to explain why this analysis fails. Finally, I will resituate humility away from the dominance given it by the so-called Protestant Principle of Paul Tillich, which asserted that we must constantly critique all presumptions toward truth and goodness in this earthly life. This principle was developed by Reinhold Niebuhr, especially in his criticism of Catholicism. He made humility an epistemological category that taught us to be critical of any unmixed good or truth in this life. He also stated that humility was the dominant virtue in the Christian life. I will argue against this by locating humility within the traditional doctrine of penance, where humility is not the end of the Christian life but, as Aquinas put it, "a door" toward other, more substantive moral virtues. The implications for how we think about war and democratic nations should be obvious. We need not accept war as a natural aspect of political life nor view democratic nations as the most superior form of political life. In fact, they are dogmatically committed to wage war against any community's substantive good that could challenge the secular nation's privileging of freedom.

The Logic of Humility: Does War Result from Making Absolute the Relative?

Is it self-evident that our parochial loyalties necessitate warfare? How did this analysis of the problem of war emerge? Exactly when this analysis became conventional wisdom is difficult to say. Hegel surely developed a version of it. It is also the inheritor of Kant's critical philosophical system, which stated that perpetual peace was possible only through cosmopolitan right. In theology, this quest for the cosmopolis lurked behind Reinhold Niebuhr's insistence that contrition and gratitude should be the dominant virtues of the Christian life. These analysts of war have suggested that once family, nation, race, or religious affiliation is granted an absolute status, people outside those social communities will be viewed as a threat; they become the enemy and war follows. Notice what this argument implies: war is a necessary feature of attachment to historical, social communities. In this view, we are faced with two possible responses: accept war as an inevitable feature of historical particularity, or eliminate war by creating a universal, cosmopolitan society. Kant argued for both. War is an inevitable feature of particularity and also a means of progress toward the cosmopolitan state. Until we reach that state, war and antagonism are necessary. But war and antagonism are also the means propelling us into the cosmopolis where finally peace will be possible.[41] Violent means will lead to a harmonious end.

For Kant, war is the means by which humanity progresses from the "state of nature" to the state of civil right to international right and finally to cosmopolitan right.[42] This journey toward the cosmopolis results from the reason inherent in political communities. Individuals "emerge from the state of lawlessness which consists solely of war" to form civil societies. In so doing, they only extend the boundary of violence from the particularity of family survival to civil survival. Now the war is not each family upon others but each civil society upon others. Eventually the boundary of violence is extended further, with each nation creating an international right. Finally the boundary will be extended to the cosmopolis creating universal right.[43] Only when each particular form of community is transformed into the larger universal cosmopolis can we have the possibility of perpetual peace.[44] Kant was skeptical that this perpetual peace would be obtained, but in his concern to curb violence he set us on this journey.

Kant's analysis of war invites us to journey away from particular forms of life to a universal one. Our moral vocation is to work toward the cosmopolis so that war will become irrelevant. This entails that we leave our particularities behind as we seek to discover the universal. Because only the universal is fundamentally true, good, and beautiful, the historical vehicles that carry the universal are constantly to be eclipsed. With religion, this means that "there is only one religion valid for all men in all times. . . . Faith and books can thus be nothing more than the accidental vehicles of religion."[45] Why? Because *true* religion will not introduce historical particularity, and any faith based on books cannot avoid historical particularity.

Because Kant's theology essentialized Christianity into a universal morality separate from its historical "accidents," he found Christianity to be a true religion, while Judaism was not.[46] For Kant, only those particularities that can be essentialized into something universal will find a place in the cosmopolis. Thus Kant envisions an inevitable violence against particular forms of life for the attainment of perpetual peace. In fact, he explicitly stated that our journey toward cosmopolis required an initial act of violence and coercion that could then never be called into question. The cosmopolitan constitution "can begin only with force and this coercion will subsequently provide a basis for public right, because an additional unifying cause must be superimposed on the differences among each person's particular desire in order to transform them into a common will."[47] This initial act of violence transforms difference into commonalty. It becomes the condition for the "free" exercise of morality.

Kant's argument for perpetual peace is ingenious. It becomes the moral argument against any possible pacifist vocation grounded in a truth claim of a particular community. For example, if a preacher somewhere in America declares that Christians should not participate in warfare, that message can seldom be heard. Even though pacifism is a reasonable interpretation of the biblical witness supported by long-standing Christian tradition, this word is exceptionally difficult to hear. This is not because we Americans are so immoral but because of our understanding of what constitutes morality is so diverse. This word will not be forcibly repressed, but it will be repressed through the freedom to speak it. We tolerate the words being spoken, but the precondition for this toleration, the *idea* of freedom grounded in an original act of violence, becomes a word so loud and noisy that it drowns out all others. This preacher will often hear responses such as, "I disagree with what you said, but I am thankful we live in a country where you are free to speak such views." Although this is meant to be a supportive statement, it actually precludes hearing the message. The initial act of coercion that creates the cosmopolis, now understood as the United States of America, so thoroughly defines our moral possibilities that even when pacifist speech is tolerated, it only reinforces the unquestioned goodness of the original act of coercion.

In the Kantian system, the original act of coercion is warranted as the means that moves us to cosmopolitan right. Kant assumed the cosmopolis is possible because "ought implies can." Because our will can obey reason's call for universality, a universal community is at least possible. Any social community short of the cosmopolis would be less than universal and thus would not provide the conditions for the autonomous exercise of the will.[48] Only the cosmopolis could finally ensure the freedom necessary for individual right.[49]

Kantian ethics on war is characterized by three points. First, war is an inevitable feature of finite loyalties. Second, the remedy for war is to transform these finite loyalties into something universal, something higher and more inclusive. Third, this remedy is possible because reason ineluctably leads us toward the cosmopolitan state.

Within Christian ethics, Reinhold Niebuhr perpetuated a version of Kantian cosmopolitanism. This may appear to be a surprising claim, for the heart of Niebuhr's pragmatic realism was his denial of the possibility of the cosmopolis. Indeed, Niebuhr denied that reason alone could lead to the formation of such a state. He wrote, "Try as he will, man seems incapable of forming an international community, with power and prestige great enough to bring social restraint upon collective egoism."[50] Niebuhr disagreed, however, only with Kant's third point, that perpetual peace in the cosmopolitan state is possible. He agreed with the first two characteristics of the Kantian analysis: war is an inevitable feature of finite loyalties, and the remedy for war is to transform these finite loyalties into something universal. The moral journey is the same as Kant's, but with Niebuhr no cosmopolis awaits us at the end of the journey.[51] Ought does not imply can.

That we are still on Kant's quest for the cosmopolis can be seen in Niebuhr's analysis of sin. It always takes the form of "translating our finite existence into a more permanent and absolute form of existence." He explains, "Ideally, men seek to subject their arbitrary and contingent existence under the dominion of absolute reality. But practically they always mix the finite with the eternal and claim for themselves, their nation, their culture, or their class the centre of existence."[52] For Niebuhr, war results from imperialist ambitions that make finite commitments to any social community absolute. Thus we mix the transcendent with the finite. The only remedy is to discover that "the organizing centre of life and history must transcend life and history, since everything which appears in time and history is too partial and incomplete to be its centre."[53]

Although war is an inevitable feature of historical particularity, Niebuhr's pragmatic realism denies that war can be remedied. The best we can do is limit it by acknowledging that our sin takes the form of making finite existence absolute. Such limitation occurs only when the "virtues" of gratitude and contrition form the center of the Christian message:

> Gratitude and contrition are the fruits of a prophetic faith which knows life in its heights and in its depths. To believe in God is to know life in its essence and not only in its momentary existence. . . . To understand life in its total dimension means contrition because every moral achievement stands under the criticism of a more essential goodness. If fully analyzed the moral achievement is not only convicted of imperfection, but of sin. It is not only wanting in perfect goodness, but there is something of the perversity of evil in it.[54]

Of course, if one accepts this analysis, one cannot accept the doctrine of the incarnation. Nor can one save the materiality of everyday existence from its necessary sacrifice to a "more essential goodness" that cannot actually exist, because this essence both transcends and calls into question every existence. The goodness of God cannot function in Niebuhr's Christian ethics. It does not exist. It is only a transcendental, idealistic essence.

If we acknowledge that our social communities are always finite and thus a priori partial, then contrition and humility become the apex of the Christian moral life. God as the absolutely transcendent Other relativizes all social particularities. This analysis led Niebuhr to denounce Catholicism: "The Catholic doctrine of the Church is in fact a constant temptation to demonic pretensions, since it claims for an institution, established in time and history, universal and absolute validity."[55]

Niebuhr has his own version of a categorical imperative: always be humble about commitments to finite, historical communities, especially the church. Yet is this not a logical contradiction, an absolute judgment grounded in Niebuhr's historical relativity? It is not, only if his judgment participates in some transcendent metaphysical realm rather than in historical boundedness. Thus implicit in Niebuhr is a metaphysics similar to Kant's, one that claims to have discovered the transcendent ground for historical experience. This ground then becomes the enabling condition of thought and a limiting condition against which knowledge, truth, and goodness cannot transgress. Truth grounded only in transcendence essentializes Christianity into an absolute critical stance against any claims for moral goodness, except, of course, for the absolute moral claim that there are no absolute moral claims to be found in history.

This means war, not because pacifism is denied, but because it is tolerated, thereby proving that the pragmatic realist form of life is more inclusive and less particular than pacifism. Since the goal remains asymptotically approaching cosmopolis, any form of life that remains parochial is morally inferior to that which appears more inclusive. Realists can tolerate pacifists, but pacifists cannot tolerate realists. Realists do not need to ask pacifists to convert to their way of life. Only pacifists can ask realists to convert. Therefore, pacifism is incorporated within realism, and realism is viewed as participating in a higher and more universal form of life. "Pacifism," writes Niebuhr, "is a reminder to the Christian community that the relative norms of social justice, which justify both coercion and resistance to coercion, are not final norms, and that Christians are in constant peril of forgetting their relative and tentative character and of making them too completely normative."[56] As with Kant, Niebuhr's appreciation of pacifism is precisely what destroys it and what renders God's goodness utterly irrelevant for everyday human existence.

WHY THE ANALYSIS FAILS

The idea that warfare results from human efforts to make absolute our relative social commitments is so common that it is seldom challenged or in need of defense. The assumption that we need tolerance and inclusivity to combat warlike pretension and that we should embody humility about the truth of our finite and historical commitments has become the norm for pacifist and warrior alike. We often view the Crusades, the Conquest, religious wars, and Jihad as proof of this analysis. This analysis fails, however, for at least three reasons. First, it uses the past to justify our present warring. Second, it cannot account for the carnage of war that has occurred since this analysis became conventional wisdom. Third, it cannot challenge the violence that forms the boundary limit for our "freedom."

War today is no longer religious or cultural; it is "nothing but the continuation of policy with other means."[57] We recognize its limited character and thus find ethnic and religious warfare repugnant. If George Bush had claimed that the Gulf War was for the purpose of defending the Christian faith against the Muslims, an outcry would have arisen against that reason for violence. Yet when George Bush said that the Gulf War was necessary "for our jobs, our way of life, our freedom and the freedom of friendly countries around the world," little outcry was heard.[58] Why? Because it seems more reasonable, more universal. Our contempt for those who would war for religious and cultural reasons does not challenge our warring for partial and limited political and economic objectives. In fact, it makes us more prone to justify our "limited" warfare.

The two centuries since Kant's analysis of war have not been marked by a steady progress toward peaceableness. If anything, the carnage of the Crusades pales in comparison to the carnage of war waged in the twentieth century by democratic nations. How do we account for this? Is it the case that we have not yet successfully taught people that, for the sake of peace, they must not make absolute that which is relative? Is it that Kantian cosmopolitanism has not yet been tried, or reason has not yet run its course? Perhaps we need another Lennon, not Vladimir but John, who will ask us to "imagine there is no country, no religion, too"? But even the popularity of the Beatles with their commitment to the modern cosmopolitan myth had no effect in curbing the modern propensity to violence. Could it be that the so-called tolerance and inclusivity of the cosmopolitan response does not limit but intensifies the spirit of warfare? In other words, the viciousness of the past century is not in spite of the cosmopolitan message but because of it.

The difficulty with Kantian cosmopolitanism is that it assumes some social space free from the relativity of historical finitude. Then the moral argument proceeds in terms of those residents of the cosmopolis whose morals are grounded in some transcendent realm and the rest of us whose morals are still firmly grounded in a local *polis*. Given these options, the residents of the cosmopolis have a distinct advantage over us parochialists. Yet if there is no cosmopolis, parochialism is not the problem. The moral argument is not between transcendent, universal awareness and local, recalcitrant particularism, between the public and the private, the universal and the sectarian, essence and existence. Instead, the moral disagreement takes place between different parochialisms. If that is the case, then those journeying toward cosmopolis lack critical self-awareness. This makes them more dangerous and more prone toward violence.

Talal Asad points this out in his commentary on the Salman Rushdie affair. When Rushdie published *The Satanic Verses,* it outraged Muslims. Many called for governments to ban the book, and a death warrant was put on Rushdie's head. In the West, this debate was framed in terms of Kantian cosmopolitanism. The West with its free speech represented the universal moment; the Muslims represented a sensuous finitude not yet enlightened. When Muslims protested in England, the leftward leaning newspaper *Independent* published an essay stating that "the present Government does not often forcefully represent the views of left-of-centre intellectuals. . . . But the recent observations of John Patten, Minister of State at the Home Office responsible for race relations, on the need for the Muslim community to integrate with British society, have broadly echoed the views of liberal opinion."[59] The *Independent* asks Muslims not to convert but to integrate. Thus, the editors must assume that "Britishness" is something more universal than the mere particularism of Islam.

But is this argument grounded in a warranted distinction between British cosmopolitanism and Islamic particularism, or is it an argument between British and Islamic particularism? If the latter, then would not the editors of the *Independent* be expected to explain why Muslims should forego one particular identity and adopt another? Should they not at least recognize that on this issue there is a conflict of particularities? Should they not seek to convert rather than to integrate Muslims? If they recognized this, they could not make an argument based on "integration" and "inclusivity." Instead, they would have to explain to the world why "Britishness" more fully participates in goodness and truth than Islam. But no such argument is found in the pages of the *Independent*, and its editors would not even allow themselves to think such a thought. Why? Is it not because the editors must believe they that live in cosmopolis? Muslims are asked to *integrate* into a more inclusive society than that which Islam provides. To do this, they must throw off laws against blasphemy and take on laws of free speech. But this argument is self-refuting. If integration requires foregoing one identity for the sake of another, how can the end result be seen as more inclusive?

Asad points out the false understanding behind this position.[60] He demonstrates that Rushdie's book is offensive precisely because it asks Muslims to do what the *Independent* has demanded: throw off Islam for British liberal individualism.[61] The moral contest is between two parochialisms, but British liberalism refuses to acknowledge the conditions of its own existence as just one more parochial identity. Therefore, it refuses to engage in moral argument for the superiority of its particular claims against those of Islam. It does not openly seek conversion but invokes the authority of "Britishness" as a formal, cosmopolitan idea. This results in an appeal to individual rights, which are viewed as nonparticular, nonpartisan. But Asad does not see these rights as nonparticular. He sees them as bearing the signs of a specific tradition that stems from Kant.

The so-called *public* use of reason that Kant asserted and upon which many arguments for free speech are based depended upon the need for a strong nation-state that would secure a public space for free-speech such that speech would pose no threat to the state. Thus, free speech depends upon the condition of the state's use of force, and that original condition cannot be fundamentally questioned. As Kant wrote, "A ruler who is himself enlightened and has no fear of phantoms, yet who likewise has at hand a well-disciplined and numerous army to guarantee public security, may say what no republic would dare to say: Argue as much as you like and about whatever you like, but obey."[62] The *Independent* invites Muslims to do the same. Asad states that in British society "individuals have the inalienable right to choose, but they must first be authoritatively constituted as persons who will make the right moral and political choices."[63] They must no longer think blasphemy matters.

The conventional analysis that war results from particular loyalties fails because it destroys the content of moral argument. It does not allow moral arguments to proceed on the basis of the truth or goodness of particular claims, which means they cannot proceed at all. Arguments based on *integration* and *inclusivity* are not moral arguments but strategies of power. Once a particular form of life is viewed as more closely approaching the cosmopolis, then the superiority of that form of life is based not on any specific account of what is good or true but on its claims for inclusivity. People no longer need to be converted, only integrated. But these claims are false. Integration brings with it an act of coercion, the foregoing of one identity for the sake of another. And this transformation occurs not on the basis of rational argument but solely through arbitrary coercion. The new identity is not viewed as true or good but as superior because it is supposedly more neutral. And this new identity is perpetuated though the sole remaining virtue possible in this polity, the virtue of humility.

HUMILITY AS A REMEDY

If the problem of war is not the establishment of the cosmopolitan state over against recalcitrant parochialisms, then this calls into question the remedy of humility. For humility, as Niebuhr defined it, asks us to distance ourselves from our local particularities for the sake of something more inclusive and universal. But if there is no cosmopolis, this is only an invitation to self-deception. *Humility* becomes a form of docility; it invites us to forget that the state's initial use of force providing the condition for our freedom is not a moment of universal necessity but a parochial assertion, the content of which is now beyond challenge. *Humility* results in a critical questioning of every social community except that one that supposedly establishes the precondition for our journey toward cosmopolis, the state. This results in a warfare that does not recognize the conditions of its own possibility, for the one thing liberal parochialism cannot tolerate is universal claims to truth based in historical communities. We are humble about our partial claims for any form of life that could be called good or true, and we are willing to universalize our partial claims upon anyone who would deny them, even to the point of waging war against them. We cannot tolerate any particular historical social institution that makes truth claims solely from the perspective of its historical tradition.

If this is the case (and this is the shape war takes in a democratic society), then when we set forth the problem of war as absolute commitments to relative historical communities, we underwrite the cosmopolitan state and its violence. This is not to deny that certain communities such as the Nazis, the Klan, or current militia groups pose a serious violent threat. The threat, however, is not that these people have made historically relative communities absolute but that they have founded these communities upon wrong and morally repugnant content. Their way of life is false and evil. They should not be tolerated as one moral option among others so long as they do not force their position upon those outside their community. They should be denounced as living illusions that perpetuate evil. To counter them requires not that we all forego our attachments to particular forms of life (or falsely assume we could) but that we argue against the content of their claims. Instead of tolerating their rhetoric in our homes, churches, and communities, we need creative ways to drown out their voices, precisely because we should not hear such evil.

Any analysis of war should divest itself of the notion that one side embodies a historical, sensuous finitude and the other a transcendent, universal moment. The remedy to war is not the establishment of a cosmopolitan state where truth and goodness can no longer be uttered. Instead, the truth claims upon which communities are based should be adjudicated on the arguments set forth by the different communities. No neutral objective and transcendent space should be assumed.

Once we free ourselves from the tyranny of cosmopolitan right, we are free to overcome our bad conscience about our commitments to historically relative communities. Because these communities give us truth upon which we can live concretely, we can be moral agents. If the moral life is grounded in the concrete material of historical communities, then the remedy for war cannot be humility *concerning* those communities. That asks us to be less than human, less than historical beings. Medieval doctrines of penance are often accused of psychological tyranny because they emphasized the thoroughness of the penitent's act of contrition.[64] But this tyranny pales in comparison to the tyranny of contrition in Niebuhrian realism. Never can I find beauty or contentment in any moral action; they all maintain "the perversity of evil." Moreover, never can I find beauty or contentment in the moral actions of others—Bartolomé de Las Casas,[65] Gandhi, Dr. King, Dorothy Day, Oscar Romero—we must be contrite even about their actions, for they likewise maintain perverse elements of evil. There can be no doctrine of the saints, no beatific vision, no going on to perfection. The Christian life can only be a form of contrition.

But this view of contrition is an aberration and an innovation within traditional doctrines of penance. Contrition is not *epistemological* humility about the truthfulness and goodness of our communities but a means for self-awareness concerning the discrepancy between the moral good our faith community offers and our performance of that good. For Reinhold Niebuhr, humility depended upon the claim that we cannot know truth or find a perfectly good act in history. But in the tradition of penance, we can be humble only because we know a truth and a perfectly good act in history. Contrition is the first step toward that perfection. If we do not know perfection, contrition has no purpose. As Dorothy Day put it, "One must be humble only from a divine motive, otherwise humility is a debasing and repulsive attitude."

Recent theological work in penance has shown how the purpose of penance is not for the sake of contrition alone but so that the penitent can be moved toward reconciliation and holiness. This assumes both are possible.[66] In the early church, this reconciliation is concretized in the kiss of peace.[67] This practice effects a new reality whereby we can be at peace with one another, not in some spiritual or transcendent realm, but as an earthly presence made possible because the finite participates in the divine. In fact, the divine is known not by abstraction *from* these particular loyalties but *only* through them. Sensuous finitude is not set in opposition to universal reason, but a particular form of life provides the possibility for divine historical performance. Contrition is not constant criticism of self, others, and local communities. It is a means for performing the divine ritual without the perversity of evil. It is possible because Jesus reveals "full humanity" to us.

War is neither inevitable nor *natural*. We are not trapped in a tragic political ontology where we must choose between love of family and local, particular communities or a cosmopolitan peace. The question of war and peace is not a question of the particular versus the universal; rather, it is a question of the content of those claims that constitute and give life to our particular communities. Once we free ourselves from the quest for cosmopolis, we can be free to return to a social ethic such as that developed by Tertullian. We are peaceable because Christ has taken away the sword from his disciples.

CRIME AND PUNISHMENT, REPENTANCE AND RECONCILIATION

Employing coercion and violence against unjust activities is not a sign of hatred. The superficial analysis of violence that finds it arising from our hatred of others does not do justice to how we get trapped in violence and coercion. Such an analysis is safe in modernity because it assures us of the adequacy of the modern nation-state's political strategy. If violence arises from our recalcitrant, particular hatreds, then the quest for cosmopolitan right in the secular state is its remedy. But this is a facile analysis of why people kill each other. The ancients rightly recognized that people use violence because of their loves, not their hates. They also realized that violence has a contagious power that seemingly erupts uncontrollably, catching up people in its wake. While ancient societies used sacrifices to contain this violence, modern societies employ a much less reasonable strategy. They teach us not to hold preferential loves but to treat each person as a unique individual who is of equal worth to every other individual. In an effort to contain violence, modern societies point away from themselves to a universal community always on the way but never here. It has been an unsuccessful strategy that has produced a nihilistic indifference. This has repercussions not only in the international role violence plays through war but also in its role internal to nation-states, both in the crime perpetuated and the means used to control it.

Even honor among thieves seems to be lost in the new indifference crime and its containment embodies in the modern era. Consider the following report from the *St. Louis Post Dispatch:* "An exchange of gang jargon between a group of youths triggered a fatal shooting inside a Northwest Plaza department store busy with last minute shoppers on Christmas Eve, authorities said Sunday. A Famous-Barr employee said he was stunned by what he called the indifference shown by the wounded youth's friends, who he said took advantage of the confusion to shoplift while showing no interest as their companion lay on the floor."[68] This report is quite telling. The gang was not bound together by bonds that would entail risking one's life for a comrade. Far from such noble sentiments, the violence here is predicated upon a complete indifference to the fate of a comrade. Although this is still sufficiently shocking that both the employee and reporter noted it, such indifference raises the question whether this kind of crime has always been with us or if it is endemic to modern societies.

Cornel West argues for the latter. Such indifference is a symptom of the nihilism present in modern culture. By *nihilism* he means "the lived experience of coping with a life of horrifying meaninglessness, hopelessness, and (most important) lovelessness."[69] This nihilism has taken root not in those communities who were excluded from the dominant cultural institutions in modern society but in those most vulnerable to those institutions. That the reported indifference of gang members to a fallen comrade takes place in a mall is itself significant. Crime and violence are not merely at the margins but at the heart of the *modern* city with its center in the local mall. The center itself invites the crime it seeks to contain.

West asks why such nihilism and hopelessness have occurred so profoundly in American culture at this historical moment. We see evidence of it in the pure desire for death and violence in school shootings. We see it present in suburban youths from the "best" schools, who quote Nietzsche in their high school yearbooks and then go on racist shooting sprees.[70] And West asks why this nihilistic hopelessness has even infected black culture. It has traditionally been a culture of hope.

Given black history in America, how can we explain the fact that "until the early seventies black Americans had the lowest suicide rate in the United States. But now young black people lead the nation in suicides." West argues that the loss of traditional cultural institutions because of the dominance of "corporate market institutions" is, in part, to blame. They create a culture preoccupied with the "provision, expansion, and intensification of pleasure." In other words, they produce a culture of desire for its own sake that rejects the past for the immediate present and views the future only as "the repetition of a hedonistically driven present." This culture undermines traditional virtues such as "love, care and service to others." And to those most vulnerable to its dominance, those in "poverty-ridden conditions, with a limited capacity to ward off self-contempt and self-hatred," it ends in nihilistic despair, indifference to goodness, truth, and beauty, and a subservience to the univocity of pleasure for its own sake.

West argues that the indifference we find present in the crime and violence of the modern era is not a result of people's *lack of access* to market institutions; it is a direct result of their *dominance*. What is true among black youth is also true throughout the American youth culture. Targeting this group for the proliferation of desire and pleasure for its own sake can only end in despair. Out of despair come not only indifference but also crime, violence, sexual promiscuity, and the slothfulness of the drug and pornography culture. Rather than merely repeating the mantra common to the United States from its earliest days, that crime is out of control, West offers a possible reason for its presence.

His analysis suggests that some alternative other than simply creating more prisons is necessary.

A common refrain in twentieth-century politics was that we must get tough on crime. This had bipartisan support. President Clinton passed his comprehensive crime bill in 1994. Two years earlier President Bush raised the issue of crime in his State of the Union address, saying, "We must do something about crime, especially violent street crime. A tired woman on her way to work at six in the morning on the subway deserves the right to get there safely. Congress, pass my comprehensive crime bill; help your country." What should we make of this?

To some degree, we must recognize that the constant refrain—"get tough on crime"—is political rhetoric in the bad sense. No one is for crime; we all fear it, and legitimately so. But precisely because those fears are legitimate, it leaves us open to be used by politicians. Getting tough on crime has always been a win-win situation for them because no one is for crime. Our fear of it works to their interests. Playing on those fears has often been a political strategy to garner support. Capitalizing on the fear of crime for political reasons has a long history. In 1929, President Herbert Hoover, in his inaugural address, expressed concern over the increasing crime rates. He appointed George W. Wickersham to head a federal commission, The National Commission on Law Observance and Enforcement, which was known as the Wickersham Commission. They published fourteen reports. One report in 1933 suggested that the crime rate revealed "something fundamentally wrong in the very heart of government and social policy in America." Over thirty years later Barry Goldwater sounded a similar theme during his campaign for the presidency when he spoke of the "growing menace of crime to personal safety, to life, to limb and to property." And in 1965 President Johnson stated, "Crime is a sore on the face of America. It is a menace on our streets. It is a corrupter of our youth. We must bring it under control. We have taken a pledge not only to reduce crime but to banish it."[71] Our own generation has launched a war on drugs that no one thinks we can win, but few think we can do without. The fear of crime is no newcomer to the political landscape in America, but the war against it seems only to perpetuate it. This makes one wonder if we are asking the right questions about crime.

The fear of crime is not merely an invention of the politicians. Crime, especially violent crime, is and has been a peculiar problem in the United States. In 1990 an estimated 2.3 million people were victims of violent crime in the United States. The homicide rate in the United States is seven times that of Finland and Canada, twenty times that of Germany, and forty times that of Japan. We have one of the highest incarceration rates in the world, which went from 230 per 100,000 persons in 1979 to 426 per 100,000 a decade later.[72] How can we make sense of our culture's high rate of crime? In truth, crime makes no sense. It makes no sense to its victims, and thus we often use the term *senseless* in descriptions of particular criminal activities. But it also makes little sense at a more theoretical level, for we have lost a theological language that would assist us in describing crime, and our responses to it, in terms of our faith. In our culture, crime is primarily understood as an activity that is against the law for which one is found guilty after due process. Crime, then, is related to law, but how do we understand law? Law for us has no foundation in the mind of God but is merely positive enactments by legislatures and others that carry the force of governmental authority. As the common cynical aphorism suggests, "Law is what the judges had for breakfast."

Crime as a mere violation of positive law bears with it a certain arbitrariness that makes it more difficult for us to know what purpose it violates. Thus, we are uncertain what is at stake in opposing crime other than securing and preserving individual rights and freedoms. What constitutes a crime appears to be that which is proscribed by the people in power. It was not a criminal act for Thomas Jefferson to own slaves, but it was a criminal act worthy of execution for a slave to escape. Such descriptions of crime are capricious.

Prior to the development of crime as a violation of positive law, theologians such as Thomas Aquinas understood law as embedded in a hierarchical structure grounded in the mind of God. Law was understood in a fourfold sense that begins with the eternal law that was in the mind of God. This was God's creative purpose, a master blueprint for creation. Below the eternal law was the natural law, which, according to Aquinas, was, "the participation in the eternal law by rational creatures." The natural law contained first principles that no reasonable person could deny, such as "Do unto others as you would have others do unto you." This was followed by the law of nations, which relied upon a universal consensus among peoples. In the fourth place in the hierarchy was human or positive law. These were those laws enacted by particular governments that were binding upon people insofar as they were consistent with the first principles.

Three fundamental assumptions lay behind this hierarchy of law. First, God had a purpose for creation, and that purpose was embodied in law. Second, this purpose was available to people through the church's teaching and through people's reasonable efforts at gaining knowledge of the law. Third, if a positive law contradicted the natural law, the positive law was invalid, and it was no crime to neglect it. When Martin Luther King Jr. made his famous statement from a Birmingham jail that "an unjust law is no law at all," he was quoting Aquinas and relying upon this theological hierarchy.

Crime made more sense theologically for Aquinas than it does for us because law was part of a grand design, grounded in God, with the purpose of guiding, directing, and teaching people God's purpose for creation. Positive law existed within the larger hierarchy. Something other than "what the judges had for breakfast" gave law its intelligibility. In fact, for a law merely to be posited (i.e., promulgated by a particular group of citizens in power) was insufficient as the foundation for law. Law had purposes that sought to direct us to virtuous ends.

Without those purposes, the law becomes arbitrary, based on nothing but the power asserted by those who make the laws and who then maintain the means to enforce them.

While law and crime may have made more theological sense to Aquinas, his world is gone forever. Those of us in the household of faith face the difficulty of making sense of crime in a political system without God's eternal law. Crime can make little sense for us, in part because the laws under which we live bear little connection with God's purposes. God as our chief end does not ground our laws; instead, they are grounded in freedom.

This creates difficulties for us to make sense of crime. For instance, criminologists often tell us that the high incarceration rate in the United States is due to the great amount of freedom our society allows. Because we do not have an oppressive society that treats criminals with a swift and decisive judgment, criminals tend to get away with more and the crime rate is high. Yet this argument makes no sense based on our unusually high incarceration rate. If we allow so much more freedom than other countries, why do we have so many more people in prison? The argument contradicts itself.

Freedom alone cannot provide a reasonable basis for criminal law. While many people recognize this contradiction, they still argue that this is the best possible world. If the good or God's purposes are the basis for law, then tyranny lurks around the corner. After all, sodomy was a capital crime in colonial America. Who wants to return to such a practice? Once again we find ourselves caught on the horns of a dilemma: either the tyranny of one community's imposed account of the good or the creation of a "neutral" public sphere where freedom alone rules. If this is our either-or, how can we make sense of the highest incarceration rate of citizens ever produced by a political formation? There must be some way out of this unpalatable either-or. We can only move beyond it when some conception of the good is able to be more determinative of our laws than is the freedom that grounds them in secular states. Yet how can this be accomplished? Its near impossibility raises a question about the appropriateness of Christian participation in the judicial and police functions of the state. Alternatives such as the victim-offender reconciliation program need to be constructed by our churches to show our neighbors that there are more productive alternatives than simply building more prisons. Perhaps from these alternatives new practices might emerge that our non-Christian neighbors will find compelling. They might see the beauty in them and develop them in ways we cannot yet recognize. We can offer them as gifts and be willing to learn from the ways others receive and develop our gifts.

People of faith must also recognize that everything we *can* do to prevent crime should *not* be done. Within a fallen creation, not every evil contingency can be prepared for without perpetuating the underlying assumption that there is nothing but power and violence. To live in hope rather than fear because Christ has redeemed the world means that we can forego arming ourselves in an effort to secure our own existence against every possible threat. To think that our only response to crime is to meet it with an equal lethal force is merely to perpetuate the nihilism that can produce the crime itself. That means some will have to die or meet injury for our convictions. For those who meet with violence and crime, we will refuse to see them only as victims but continue to believe that God even raises the dead. Crime and violence cannot have the last word. It stands in need of redemption, and that redemption is possible.

To proclaim this is not to deny the inequities in crime and violence people face each day. Some, especially the poor, are more at risk than others. I learned this by living for three years next to a house where my neighbors were drug dealers. This was a poor neighborhood close to a major university. The houses were owned primarily by absentee landlords who were well-respected civic leaders. Some were regular churchgoers. They seldom even came into this neighborhood, and if they did, they were gone before nightfall. They would not return calls when the neighborhood watch complained about the illegal activities going on in their houses. They refused any accountability.

The house of our drug-dealing neighbors functioned as a quasi-church. It was a "house of hospitality" where rich and poor, educated and uneducated, white and black, regularly gathered. Sitting on our front porch, we saw first-hand how their activities worked. The supplier would drive up in an automobile. As he brought in fresh supplies, another lookout would circle the neighborhood until his work was finished. The days after his visit would see increased activities, as persons "from every tribe and nation"—including students from the local university—descended on the home to be united around their passion for these drugs. But, of course, this practice of hospitality came with a price. It was a false "catholicity." It did not produce trust. Handguns and other weapons were regularly seen, even though children were also ever present in this house and neighborhood. We let our neighbors know that we were not oblivious to their activities.

One night our family life was disrupted as a cinder block came flying through the window of our daughters' room, landing on the pillow of our eldest daughter's bed as she brushed her teeth preparing for bed. A few minutes later, and serious injury, if not death, would have been the result. Our second daughter, lying in her crib, was covered in glass as the force of the cinder block shattered the window, sending fragments throughout the room.[73] After the initial shock, fear and a desire for retaliation welled up within me. Such desire and passion do not oppose Christian faithfulness. It emerged out of my love for my children, a good and holy desire. But such a passion also tempted me to desire the death of the man who did this to my family. Even though a dispassionate passivity toward such violence would be a worse form of faithlessness, to desire another's death is not appropriate for Christian faithfulness. What I wanted was not his death but his conversion. I wanted him not to be this kind of person. His callous disregard for my children's lives violated God's good purposes.

Only contingent circumstances prevented his actions from doing serious bodily harm. Anyone who would not have my same desire would be incapable of loving those closest to him or her. My desire for vengeance arose out of my love for my family. But what prevented such retaliation? It is surely not just the threat of law. Although the police regularly visited our neighborhood, their visits had little effect. They could not be present around the clock, and a well-placed system of observation by the drug dealers was in place. The majority of everyday life in this neighborhood existed beyond the boundaries of the law. Retaliation was not uncommon.

Vengeance and retaliation were absent not because we feared the law or because we handed our "will" over to some "commonweal," trusting that it would protect us. Even in their good-faith efforts, the local authorities were ineffective. Retaliation was not possible because we were part of a prayer group that did not fear coming to our home regularly. We were not alone. Others who loved us, cared for us, and participated in our lives were a witness, letting our neighbors know that they could not terrorize us in private. Our friends made their lives publicly accountable. They learned our neighbors' names and heard our stories. We could have been one more statistic decried by politicians, an object lesson for the reason why increased police presence might be necessary, but faithful friends would not let this happen anonymously. They were present to us and to our neighborhood. I cannot help but think that this gave witness to our neighbors. There was something compelling about the beauty of friendship that refused to abandon others in the midst of terror. Friendship was a stronger and more palpable presence than police who came with sirens wailing.

The drug dealers in our neighborhood could not accomplish their work without all the various (distorted) levels that made their activities and our "neighborhood" possible: the absentee landlords, churches who refused to hold these "respected" citizens accountable, the college students looking for recreation, university officials who looked the other way, and other neighbors who allowed such activities to take place without any public utterance. But the church's task is not simply to seek the punishment of offenders; it is to redeem and restore such neighborhoods. Thus, rather than merely seeking retaliation, the faithful must remember that ministry to the criminal and to the imprisoned is part of their mission. This does not imply a passive tolerance of injustice, but confronting it with truth and charity. We Christians have ourselves been in the place of the criminal.

Christianity itself had a history of being a crime. The early Christians were accused of atheism for their rejection of the Roman gods, and this charge was true. Some were even killed for this crime. Christians call such people martyrs, but the governing authorities called them criminals. But this was not limited to the second century. On July 1, 1535, Thomas More was executed by Henry VIII for opposing the act of supremacy that made the king the head of the church. Abolitionists were imprisoned during the slavocracy in the United

States. Harriet Tubman helped three hundred slaves escape the South through the underground railroad. She had a bounty of $40,000 on her head. Dorothy Day, a Catholic layperson who began hospitality houses for the poor and a magazine known as the *Catholic Worker,* was imprisoned for her labor activity in the early decades of this century. During World War II, one thousand United Methodist young men refused to participate in the war and were sent to alternative service camps.

Countless numbers of Christians went to jail during the Civil Rights struggle in the 1960s, including Martin Luther King Jr. on Good Friday in 1963, when he wrote his famous "Letter from a Birmingham Jail." Christians went to jail in the 1980s for participating in the sanctuary movement that provided haven to refugees fleeing from places such as El Salvador and Guatemala. Christians have been jailed for protesting the state's war-making power. It was also Christians who were willing to be the executioners, jailers, judges, and juries in all these cases. This should cause us pause in too quickly taking our place within the prison and the judicial system in a re-Hellenized culture.

Christianity was born out of the imprisonment and execution of an innocent person. Given our history, we cannot seek the solution to crime in a punitive prison industry. Although Christians and other innocent persons have often been labeled as criminals, this does not imply that all criminals are unjustly persecuted. Some people do evil things that require the kind of correction imprisonment could potentially bring. Imprisonment should not be a time of punitive retribution but an opportunity for people to face the reality of the evil they have committed in hope that they might yet repent and turn toward the good. If we have no account of the good, how can this occur?

Conclusion

The goodness of God is a discovery. This qualifies what Christians can mean by *ethics*. Because God's goodness is discovered, we cannot assume that the good is an achievement of the human will. Christian ethics cannot be based on the assumption that a free will chooses to live by a law consistent with a universal demand. Law and freedom do not have such a central role for the moral life within God's good economy. Human creatures as self-legislating beings do not contain the moral resources to enact goodness. Acts of will alone do not constitute moral goodness. It is discovered, and this requires participation in the life of God.

Of course, all of creation participates in God's life; that is why it is called creation. God alone gives life. God does not fashion being by giving form to a preexisting and inert matter. Nothing preexists God. And even this creedal expression must be explained in such a way that the *nothing* that preexists God is not read as a potentiality God infuses or contains. Such a *meontics* leads to necessary relationships between God and that which is "outside" God that require God to *contain* a threatening chaos. Such theologies that posit an "outside" to God coeternal with God inevitably assume that strife defines being. Violence constitutes ontology. Such theologies also inevitably inscribe a lack into God's own being that must then be overcome. But for Christian orthodoxy, no "outside of" God exists. That is why Christian theologians properly claim that God's essence is God's existence and that God creates *ex nihilo*. No being is coeternal with God, not even a being we might designate as *nothing*. Only God is. Good, then, cannot be a function of a category called *being* more encompassing than God. Ethics cannot be the province of a philosophical discourse that brackets out theological consideration, unless philosophers assume a being greater than God giving access to goodness. Once we realize, following

Anselm, that only unreasonable persons could claim such an account of being, then we realize that any discourse about the good must also entail discourse about God.

Kant himself was led to this realization. Beginning with pure reason grounded in beings like us, he asked if we could think God and argued that we could not. Then, moving to practical reason, which assumed freedom and goodness as mere facts, he was unable to think them without God. God was a necessary thought, but this thought of God did not treat goodness as a discovery. Instead Kant "discovered" a moral faculty in human creatures. Its secure presence made the thought of God possible. Kant could not have reversed the poles of his discovery. He could not have found that God made the moral faculty in us secure, for the very thought of God would have called that security into question. God cannot be a self-possession such as the freedom for an autonomous employment of reason and will can be. Nietzsche served Christian theology well by revealing that Kant did not discover this secure moral faculty but invented it. Kant invented it because he did not think we could live in a world without *good* and *evil.* Nietzsche thought we had already moved beyond—or rather revolved and returned to—that world. The world revolves around a tragic axis where we are caught between eternal grief and eternal joy. There is no redemption beyond this tragic existence. All we can do is make it as beautiful as possible. Beauty remains, but truth and goodness exist with God.

Are we left with only the play of beauty, the mere joy of giving multiple forms and meanings to reality, which is nothing but those multiple forms and meanings? Has the quest for goodness disappeared? No, it is disappearing, but it has not disappeared. We still use the terms. We are still shocked by gang members who leave a comrade dying on the mall floor while they use the confusion to loot stores. Nietzsche may be right; we still use these terms because "people like us" need them. But why is this a criticism? Why should Nietzsche's contempt for the "mass like herds" lead us to repeat the Western heroic ascent out of the cave one more time and look for someone not "like us" who has moved beyond good and evil? Kant may have failed in his explanation of the relationship between God and the good, setting us out on a quest for freedom instead of a quest for goodness, but he at least set us out on a journey. With Nietzsche no quest remains. There is no up or down, left or right. We are on a little blue ball spinning through space with no apparent direction.

Kant's quest ends in failure. The journey to freedom ends when progress becomes our fate. Nietzsche resolves the failure by doing away with the quest. The social and political formations within which we live bear traces of both Kant's failed quest and Nietzsche's postmodern vision. Neither can be nor should be destroyed. To put forth the next new development after Kant is only to remain trapped in the modern, in its ceaseless progress, in the new and improved. To destroy Nietzsche's postmodern vision would be to underwrite it; to put forth an assertion of will against it can only confirm it, precisely because it is the recognition that all we have is the assertion of will to make the passions that rule us beautiful. Yet neither Kant's journey nor Nietzsche's vision can escape their relationships with social and political formations. Every *ethic* assumes a sociology. Kant's journey ends in the colossus of the state claiming the mantle of divinity. Nietzsche's postmodern vision is trivialized by the infinite exchange of signs that serves the interest of the global market. The loss of the true and good does not make beauty possible; it serves the interest of *kitsch*.

A different journey and vision are present in the church, even when those persons who constitute the church do not always recognize them. This journey and vision are so much a part of the church's life that its architecture, its liturgical practices, its ordinary life bear witness to them. This is a journey toward the vision of the Triune God, a journey that still holds forth the possibility of the beatific vision. Goodness cannot be adequately thought outside this journey. To think goodness within this journey and vision is to think it as gift. Goodness as a gift is difficult to think. If the good is not a free choice I make for myself, then can it be good? The first thought that makes this possible is to think the good other than as merely an anthropological predicate. Goodness is not predicated upon any secure possession of the human subject. The good is a transcendental predicate of being, but being here does not describe a secure creaturely existence. Good is theological. It makes sense when we adhere to the orthodox Christian claims that God creates *ex nihilo* and that God's essence is God's existence. A real distinction exists between God's being and creaturely being such that goodness as a transcendental predicate of being says something first about God and only derivatively about us. Goodness is not, first of all, anthropological; it is theological. Then, because of God's goodness, it can also be anthropological. We do not know it in its fullness. Only God is the full intensity of goodness. But because God is this, we know it analogically.

Goodness is. People like us cannot do without it. Yet every attempt to explain it fails. It either becomes reduced to a function of the useful or is dismissed altogether as a sign of immaturity. Yet when we try to move beyond it, we cannot seem to do so. The word haunts us. If goodness is theological, this poses no problem. It is what we would have expected, for goodness is secure only in God; our goodness is a participation in God's goodness, and that can never be our secure possession. For us, goodness is a fragile thing. We will constantly seek it and need to rethink it, develop new practices that direct us toward it. But not even the language of *virtue* can adequately account for goodness as theological. Gifts, beatitudes, and theological virtues must be added to our language to reflect our goodness as a gift that is discovered. To explain these we refer to the Holy Spirit, who *infuses* a goodness into us that makes us better than we know we are by ourselves. This *better* is what theologians mean by *grace*. People find themselves caught up in a journey that results in the cultivation of gifts and beatitudes they did not know were possible. They discover that this journey was possible only through friendship. Where did this come from? It is no irrational assertion to answer, "the Holy Spirit." The mission of the Holy Spirit is to move us toward the charity that defines the relationship between Father and Son, a charity so full that it is thoroughly one and yet cannot be contained within a single origin or between an original and copy but always, eternally, exceeds that relationship into another. The Holy Spirit is that relationship.

The Spirit catches us up into the life of God. That it results in ecstatic manifestations is a sign of this reality. That such manifestations worry us moderns is a sign that we want a self-secure morality free from external possession, but the Spirit troubles all such self-security. The Spirit's possession is not catastrophic. It does not destroy our nature, resulting in "unnatural excesses." The Spirit is not Dionysius. It is the Spirit of Jesus Christ. He is the journey's end.

That Christ is the journey's end does not contain the journey within a totalizing narrative easily set forth, for Christ is true God and true humanity where through the hypostatic union what is attributed to one nature is attributed to the other as well. Christ makes possible a journey into the infinity that is God, an infinite desire that can never be satisfied, never fully completed or articulated, yet never lacking. Just as his physical body can be indefinitely repeated, but each repetition is his body without remainder, so Jesus is the sign that can be indefinitely proclaimed and each proclamation is God's Word without remainder. The church enacts this even when people are sleeping, children crying, and believers skeptical. It occurs in the midst of the confusion of everyday life. But what the church enacts it is also called to embody. This is signified in the sacraments of baptism and Eucharist. Baptism is accomplished once. God works through the Holy Spirit to graft believers into the Triune Life through Christ's sacrifice. His humanity becomes our humanity. Just as his humanity is *enhypostatic*—that is, the center of his person is not found in an independent human subjectivity but in the Divine Word that makes his life possible—so our lives become enhypostatic as well, but only through him. What can occur only once at baptism is then repeated in the Eucharist, where we repeat this event again and again in an effort to live into our baptism. Repentance and reconciliation (including acts of satisfaction) are the gracious means by which we participate in this movement from baptism to Eucharist and back to baptism.

The church is the only social formation that points us toward the vision of God. If this vision is to be seen, then the church cannot be ruled by the Protestant Principle, where every historical representation of God is placed under erasure. The goodness of God is analogical. That means that the relationship between our goodness and our historical presentations of God's goodness are not identical with God's. God cannot be so securely possessed. It also means that the relationship between our goodness and our historical presentations of God's goodness are not so radically other that no truthful relationship exists between them. That would result in silence. God's Word could not be proclaimed;

the sacraments could not be celebrated as God's presence. The church is not an institution like the nation-state and global market, that finds its authority in its ability for self-critique and permanent revolution. Such an understanding of social formations can produce only people on a quest for freedom or the useful. The church produces people on a quest for truth, goodness, and beauty, and thus it still believes that God speaks, that God is present. Is this a mere assertion? How would we know?

We cannot know with certainty any more than we can know with thoroughgoing certainty what the shape of the universe is or what the relationship between genetic structure and human behavior is. That the church *makes* God present is a theological confession. Its reasonableness can be assessed only in terms of the political and social formations such an idea requires. The church is not a self-contained society, nor is the church a mystical communion with no relations to temporal social and political formations. Both understandings of the church remove it from its relationships to other social formations, which is where we discover the church's truth. The church is a nonnecessary formation grounded in charity. It exists within kinship systems, nation-state and other political systems, and market exchanges, but it is not defined by any of those systems. It defines them. The reason is that charity is the basis for our existence. No institution or social formation can do without it; even the most corrupt form of social formation will eventually have to bear witness to the primacy of charity over power, will, and coercion. Only the church can explain why that is so.

The task of Christian ethics is to explain the church's relationship to other social formations as they develop, die, and mutate into different forms. It will do this through recognizing God's goodness as the measure against which all things are measured (including the church). This task will remain as long as those other formations exist. It is a task where our primary vocation is to bear witness to God's goodness. Such a goodness is not natural to us, although God seeks to share it with us. It is a gift, the gift of Jesus Christ. He is God's goodness, for God's goodness is God's own self.

Notes

INTRODUCTION

1. Gianni Vattimo, in *The End of Modernity,* trans. J. R. Snyder (Baltimore: Johns Hopkins University Press, 1989), discusses "the crisis of humanism."

2. Walter M. Miller, *A Canticle for Leibowitz* (New York: Bantam Books, 1976), 296–97.

3. See Jan Aertsen, *Nature and Creature: Thomas Aquinas's Way of Thought* (Leiden: E. J. Brill, 1988), 141.

4. See Catherine Pickstock and John Milbank, *Truth in Aquinas* (London: Routledge, 2000), 5–9 for an excellent discussion and defense of truth as correspondence.

5. Thomas Aquinas, *Summa Theologica,* trans. Fathers of the English Dominican Province (Westminster, Md.: Christian Classics, 1948), I q. 5, a 4, ad 1. See also Catherine Pickstock and John Milbank, *Truth in Aquinas,* 7–8. Commenting on this passage in the *Summa,* they state, "Thus Beauty shows Goodness through itself and the Good leads to the True. . . ."

6. Aquinas, *Summa Theologica* I, q. 5, a. 4 ad 1.

7. Francesca Murphy, *The Beauty of Christ,* (Edinburgh: T & T Clark, 1995), 216.

8. Aertsen, *Nature and Creature,* 145.

9. Aquinas, *Summa Theologica,* q. 6, a 2, resp.

10. Yves Congar, *I Believe in the Holy Spirit,* trans. David Smith (New York: A Crossroad Herder Book, 1997), 12.

11. Ibid., 57.

12. Iris Murdoch, *The Sovereignty of Good* (London: Routledge & Kegan Paul, 1970), 79.

13. Emmanuel Katongole, *Beyond Universal Reason: The Relations between Religion and Ethics in the Work of Stanley Hauerwas* (Notre Dame, Ind.: University of Notre Dame Press, 2000), 13.

14. An important exception to this is the work of the philosopher Alasdair MacIntyre, who has argued that "what philosophy is and what it can legitimately hope to achieve, has to be understood in the light afforded by the Christian gospel." He explains this position in his essay, "How Can We Learn What *Veritatis Splendor* Has to Teach Us?" *The Thomist* 58 (1994): 171–95.

CHAPTER 1

1. Friedrich Nietzsche, *Beyond Good and Evil*, trans. Helen Zimmern (New York: Modern Library, 1927), 384.

2. Ibid., 578.

3. William K. Frankena, *Ethics*, 2d ed. (Englewood Cliffs, N.J.: Prentice Hall, 1973), 4.

4. Stephen Layman, *The Shape of the Good* (Notre Dame, Ind.: University of Notre Dame Press, 1991), 59–84, 85–121.

5. H. Richard Niebuhr, *The Responsible Self* (New York: Harper & Row, 1963), 68.

6. Paul Ramsey, "The Case of the Curious Exception," in *Norm and Context in Christian Ethics,* ed. Gene H. Outka and Paul Ramsey (New York: Scribner, 1968), 67–115.

7. Albert Jonsen and Stephen Toulmin, *The Abuse of Casuistry: A History of Moral Reasoning* (Berkeley and Los Angeles: University of California Press, 1988), 35.

8. Graham Greene, *The Power and the Glory* (London: Penguin Books, 1971), 190–96.

9. John D. Caputo, *Against Ethics: Contributions to a Poetics of Obligation with Constant Reference to Deconstruction* (Indianapolis: Indiana University Press, 1993), 17.

10. Walter Kaufmann, *Tragedy and Philosophy* (Princeton, N.J.: Princeton University Press, 1979), 88.

11. Louis A. Ruprecht, Jr., *Tragic Posture and Tragic Vision: Against the Modern Failure of Nerve* (New York: Continuum, 1994), 97.

12. Ibid., 229

13. Robert R. Williams, "Sin and Evil," in *Christian Theology,* ed. Hodgson and King, 211.

14. Ibid., 208, 211, 214, 216, 219.

15. Ibid., 214.

16. Ibid., 218.

17. Schleiermacher, *The Christian Faith* (Edinburgh: T & T Clark, 1986), 270.

18. Ibid., 282–83.

19. Ibid., 264–68.

20. Ibid., 273.

21. Karl Barth, *Church Dogmatics* IV.1 (Edinburgh: T & T Clark), 359.

22. Ibid., 372.

23. Servais Pinckaer, *The Sources of Christian Ethics* (Washington, D.C.: Catholic University of America Press, 1995), 168–90.

24. For a refined development of this position by a Protestant theologian see Edward Farley's *Good & Evil: Interpreting a Human Condition* (Minneapolis: Fortress Press, 1990).

Farley envisions social and human reality as bounded by a tragic structure because of the dialectic between finitude and transcendence. For a similar development of this theme, see Wendy Farley's *Tragic Vision and Divine Compassion: A Contemporary Theodicy* (Louisville: Westminster/John Knox Press, 1990), particularly 60–65, where both creation and human freedom are viewed as tragic structures.

25. I shall argue in the next chapter, following John Milbank, for an appropriate use of the term "church and society." In critiquing that language here, I am concerned with Karl Barth's worry about the "copulative and" in Protestant theology that adds sources of a non-theological natural knowledge to the insights of sacred doctrine. Thus "society" is construed as accessible to us through sociological methods. Sociology presents society to us and then theology can work on that which is presented. Barth recognized that this was a fatal error in Christian theology that rendered it apolitical and asocial. John Milbank has developed a convincing argument against this understanding of "society." However, Milbank, unlike Barth, argues theology must use analogical speech about God, which is other than the *analogia fidei* that requires language such as "church and society," but now not in any sense conceding an autonomous space to a purely natural depiction of society.

26. Caputo, *Against Ethics,* 33.

27. Plato, *The Republic,* 515c.

28. Ibid., 717c.

29. James C. Edwards, *Ethics without Philosophy: Wittgenstein and the Moral Life* (Tampa: University Presses of Florida, 1985), 71.

30. Aristotle, *Nicomachean Ethics,* 1094a; *Politics,* 1252a.

31. Aristotle, *Nicomachean Ethics,* 1096a25.

32. Ibid., 1098a15.

33. Raimond Gaita, *Good and Evil: An Absolute Conception* (New York: Macmillan, 1991), 202–20.

34. Catherine Pickstock, *After Writing: On the Liturgical Consummation of Philosophy* (Oxford: Blackwell, 1998), xv. This is the argument she makes throughout the book.

35. Murdoch, *The Sovereignty of Good,* esp. 73–76, 80–81.

36. Ibid., 80–81.

37. This point cannot be developed here. I hope to have the occasion to develop it more fully in a future work on the truthfulness of God. Etienne Gilson's *Being and Some Philoso-*

phers (Toronto: Pontifical Institute of Medieval Studies, 1949) explains this critique more fully. It is a "genealogy" before genealogy was popular. In it Gilson argues that Scotus begot Suarez, who begot Kleutgen, who begot Wolff, who (oddly enough with Hume) begot Kant.

CHAPTER 2

1. John H. Zammito, *The Genesis of Kant's Critique of Judgment* (Chicago: University of Chicago Press, 1992), 242.

2. Herbert Schnadelbach, *Philosophy in Germany, 1831–1933* (New York: Cambridge University Press, 1984), 17.

3. Zammito, *Genesis of Kant's Critique,* 241.

4. Ibid., 253: "The kind of God Kant required in his ethico-theology was the 'living' God of the Christian tradition, with a providential and personal character, who 'created' the world."

5. Gilson gives a fuller discussion of this point in *Being and Some Philosophers,* 106–34.

6. Karl Barth, "The Gift of Freedom," quoted in John Webster's *Barth's Moral Theology: Human Action in Barth's Thought* (Grand Rapids: Eerdmans, 1998), 104. For Barth's development of dogmatics as ethics, see *Church Dogmatics* II/2, 515–52.

7. John Webster states, "From the beginning Barth believed that because of who God is, we may not pursue talk of divine action in isolation from talk of the human ethical realm." This is a consistent theme in Barth's work, and whoever does not see it has not read Barth with care. Webster, *Barth's Moral Theology,* 19.

8. For Barth, the central dogma whereby "ethics is a task of the doctrine of God" is election. See *Church Dogmatics* II/2, 508–27. Barth discusses the benefits of Roman Catholic moral theology over and against neo-Protestant ethics and argues that if forced to choose between these two options, he would choose Roman Catholic moral theology. The reason he cannot be for Roman Catholic moral theology, however, is because "this Roman Catholic coordination of moral philosophy and moral theology is based on the basic view of the harmony which is achieved in the concept of being between nature and supernature, reason and revelation, man and God. And it is quite impossible to see how in this basic view grace can really emerge as grace and the command as command" (ibid., 530). For Barth this command as command—with no prior framework within which it can be made intelligible—is the dogma of election.

9. Webster, *Barth's Moral Theology,* 22.

10. See the limited role Mary plays in Barth's Christology, which can be found in *Church Dogmatics* IV/I, 189. Barth was concerned about using "tradition" as a source for theology. He thought this led theologians to falsely think that church makes Scripture rather than Scripture making church. Such a thought ineluctably led, for Barth, to the dogma of infallibility. See *Church Dogmatics* I/2, 544–72. In *Church Dogmatics* I/2 Barth states, "We do not say that, armed with the conception of an outpouring of the Holy Ghost upon the Church and its office, one can overlook for a moment the human fallibility of everything that the Church says about God" (755). Barth finds Protestantism superior to Catholicism because it has "no teaching office" and thus "Protestant theology has a door open to freedom" (*Church Dogmatics* II/1, 585). But notice how, as usual, Barth then qualifies these claims on page 747 by warming up to Luther's idea that "doctrine is not sinful or culpable" even though this comes close "to the Catholic doctrine of the infallibility of the Church's teaching office." Even though Barth appears at many places to reject transubstantiation, he comes quite close to arguing for something like it with respect to the preaching of the Word. He states that "The Word of God is God Himself in the proclamation of the Church of Jesus Christ" (ibid., 743).

11. Von Balthasar writes against Barth's preoccupation with not absolutizing anything finite in history: "But we reply: Does the Church—knowing as she does that she has been founded by Christ—not have the right to regard herself as true? Can she relativize herself without abrogating her obedience to her Lord? And where would such self-relativization ever come to an end? The 'absoluteness' that the Catholic Church must claim for herself really represents her obedience, her refusal to countenance any detriment or constriction of the freedom of God's grace. The Church has never equated the place of her visibility with that of the elect and justified. And the certainty that she possesses depends entirely on her mission and charge. For every member of the Church, even for the infallible Pope, the essence of the Church is the

promise of salvation and not its 'guarantee.' The Catholic knows nothing of this attempt to 'lay hands on God'." Hans Urs von Balthasar, *The Theology of Karl Barth* (San Francisco: Communio Books, Ignatius Press, 1992), 54. As a member of a Protestant tradition, readers might be surprised that I defend von Balthasar's reading of dogmas against that of Barth, but I am a United Methodist. We are a holiness sect that believes in perfection. Thus I find my tradition more in continuity with something like the infallibility present in Catholic dogma than in the dialectical emphasis in some Reformed traditions that refuse any historical presentation of the true and the good.

12. See, among other places, *Church Dogmatics* II/1, 127–28.

13. To argue that Barth did not incorporate Aquinas into his theology is not to assert that he could not be so incorporated within Barthianism. In fact, Eugene Rogers has argued that the way in which Barth reread Anselm against the scholastics could also be done with Aquinas. For a discussion of this see, Eugene Rogers's *Thomas Aquinas and Karl Barth: Sacred Doctrine and the Natural Knowledge of God* (Notre Dame, Ind.: University of Notre Dame Press, 1995). This would require, however, that Barth take more seriously than he did the role of virtue, the sacraments, and the church as a material and historical reality re-presenting the body of Christ.

14. John Milbank, *The Word Made Strange: Theology, Language, Culture* (Oxford: Basil Blackwell, 1997), 3.

15. As Milbank puts it, "Kant was metaphysically dogmatic in affirming that [the extrapolation of categories from our material, finite temporal experience] do not at all apply precisely because he believed (unlike Aquinas) that he had direct cognitive access in practical reason to what the immaterial and atemporal is like" (ibid., 12).

16. For Barth's discussion of this, see *Church Dogmatics* II.1. When Barth read Gottlieb Söhngen's account of the analogy of being, he was willing to entertain the possibility of a Christian interpretation of the analogy of being solely on the basis that this conflicted with its traditional account found in Catholic theologians such as Thomas Aquinas. See Gottlieb Söhngen's "Analogia Fidei: Gottähnlichkeit allein aus Glauben," *Catholica* (1934): 3. Barth may have moved from his denunciation of the

analogia entis as the antichrist (*Church Dogmatics* I.1) to an appreciation for an analogy of faith that made possible his statement, "the covenant is the internal basis for creation and creation is the external basis for the covenant" (*Church Dogmatics* III.1), but this did not lessen his concern that Catholicism was too willing to speak also of being, nature, culture, and society without explicit reference to Christology.

17. Karl Barth, "Kant," in *From Rousseau to Ritschl* (Ayer Company, Publishers, Inc., 1971), 167.

18. Ibid., 150–87.

19. Michael L. Budde, "Pledging Allegiance: Reflections on Discipleship and the Church after Rwanda," in *The Church as Counterculture*, ed. Michael L. Budde and Robert W. Brimlow (Albany, New York: SUNY Press, 2000), 214.

20. See *Church Dogmatics* II/1, 172–78.

21. John Milbank, "The Theological Critique of Philosophy," in *Radical Orthodoxy* (Routledge, 1999), 33.

22. John Milbank, *Theology and Social Theory: Beyond Secular Reason* (Oxford: Basil Blackwell, 1990), 221. This does not imply that Milbank denies the gratuity of the Christ event. He simply refuses to separate creation from redemption. Both re-present the same gracious event. To put it in his own words, he "supernaturalizes the natural."

23. Or if the reader prefers, I could equally say, "Barth's radical move to make dogmatics ethics avoids thinking in terms of both a both/and and an either/or."

24. This led von Balthasar to his well-known thesis that the early Barth was still indebted to an idealistic dialectic that was eschewed after Barth's book on Anselm where Barth began to think and work analogically. For an alternative reading of Barth, see Bruce McCormack's *Karl Barth's Critically Realistic Dialectical Theology* (Oxford: Clarendon Press, 1995).

25. Hans Urs von Balthasar, *The Theology of Karl Barth,* 82, 91, 103. Von Balthasar suggests that Barth's Christology bears elements of Monophysitism.

26. For a helpful discussion of the political implications of the significance of Henri de Lubac's challenge to the scholastic nature/grace distinction, see Joseph A. Komonchak's "Theology and Culture at Mid-Century: The Example of Henri De Lubac," *Theological Studies* 51 (1990): 579–602.

27. See Eugene Rogers's *Thomas Aquinas and Karl Barth: Sacred Doctrine and the Natural Knowledge of God*, 73–75, 183–202.

28. Kant, *Critique of Pure Reason*, 501.

29. Thomas Aquinas, "De Malo," q. 16, a. 7, ad. 15, quoted in Eberhard Jüngel, *God As the Mystery of the World* (Grand Rapids: Eerdmans, 1983), 34.

30. Immanuel Kant, *Critique of Pure Reason*, trans. Lewis White Beck (New York: Macmillan, 1993), 526.

31. Kant, *Critique of Practical Reason*, 3.

32. Ibid., 130–38.

33. Immanuel Kant, *The Metaphysics of Morals*, trans. Mary Gregor (Cambridge: Cambridge University Press, 1991), 183. Kant states, "When a thoughtful man has overcome incentives to vice and is aware of having done his often bitter duty, he finds himself in a state that could well be called happiness, a state of contentment and peace of soul in which virtue is its own reward." In *Lecture on Ethics*, trans. Louis Infield (Indianapolis: Hackett Publishing Co., 1963), Kant discusses the *summum bonum* of the ancients and relates it to Christian notions of holiness. Both are unachievable ideals yet nevertheless necessary for a complete moral system. For Kant, this state of blessedness can never be pure gift: "Man can hope to be happy only in so far as he makes himself worthy of being happy, for this is the condition of happiness which reason itself proposes" (11).

34. Immanuel Kant, *Lectures on Philosophical Theology*, trans. Allen Wood (Ithaca: Cornell University Press, 1978), 110.

35. Ibid., 94.

36. Kant, *Critique of Practical Reason*, 4. The German states, *"Die Möglichkeit derselben wird dadurch bewiesen, daß Freiheit wirlich ist; denn diese Idee offenbaret sich durchs moralishce Gesetz"* (*Kritik der praktischen Vernunft*, in *Werke VII, Schriften zur Ethic und Religionsphilosophie*, I [Wiesbaden: Insel Verlag, 1956]), 108. Although *offenbaren* is the same verb used by theologians to describe the revelation of God in Jesus, I am not arguing that Kant intentionally chose this term. I am, however, arguing that his system presupposes a similar *revelation* at its base as does theology. This revelation is explicitly argued for in Kant's preface to *Critique of Practical Reason*. Thus his ethics is no more, nor less, reasonable than is Christianity.

37. Kant, *Critique of Practical Reason*, 4.

38. Immanuel Kant, *Critique of Judgment*, trans. James Creed Meredith (Oxford: Clarendon, 1991), 140.

39. Ibid.

40. Quoted in von Balthasar, *The Theology of Karl Barth*, 399.

41. Catherine Pickstock, *After Writing: On the Liturgical Consummation of Philosophy* (Oxford: Blackwell, 1998), xv.

42. Mariá Clara Bingemer, "Women in the Future of the Theology of Liberation," in *Expanding the View: Gustavo Gutiérrez and the Future of Liberation Theology*, ed. Marc H. Ellis and Otto Maduro (Maryknoll, N.Y.: Orbis, 1990), 188; and "A Post-Christian and Postmodern Christianism," in *Liberation Theologies, Postmodernity, and the Americas*, ed. David Batstone, et al. (New York: Routledge, 1997), 89–90.

43. Max L. Stackhouse, *Creeds, Society, and Human Rights* (Grand Rapids: Eerdmans, 1984), 1.

44. Joan Lockwood O'Donovan, "Historical Prolegomena to a Theological Review of 'Human Rights,'" *Studies in Christian Ethics* 9.2 (1996): 52.

45. Stackhouse, *Creeds, Society, and Human Rights*, 2.

46. Relativism as a moral theory is *silly* because it is self-contradictory. No one can actually hold to such a position. As Stanley Fish has argued, one need not dispute relativism because it makes no sense to claim to be a relativist in the first place. His *"Is There a Text in This Class?"* (Cambridge: Harvard University Press, 1980), which for some strange reason has been used by many as a defense of a thoroughgoing relativism when Fish's point is exactly the opposite. Someone who says "everything is relative" is as silly as someone who says "we must be more clear about our ambiguity." That both statements are regularly uttered within contemporary theology and church practice simply shows the current intellectual crisis.

47. Stackhouse, *Creeds, Society, and Human Rights*, 2.

48. Max L. Stackhouse and Dennis McCann, "A Postcommunist Manifesto: Public Theology after the Collapse of Socialism," in *On Moral Business: Classical and Contemporary Resources for Ethics in Economic Life*, ed. Max L. Stackhouse (Grand Rapids: Eerdmans, 1995), 952.

49. Ibid., 951.

50. Ronald F. Thiemann, *Religion in Public Life: A Dilemma for Democracy* (Washington, D.C.: Georgetown University Press, 1996), 37.

51. Ibid., 4.

52. Ibid., 147.

53. A splendid account of how this distinction became normative in Christian ethics may be found in Emmanuel Katongole's *Beyond Universal Reason: The Relation between Religion and Ethics in the Work of Stanley Hauerwas* (Notre Dame, Ind.: University of Notre Dame Press, 2000), 189–203.

54. Thiemann, *Religion in Public Life*, 171.

55. Ibid., 126.

56. Ibid., 135.

57. Ibid., 21.

58. Ibid., 102.

59. Immanuel Kant, "What Is Enlightenment?" in *Foundations of the Metaphysics of Morals*, trans. Lewis White Beck (New York: Macmillan Publishing Co., 1987), 87.

60. Thiemann, *Religion in Public Life*, 104.

61. Ibid., 156.

63. Ibid., 160–61.

62. Ismael Garcia, *Dignidad: Ethics through Hispanic Eyes* (Nashville: Abingdon Press, 1997), 34–40.

64. Ibid., 44.

65. "The sphere that we are deserting, within whose boundaries the sale and purchase of labour-power goes on, is in fact a Eden of the innate rights of man. There alone rule Freedom, Equality, Property and Bentham. Freedom because both buyer and seller of a commodity, say of labour-power, are constrained only by their own free will. They contract as free agents, and the agreement they come to is but the form in which they give the expression to their common will. Equality, because each enters into relation with the other, as with a simple owner of commodities, and they exchange equivalent for equivalent. Property because each disposes only of what is his own. And Bentham because each looks only to himself." Karl Marx, *Capital*, vol. 1, trans. Samuel Moore and Edward Aveling (New York: International Publishers, 1973), 1:176.

66. Garcia, *Dignidad*, 73.

67. Ibid., 75.

68. Ibid., 67.

69. Ibid., 85.

70. William T. Cavanaugh, *Torture and Eucharist* (Oxford: Blackwell, 1998), 3.

71. Garcia uses the excellent film *Mi Familia* to explain *dignidad*. That film depicts the story of a father, who finds dignity in his work, and his children, who have different conceptions of *dignidad*. One son, Chucho, rejects his father's world and takes on the customs of an all-American Elvis Presley persona. The result is a fight between the father and son, which is obviously an intergenerational conflict based on the father's tradition and the son's assimilation. Surprisingly, Garcia reproaches the father for his "disregard for Chucho's autonomy and sense of dignity" (Garcia, *Dignidad*, 67). With that, Garcia sides with the modern assimilation desired by Chucho against the father's tradition.

72. Cavanaugh, *Torture and Eucharist*, 249.

73. John Milbank, *Theology and Social Theory: Beyond Secular Reason* (Oxford: Basil Blackwell, 1990), 1.

74. Ernst Troeltsch, *Protestantism and Progress: The Significance of Protestantism for the Rise of the Modern World* (Philadelphia: Fortress, 1986), 100–101.

75. H. Richard Niebuhr, *Christ and Culture* (New York: Harper & Row, 1951), 28–29.

76. Jakob Burkhardt, in his 1943 book *Force and Freedom*, defined culture as "the sum of all that has *spontaneously* arisen for the advancement of material life and as an expression of spiritual and moral life—all social intercourse, technologies, arts, literature and sciences. It is the realm of the variable free, not necessarily universal, of all that cannot lay claim to compulsive authority" (cited in Niebuhr, *Christ and Culture*, 31).

77. Ibid., 32.

78. Glen H. Stassen, D. M. Yeager, and John Howard Yoder, *Authentic Transformation: A New Vision of Christ and Culture* (Nashville: Abingdon, 1996), 54–55.

79. Yoder explained, "In the course of the argument, we observed that each position was measured by Niebuhr according to the consistency with which a thinker responds to the entire realm of values called 'the world' or 'culture.' Should anyone not have the same attitude toward every part of culture, this is itself evidence of inconsistency. Tertullian was a radical critic of culture, and yet he 'could not extricate' himself from it (p. 55) but in fact used Latin philosophical terms in his writing. This is clearly reported as a limitation, not of the

validity of H. Richard Niebuhr's concept, but of Tertullian's intelligence or integrity" (ibid.).

80. H. Richard Niebuhr, *Radical Monotheism and Western Culture* (New York: Harper Torchbooks, 1960), 59.

81. Ibid., 126.

82. Ibid., 96–97.

83. Immanuel Kant, *Religion within the Limits of Reason Alone,* trans. Theodore M. Greene and H. H. Hudson (San Francisco: Harper Torchbooks, 1960), 112.

84. Servais Pinckaers, *The Sources of Christian Ethics,* trans. Mary Thomas Noble (Washington, D.C.: Catholic University of America Press, 1995), 231. This obsession with legal obligations was mirrored by Protestant moral theology in its appropriation of Kantianism during the nineteenth century.

85. Ibid., 234.

86. I recognize that not all moral theologians make a firm distinction between Aquinas and Kant here. For instance, Charles E. Curran states, "Thomas Aquinas anticipated many moderns by basing his ethics on the human being who is an image of God precisely insofar as being endowed with intellect, free will, and the power of self-determination." *Moral Theology: A Continuing Journey* (Notre Dame, Ind.: University of Notre Dame Press, 1982), 117. He bases this statement on a reading of the prologue to the *prima secundae,* where Aquinas states that human creatures are created in the image of God *"quasi liberum arbitrium habens et suorum operum potestatem."* To interpret *habens suorum et operum potestatem* as self-determination seems to me a rather large leap—a leap from Aquinas to Kant. In fact, as I hope to show in the argument that follows, Aquinas precisely denies this power as a power of self-determination, which is the reason the theological virtues, gifts, fruits, and beatitudes are necessary for the completion of the moral life. It seems to me that it is precisely because Curran has misread Aquinas here and views him as consistent with a Kantian account of moral agency that he can make such statements as "I deny that on the level of material content (actions, virtues, attitudes and dispositions) there is anything distinctively Christian" (43).

87. Aquinas, *Summa Theologica,* 1–2.1.

88. In developing this point further in Question 1.4, Aquinas suggests that "if there would be no ultimate end there would be no appetite." The reason for this is that if no end exists, then there would be no desire elicited. Nor would there be the possibility of rest. Note the similarity here between Aquinas and Bingemer, when she states, "God can only be, in the beginning, the object of desire." Bingemer, "A Post-Christian and Postmodern Christianism," 178.

89. Aquinas, *Summa Theologica,* 1–2.2.6, ad 2 (my translation).

90. He writes, *"Non solum potentia aut habitus aut actus sed etiam objectum, quod est extrinsecum"* (ibid., 1–2.2.6, ad 1).

91. Stanley Hauerwas's Gifford Lectures (*With the Grain of the Universe* [Grand Rapids: Brazos Press, 2001]) suggest that this reading of Barth is incorrect. Barth, suggests Hauerwas, is the "natural" theologian par excellence. Hauerwas's reading of Barth is intriguing. If he is correct, it does not qualify the heart of the position I am advocating; it only means that Barth can be more closely related to this Thomistic ethic than Barth himself recognized. That is a position for which I have great sympathy.

92. Henri de Lubac, *Mystery of the Supernatural* (New York: Herder & Herder, 1967), 123.

93. Aquinas, *Summa Theologica,* 3.1.2, resp. Aquinas connects the theological virtues of faith, hope, and charity with the incarnation and the possibility of "well-doing." The significance of the incarnation for the moral life is emphasized by quoting Augustine, "The human creature who might be seen was not to be followed; but God was to be followed, Who could not be seen. And therefore God was made human, that He Who might be seen by the human creature, and Whom the human creature might follow might be shown to the human creature" (3.1.2, resp.).

94. Kant, *Critique of Judgment,* par. 26, quoted in Zammito, *Genesis of Kant's Critique,* 281.

95. Aquinas, *Summa Theologica,* 1–2.3.1, resp.

96. Ibid., 1–2.3.1, ad 1.

97. Aquinas, *Summa Theologica,* 1–2.106.1, rep. obj. 2.

98. Ibid., 1–2.108.1, resp.

99. Ibid., 1–2.106.2, ad 2.

100. Pinckaers, *Sources of Christian Ethics,* 211.

101. John Howard Yoder, *For the Nations: Essays Public and Evangelical* (Grand Rapids: Eerdmans, 1997), 3–5, esp. nn. 6–7.

102. John Howard Yoder, *The Priestly Kingdom: Social Ethics As Gospel* (Notre Dame, Ind.: University of Notre Dame Press, 1984), 158–59.

103. Yoder, *Priestly Kingdom,* 156.

104. Ibid., 158–59.

105. In *Priestly Kingdom* Yoder writes, "If we claim for democracy the status of a social institution *sui generis,* we shall inflate ourselves and destroy our neighbors through the demonic demands of the claims we make for our system and we shall pollute our Christian faith by making of it a civil religion. If on the other hand we protect ourselves from the Constantinianism of that view of democracy, we may find the realistic liberty to foster and celebrate relative democratization as one of the prophetic ministries of a servant people in a world we do not control" (166). Yoder writes more favorably of democracy in his "Sacrament As Social Process," where he notes, "What New Testament believers were doing in these several practices [fraternal admonition, the universality of charisma, the Spirit's freedom in the meeting] can be spoken of in social process terms easily translated into nonreligious terms. The multiplicity of gifts is a model for the empowerment of the humble and the end of hierarchy in social process. Dialogue under the Holy Spirit is the ground floor of the notion of democracy. The admonition to bind or loose at the point of offense is the foundation for what now would be called conflict resolution and consciousness raising." *The Royal Priesthood: Essays Ecclesiological and Ecumenical,* ed. Michael Cartwright (Scottsdale, Pa.: Herald Press, 1994), 364. This seems to be a more positive construal of democracy than was found in *Priestly Kingdom,* but what Yoder means by *democracy* even here must be carefully considered.

106. Yoder, *Priestly Kingdom,* 163.

107. Ibid., 164.

108. The answer is yes and no. At times Yoder argues as though *Christendom* were a seamless whole running from Constantine to the Reformation. Thus, he states that the fall for the Anabaptists signifies the "fusion of church and society of which Constantine was the architect, Eusebius the priest, Augustine the apologete, and the Crusaders and Inquisition the culmination" (*Royal Priesthood,* 89). In this same work he also speaks of the "otherness of the Church in the Middle Ages" that produced a visible ecclesial hierarchy in opposition to that of the princes. And this was preferable to the subordination of the church to the nation under the Protestant Reformation (58–60).

109. Ernst Kantorowicz, *The King's Two Bodies: A Study in Medieval Political Theology* (Princeton: Princeton University Press, 1985), 144.

110. Reinhold Niebuhr, *An Interpretation of Christian Ethics* (San Francisco: Harper & Row, 1963), 143.

111. Yoder, *Royal Priesthood,* 250.

112. Yoder, *Priestly Kingdom,* 23.

113. Ibid., 16.

114. Yoder, *Royal Priesthood,* 244.

115. Ibid., 238.

116. Ibid., 225.

117. Perhaps the best account of the modern and its relationship to progress and the new can be found in Gianni Vattimo's *The End of Modernity,* trans. J. R. Snyder (Baltimore: Johns Hopkins University Press, 1989). He finds a relationship between modernity, secularization, progress, and the new, which he defines on p. 101.

118. Yoder, *Royal Priesthood,* 268.

119. John Howard Yoder, *Preface to Theology: Christology and Theological Method* (Elkhart, Ind.: distributed by Co-op Bookstore, 1981), 85.

120. John Howard Yoder, *Body Politics* (Nashville: Abingdon, 1992), 15.

121. Ibid., 20.

122. Ibid., 72.

123. Yoder, *For the Nations,* 44.

124. Yoder, *Royal Priesthood,* 249.

125. Ibid., 246n.5.

126. David Yeago, "The New Testament and the Nicene Dogma," in *The Theological Interpretation of Scripture,* ed. Stephen E. Fowl (London: Blackwell, 1997), 88.

127. Yoder, *Royal Priesthood,* 352.

128. Yoder, *For the Nations,* 46.

129. Oliver O'Donovan, *The Desire of the Nations: Rediscovering the Roots of Political Theology* (Cambridge: Cambridge University Press, 1996), 49.

130. Ibid., 20.

131. Ibid., 82.

132. Ibid., 123.

133. Ibid.

134. Oliver O'Donovan, "Response to Respondents: Behold the Lamb," *Studies in Christian Ethics* 11.2 (1998): 101. In *Desire of*

the Nations O'Donovan both critiques the command and obedience model that dominated understandings of the monarchy in the later Middle Ages and suggests that "nothing in modern democracy has changed the fact that political existence depends upon structures of command and obedience. If modern democracy has broadened the extent to which citizens find themselves sometimes commanding as well as obeying, and if it has developed expectations about the duty of those who command to consult first, one would expect to find these elements present in a more developed reference to political authority. But the whole problematic is strikingly absent" (18).

135. Ibid.

136. An example of what I think O'Donovan means here is found in the state of Texas's recent execution of a convicted murderer who had an IQ of less than 70. Once the formal, bureaucratic process becomes the standard for *justice,* then the human act of deliberating gets turned over and subordinated to it. Consistency with the process becomes the norm. The possibility of taking into account significant differences even among murderers is abandoned.

137. O'Donovan, "Response to Respondents," 104.

138. O'Donovan, *Desire of the Nations,* 197; Augustine, *De perfectione justitiae hominis,* 15.35.

139. O'Donovan, *Desire of the Nations,* 243.

140. Arne Rasmussen, "Not All Justifications of Christendom Are Created Equal: A Response to Oliver O'Donovan," *Studies in Christian Ethics* 11.2 (1998): 75–76.

141. O'Donovan, *Desire of the Nations,* 244; Rasmussen, "Not All Justifications," 74.

142. Stanley Hauerwas and James Fodor, "Remaining in Babylon: Oliver O'Donovan's Defense of Christendom," *Studies in Christian Ethics* 11.2 (1998): 31.

143. Stanley Hauerwas, *Wilderness Wanderings* (Boulder, Colo.: Westview, 1997), 10.

144. Ibid., 6.

145. For instance, in response to Robert Jenson's call for Hauerwas to attend more to the dogmatic tradition (or at least to systematic theology) Hauerwas does not refute the need for such dogmatic reflection. He draws upon Milbank's development of the doctrine of the Trinity to explain why we need dogma without an overarching system that becomes more basic

to theology than the particular dogmas themselves. "Creation, Contingency, and Truthful Nonviolence: A Milbankian Reflection," in Hauerwas, *Wilderness Wanderings,* 188–99.

146. Hauerwas writes, "Questions of dogmatics cannot be separated from how we think about war, the holocaust, suicide, and a host of other questions. That is the task I have tried to perform." Stanley Hauerwas, *Against the Nations* (Minneapolis: Winston, 1985), 9.

147. Stanley Hauerwas, *Dispatches from the Front: Theological Engagements with the Secular* (Durham: Duke University Press, 1994), 94.

148. Ibid., 105.

149. Hauerwas, *Wilderness Wanderings,* 57.

150. He explained earlier what he meant by liberalism: "In the most general terms I understand liberalism to be that impulse deriving from the Enlightenment project to free all people from the chains of their historical particularity in the name of freedom. As an epistemological position liberalism is the attempt to defend a foundationalism in order to free reason from being determined by any particularistic tradition. Politically liberalism makes the individual the supreme unit of society, thus making the political task the securing of cooperation between arbitrary units of desire." Hauerwas, *Against the Nations,* 18.

151. Ibid.

152. The language of simple and complex space can be found in John Milbank's essay, "On Complex Space" (in *The Word Made Strange*). Simple space reflects modern political arrangements that are defined by a central authority and individuals who are all indebted to that authority (a description Michel Foucault made famous in his account of the panopticon in *Discipline and Punishment*). Complex space is more medieval in that it does not allow for a single hierarchical ordering but assumes complex overlapping hierarchies so that no single institution has the ability to survey the whole. Michel Foucault, *Discipline and Punishment: The Birth of the Prison,* trans. Alan Sheridan (New York: Vintage Books, 1979).

153. Hauerwas, *Wilderness Wanderings,* 191.

154. Hauerwas, *Against the Nations,* 19.

155. Hauerwas, *Dispatches from the Front,* 105.

156. This is a historical judgment that is not in the purview of this study to examine.

CHAPTER 3

1. Jean-Luc Marion, *God without Being,* trans. Thomas A. Carlson (Chicago: University of Chicago Press, 1991). "The Christian religion, does not think God starting from the *causa sui,* because it does not think God starting from the cause, or within the theoretical space defined by metaphysics, or even starting from the concept, but indeed starting from God alone, grasped to the extent that he inaugurates by himself the knowledge in which he yields himself—reveals himself" (36).

2. Here I disagree with Jean-Luc Marion precisely because I find John Milbank's work able to avoid what Marion rightly wants to avoid (see above) and yet also maintain a place for an ontology (and thus an ethics) that does not subordinate theology to metaphysics. John Milbank, "Only Theology Overcomes Metaphysics," in *The Word Made Strange.*

3. I am obviously indebted to Alasdair MacIntyre for this way of putting things, although he did not quite put it as I have. As a philosopher he did not argue, at least in *After Virtue,* that human nature as it should be comes to us as a gift in Jesus. Alasdair MacIntyre, *After Virtue* (Notre Dame, Ind.: University of Notre Dame Press, 1981).

4. Robert Sokolowski, *The God of Faith and Reason: Foundations of Christian Theology* (Washington, D.C.: Catholic University of America Press, 1995), 38

5. Gregory of Nazianzus, "Fifth Theological Oration," in *Christology of the Later Fathers,* Library of Christian Classics (Philadelphia: Westminster, 1944), 199.

6. Richard B. Hays, *The Moral Vision of the New Testament* (San Francisco: Harper, 1996), 158–69.

7. My understanding of Jesus and the church is indebted to the work of John Howard Yoder, especially his *Politics of Jesus* (Grand Rapids: Eerdmans, 1972), as well as Gerhard Lohfink, *Jesus and Community* (Philadelphia: Fortress, 1984); Luke Timothy Johnson, *The Gospel of Luke,* ed. Daniel J. Harrington (Collegeville, Minn.: Liturgical Press, 1991) and *The Acts of the Apostles* (Collegeville, Minn.: Liturgical Press, 1992); Geoffrey Wainwright, *Doxology: The Praise of God in Worship, Doctrine and Life* (New York: Oxford University Press, 1980), esp. 45–149. The above summary of the significance of Jesus and church for social

ethics is not intended to function as a complete description of the above authors' positions, nor do I mean to suggest that they will agree with my narration of that significance or with one another. I seek only to let the reader know the influences on my development of the centrality of Jesus and church.

8. A critique of the privation argument may be found in Kathleen Sand, *Escape from Paradise* (Minneapolis: Fortress, 1994), x. She dismisses the privation argument on the assumption that it produces an "intellectual and moral posture of neutrality" toward the world as it is. She describes it as a "liberal idea" because she sees it fundamentally in terms of Plato's understanding of error as a lack of wisdom. That, however, is not Augustine and Aquinas's privation theory. Nor does their privation theory lend itself to a "posture of neutrality." In fact, Sand's own advocacy of a recovery of tragedy inevitably leads to a *posture of neutrality* much more than traditional Christian reflection would allow. What benefit is there to the moral life to acknowledge irresolvable and irredeemable conflict between good and evil?

9. Kant equates hierarchy with Judaism and egalitarianism with true morality. Interestingly, those who dismiss hierarchy as part of the Western, white, patriarchal system fail to acknowledge that, at least in the Kantian wing of that system, egalitarianism *is* the white patriarchal system. Immanuel Kant, *Religion within the Limits of Reason Alone,* trans. Theodore M. Greene and H. H. Hudson (San Francisco: Harper Torchbooks, 1960), 73–78.

10. Both in *Religion within the Limits of Reason Alone* and in *Foundations of the Metaphysics of Morals,* Kant is clear that divine cooperation cannot be a factor in the moral life. In his *Lecture on Ethics,* however, Kant does speak of divine aid. Here he argues that the "ideal of the Gospels is complete in every respect" because unlike other forms of ethics it does not accommodate ethics to nature but seeks "the greatest purity and the greatest happiness" (i.e. "holiness"). He adds, Christianity "commands man to be holy, but as he is imperfect it gives him a prop, namely divine aid." *Lecture on Ethics,* trans. Louis Infeld (Indianapolis: Hackett Publishing Co., 1963), 11. Yet this divine aid functions only to ensure that, if we have done all in our power to achieve the highest good but historical contingencies prevent our accomplishment of the task, God "will make

up our shortcomings." This divine aid in no way conflicts with our autonomous use of reason and exercise of free will.

11. Kant does not explicitly put the matter this way, but I think it is a fair extrapolation of his statements in *Religion Within the Limits of Reason Alone,* 5–6; *Critique of Practical Reason,* 132; and *Critique of Judgment,* trans. James Creed Meredith (Oxford: Clarendon, 1991), 127–28.

12. Quoted in John H. Zammito, *The Genesis of Kant's Critique of Judgment* (Chicago: University of Chicago Press, 1992), 39.

13. Quoted in Theodore Greene's introduction to *Religion within the Limits of Reason Alone,* lix.

14. Kant, *Religion Within the Limits of Reason Alone,* 125.

15. Immanuel Kant, *Lectures on Philosophical Theology,* trans. Allen Wood (Ithaca: Cornell University Press, 1978), 155.

16. Kant, *Religion Within the Limits of Reason Alone,* 112.

17. John Paul II, *Encyclical Veritatis Splendor* (Washington, D.C.: United States Catholic Conference, 1993), par. 79.

18. John Milbank, "On Complex Space," in *The Word Made Strange;* Oliver O'Donovan, "The Death Penalty in Evangelium Vitae," in *Ecumenical Ventures in Ethics: Protestants Engage Pope John Paul II's Moral Encyclicals,* ed. Reinhard Hütter and Theodore Dieter (Grand Rapids: Eerdmans, 1998); Michael Budde, *The (Magic) Kingdom of God: Christianity and Global Cultural Industries* (Boulder, Colo.: Westview, 1997); Jean Bethke Elshtain, "A Pope for All Seasons? The Many-Sidedness of John Paul II," in *Ecumenical Ventures in Ethics.*

19. *Veritatis Splendor,* par. 8.

20. Ibid., par. 9.

21. "Veritatis Splendor," in *Considering Veritatis Splendor,* John Wilkins, ed. (Cleveland: Pilgrim Press, 1996), 95.

22. John A. Gallagher, *Time Past, Time Future: An Historical Study of Catholic Moral Theology* (New York: Paulist Press, 1990); John Mahoney, *The Making of Moral Theology: A Study of the Roman Catholic Tradition* (Oxford: Clarendon, 1987); and Servais Pinckaers, *The Sources of Christian Ethics,* trans. Mary Thomas Noble (Washington, D.C.: Catholic University of America Press, 1995), 191–280.

23. Peter Knauer, "The Hermeneutic Function of the Principle of Double Effect," *Readings in Moral Theology No. 1: Moral Norms and Catholic Tradition,* ed. Charles E. Curran and Richard A. McCormick (New York: Paulist Press, 1979), 1.

24. Ibid., 5.

25. Ibid.

26. Ibid., 6.

27. Richard A. McCormick, "Some Early Reactions to *Veritatis Splendor,*" *Theological Studies* 55 (1994): 499.

28. I hope this way of putting it is consistent with McCormick's statement, "When there is no commensurate reason in the sense just described"—i.e., "the action does justice to the universally formulated premoral value or value-complex sought in the action, in the long run and overall"—"then the evil effect or harm is direct in the moral sense and constitutes the very object of the act. When there is a commensurate reason, that constitutes the object and the evil effect is morally indirect" (ibid.).

29. John Paul II, *Veritatis Splendor,* par. 78.

30. Martin Rhonheimer, "'Intrinsically Evil Acts' and the Moral Viewpoint: Clarifying a Central Teaching of *Veritatis Splendor,*" *The Thomist* 58.1 (1994): 5.

31. Aquinas, *Summa Theologica,* 1–2.18.6.

32. The proportionalist argument seems to find a home in our culture because it can give Catholics reasons for using artificial contraception and still be faithful Catholics. That many Catholics still need a commensurate reason to dissent against the church's teaching is surely a residual sign of their great faithfulness to the church and its teachings. Yet, the development of this moral rationality creates more problems than it resolves. It inexplicably assumes that all *natural* child family planning is good and all *artificial* contraception evil, both of which are open to debate. The proportionalist argument further permits (evil) artificial contraception when a commensurate reason is present, which is the very kind of casuistry Luther rightly protested against. However, the Protestant tradition's uncritical acceptance of artificial contraception is not without problems, since, from a historical perspective, artificial contraception was promoted in order to limit the population of the poor in the interests of a free market. Paul Ramsey has made a good defense of the Protestant position on artificial contraception that is also sensitive to the

importance of procreation in his article, "The Covenant of Marriage and Right Means," in *The Essential Paul Ramsey*, ed. William Werpehowski and Stephen D. Crocco (New Haven: Yale University Press, 1994), 137–50.

33. John Paul II, *Veritatis Splendor,* par. 80.

34. Willfred Parson, "Peace in the Atomic Age," Catholic Association for International Peace (1947); Roland Bainton, *Christian Attitudes toward War and Peace* (Nashville: Abingdon, 1964), 234.

35. John Paul II, *Veritatis Splendor,* par. 103.

36. Ibid., par. 88.

37. Ibid., par. 86.

38. McCormick, "Some Early Reactions," 499.

39. For a defense of this possibility, which was unfortunately characterized as Kantian during his time, see Maurice Blondel, *Action: Essay on a Critique of Life and a Science of Practice,* trans. Oliva Blanchette (Notre Dame, Ind.: University of Notre Dame Press, 1984). Blondel argues that action flows from the infinite to the infinite and cannot be understood separate from God. Unlike Kant, he realizes that there is no freedom in an infinite possibility of willing but that freedom exists in willing the Infinite.

40. Zammito, *Genesis of Kant's Critique,* 239–40.

41. Friedrich Nietzsche, *Thus Spake Zarathustra,* in *The Portable Nietzsche,* trans. Walter Kaufmann (New York: Penguin, 1983), 150–51. I remain indebted to Professor Michael Gillespie for opening up *Thus Spake Zarathustra* to me.

42. Paragraph 86 in *Veritatis Splendor* seems quite consistent with the argument in chapter 1 of Dietrich Bonhoeffer, *Ethics,* trans. Eberhard Bethge (New York: Macmillan, 1965).

43. Bonhoeffer, *Ethics,* 17.

44. This lovely phrase comes from a brilliant lecture presented by Phillip Blond at Duke Divinity School (March 12, 1993). Copies of the lecture are available on audiocassette through the media center of Duke Divinity School.

45. Waldo Beech and H. Richard Niebuhr, *Christian Ethics: Sources of the Living Tradition* (New York: Alfred A. Knopf, 1973), 9.

46. Bonhoeffer, *Ethics,* 25.

47. Friedrich Nietzsche, *Beyond Good and Evil,* trans. Helen Zimmern (New York: Modern Library), 433.

48. Friedrich Nietzsche, *On the Genealogy of Morals,* trans. Walter Kaufmann (New York: Vintage Books, 1989), 35

49. Friedrich Nietzsche, *Antichrist,* in *The Portable Nietzsche,* 617 (par. 42).

50. Walter Kaufmann, *Nietzsche: Philosopher, Psychologist, Antichrist* (Princeton: Princeton University Press, 1974), 346–47. Nietzsche criticized Dante, Aquinas, and Tertullian for their not only positing the concept of hell but also taking pleasure in it. Nietzsche finds Christianity vengeful because Dante can inscribe over the entrance to hell, "I too was created by eternal love." Nietzsche, *Genealogy of Morals,* 49–51.

51. I am thinking in particular of contemporary New Testament scholars who are meeting Jesus again for the first time and giving us one more *timely* Christology. I also have in mind bishops who claim to know how Christianity must change or die by also giving us one more *timely* Christology.

52. Nietzsche, *Beyond Good and Evil,* 433.

53. This is the reason arguments such as Marjorie Hewitt Suchocki's *The Fall to Violence: Original Sin in Relational Theology* (New York: Continuum, 1994) are unpersuasive. She begins by assuming that there was in Christianity a single, monolithic, and hegemonic interpretation of the fall that descended intact from Augustine to Reinhold Niebuhr, then positions her own account of it as an alternative to this other monolithic, hegemonic accept. But Augustine himself gave several interpretations of the fall, some of them quite close to her own alternative reading. Although she is correct to argue that Augustine would never have made sin fundamentally against creation rather than the Creator, nor could he have argued that the world affects God in the way she suggests it does.

54. Augustine, *Confessions,* 10.30.

55. Augustine, *City of God,* 14.10, ed. and trans. Marcus Dods, in *A Select Library of the Nicene and Post-Nicene Fathers,* ed. Philip Schaff, 1st series, 14 vols. (Grand Rapids: Eerdmans, 1979), 2:274.

56. The phrase "participation in God" will be important for the next major move in this book. The doctrine of penance assumes the possibility that through liturgical enactments we

can participate in God. Such participation is not an intrinsic feature of our being; it is performed.

57. Augustine, *On the Trinity* 11.5, ed. Philip Schaff, trans. Arthur West Haddan, in *Nicene and Post-Nicene Fathers* (Peabody, Mass.: Hendrickson, 1994), 149.

58. Irenaeus, *Against Heresies*, "The Myth of Ialdabaoth," 1.30; and Tertullian, *Against All Heresies*, trans. A. Cleveland Coxe, in *The Ante-Nicene Fathers: The Writings of the Fathers Down to A.D. 325*, ed. Alexander Roberts and James Donaldson, 10 vols. (Grand Rapids: Eerdmans, 1989) 3.

59. Irenaeus, *Against Heresies*, 1.30.7.

60. Tertullian, *Against All Heresies*, 650.

61. Ibid.

62. Augustine addressed evil as a privation of the good and the intrinsic goodness of God's creation in *Enchiridion on Faith, Hope, and Love*, trans. Henry Paolucci (Washington, D.C.: Regnery Gateway, 1996), 15; Aquinas, *Summa Theologica*, 1–1.49.1. Aquinas also addressed the relationship between goodness and God's love in *Summa Theologica*, 1–2.110.1.

63. An interesting defense of Hannah Arendt's famous and controversial phrase "the banality of evil" as made by Jean Bethke Elshtain in *Augustine and the Limits of Politics* (Notre Dame, Ind.: University of Notre Dame Press, 1995).

64. Stanley Hauerwas, *Truthfulness and Tragedy* (Notre Dame, Ind.: University of Notre Dame Press, 1985), 90.

65. Robert C. Batchelder, *The Irreversible Decision* (Boston: Houghton Mifflin, 1962), 15.

66. Ibid., 15 and 26.

67. Kyoko and Mark Seldon, *The Atomic Bomb* (Armonk, N.Y.: M.E. Sharpe, 1989), xxv, xx.

68. Mary Midgley, *Can't We Make Moral Judgments?* (New York: St. Martin's Press, 1991), 12.

CHAPTER 4

1. James Dallen, *The Reconciling Community: The Rite of Penance* (Collegeville, Minn.: Liturgical Press, 1991), 261.

2. Marlin Jeshke, *Disciplining in the Church: Recovering a Ministry of the Gospel* (Scottsdale, Pa.: Herald, 1988); John Howard Yoder, "The Hermeneutics of Peoplehood," in *Priestly Kingdom*.

3. H. Richard Niebuhr, *Christ and Culture*, 45.

4. Quoted in Hugo Rahner, *Church and State in Early Christianity*, trans. Lee Donald Davis (San Francisco: Ignatius Press, 1992), 28.

5. In his *On Idolatry*, the vocations of artificers, astrologers, schoolmasters and professors of literature, traders, proprietors of prostitution houses, gladiator trainers, and military service are to be abandoned because of their relationship with idolatry before one comes over to the school of Christ. Tertullian, *On Idolatry*, trans. S. Thelwall, in *The Ante-Nicene Fathers: The Writings of the Fathers Down to A.D. 325*, ed. Alexander Roberts and James Donaldson, 10 vols. (Grand Rapids: Eerdmans, 1989).

6. Tertullian, *On Repentance*, trans. S. Thelwall, in *The Ante-Nicene Fathers: The Writings of the Fathers Down to A.D. 325*, 3:664; Oscar D. Watkins, *A History of Penance: Being a Study of the Authorities* (New York: Longmans, Green, 1920), 116.

7. Tertullian, *On Repentance*, 3:664.

8. Gregory Thaumaturgus, bishop of Neo-Caesarea, explained five grades of penance that the penitent must go through. Joseph A. Favazza, *The Order of Penitents: Historical Roots and Pastoral Future* (Collegeville, Minn.: Liturgical Press, 1988). The five grades for the penitent are usually described as mourners, who confess their sins and enter into time of mourning; hearers, who stand in the narthex of the church and hear what occurs in worship; fallers, who can sit in the nave of the church but do so on their knees and are not yet ready to participate in the sacred mysteries of the church; bystanders, who can stand in the nave; and full participants, who are once again readmitted into the full participation in the church's sacred mysteries.

9. Augustine, *Faith and Works*, trans. Marie Liguori, Fathers of the Church (Washington, D.C.: Catholic University of America Press, 1985), 241.

10. Augustine, *Enchiridion on Faith, Hope, and Love*, 10–11, 15, 51.

11. Ibid., 124.

12. Augustine, *Faith and Works*, 234.

13. Augustine, *Of the Morals of the Catholic Church*, trans. Richard Stothert, in *Nicene and Post-Nicene Fathers* (Grand Rapids: Eerdmans, 1989), 4:47.

14. Ibid.

15. Ibid.

16. Aquinas, *Summa Theologica,* 3.60.3.

17. Ibid., 3.60.5.

18. Ibid., 3.63.5.

19. Ibid., 3.61.1.

20. Ibid., 3.64.2.

21. Ibid.

22. Thomas N. Tentler, *Sin and Confession on the Eve of the Reformation* (Princeton: Princeton University Press, 1977), 22.

23. Alasdair MacIntyre, *A Short History of Ethics* (New York: Collier, 1966), 121–22.

24. Reinhard Hütter, *Suffering Divine Things* (Grand Rapids: Eerdmans, 1999), 129–30.

25. Ibid., 131.

26. Reinhard Hütter, "'God's Law' in *Veritatis Splendor,*" in *Ecumenical Ventures in Ethics,* 94–95.

27. Martin Luther, *Luther's Works,* ed. and trans. Theodore Bachmann (St. Louis: Concordia Publishing House, 1955–86), 35:38.

28. Martin Luther, *Martin Luther: Selections from His Writings,* ed. John Dillenberger (New York: Anchor Books, 1961), 292.

29. Luther, *Luther's Works,* 35:32.

30. Ibid.

31. Ibid., 35:34.

32. Ibid., 35:36.

33. Luther, "Babylonian Captivity of the Church," in Dillenberger, p. 316.

34. Ibid., 316–21.

35. John Calvin, *The Institutes of the Christian Religion,* ed. John T. McNeill, trans. Ford Lewis Battles (Philadelphia: Westminster, 1960), 1:602.

36. Ibid., 1:651.

37. Ibid.

38. Ibid., 1:624, 653.

39. Ibid., 1:632.

40. Talal Asad, *Genealogies of Religion: Discipline and Reasons of Power in Christianity and Islam* (Baltimore: John Hopkins University Press, 1993), 72.

41. Blaise Pascal, *Provincial Letters,* trans. Thomas M'Crie (Boston: Houghton, Osgood, 1880), 217–18.

42. Henry Davis, *Moral and Pastoral Theology: A Summary* (New York: Sheed & Ward, 1952), xxviii.

43. Hegel writes, "The state is absolutely rational inasmuch as it is the actuality of the substantial will which it possesses in the particular self-consciousness once that consciousness has been raised to consciousness of its universality. . . . this final end has supreme right against the individual, whose supreme duty is to be a member of the state." Georg Wilhelm Friedrich Hegel, *Philosophy of Right,* trans. T. M. Knox (New York: Oxford University Press, 1952), 155–56.

44. Stanley Hauerwas, *Sanctify Them in the Truth: Holiness Exemplified* (Nashville: Abingdon, 1999), 128.

CHAPTER 5

1. Another way of putting this would be that our making or *poiesis* must always be subordinated to the *pathos* that the Holy Spirit produces within the church. Reinhard Hütter defines pathos as "suffering, undergoing" as against "doing." Reinhard Hütter, *Suffering Divine Things,* 29.

2. Gerhard Lohfink, *Does God Need the Church?* (Collegeville, Minn.: Liturgical Press, 1999).

3. The following discussion relies on Gerhard Lohfink's *Jesus and Community* (Philadelphia: Fortress, 1984).

4. This quote comes from a subheading in Lohfink, *Does God Need the Church?* 106.

5. Ibid., 106–17.

6. Ibid., 118.

7. Ibid., 163.

8. Luke Timothy Johnson, *The Gospel of Luke,* ed. Daniel J. Harrington (Collegeville, Minn.: Liturgical Press, 1991), 134.

9. Lohfink, *Does God Need the Church?* 194.

10. Ibid., 180.

11. John Milbank, "A Midwinter Sacrifice," *Studies in Christian Ethics* 10.2 (1997): 13–39.

12. Luke Timothy Johnson, *The Acts of the Apostles* (Collegeville, Minn.: Liturgical Press, 1992), 88–89.

13. Albert Schweitzer, *The Quest of the Historical Jesus* (Baltimore: Johns Hopkins University Press, 1998), 365.

14. Schweitzer began his book with a tribute to German theology and civilization for its unique contribution to theology and history by disclosing how "the ideas of Jesus were taken possession by the Greek spirit." To his credit, he also showed how they were taken possession by the German spirit. But the latter, unlike the former, is not subjected to crit-

icism. Of course, Schweitzer did not see how the very act of thinking Jesus within the context of the *ecclesia* in every culture and context is itself an intrinsic feature of the historical Jesus. Thus, all that he can finally give us is a Jesus who fits well the metaphysical spirit of German idealism (ibid., 399).

15. Richard B. Hays, *The Moral Vision of the New Testament: Community, Cross, New Creation* (San Francisco: HarperCollins, 1996), 198.

16. Lohfink, *Does God Need the Church?* 211.

17. John D. Zizioulas, *Being As Communion* (Crestwood, N.Y.: St. Vladimir's Press, 1985), 171–208.

18. I use the Greek terms to avoid the suggestion that the only way to be sustained in these necessary exchanges is to embrace the current social formations of the global capitalist market and the liberal nation-state. That we need some such formations for everyday life does not imply that we need these particular versions as they now exist. In fact, I am suggesting that the very presence of the church gives us wisdom to discern how the global market and the nation-state have become disordered, seeking from us more (and less) than they should.

19. Greg Jones gives an excellent discussion of "practicing forgiveness" in *Embodying Forgiveness: A Theological Analysis* (Grand Rapids: Eerdmans, 1995).

20. Aquinas, *Summa Theologica* (Cambridge: Blackfriars, 1966), 1–2.113.5: *Recessus autem et accessus in motu liberi arbitrii accipitur secundem detestationem et desiderium.*

21. Herbert McCabe, *God Matters* (Springfield, Ill.: Templegate, 1987), 228.

22. Francesca Aran Murphy, *Christ the Form of Beauty: A Study in Theology and Literature* (Edinburgh: T. & T. Clark, 1995).

23. Yves Congar, *I Believe in the Holy Spirit* (New York: Crossroad-Herder, 1997), 75.

24. Henry Davis, *Moral and Pastoral Theology: A Summary* (New York: Sheed & Ward, 1952), 33.

25. All these definitions of the seven deadly sins come from ibid., 22–23.

26. Ralph McInerny, *Ethica Thomistica* (Washington, D. C.: Catholic University of America Press, 1982), 2.

27. *"Unde oportet quod ultima perfectio hominis sit per cognitionem alicujus rei quae sit supra intellectum humanum."*

28. 1–2.4.8 resp.

29. 1–2.65.3, resp.

30. 1–2.68.2, resp.

31. The discussion of the beatitudes in Augustine comes from his *Commentary on the Sermon on the Mount,* trans. Denis J. Kavanaugh (New York: Fathers of the Church, 1951), 3:19–39. His discussion of the gifts can be found in *De doctrina christiana* 2.7.9–11. Aquinas's account of the gifts and beatitudes is found in *Summa* Ia IIae, qq. 68–69. I am indebted to Servais Pinckaers's presentation of this in his *The Sources of Christian Ethics,* trans. Mary Thomas Noble (Washington, D.C.: Catholic University of America Press, 1995), 156–69.

32. John Wesley, "Sermon on the Mount," in *The Works of John Wesley,* ed. Albert Outler (Nashville: Abingdon, 1984), 1:447.

33. My own reflections on the Ten Commandments have been greatly informed by James William McClendon Jr., *Systematic Theology: Ethics* (Nashville: Abingdon, 1986), 177–84.

34. Walter M. Miller, *A Canticle for Leibowitz* (New York: Bantam Books, 1976), 260.

35. Tertullian, *Apology,* in *The Ante-Nicene Fathers: The Writings of the Fathers Down to* A.D. *325* (Grand Rapids: Eerdmans, 1989), 3:49.

36. Augustine, *City of God,* 413.

37. Immanuel Kant, *The Metaphysics of Morals,* trans. Mary Gregor (Cambridge: Cambridge University Press, 1991), 96–98.

38. Mary Daly, *Beyond God the Father* (Boston: Beacon, 1973), 195.

39. Jean Belhke Elshtain, *Augustine and the Limits of Politics,* 29.

40. Gerhard Lohfink, *Jesus and Community,* 48–49.

41. United States Catholic Conference, *Catechism of the Catholic Church* (Chicago: Thomas More, 1994), par. 2214. This statement in the *Catechism* draws on Ephesians 3:14–15, which states, "For this reason I bow my knees before the Father, from whom every family in heaven and on earth is named."

42. Michael Ignatieff, *The Needs of Strangers* (New York: Viking, 1985), 10.

43. Jean Bethke Elshtain, *Democracy on Trial* (New York: Basic Books, 1995), 41.

44. Aquinas, *Summa Theologica,* 2–2.66.7.

45. *Catechism,* par. 2263.
46. Ibid., par. 2262.
47. Ibid., par. 2307.
48. Ibid., par. 2305 and 2306.
49. Aquinas, *Summa Theologica,* 2–2.40.2.
50. Of course, a counsel like *celibacy* would not be extended to all the faithful, but obedience and perhaps the kind of poverty that assumes sharing of possessions certainly should be.
51. Karl von Clausewitz, *On War,* trans. Michael Howard and Peter Paret (Princeton: Princeton University Press, 1989), 69.

CHAPTER 6

1. Karl Barth, *Church Dogmatics* II/1, ed. G. W. Bromiley and T. F. Torrance, trans. G. W. Bromiley (Edinburgh: T. & T. Clark, 1956), 428.
2. I am indebted to David McCarthy for this way of putting things. See his *Sex and Love in the Home* (London: SCM Press, 2001).
3. David Hunter, *Marriage in the Early Church* (Minneapolis: Fortress, 1992), 7–8.
4. John T. Noonan, *Contraception* (New York: New American Library, 1967), 39.
5. Quoted in ibid., 69.
6. Noonan writes, "Virtually without exception the Gnostics challenged marriage as a child-related institution" (ibid., 79).
7. Ibid., 78–84.
8. Tertullian's letter to his wife in Hunter, *Marriage in the Early Church,* 35–38.
9. A good interpretation of this is given by Richard B. Hays, *The Moral Vision of the New Testament* (San Francisco: Harper, 1996), 47.
10. Quoted in Hunter, *Marriage in the Early Church,* 61.
11. Quoted in ibid., 55.
12. Ibid., 73–75.
13. John Updike, "Even the Bible Is Soft on Sex," *New York Times Book Review* (June 20, 1993), 3.
14. The "Religious Declaration on Sexual Morality, Justice and Healing" was published on January 20, 2000. Signed by over eight hundred religious leaders, this declaration said, "All persons have the right and responsibility to lead sexual lives that express love, justice, mutuality, commitment, consent and pleasure." How one can have a *right* to sexual pleasure was not delineated. I am baffled as to what it could possibly mean.

15. John Milbank, *The Word Made Strange,* 194.
16. Gregory of Nyssa, *The Life of Moses,* trans. Abraham J. Malherbe and Everett Ferguson, in *The Classics of Western Spirituality* (New York: Paulist Press, 1978), 116.
17. Michel Foucault, *The History of Sexuality,* vol. 1, trans. Robert Hurley (New York: Vintage Books, 1980), 12.
18. Quoted in Hunter, *Marriage in the Early Church,* 99.
19. Augustine, *The Good of Marriage,* trans. Charles T. Wilcox, in *Saint Augustine: Treatises on Marriage and Other Subjects* (Washington, D.C.: Catholic University of America Press, 1955), 42.
20. Ibid., 36.
21. Ibid., 14.
22. United States Catholic Conference, *Catechism of the Catholic Church* (Chicago: Thomas More, 1994), par. 2346.
23. Bertrand Russell, *Marriage and Morals* (New York: Liveright, 1970), 106.
24. Ibid., 144.
25. Ibid., 216–17.
26. Stanley Hauerwas, *Unleashing the Scriptures* (Nashville: Abingdon, 1993), 120.
27. Quoted in Robert Moats Miller, *Bishop G. Bromley Oxnam: Paladin of Liberal Protestantism* (Nashville: Abingdon, 1990), 461.
28. Cornel West, *Prophesy Deliverance: An Afro-American Revolutionary Christianity* (Philadelphia: Westminster, 1982), 49.
29. Ibid., 61.
30. Stanley Hauerwas has consistently made this argument in all his work. In *Peaceable Kingdom* he argues that "the fundamental nature of our sin is self-deception." Although he usually refers to the faithful by the pronoun *our,* here he must mean modern liberals. Yet self-deception characterizes liberal society in ways that it might not characterize other societies. For instance, Masama Nakashima suggested to me that this particular understanding of the fundamental nature of sin would not be the same in Japan, where liberalism was once not so formative. This did not prevent the Japanese from producing their own form of sin and "racism," but perhaps calling Japanese imperialism a species of *racism* might be a category mistake that will not allow the Japanese to own their own history truthfully. The problem with calling what the Japanese did to the Koreans *racism* is that that history gets scripted into the West-

ern history of race. Unfortunately, the dominant solution to racism is merely to advocate more "freedom and equality," which is the discourse of the dominant culture that produced racism in the first place. Once the history of Japanese imperialism is described as racism, the solution will be to become more like liberal Western society to redress its own past evils, evils that do indeed need to be redeemed.

31. Malcolm X, *The Autobiography of Malcolm X* (New York: Ballantine, 1992), 183.

32. Stanley Hauerwas, *Dispatches from the Front: Theological Engagements with the Secular* (Durham: Duke University Press, 1994), 88.

33. These quotes come, respectively, from James Cone, *Black Theology and Black Power* (Maryknoll, N.Y.: Orbis, 1997), 21, 24, 40, 53, 20; and James Cone, *A Black Theology of Liberation* (Maryknoll, N.Y.: Orbis, 1993), 9.

34. Cone, *Black Theology and Black Power*, 27.

35. Ibid., 63.

36. This theological indifference is similar to the reaction of the Klan to Malcolm X. They misunderstood him and were favorably disposed to their perception of some of his political statements. As a result, they approached him with a political "compromise"—you take New York, and we'll take Montana.

37. Cone, *Black Theology and Black Power*, 41.

38. Ibid., 24.

39. Ibid., 26.

40. This seems to be the heart of the argument in the statement put forth as "The Ramsey Colloquium," *First Things* 41 (March 1994): 15–20.

41. The editors initially invited an essay by Stanley Hauerwas to be included in the collection. Although Hauerwas's essay defended a form of gay unions, it asked some critical questions and did not fit the standard liberal Protestant defense of gay unions based on a creation spirituality, a strong law/gospel distinction, the primacy of personal experience, grace understood as acceptance, and the normative role for North American pluralism. For that reason, one editor disinvited Hauerwas's contribution, which is now published in his *A Better Hope: Resources for a Church Confronting Capitalism, Democracy, and Postmodernity* (Grand Rapids: Brazos, 2000), 47–51. I relate this because, as Hauerwas himself taught me, liberalism becomes violent precisely because it

subordinates truth to utility. Therefore, I think it necessary to confess that a work like *The Loyal Opposition* is born out of a form of censorship. This would not be so troubling if liberals would come clean and recognize that they are just as dogmatic and magisterial as any other tradition. If, for instance, like Roman Catholics they placed an *imprimatur* within the pages of books officially sanctioned by their tradition, they would be more truthful. What makes this form of liberalism so insidious is that it practices censorship without the courage to state publicly that it does so. Therefore, its official dogmas are less subject to scrutiny.

42. Tex Sample, "Introduction," in *The Loyal Opposition: Struggling with the Church on Homosexuality*, ed. Tex Sample and Amy E. DeLong (Nashville: Abingdon, 2000), 16.

43. Victor Paul Furnish, "The Loyal Opposition and Scripture," in *The Loyal Opposition*, 36.

44. Ibid., 39.

45. Ibid., 41.

46. Ibid., 44.

47. Ibid., 154.

48. Roy I. Sano, "Unity with Integrity in God's Mission," in *The Loyal Opposition*, 49.

49. Dale Dunlap, "Homosexuality and the Social Principles," in *The Loyal Opposition*, 77–78.

50. Hays, *Moral Vision*, 390.

51. Hütter, *Suffering Divine Things*, 130.

52. James A. Brundage, *Law, Sex, and Christian Society in Medieval Europe* (Chicago: University of Chicago Press, 1987), 122.

53. Hays, *Moral Vision*, 381.

54. Friedrich Nietzsche, *The Birth of Tragedy*, trans. Clifton P. Fadiman (New York: The Modern Library, 1927), 995.

55. Dale Martin, "Heterosexism and the Interpretation of Romans 1:18–32," *Journal of Biblical Interpretation* 3 (1995): 337.

56. Ibid., 339.

57. Ibid., 342.

58. Hays, *Moral Vision*, 387.

59. Rogers, *Sexuality and the Christian Body*, 35.

60. Ibid., 27.

61. This is what Lisa Cahill finds him doing in "The Defense of Moral Practices," *Modern Theology* 16.3 (2000): 347–52. Cahill notes that, unlike fertility-cult spirituality, sexuality should not have a central role in Christian spirituality. I agree with her concern but do not see

Rogers in disagreement. That marriage is a monastic practice would seem to avoid any hint of assuming that sexual intercourse itself gives a privileged access to God. Rogers argues that our relationship to God requires bodies, but that does not mean it requires sexual activity.

62. Bernd Wannenwetsch, "Old Docetism— New Morality," *Modern Theology* 16.3 (2000): 353–65.

63. René Girard, *Violence and the Sacred*, trans. Patrick Gregory (Baltimore: Johns Hopkins University Press, 1977), 227. Girard argues, "If there were no incest prohibitions there would be no biological laws."

64. Wannenwetsch, "Old Docetism," 362.

65. Rogers, "The Liturgical Body," *Modern Theology* 16.3, (2000), 370–71.

66. I am not asking whether homosexuality is practiced in Africa, Asia, and Latin America; it is. I am asking why the North American church seeks to accommodate as it does and the church in these other places does not.

67. Quoted in Michael J. Gorman, *Abortion and the Early Church* (New York: Paulist Press, 1982), 20.

68. Tertullian, quoted in ibid., 20.

69. Origen, *Contra Celsum,* trans. Henry Chadwick (Cambridge: Cambridge University Press, 1953), 3.7.

70. Catharine A. MacKinnon, *Feminism Unmodified: Discourses on Life and Law* (Cambridge: Harvard University Press, 1987), 99.

71. David Ricardo, *Principles of Political Economy and Taxation* (London: J. Murray, 1817), 94.

72. John Paul II, *Encyclical Evangelium Vitae,* no. 59.

73. Jeremy Taylor, *Holy Living and Dying with Prayers containing the Whole Duty of a Christian* (New York: Appleton and Co., 1859), 42–57.

74. Taylor himself was no stranger to death and suffering, having faced imprisonment and poverty and having buried two sons.

75. Peter Laslett, *A Fresh Map of Life: The Emergence of the Third Age* (London: Weidenfeld & Nicolson, 1989).

76. Another problem with this interpretation is that it seems to be false. Sociological interpretations of statistics do not show direct correlations between increased life expectancy and modernization and industrialization. Laslett, *Fresh Map,* 83.

77. Richard Disney, *Can We Afford to Grow Older?* (Cambridge: MIT Press, 1996), 17. Such "conventional approaches to the 'economics of aging'" then give rise to discussions of aging in a burden-of-dependency model that uses "static (within period) measures of the burden, calculated with varying degrees of sophistication" (12). It should be noted that Disney's work develops a different model than the burden-of-dependency model, although he does assume that the retired are a *burden* in this putatively neutral, technical sense.

78. A good analysis of the marginalist revolution is given by Simon Clarke, *Marx, Marginalism and Modern Sociology: From Adam Smith to Max Weber* (London: Macmillan, 1982), esp. 145–85.

79. This language is prevalent not only with economists but also with sociologists. For example, one sociological analysis of care for the elderly begins by stating, "In the United States today, programs for the old and for the young compete for the same limited resources. If real economic growth remains relatively low, increased outlays for the elderly can only come at the expense of other social goods, including programs for children." Ronald J. Angel and Jacqueline L. Angel, *Who Will Care for Us? Aging and Long-Term Care in Multicultural America* (New York: New York University Presses, 1997), xxi.

80. Clarke, *Marx,* 153.

81. Joseph E. Stiglitz, *Economics,* 2d ed. (New York: W.W. Norton, 1997), 920. Stiglitz served as President Clinton's chairman of the council of economic advisers as well as chief economist at the World Bank.

82. The one exception would be taxation, but what impacts us directly is the amount we will be taxed. We have little recourse as to how those taxes will be utilized, for all the political options present accept the basis of marginalist rationality.

83. A fuller explanation of this point is given by Michael Sandel, *Democracy's Discontent: America in Search of a Public Philosophy* (Cambridge: Harvard University Press, 1996), esp. chapter 1, "The Public Philosophy of Contemporary Liberalism" (3–24).

84. I recognize that many theologians would find this claim objectionable, but John Milbank's argument in *Theology and Social Theory: Beyond Secular Reason* (Oxford: Basil Blackwell, 1990) is convincing on this point.

Milbank writes, "The pathos of modern theology is its false humility. For theology, this must be a fatal disease, because once theology surrenders its claim to be a meta-discourse, it cannot any longer articulate the word of the creator God, but is bound to turn into the oracular voice of some finite idol. . . . If theology no longer seeks to position, qualify or criticize other discourses, then it is inevitable that these discourses will position theology: for the necessity of an ultimate organizing logic cannot be wished away" (1).

85. Barth, *Church Dogmatics* IV/1, 281.

86. The language comes from the Anglican and the United Methodist Articles of Religion. The expression is ecumenical. I do not intend to eclipse the "not-yet" character of this eschatological claim into a fully realized eschatology. The very effort to subordinate an economic analysis of aging to theological considerations is a sign of this "not-yet" character present in these claims.

87. Milbank, *Theology and Social Theory,* 116.

88. Aquinas, *Summa Theologica,* 1–2.108.

89. Oliver O'Donovan has persuasively narrated the political implications of Christ's victory in *The Desire of the Nations: Rediscovering the Roots of Political Theology* (Cambridge: Cambridge University Press, 1996). I was impressed especially by his discussion of how Christ's subjection of the "principalities and powers" should shape our view of secular authority (146). I would extend his analysis to the family. As Christ subjects (and will subject) all nations to his authority, so also does he (and will he) subject the family. To understand how he subjects the family to his authority, we must be attentive to the scriptural narratives that characterize the subordination of the family to Christ's mission.

90. Raniero Cantalamessa, *Mary: Mirror of the Church,* trans. Frances Lonergan Villa (Collegeville, Minn.: Liturgical Press, 1992), 121.

91. Augustine, *Sermons* 72A, quoted in ibid., 69.

92. Augustine, *Faith and the Creed,* trans. Robert D. Russell, in *St. Augustine's Treatises on Marriage and Other Subjects* (Washington: Catholic University of America Press, 1985), 27:325.

93. That the disciples took Jesus' bequeathment seriously is found in Acts 1:12–14, where Luke tells us that Mary was with the disciples when they returned to Jerusalem after the ascension.

94. *Lumen Gentium,* The Dogmatic Constitution on the Church, Vatican Council II, November 21, 1964, par. 63.

CHAPTER 7

1. Yoder, *Politics of Jesus,* 11.

2. Ibid., 29.

3. Pickstock, *After Writing.*

4. Joseph Fitzmyer's discussion in *The Gospel According to Luke I–IX,* Anchor Bible (Garden City, N.Y.: Doubleday, 1981), 293.

5. Luke Timothy Johnson, *The Gospel of Luke,* 102.

6. Ibid., 342.

7. *Papal Documents from Rerum Novarum through Centisimus Annas,* par. 39, in *Proclaiming Justice and Peace,* ed. Michael Walsh and Brian Davies (Mystic, Conn.: Twenty-Third Publications, 1991), 31

8. Quoted in *Church and State in the Modern Age: A Documentary History,* ed. J. F. Maclear (Oxford: Oxford University Press, 1995), 349–51.

9. I do not mean to be unduly critical in offering such a statement, but such a statement does seem fitting with apologies for the Orthodox Church as one finds in John Meyendorff's *Imperial Unity and Christian Divisions* (New York: St. Vladimir's Seminary Press, 1989). Vigen Guroian's *Incarnate Love: Essays in Orthodox Ethics* (Notre Dame, Ind.: University of Notre Dame Press, 1987) provides a different account of the relationship between the Orthodox Church and the "imperial" power than one finds in Meyendorff. Nor do I wish to neglect the reality that Protestant denominations in the United States of America have been as committed to using the state as the means by which the gospel is mediated to the world as the Orthodox in Eastern Europe. In fact, although their theories as to how this works differ, mainline American Protestant Christianity has been more prone to serve the interests of the state in the latter part of the twentieth century than has the Orthodox Church in Eastern Europe.

10. Luke Timothy Johnson, *Sharing Possessions: Mandate and Symbol of Faith* (Philadelphia: Fortress, 1981), 128.

11. Ibid., 132.

12. This is another reason to wonder about Johnson's reading of Acts 2 and 4. Was Plato serious in his espousal of common ownership in *Republic* 5? Notice that Luke does not go as far as Plato and argue for the common ownership of spouses and children.

13. Michael Grant, *Constantine the Great: The Man and His Times* (New York: Charles Scribner's Sons, 1994), 130.

14. Justo L. Gonzalez, *Faith and Wealth* (San Francisco: Harper & Row, 1990), 112.

15. Quoted in Waldo Beach and H. Richard Niebuhr, *Christian Ethics: Sources of the Living Tradition* (New York: Alfred A. Knopf, 1973), 96–97.

16. Quoted in Gonzalez, *Faith and Wealth*, 118.

17. Ibid., 120–21.

18. Tertullian, *On Idolatry*, 3:61.

19. Ibid., 3:67.

20. Aquinas, *Summa Theologica*, 2–2.78.

21. Ibid., 2–2.2, rep. 1.

22. Ibid., 2–2.2, rep. 5.

23. Ibid., 2–2.4.

24. Robert Heilbronner, *The Worldly Philosophers: The Lives, Times and Ideas of The Great Economic Thinkers* (New York: Simon & Schuster, 1986), 18–21.

25. Max Weber, *The Protestant Ethic and the Spirit of Capitalism*, trans. Talcott Parsons (New York: Charles Scribner's Sons, 1958), 116–17.

26. Sandra Cavallo, *Charity and Power in Early Modern Italy: Benefactors and Their Motives in Turin, 1541–1789* (Cambridge: Cambridge University Press, 1995).

27. Eamon Duffy, *The Stripping of the Altars* (New Haven: Yale University Press, 1992), 127.

28. John Bossy, *Christianity in the West, 1400–1700* (Oxford: Oxford University Press, 1985).

29. Weber, *Protestant Ethic,* 108.

30. John Calvin, "On Usury," quoted in *From Christ to the World: Introductory Readings in Christian Ethics,* ed. Wayne G. Boulton, Thomas D. Kennedy, and Allen Verhey (Grand Rapids: Eerdmans, 1994), 453.

31. Ibid., 455.

32. Pickstock, *After Writing,* 3.

33. Robert Skidelsky, *John Maynard Keynes: The Economist As Saviour, 1920–1937* (London: Penguin, 1992), 170.

34. Milbank, *Theology and Social Theory,* 97–98.

35. The Guarifuna are a dispersed people, remnants of the slave trade who are more committed to being Guarifuna than to the current national boundaries that define Central and South America. Thus, they live transnationally. An account of the Guarifuna is given by Nancie L. Solien Gonzalez in *Le Estructura Del Grupo Familiar Entre Los Caribes Negros,* Seminario De Integracion Social Guatemalteca, pub. no. 39 (1979).

36. Reinhold Niebuhr, *The Nature and Destiny of Man,* 2 vols. (New York: Charles Scribner's Sons, 1964), 2:266.

37. The last pair of terms comes from Gilles Deleuze and Felix Guattari's "Micropolitics and Segmentarity," in *A Thousand Plateaus: Capitalism and Schizophrenia,* trans. Brian Massumi (Minneapolis: University of Minnesota Press, 1987).

38. Immanuel Wallerstein, *The Modern World System I: Capitalist Agriculture and the Origins of the European World Economy in the Sixteenth Century* (San Diego: Academic Press, 1974), 133–62.

39. Of course, the nation-state also assisted the development of a global capitalist economy. Ernest Mandel calls the nation-state the "midwife of modern capitalism." *Late Capitalism,* trans. Joris deBres (London: Humanities Press, 1975), 54.

40. Daniel Yegin, "Oil: The Strategic Prize," in *The Gulf War Reader: History, Documents, Opinions,* ed. Micah L. Sifry and Christopher Cerf (New York: Random House, 1991), 24.

41. See James Morgan, "Adventures in the Food Chain," *The Atlantic* 296.6 (June 1992): 30–49 for how Wal-Mart has been so effective.

42. See chs. 9 and 10 in Anthony Giddens, *The Nation, State, and Violence* (Berkeley: University of California Press, 1987).

43. David Siegel and Joy Hackel, "El Salvador: Countersurgency Revisited," in *Low Intensity Warfare: Counterinsurgency, Proinsurgency, and Antiterrorism in the Eighties,* ed. Michael T. Klare and Peter Kornbluh (New York: Pantheon Books, 1988), 122.

44. Georg Wilhelm Friedrich Hegel, *Philosophy of Right,* trans. T. M. Knox (London: Oxford University Press, 1952), 210.

45. Michael Allen Gillespie, *Hegel, Heidegger, and the Ground of History* (Chicago: University of Chicago Press, 1984), 41. Gillespie adds, "Hegel thus concluded . . . that it is only through war that bourgeois man is elevated

above his own self-interest to concern himself with the state, and even in such cases his patriotism is bound up with his economic and personal well-being. Thus unless reconciled with the true principles of a free and rational government, this society can never constitute a true ethical community and consequently its members cannot achieve true freedom and humanity but remained trapped in the loneliness of their individuality and the slavery of natural desire."

46. A. Sivanandan, *Communities of Resistance: Writings on Black Struggles for Socialism* (London: Verso, 1990), 184.

47. Robert J. S. Ross and Kent C. Trachte, *Global Capitalism: The New Leviathan* (Albany: State University of New York Press, 1990), 124–27.

48. Karl Marx, *Capital*, trans. Samuel Moore and Edward Aveling (New York: International Publishers, 1973), 1:171–75.

49. Alasdair MacIntyre, *Whose Justice? Which Rationality?* (Notre Dame, Ind.: University of Notre Dame Press, 1988), 161.

50. Cited in Brian Tierney, *The Crisis of Church and State 1050–1300* (Englewood Cliffs, N.J.: Prentice-Hall, 1964), 49.

51. For the specific numbers of slaves imported to the U.S., see "Slavery and Southern Development," in Jeremy Atack and Peter Passell, *A New Economic View of American History* (New York: W. W. Norton and Co., 1994), 299–326. This information comes from C. Eric Wolfe, *Europe: A People without History* (Berkeley: University of California Press, 1982); and Eduardo H. Galeano, *The Open Veins of Latin America: Five Centuries of the Pillage of a Continent*, trans. Cedric Belfrage (New York: Monthly Review Press, 1973, 1977).

52. Quoted in Gustavo Gutiérrez, *Las Casas: In Search of the Poor of Jesus Christ* (Maryknoll, N.Y.: Orbis, 1993), 29.

53. Frederick Jameson, *The Political Unconscious: Narrative as a Socially Symbolic Act* (Ithaca: Cornell University Press, 1981), 31.

54. Robert Nelson, *Reaching for Heaven on Earth: The Theological Meaning of Economics* (Savage, Md.: Rowman & Littlefield, 1991), 119–25, 218, 250, 302.

55. Ibid.

CHAPTER 8

1. Raymond Brown, *The Gospel According to John XIII–XXI*, Anchor Bible (Garden City, N.Y.: Doubleday, 1970), 890.

2. Quoted in Hugo Rahner, *Church and State in Early Christianity*, trans. Leo Donald Davis (San Francisco: Ignatius Press, 1992), 23.

3. Ibid., 28.

4. Ibid., xvi.

5. Jean Bethke Elshtain, *Public Man, Private Woman: Women in Social and Political Thought* (Princeton: Princeton University Press, 1981), 56.

6. Ibid., 12.

7. Ibid., 59.

8. Milbank, *Theology and Social Theory*, 389.

9. Alasdair MacIntyre, "The Augustinian Alternative," in *Which Justice? Whose Rationality?* (Notre Dame, Ind.: University of Notre Dame Press, 1988), 153.

10. Brian Tierney, *The Crisis of Church and State 1050–1300* (Englewood Cliffs, N.J.: Prentice-Hall, 1964), 62.

11. MacIntyre, *Which Justice?* 161.

12. Augustine, *The Trinity*, trans. John Burnaby, in *Augustine: Later Works*, Library of Christian Classics (Philadelphia: Westminster, 1960), 65–66.

13. Of course, this is not to deny that the church, in both its Catholic and Protestant variants, has commanded troops in the past, which is a sign of apostasy.

14. Tertullian, *On Idolatry*, 73.

15. Shalom Spiegel, *The Last Trial*, trans. Judah Goldin (New York: Pantheon Books, 1967), 64.

16. Joanne Carlson Brown and Rebecca Parker, "For God So Loved the World?" in *Christianity, Patriarchy, and Abuse: A Feminist Critique*, ed. Joanne Carlson Brown and Carole R. Bohn (New York: Pilgrim Press, 1989), 7.

17. Anselm, *Why God Became Man*, trans. and ed. Eugene R. Fairweather, in *A Scholastic Miscellany*, Library of Christian Classics (Philadelphia: Westminster, 1956), 111–15.

18. Ibid., 112.

19. Ibid., 113, 115.

20. Ibid., 122–24.

21. René Girard, *Violence and the Sacred*, trans. Patrick Gregory (Baltimore: Johns Hopkins University Press, 1977), 8.

22. Ibid., 20.

23. Brown and Parker, "For God So Loved the World?" 27.

24. John Milbank, "A Midwinter Sacrifice," 34–35.

25. Ibid.

26. Susan Niditch, *War in the Hebrew Bible: A Study in the Ethics of Violence* (New York: Oxford University Press, 1993), 49–50.

27. Ben C. Ollenburger, "Peace and God's Action Against Chaos in the Old Testament," in *The Church's Peace Witness,* ed. Marlin Miller and Barbara Nelson Gingerich (Grand Rapids: Eerdmans, 1994), 86.

28. Cicero, *De Officiis* 1.7.23: "He who does not prevent or oppose wrong if he can, is just as guilty or wrong as if he deserted his parents or his friends or his country." Trans. Walter Miller in *Loeb Classical Library* (Cambridge: Harvard University Press, 1990), 86.

29. Ibid., 1.11.33. 35.

30. John Helgeland, Robert Daly, and J. Patout Burns, *Christians and the Military: The Early Experience* (Philadelphia: Fortress, 1958).

31. Roland Bainton, *Christian Attitudes toward War and Peace* (Nashville: Abingdon, 1988), 92.

32. Oliver O'Donovan, *The Desire of the Nations: Rediscovering the Roots of Political Theology* (Cambridge: Cambridge University Press, 1996), 7.

33. Rahner, *Church and State,* xvi.

34. Francisco de Vitoria, "On the Law of War," in *Vitoria: Political Writings,* trans. and ed. Anthony Pagdes and Jeremy Lawrance, Cambridge Texts in the History of Political Thought (Cambridge: Cambridge University Press, 1991), 296.

35. Martin Luther, "On Secular Authority," in *Martin Luther: Selections from His Writings,* ed. John Dillenberger, trans. Bertram Lee Woof (New York: Anchor Books, 1961), 379.

36. Ibid., 366.

37. Ibid., 384.

38. Quoted in Michael Sandel, *Democracy's Discontent: America in Search of a Public Philosophy* (Cambridge: Harvard University Press, 1996), 63.

39. Luther denies that it is contrary to the vocation of the apostles (and by extension to all the clergy) to bear the sword. They do not use it only for tactical reasons. If they do use it, "it is not contrary to their calling." Luther, "On Secular Authority," 379.

40. William T. Cavanaugh, "'A Fire Strong Enough to Consume the House': The Wars of Religion and the Rise of the State," *Modern Theology* 11.4 (1995): 398, 405.

41. A fuller statement of Kant's views is given in his "Idea for a Universal History with a Cosmopolitan Intent," in Immanuel Kant, *Perpetual Peace and Other Essays,* trans. Ted Humphrey (Indianapolis: Hackett, 1992), 35. As I have already mentioned, in his *Metaphysics of Morals* Kant expressed deep reservations about the possibility of ever actually attaining perpetual peace (xx).

42. Kant, *Perpetual Peace,* 124–25.

43. Kant writes, "Reason can provide related nations with no other means for emerging from the state of lawlessness, which consists solely of war, than that they give up their savage (lawless) freedom, just as individual persons do, and by accommodating themselves to the constraints of common law, establish a nation of people that continually growing will finally include all the people of the earth" (ibid., 117).

44. Ibid., 120.

45. Ibid., 125.

46. Ibid., 125. This also explains why Kant wrote, "Judaism has not allowed its organization to become religious." Why? "Judaism fell so far short of constituting an era suited to the requirements of the church universal or of setting up this universal church itself during its time, as actually to exclude from its communion the entire human race, on the ground that is was a special people chosen by God for Himself." Immanuel Kant, *Religion within the Limits of Reason Alone,* trans. Theodore M. Greene and Hoyt H. Hudson (San Francisco: Harper Torchbooks, 1960), 116–17.

47. Kant, *Perpetual Peace,* 128.

48. Kant writes, "Pure reason alone is practical of itself, and it gives (to man) a universal law, which we call the moral law. . . . Now this principle of morality, on account of the universality of its legislation which makes it the formal supreme determining ground of the will regardless of any subjective differences among men, is declared by reason to be always for all rational beings in so far as they have a will, i.e., faculty of determining their causality through the representation of a rule." Immanuel Kant, *Critique of Practical Reason,* 32. The logic of freedom requires the possibility of a cosmopolitan state.

49. Kant defines freedom as "the privilege not to obey any external laws except those to which I have been able to give my consent" (*Perpetual Peace,* 112). This idea of freedom makes the cosmopolis both possible and necessary, for only it can secure individual freedom from all threats. In the cosmopolis, a single authority is granted the right of coercion, and that right can never be challenged, for reason itself makes this right possible and all reasonable people would consent to it. This act of coercion is not a threat to, but a condition for, individual freedom (33).

50. Reinhold Niebuhr, *Moral Man and Immoral Society* (New York: Charles Scribner's Sons, 1960), 48; 23–50.

51. On the similarity of the journey, ibid., 29–30; on its inevitable failure, 45, 47.

52. Reinhold Niebuhr, *An Interpretation of Christian Ethics* (San Francisco: Harper & Row, 1963), 52. My analysis might appear to fail to take into account Niebuhr's criticism of Kant in *The Nature and Destiny of Man,* 2 vols. (New York: Charles Scribner's Sons, 1964), 1:118–20. Yet Niebuhr's critique of Kant does not challenge the overall schema of the relationship between Kant's ethics and politics. Thus, Niebuhr continues to assume that our absolute commitment to finite particularities results in our wickedness.

53. Niebuhr, *Interpretation of Christian Ethics,* 52.

54. Ibid., 134.

55. Ibid., 143. He adds, "There is no question that the essential genius of the Christian faith is set against the religious sanctification of partial and relative values" (144).

56. Reinhold Niebuhr, "Why the Christian Church Is Not Pacifist," in *The Essential Reinhold Niebuhr,* ed. Robert MacAfee Brown (New Haven: Yale University Press, 1986), 104.

57. Karl von Clausewitz, *On War,* trans. Michael Howard and Peter Paret (Princeton: Princeton University Press, 1989), 69.

58. Quoted in Kenneth Vaux, *Ethics and the Gulf War* (Boulder, Colo.: Westview, 1992), 18.

59. Quoted in Asad, *Genealogies of Religion,* 240.

60. Asad writes, "The idea of freedom appears to consist of two interconnected ideas, tolerance and obligation. . . . 'Tolerance' requires acceptance of diversity . . . based on the individual's right to believe, act, and speak as he or she chooses. But rights create 'obligations,' above all the obligation to respect the rights of others—'respect for the safety of their property,' no less than for their right to speak and write 'freely.' Rights of course, have to be created before the obligation to respect them can arise. And it is inevitable that some rights will conflict with others. But Patten does not point out that respect for property rights (as opposed to the right to choose and follow one's faith) takes precedence in the British way of life over the right to speak and write freely. Thus, the laws on patents, copyright, contracts in restraint of trade, protection of trade secrets and intellectual property all involve restrictions on free expression in Britain. Unlike other restrictions, such as those relating to blasphemy or incitement to hatred, which arise because of undesirable *consequences* that public communication is assumed to have, these are property rights that consist in precisely in limiting free expression. . . . What is also not immediately clear from Patten's statements is whether 'diversity' is an intrinsic feature of the British way of life or something allowed only when divergences do not contradict an essential—and therefore unchangeable—Britishness" (ibid., 244–45).

61. Ibid., 295.

62. Immanuel Kant, "What Is Enlightenment?" in *Foundations at the Metaphysics of Morals,* trans. Lewis White Beck, in the Library of Liberal Arts (New York: Macmillan Publishing Co., 1987), 87. Ernst Cassirer made a similar point some eighty years earlier when he recognized that "the only route to autonomy is through compulsion" (*Kant's Life and Thought,* trans. James Haden [New Haven: Yale University Press, 1981], 224).

63. Asad, *Genealogies of Religion,* 276.

64. Ernst Troeltsch, *The Social Teaching of the Christian Churches,* trans. Olive Wyon (Chicago: University of Chicago Press, 1981), 55, 57, 234.

65. A critical view of Las Casas is given by Martin Marty's foreword to Bartolomé de Las Casas, *In Defense of the Indians,* trans. Stafford Poole (Dekalb: Northern Illinois University Press, 1992), xvi. One wonders if a commitment to the Protestant Principle and Niebuhrian humility motivate Marty to look for the "cosmic flaw" in Las Casas. A more sympathetic view is seen in Gustavo Gutiérrez, *Las Casas: In Search*

of the Poor of Jesus Christ (New York: Orbis, 1993), 312–30.

66. James Dallen discusses the place of reconciliation in the doctrine of repentance in *The Reconciling Community: The Rite of Penance* (Collegeville, Minn.: Liturgical Press, 1991), 17–24.

67. Ibid., 23.

68. *St. Louis Post Dispatch* (December 16, 1994): 1.

69. Cornel West, *Race Matters* (Boston: Beacon, 1993), 14.

70. Such was the case with the tragic killing of Ricky Birdsong in my own Skokie, Illinois, neighborhood.

71. Lawrence M. Friedman, *Crime and Punishment in American History* (New York: Basic Books, 1993), 274.

72. Nils Christie, *Crime Control As Industry* (London: Routledge, 1993), 31, 48.

73. We placed security glass on all our windows after this event, which thwarted six other attempts to throw cinder blocks at us.

Name Index

Subject Index